327.12
Bourke, Sean
   The springing of George Blake

Date Due

CUMBERLAND COUNTY LIBRARY
BRIDGETON, N.J.   08302

PRINTED IN U.S.A.

The Springing of George Blake

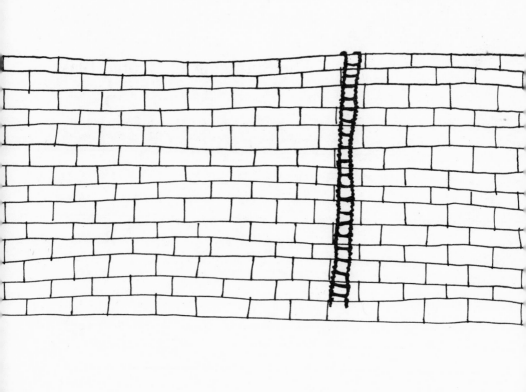

The Springing of
George Blake

SEAN BOURKE

NEW YORK · THE VIKING PRESS

TO LARISA

ДЛЯ ЛАРИСЕ

Preface

In May 1961 a Foreign Office man named George Blake, who had ✠✠ ✠✠
been serving in Berlin at the time of his arrest, was tried at the Old ✠✠ ✠✠
Bailey on five counts of spying for the Soviet Union. He was found
guilty and sentenced to the longest term of imprisonment ever imposed under English law—forty-two years. This was more than a
third as much again as the sentences given to the leaders of the Great
Train Robbery gang. At his trial it emerged that Blake had been a
double agent for at least nine years and had "blown" the network
of Western secret agents operating on the Continent of Europe and
elsewhere. He had, on his own admission, handed to his Russian
contacts "every document of any importance that came into my hands."

On October 22, 1966, Blake escaped from Wormwood Scrubs
Prison in London. There was an immediate international furor. Every
port, airport, and landing-strip throughout the British Isles was put
under strict round-the-clock surveillance. Watch was kept on every
Eastern European embassy and consulate in London. The authorities
believed at first that high-level KGB agents had engineered the daring
coup. While the hue and cry mounted, Blake was living quietly in a
flatlet in Highlever Road, a few minutes' walk from Wormwood
Scrubs Prison.

This is my account of how I planned and engineered George Blake's
escape from prison and of how I spirited him out of England and then
to Moscow. It is also the story of how, a few weeks later, I followed
him to Moscow by way of Paris and of the extraordinary two years

I spent in Moscow until my return to Dublin on October 22, 1968, the second anniversary of the jailbreak.

The manuscript of this book was written in my own hand in Moscow between March and October 1968. At that time I had no reason to believe that I would ever be permitted to return to the West and, as the reader will discover, I gave the manuscript to my brother Kevin for him to smuggle out of Moscow, though, in the event, the attempt was unsuccessful. The nine exercise books that contained my manuscript were confiscated at Moscow Airport and handed over to the KGB.

Shortly after my return to Dublin I wrote to Stanislav at the KGB Headquarters in Moscow and asked for my manuscript to be returned to me. My letter received no answer. I wrote three further letters but received a reply to none of them. Then, entirely unexpectedly, a somewhat tattered parcel was delivered to the offices of my solicitor in Dublin. It contained my original manuscript, from which had been removed the entire final section, which deals with my experiences in Moscow. The rest of the book had been heavily censored by another hand, which I am sure was that of George Blake himself. I have reproduced in this book a number of pages of the original, in the form in which it eventually reached me in Dublin.

SEAN BOURKE

Dublin
January 1970

Contents

Plates

Following page 178

Sean Bourke
George Blake
One of the cell blocks at Wormwood Scrubs Prison
The entrance to Wormwood Scrubs Prison
George Blake with his mother, when he returned from Korea in 1953
Prisoners in the yard at Wormwood Scrubs Prison
The receipt for the two-way radio
Wormwood Scrubs Prison. The installation of arc lamps was part of
the security arrangements made *after* the escape of George Blake
Wormwood Scrubs Prison. The dotted line shows George Blake's
escape route
Two pages from the original manuscript, showing the extent of the
alterations made in Moscow
Sean Bourke at Shannon Airport, after his return from Moscow

ILLUSTRATIONS

The Springing of George Blake

"Will You Help Me Escape?"

The first Monday morning of September 1965 was just like any other
Monday morning at Her Majesty's Prison Wormwood Scrubs, London W. 12. The big brass bell on the ground floor of D-Hall clanged
noisily and reverberated throughout the huge building, harsh and
commanding. Three hundred prisoners stirred and reluctantly opened
their eyes. It was six-thirty, the beginning of another day behind bars.

I lay in bed for a few minutes, staring up at the solid brick ceiling
of my cell, arched and whitewashed. The light from the sixty-watt
bulb, switched on by the night patrol half an hour before, was painful
to the eyes so early in the morning, though by this stage in my sentence I hardly noticed it any more.

I was now into the last ten months of my seven years, minus three
for parole, and this morning I could afford the luxury of reflecting on
what had been and what lay ahead. It seemed to have gone quickly,
but then it always did after you had done it.

I would leave prison at the age of thirty-two, and I would then have
spent a total of nine years in penal institutions. I cast my mind back
over the years and the crimes. It began with playing truant from
school in 1943, at the age of ten, because I hated the Christian Brothers whose responsibility it was to educate me. In the early stages I and
the other boys in the gang would be quickly rounded up by the school
policeman and taken back to face our beating from the head brother.
But the more I was beaten the greater grew my hatred, and after a
while I was no longer content just to play truant but began to run

away from home and to sleep in haybarns and derelict houses and empty railway wagons parked in the sidings across the field from our street.

But when you're on the run you still have to eat, and that was where my criminal career began. A loaf of bread lying unattended on the back seat of a motorcar was tempting to a hungry boy. One loaf of bread led to another and then to another, and before long there were three of us standing before the District Justice at Limerick Juvenile Court. "This sort of behaviour cannot be tolerated. It is time you boys were taught a severe lesson. You will go to Daingean for three years."

Daingean! The word struck the same sort of terror into the hearts of Irish boys as Alcatraz once did to America's public enemies or Dartmoor to London's hardened criminals. Daingean! My mother sobbed, and an older brother put a comforting arm around my shoulder. And Daingean deserved its reputation. It was a reformatory situated in the small village of Daingean in County Offaly. It was surrounded by a twenty-foot-high wall and was as grim on the inside as it looked from the outside. It was run by an order of priests and brothers called the Oblates of Mary Immaculate.

The only rules were the Ten Commandments. To fail to carry out an order rendered you liable under the Fourth Commandment. An immodest word or gesture, and you had sinned against the Sixth. The least transgression brought a beating. And the age-old principle that a man should not be punished twice for the same offence did not apply. You were first beaten by the Prefect of Discipline and then by the brother in charge of your working party, and after that any other brother who happened to come across you in the exercise yard might take it into his head to make his own contribution to saving your immortal soul by giving you yet another beating.

The policy of spiritual reclamation extended to the diet. Breakfast and supper were identical: porridge, bread and dripping, and luke-warm, unsweetened tea in a rusty tin mug. Dinner consisted of cabbage water made from the thick green outer leaves of the cabbage, and floating in the cabbage water would be bad potatoes still in their jackets. You got meat once a year, on Christmas Day.

A boy who tried to escape would be flogged and would have his head shaved and would be made to kneel on the concrete floor of the dining-hall for a whole week on a diet of bread and water three times a day.

I heard the man in the next cell moving about, and presently I knew that he had picked up his chamber pot and was urinating into it. I would lie in bed a few more minutes. The screws didn't unlock the cell doors until seven o'clock. I continued to stare at the ceiling.

After Daingean, of course, it had to be the boat for England. But old habits die hard. Within a couple of years there was a charge of receiving a wireless set. A year on the run and then, inevitably, capture. "What you need," the judge said, "is a period of strict discipline. I will send you for Borstal training." That could mean anything from one to three years. I was released on licence after only fifteen months. In contrast to the people of Daingean, the staff at the Borstal were decent, fair-minded people.

But enough was enough. I was now twenty-one and the time had come to settle down. I went to a town called Crawley in Sussex. I began by digging trenches on a building site and graduated to the wages office at a local factory. For the next six years I led a hard-working, law-abiding life, and nobody knew anything about my past. Then the local police found out that I had been to Borstal, and that was the beginning of the end. My neighbours were asked questions about me, and gradually these questions filtered back to me.

In one particular incident I issued a writ against a policeman, and the case was down for hearing in the High Court. Shortly afterwards the policeman received a home-made bomb through the post. Because of the writ I was the immediate suspect. I was arrested and put on trial at the Sussex Assizes. I pleaded not guilty, but the jury decided otherwise, and I got seven years.

I had been taken to Wandsworth Prison at the end of my trial and had stayed there for eight weeks before being transferred to Wormwood Scrubs. Wandsworth was a filthy, depressing place, and the screws hated it as much as the prisoners did. When my landing officer came to tell me of the decision to transfer me, I asked him if this would be an improvement. He turned his pale, sad face towards the distant roof and, with what seemed like despair in his voice, he said, "Anything would be better than this fucking place."

Things were different at Wormwood Scrubs. I spent the first two years in the Tailor's Shop, where I became head cutter, and then I was made editor of the prison magazine, *New Horizon*. As editor of the magazine I was the most highly privileged prisoner in Wormwood

Scrubs. The editorship was a full-time job, and I had my own private office in D-Hall. My task was to produce a twenty-four-page duplicated magazine once a month. Since I was a competent touch-typist the work came very easy to me, and cutting the stencils was a simple matter. Duplicating the two hundred copies of the magazine was only a day's work. The real labour lay in trying to persuade the other prisoners to write letters and articles and then having to rewrite most of what they contributed.

The editorship carried a blue-band with it. This was a three-inch band of blue cloth that you fixed round your left upper arm. A blueband, or Leader as he was called, could go anywhere in the prison without an escort. Indeed, he could even escort other prisoners.

I was feeling very happy this morning. In exactly one month I would appear before the Hostel Board. If I was accepted I would spend the last seven or eight months of my sentence living in the prison Hostel and going out to work each day in the outside world among ordinary people. I could stay out all day provided I was back in the hostel by ten-forty-five, and at weekends I could go away.

In the meantime there was work to be done. The first Monday of the month was distribution day. There were two hundred copies of *New Horizon* waiting in my office to be distributed throughout the prison. And then I would have to start work on the October issue.

The landing officers were shouting down to the Duty Principal Officer on the ground floor (the Ones) to tell him how many prisoners were in their cells on each landing. "Seventy on the Ones, sir." "Seventy on the Twos, sir." "Eighty on the Threes, sir." "Eighty-two on the Fours, sir." There was a slight pause as the P.O. added up these figures and checked them against the total on the roll. "Slop out!" he shouted, and the screws began unlocking the cell doors.

I joined the queue in the recess to empty my chamber pot into the large sink provided for the purpose and then went back to my cell. Ten minutes later the bell rang on the Ones again and the desk officer shouted, "Breakfast—lead on!" The prisoners headed for the narrow iron stairs leading down to the ground floor.

My table in D-Hall was Number 12, and I shared it with three rapists, an embezzler, a bank robber, and four murderers. Before going to my table I took my blue-band from its numbered hook on the rack near the duty officer's desk. The table orderly laid the table and then fetched the two tea jugs and the bread and margarine from the hotplate. When he brought the goulash there were the usual caustic remarks. This goulash was a strange concoction made up from the leftovers of the previous day's meals, and hardly anybody ate it.

As soon as the screw had checked the roll by counting the men at each table, I headed straight for my office.

Wormwood Scrubs is comprised of four huge oblong cell blocks built parallel to each other, with other buildings and workshops and the exercise yards between them, the whole lot surrounded by a twenty-foot-high wall. The cell blocks are identical, with their four landings and a turret at each corner. The turrets have a small room at the level of each landing. These rooms are used as offices by the landing officers or as storerooms. My office was one of these turret rooms at the north end of Three landing.

I had long ago made myself comfortable here, with good furniture and curtains and a carpet on the floor and a gas ring on which I could make my own meals to supplement the prison food. As a non-smoker I was able to spend my entire salary of eight shillings a week on food-stuffs from the canteen.

In the office I made myself a cup of coffee and sat down at my desk. Through the window in front of me I had an excellent view, over the top of the north perimeter wall, of the large park from which the prison took its name. Just a few yards beyond the wall were the white H-shaped goalposts which were used at weekends by some local Irish hurling clubs. I had promised myself that as soon as I was free I would stand near those goalposts and look up at the window of the magazine office and see what it felt like to be viewing Wormwood Scrubs Prison from the outside.

The bell rang down on the Ones and the screw shouted, "On the yard!" The prisoners were going to work. I would allow them about ten minutes to settle in their various workshops and then I would do my rounds of the prison to distribute the magazines. I made myself another cup of coffee and continued to gaze out at the park. How soon would I be out there standing near those hurling goalposts? Two months' time, or ten months'? It depended on the Hostel Board.

I gathered up the magazines and left D-Hall. An hour and a half later I was back, exhausted, my task done. I made myself another cup of coffee and put my feet up on the desk. I would have a couple of days off before starting work on the October issue. After all, I was my own boss.

I looked at my alarm clock perched on top of the bookshelf: eleven-fifteen. Lunch was at eleven-thirty, but I would make my way down to the Ones at about eleven-twenty. The reason for this was that I enjoyed a little stroll on the ground floor before lunch began and while the others were queuing up. For the past few months I had been sharing this daily stroll with a man for whom I had a great deal of sympathy. His name was George Blake.

In May 1961 he had been charged at the Old Bailey on five counts of spying for the Russians and had been sentenced to an unprecedented forty-two years' imprisonment. He had been in the Foreign Office and at the time of his offences was working as a British Secret Service agent in Berlin. He was what is popularly called a double agent.

I had been on friendly terms with him since shortly after my arrival at Wormwood Scrubs nearly four years before. We met during an extramural course in English literature being run at the prison by London University. Though he was serving the longest prison sentence ever passed in a British court of law, Blake *did his bird*—his sentence—better than any other prisoner I had met. I had known men serving a mere six months or a year who wanted the whole world to share their sorrow. Not so Blake. But then I had always noticed that it was characteristic of the educated and well-bred prisoner that he could do his bird with apparent ease while most of the others complained.

With full remission, Blake would have to serve twenty-eight years of his forty-two-year sentence. Since he was thirty-eight years of age when he was sentenced, this meant that he would be sixty-six before he was released.

Whatever private agonies went through his mind in the solitude of his darkened cell at night at the awful prospect before him, he showed no signs of them to his fellow prisoners. Indeed, it was they who frequently came to him in search of a shoulder to cry on, and I always marvelled at the sight of this man-without-hope giving help and advice and comfort to young fellows in their twenties whose grandchildren would be in Borstal before Blake again saw the light of day as a free man. Blake was one of that all too rare breed of men—a good listener. And in prison such men were in especially great demand.

Blake was at this time studying Arabic literature, and a couple of months before he had been given permission to study in his cell two days a week instead of going to the Mailbag Shop. He would be in his cell today, Monday, and since he would get to lunch sooner, I would be able to have a longer chat with him than usual.

I locked the office and went down to the Ones. I walked up and down for a few minutes at the north end of the hall, where there were no tables. There was a trickle of prisoners arriving early for lunch. They were mostly red-bands, who worked on their own without the supervision of a screw. They were always early.

Blake's cell was on the Ones, Number 8, where they could keep close watch on him. He was the only prisoner in D-Hall who could not be entrusted to a Leader. He was accompanied by a screw everywhere he went outside the Hall.

As I turned round at the end of the hall to walk back towards Table 14, I saw Blake emerge from his cell. Number 8 was down at the south end. As he got closer I noticed that he had his hands pulled well down behind his back; his head was bent forward, and there was a look of deep concentration on his face. I had never seen him look like this before. He usually walked through the hall with his head held high, a broad smile on his face. I suspected immediately that something was wrong.

When he reached the spot where I had stopped to wait for him he raised his head suddenly and looked me straight in the face. He was frowning deeply. Without any preliminaries he said, "Mr. Bourke, I have something very important to discuss with you." He had not addressed me as "Mr. Bourke" for some years, not since we had become friends.

"Oh, what is it?"

We started to walk towards the end of the hall.

"I have a proposition to put to you," he said, his arms still pulled firmly behind his back, his eyes once again on the floor. "Before I put my proposition to you," he went on, "there are two preliminary points I should like to make. First of all, I possess no capital. I have no money at all, but I do represent in my person a fairly substantial sum of money. There are certain things I can do, such as writing about my experiences, which would have a very ready market. Do you understand this?"

"Yes," I said.

"The second point," he went on, "is this: if you refuse to accept my proposition I shall perfectly understand and shall not think any the less of you for it. All I ask is that you don't make up your mind straightaway, but think it over for a few days. Have I made myself perfectly clear?"

"Yes, perfectly clear."

I noticed that he had started to turn round about ten yards short of Table 14, where a few men were now sitting down to lunch.

"Good," he said.

We walked in silence for a few yards as he carefully formulated his next words.

"I have now been in prison for more than four years. From the outset my sentence has always seemed to me to be a bit unreal, and I had hoped for some sort of relief, such as an exchange of prisoners with the Russians or something like that. However, I now have good reason to believe that such an exchange will not take place. I have therefore decided that the time has come for me to leave here—er—under my own steam, as it were. I am asking you to help me escape."

I said nothing. I was too surprised and confused to speak. There had been no forewarning of this, not the slightest hint in that smiling face over the years. The most notorious spy in the Western world had just asked me to spring him from jail!

"As I said," Blake went on, "you don't have to give me your answer straightaway. Think it over for a few days."

I stopped abruptly and turned to face him. "George I don't have to think it over. I have already made up my mind."

"Oh?" His face clouded apprehensively. "What have you decided?"

"I'm your man!"

His face lit up.

"Just one thing," I said.

"What's that?"

"Don't mention money any more."

All that afternoon I kept turning Blake's words over in my mind, and I realized that from now on I would be able to think of little else. Why had I agreed to undertake this dangerous mission? And so readily? I liked Blake. You couldn't help liking him. Virtually everyone at the prison, both inmates and authorities, were deeply impressed by Blake's charm and good manners and by his humanitarian concern for the well-being of his fellow men. But was that enough? There were quite a few people in D-Hall that I liked, but I was not sure that I would so readily have agreed to do the same for them. The length of his sentence was a factor certainly, and of course he was not an ordinary criminal but a prisoner of conscience.

But no, I had to be honest with myself. In the solitude of my tiny office there could be no hope of evading the truth. I had accepted this mission partly because I saw in it an opportunity to strike a blow against authority.

For the next month Blake and I spent many hours discussing our plans. There were three alternatives: A) to escape during the film show in D-Rec on a Saturday night; B) to make a dash for the wall while on the way to the library on a Saturday afternoon; C) to do the same thing while sitting on the grass near the north wall with all the other prisoners on a Sunday afternoon. All three plans would involve me throwing a rope ladder over the wall from the outside.

We calculated that we would need about seven hundred pounds to finance the project, and Blake decided that I should ask his mother for the money when I left the prison. He would find some way of letting her know on her next visit what our intentions were.

BOOK ONE

1

Last Days in D-Hall

Blake was very pleased when I told him that I had got the Hostel.

"And how long before you move?" I asked.

"At least a month," I told him. "Maybe even longer. We will have plenty of warning. I shall have to see the man from the Ministry of Labour and then later go for an interview with my prospective employer."

"Good," he said. "So we have plenty of time to make our final preparations. We must go over everything again in minute detail. There must be no room for error after your departure, and our communications must be clear and effective. Once you go on the Hostel we shall not see each other again unless the operation succeeds."

"Right," I agreed, "and for the next month we must keep a close watch on routine and note any changes or even rumours of changes. You should go to the cinema frequently so that they will get used to seeing you there, and I shall make a point of studying the prison at six o'clock on Saturday evenings. I shall do this by offering to take the tea buckets and trays back to the kitchen for the hotplate Leader."

"That's a good idea," Blake said.

"Well," I said, smiling, "it is now, we hope, just a matter of time."

"Perhaps December or January?" Blake suggested hopefully.

"Perhaps," I said. "Perhaps."

During the first week in November I was seen by the man from the local Ministry of Labour office. He took all my particulars and said he would try to fix me up as soon as possible. Things were now definitely moving. It was time for a last really exhaustive look at our plans.

"Most important of all, Sean," said Blake, "is communication. We must each know what the other is talking about. There must be no slip-ups here. All reference to Plan A, then, is reference to my departure from the cinema at six o'clock on a Saturday evening. Plan B means that I make my getaway on the way to the library at two o'clock on a Saturday afternoon. And Plan C is when I'm out near the north wall on a Sunday afternoon with the rest of D-Hall."

"I've got all that," I said.

"And the code?" Blake asked.

"Yes," I said. "You will send me a message in the first instance. It will be, 'Have you got the book *A Thousand and One Nights* yet?' This will mean that you, for your part, are all set to go. Then when I've got everything ready for the operation I'll send you a message saying, 'I've got that book *A Thousand and One Nights*, and I'll let you have it on Saturday.' This will mean that I'm going to do the job that Saturday. Then, finally, you will acknowledge my signal by saying, 'Thank you for getting me that book. I look forward to having it on Saturday.' That's it."

"Good." Blake smiled.

"And," I added, "all messages go through Peter Martin." Peter Martin was a twenty-six-year-old Londoner who was a close friend of both Blake and myself. He was a professional criminal who specialized in banks and post offices and was at that time serving a six-year sentence. We knew we could trust him completely.

"Of course." Blake paused. "And now I'll tell you how I propose to let my mother know that I'm sending you along to see her. I've got some snapshots of my family in my cell. If I cut one of these snapshots in two pieces and give one of the pieces to my mother and the other piece to you, when you meet you could put the two pieces together, and that would convince my mother beyond doubt."

"A good idea," I said. "And how would you go about letting your mother have her half of the photograph?"

"I have also thought of that. I shall just slip it to her on a visit."

I looked at him. "But your visits are special affairs. You see your mother in a special room away from all the other prisoners, and you have a screw watching over you."

"That's right," he said. "But the officer is very friendly about it. He sits as far away from us as possible and doesn't go out of his way to watch our every action and listen to our every word." He then went on to explain that he would have no difficulty in pressing part of the small snapshot into her hand as they sat together at the table laughing and joking and eating chocolates.

"The atmosphere is really very relaxed and informal, and my mother and I exchange an occasional word or two in Dutch. In this way I can give her a hint of what to expect. I can say a few words in Dutch like, 'A man will call to see you and you are to trust him because he will be acting for me.' She will probably guess straightaway that I'm planning to escape. And, of course, you will give her all the details she needs to know."

"Sounds easy," I said thoughtfully.

"All right," said Blake finally, "let's go to my cell and have a look at some snapshots."

In the cell Blake emptied one of those yellow Kodak envelopes onto the table and selected a photograph showing his three young sons playing in a garden. (He was devoted to his family but had nevertheless suggested to his wife that because of his imprisonment she start divorce proceedings. She had done so, and they were subsequently divorced.) He held it up and looked at me silently. I nodded my approval. With a small scissors he cut the photograph in two halves vertically so that the head of the boy in the middle was divided. He handed me one of the pieces, and I immediately put it in my pocket. The other piece he put back in the envelope. Very conscious of the possibility that his cell was bugged, we spoke not a word until we were out in the hall again.

When we were well clear of the cell Blake turned to me. "Well, that's about everything. My mother is coming to see me next Tuesday, and I shall pass my half of the snapshot to her then."

Mrs. Blake did, in fact, visit the prison the following Tuesday, and Blake successfully passed on the half of the photograph.

In the last week of November the Principal Officer in charge of the Hostel under the Assistant Governor (the Hostel Warden, as he was called) told me that a job had been got for me at the Lucas car-accessory factory in Acton, about a mile from the prison. I had to be at Reception at eight o'clock next morning to change into my civvies in preparation for an interview at the factory.

The Hostel P.O. picked me up at Reception and took me to the main gate. He had an official-looking form in his hand. "This," he announced, "is your parole form. You're on parole until one o'clock. I'll have to get one of the Governors to sign it. Here's your letter of introduction." He handed me a long brown envelope. "And here's five bob expenses." He handed me two half crowns. "I'm lending you this myself so that we won't have to go through all the red tape of getting an advance from the Steward—he's responsible for the hostellers' money. You can pay me back out of your first week's wages."

Mr. Ware, the man in charge of the Borstal Wing, was the first of the Governors to come through the gate that morning, and the P.O. got him to sign my parole form.

"Good luck, Bourke." He grinned as he signed the form.

"Thank you, sir."

The gatekeeper unlocked the small door for pedestrians.

"Straight across the road," said the P.O. "Number Seven bus takes you to the factory gate. You're on your own. Good luck."

I stepped through the door and walked in the free world for the first time in four years. After the greyness of prison the world outside seemed a dazzling panorama of colour. There were several new designs of motorcar, and girls' skirts were shorter than they had been before. I thought everybody must be looking at me, but nobody noticed me at all. I caught a Number Seven bus and got out at the bottom of East Acton Lane.

The factory was just across the road in Warple Way. I was handed from Reception to Personnel and then to an assistant foreman, who led me through a labyrinth of corridors and passages, through lines of deafening machines with their masked and goggled attendants, through steaming, sulphurous process plants. After the peace and tranquillity of that little editorial office in D-Hall, the free world was going to exact its price.

Presently we came to a cagelike office, fashioned of sheet metal and glass, in the middle of the floor deep down in the factory's bowels. Here sat my future boss, the general foreman in charge of all stores. I would be one of several hundred men working under him.

He shook me firmly by the hand. "Please sit down," he said with a smile.

His assistant handed him the letter of introduction, which he read slowly. Then he looked up at me. "Well, Mr. Bourke," he began, "we have a five-day week, Monday to Friday, and the hours are seven-thirty to four-thirty. Your wages will be about sixteen pounds a week. You can work overtime if you want to. That's entirely up to you. You'll be working in 224 Stores, which is responsible for feeding the production lines that make electrical switchgear for military fighting vehicles—tanks, armoured cars, that sort of thing. It's a nice stores, a pleasant place to work, and you'll find the other people there very easy to get on with."

The letter of introduction was lying open on his desk. He looked down at it and then looked at me again. "By the way," he said, spreading his open hand over the letter, "nobody." He looked me straight in the face, and his expression was quite solemn. "Nobody," he repeated.

I nodded. "Thank you," I said.

That was the only reference made to my past life during all the time I worked at that factory. It was Wednesday, and we agreed that I should start work the following Monday.

On the way back to the prison I called in at the Western public house for a drink. The Western is on the roundabout where Westway meets Western Avenue. It is only a ten-minute walk from Wormwood Scrubs Prison. In addition to the five shillings given to me by the P.O. I had a couple of pound notes that I had brought with me from D-Hall. I had a meal and about six double whiskies, and at one o'clock I was ringing the bell at the prison gate and asking to be let in.

The Hostel P.O. was very pleased to hear that I had got the job. "When do you start?" he asked.

"Monday."

"Good. You can move into the Hostel on Friday. You'll have the whole weekend to settle in."

Later I met Blake in the Hall and gave him the news. We talked for about half an hour, and I knew that he was worried about my drink-induced gaiety, though he made no reference to it. He would now, I thought, look upon my partiality to a drop of the hard stuff as an additional hazard.

After lunch on Friday I was hanging about the south end of D-Hall near the gate leading to the Reception, the gate that Blake would use on his way to the library if Plan B were ever employed. My bundle rested on a table, and beside it was the pillowcase containing those items with which I had been issued on the day of my arrival: razor, shaving brush, nail brush, and so on. The screw shouted, "Exercise! Everybody on the yard!" The prisoners started to drift slowly, resignedly, towards that side gate leading to the exercise yard. One or two threw a reluctant glance in my direction and wished they were me.

Blake emerged from his cell and walked towards me. We shook hands. "Good luck, Sean," he said. Then, still clutching my hand, he added slowly, "I hope we meet again." He unbuttoned the flap of his breast pocket. "I would like you to have this as a souvenir," he said, handing me a postcard. "I think the theme is no longer appropriate." He then turned his back and headed for the exercise yard.

"I'll be seeing you," I called after him, but he didn't look back. I looked at the postcard. It was a print showing a monkey sitting in a garden of flowers. Round the monkey's neck was an iron collar, which was connected by a thick chain to a heavy garden roller. On the monkey's face was an expression of the most pitiable agony and despair.

The D-Hall Leader came up to me.

"Hello, Sean. All ready to go?"

"Yes."

"In that case, I'll have your band."

"Oh, of course." I unbuttoned my blue-band and surrendered it.

He stuck it in his pocket. "I'll hang it on the rack for you later," he said. "And now I'll take you across to the Reception. The P.O. asked me to tell you that he'll be along to collect you at two o'clock. That should give you plenty of time to change into your civvies and be cleared by Reception."

And so for the first time in two years I found myself being escorted by another prisoner. The situation was a little bizarre. *I* would be walking free through the streets of London within an hour, but at this moment I was being guarded by a man who was himself serving life imprisonment and who carried in his pocket the blue-band I had just surrendered to him.

A screw unlocked the gate for us, and I walked out of D-Hall for the last time. I didn't look back.

2
Back to the World

I changed into my civvies in Reception, and shortly afterwards the
Hostel P.O. came to collect me. We sat in his office in the Hostel, he on
one side of the desk, I on the other. On the desk was a small canvas
bag secured by a pull-through cord, some money, and several documents.

"Well now, Bourke," the P.O. began, "the rules are simple. You
have your breakfast here in the Hostel and also your dinner in the
evening. Your lunch, of course, you have at your place of work. You
must be back in the prison by ten-forty-five each night. You can have
weekend leave from Friday evening to Sunday evening to go home to
your family or to an address approved by the Home Office. Such an
address would have to be checked out by the local police and probation
service. Saving is compulsory. On Friday evening you will hand in
your wages to me here, and you will be given three pounds pocket
money. Another three pounds will be deducted for your board and
lodging. The balance will be saved for your release." He picked up the
canvas bag and untied the cord. "Your valuables," he announced and
emptied the bag on the desk. There was a watch, a pair of cuff-links, a
High Court writ, and an Irish ten-pound note.

The English had insisted on treating this Irish banknote as a *valu-
able* instead of as cash. If they had treated it as cash it would now be
with the Steward as part of my compulsory savings. As it was, it
looked like I was going to have plenty of spending money for my first
weekend of freedom.

He then picked up two hard-covered passes. "This," he said, handing me the smaller of the two, "is your daily pass. And this other one is for weekends. Please sign both. When you come back into the prison you leave your pass at the gatehouse in the rack provided. And this"—he picked up the three pound notes—"is your first week's allowance, in advance. You now owe the Steward three pounds." He paused and looked thoughtful. "That reminds me," he said, grinning, "you owe *me* five bob." He took back one of the pound notes and gave me fifteen shillings in change from his pocket. Then he glanced at the Irish ten-pound note and smiled. "By the way," he said, "before I forget, booze is not allowed inside the prison walls."

The Hostel was next to the Reception, at the front of the prison, its door a few yards from the perimeter wall. It consisted of one wing of an L-shaped building two stories high. The other wing was the Officers' Mess. When I first moved in, the upper floor of the Hostel wing was still part of the Officers' Mess and was being used to accommodate bachelor screws. Later it was taken over to increase the capacity of the Hostel. The front door led straight into a tiled corridor that ran the full length of the building. The rooms were on either side of the corridor, and down at the end were the kitchen and the sitting-room. There were three men to a room.

My room was the first on the left inside the door, and I shared it with a murderer and a rapist. The cooking and cleaning were done by a red-band prisoner from D-Hall, who had a room of his own in the Hostel. It was the policy of the authorities to appoint a man to this job who was himself due to go before the Hostel Board within a couple of months. Such a man, they considered, would be less inclined to fiddle.

That evening I went to the Western again and drank at least a full bottle of whisky. Prolonged abstinence reduces one's capacity for drink, and I often marvelled afterwards that I did not lose the Hostel on my first day. Some animal instinct for survival made me walk straight and orderly through the prison gate that night. Nor was that the only time I got drunk before Blake's escape. No matter how much willpower a man thinks he has got, he will do and say things when he is drunk that he will later regret, and I am no exception. But if you hold something sacred, no amount of drink will loosen your tongue on the subject. My deep-rooted appreciation of the importance of Blake's escape served as a bulwark against the swollen tides of alcohol during my months on the Hostel, and afterwards.

On the Saturday morning I caught a train to Crawley in Sussex. As I alighted on the platform I noticed a detective from the local force standing a few yards from the barrier. His hair had greyed a little more in the past four years. The police would have been informed as a matter of routine that somebody from their *manor* had just been released to the Hostel. Since the charge had been one of attempting to kill a policeman by means of a home-made bomb sent through the post, this slight show of unease was perhaps understandable.

I walked down the main street towards Queen's Square. One or two people recognized me and promptly got into a huddle to point and whisper. (I had always thought that that sort of thing only happened in films.) In a pub the landlord did his best to be kind. There was no reference to prison, of course. "Ah, Sean, how are you? Have a drink. You've put on a bit of weight. How've you been keeping? Glad to see you again. Are you living in Crawley now? There's plenty of jobs around here these days. No trouble getting a job, that's for sure."

A big Irish labourer in a blue suit came up to me, depositing his pint of Guinness next to my own drink. "Excuse me," he said, "aren't you Sean Bourke?"

"I am."

"I hope you don't mind me asking. I don't know you at all myself, but I've heard people talking about you in the pubs."

"Have you?"

"Yes, I have. Tell me, don't you—er—feel embarrassed at all, coming in here to a pub, like, and meeting people and that sort of thing?"

"No. If I felt embarrassed I wouldn't be here."

"Is that so? Well, I just thought that, like, you might feel . . ."

"Not only am I not embarrassed, my friend, but I intend to write a book about it someday."

"Is that so?"

"Yes, it is."

When I left the pub I caught a taxi to Langley Green, one of the outlying neighbourhoods. I paid the cabbie off some distance from the house and finished the journey on foot. I rang the bell and waited. I heard hurried footsteps in the hall and then the door opened. For the first few seconds she didn't seem to recognize me, then her mouth fell open but no sound came out of it.

"Hello," I said.

"Hello, Sean."

She had changed too. But then she had been only twenty-one when I went to prison. Now she was twenty-five. We stood there facing each other silently for what seemed a long time, and I knew instinctively that my arrival was not going to be a cause for rejoicing.

"Er—come in." She stepped back and held the door open.

I needed no help to find the sitting-room. We didn't shake hands or come into contact in any way.

"Sit down," she said. She hadn't smiled. She just looked thoughtful and frowned a little. "Can I get you a cup of tea?"

"No, thanks."

"Sean—" she began.

I forced a laugh. "Well," I said, looking around at the room, "according to the storybooks, this is where one of us must say, 'it's been a long time,' or does that sound a bit corny?"

She looked down at her hands, clasping and unclasping them nervously. "Sean," she said in a whisper without looking up, "I'm sorry. That's all I can say."

"There's no need for you to be sorry. It was I who went to jail, not you. But one letter, just one letter, would have been welcome. Even if it was only to say good-bye."

"You've no idea what it was like with the neighbours—the giggling and the pointing and the whispering—and all the time—"

"You could have written one letter without telling your neighbours about it."

She looked more distressed than ever. "My mother didn't want me to."

"Where's your mother now?"

"Out shopping."

There was a scraping sound at the back door like somebody trying to rub off the paint. She gave me a nervous look, started to say something, and then went to the door. When she reappeared she was holding a small boy by the hand.

"Ah, another nephew!" I smiled.

She stood there looking down at me, still holding the child by the hand. "No, Sean. He's not my nephew. He's my son."

I gripped the arms of the chair a little harder for a moment and then stood up.

"I've been trying to tell you. I've been married for three years."

We stood there facing each other in silence for a full minute, she with her eyes cast down at the child. Then I started to walk towards the hall.

At the door she gripped my arm, our first contact that afternoon. "Sean, I'm sorry. I really am sorry." And I could see by her eyes that she was.

"Don't be sorry," I said. "In a way this makes things easier. The last obstacle has been removed. You'll probably never know how lucky you are. Good-bye."

I walked back to the town centre.

Next day was Sunday, and I decided not to waste it. I took my pass from the rack at the gatehouse and the screw let me out, having first noted in his ledger my name and the time of my exit. I turned right in Du Cane Road and walked to the bottom, to where it joined the East Acton shopping centre, in Old Oak Road. Erconwald Street joins the shopping centre at the same point, forming a V with Du Cane Road. I walked up Erconwald Street, past the East Acton Underground station, to Braybrook Street, which borders the western edge of Wormwood Scrubs park. The prison wall loomed up ahead of me to the right; the huge parallel cell blocks looked as ugly from the outside as they looked from within. My eyes went to the turrets of D-Hall and found the window of the magazine office on the Threes. I walked across the park towards the white-painted, H-shaped goalposts. There was no game in progress. I stood in the centre of the pitch and looked up at that window for a full minute. It was a pleasant feeling but at the same time a guilty one. The cell windows on the Threes and Fours were visible over the top of the wall, and I could not escape the painful truth that my present happiness was built on the knowledge that behind each of those barred windows there languished a captive man and I was no longer one of them. I was free. I could look at a prison wall and derive a comfort from it that was possible only to a man who had himself tasted captivity.

I spent most of that day reconnoitring the area immediately around the prison, only breaking off for an hour to go back to the Hostel for lunch. The prison was bordered on the front by Du Cane Road, which ran from Old Oak Common Lane in the west to Wood Lane in the

WORMWOOD SCRUBS

HAMMERSMITH HOSPITAL

ARTILLERY ROAD

CAR

Telephone kiosk

College

D HALL

Hostel

C HALL

B HALL

A HALL

Governor's house

PATH

Main gate

Street gate

Officers' houses

PATH

DU CANE ROAD

CENTRAL LINE UNDERGROUND

N

east. The western wall of the prison was on a narrow strip of private land behind a row of screws' cottages in Wulfstan Street (Wulfstan Street was one of two streets connecting Du Cane Road to Erconwald Street. The other was Fitz Neal Street.) The east wall, behind D-Hall, was separated from Hammersmith Hospital by a small private road leading from Du Cane Road straight to the park at the back. This road was called Artillery Road. The north wall of the prison was entirely on the park. The park itself was, I discovered, slightly larger than my original estimate of half a mile square. It was bordered on the west by Braybrook Street and on the east by Scrubs Lane, which connected Wood Lane to the Harrow Road. The northern edge of the park was bordered by an iron fence separating it from some railway lines. The railway lines were much lower than the level of the park to enable them to go under a bridge at Old Oak Common Lane, resulting in an embankment between the fence and the lines themselves. This embankment was divided into allotments, and here and there was a small toolshed belonging to the gardeners. The prison was near the western edge of the park, and the remainder of the park to the east was hidden from Du Cane Road by Hammersmith Hospital, St. Dunstan's Grammar School, and a private sports ground. The south wall of the prison was separated from Du Cane Road by a strip of land about thirty yards wide belonging to the Home Office. On this land were built screws' flats, on either side of the forecourt, their doors leading onto Du Cane Road. In the forecourt itself, to the left, were the Officers' Club and a house occupied by some of the nurses working in the prison hospital. To the right was a large unoccupied house, which had at one time been the Chaplain's residence. The screws' flats to the left of the forecourt stretched the full extent of the perimeter wall, concealing it from the road. To the right of the forecourt they went only halfway, the remainder of the space being occupied by the Governor's and the Principal Medical Officer's semi-detached houses and, down at the corner near Artillery Road, a couple of prefabs occupied by P.O.s. The street gate of the forecourt was never shut, day or night. There would be no point.

I walked through every street in the neighbourhood, making a careful note of all their features, the location of schools, shops, car parks, the density of vehicular and pedestrian traffic, the location of pedestrian crossings and traffic lights, and anything else that I considered might have the slightest effect on a getaway. I then went to a shop and bought a street map of Hammersmith and district as well as an "A to Z" of London. I spent the whole evening in my room at the Hostel, studying these maps and making notes. The other two occupants of the room were on weekend leave and would not be back much before ten-thirty.

Once Blake was over the wall there were, it seemed to me, three ways of getting us out of the immediate vicinity of the prison. Running across to the railway lines at the north edge of the park would serve no purpose at all. That was out. I could leave the getaway car parked in one of three places: Braybrook Street on the western edge of the park, Scrubs Lane on the eastern edge, or Artillery Road. Since the prison was quite near Braybrook Street, there seemed little sense in running virtually the whole width of the park to Scrubs Lane. Such a run would take nearly ten minutes, and if the alarm was raised immediately (and I had to allow that it would be) a run to Scrubs Lane would almost certainly be a run into the arms of the law. And Braybrook Street was the beginning of a council estate. There were children playing in the streets and housewives gossiping over garden fences, and between the prison wall and Braybrook Street there might be several people exercising their dogs.

It seemed to me as I studied my maps that the most sensible route might be along Artillery Road. The sooner we got inside the getaway car the better would be our chances. Whether we turned right or left in Du Cane Road would to some extent depend on the location of the hideout. Turning left would be infinitely preferable as it would involve breaking into only one lane of traffic, while turning right would mean an uncertain and dangerous wait for a simultaneous gap in *both* lanes.

I spent every evening of the following week plodding around Hammersmith and the surrounding districts, from the Harrow Road in the north to Uxbridge Road in the south, from Ladbroke Grove in the east to Horn Lane in the west. The only way to get to know a district thoroughly is on foot, and at the end of the first week I was a tired but satisfied man.

On my maps I had marked every traffic light, pedestrian crossing, school, playground, car park, bus route, Underground station, one-way street, cinema, church, pub, and police station. Most of these could, one way or another, affect the speed of a getaway. The cinemas, churches, and pubs might be places of temporary refuge if pursuit got too hot, and Underground stations would be ideal terminal points. The police stations were, of course, of special importance. The three nearest ones to the prison were in the Harrow Road to the north, Acton High Street to the southwest, and Shepherd's Bush immediately to the south. The latter was the prison's "local" station and was situated in Uxbridge Road at the junction with Loftus Road. This station would get my special attention later on. The visiting hours at Hammersmith Hospital, I discovered from the gatekeeper, were from seven to eight every evening of the week. This was to prove one of the most important factors in the escape.

3

An Approach to Blake's Family

A week after I entered the Hostel the agreed signal came from Blake.
A trusty who was casually strolling past the Hostel building told me
that Peter Martin had inquired if I could get him the book *A Thousand and One Nights*. I immediately wrote a brief letter to Blake's
mother in Radlett, Hertfordshire:

> Dear Mrs. Blake:
>   You will have been expecting to hear from me. I am acting
> on your son's behalf. Could you please meet me outside Golder's
> Green Underground station this Friday evening at 8 P.M. Please
> bring your half of the photograph.
>
>   Sean Bourke

On Friday I caught a tube to Golder's Green and got there at a
quarter to eight. I waited at the far side of the street outside the Hippodrome Theatre. At five minutes to eight Mrs. Blake got off a Green-
line country bus and stood near the entrance to the station. I recognized her from a photograph Blake had shown me in his cell. I carefully observed everybody else who got off the bus with her, and she
did not appear to be followed. I kept her under observation for another
ten minutes, carefully scrutinizing everyone in the vicinity. Then I
crossed to the station.

I walked up to her and raised my hat. "Good evening, Mrs. Blake?"
"Yes." She gave me a keen look. She seemed nervous.
"I'm Sean Bourke, madam. Shall we take a little walk?"

"Yes."

"It would be a good idea for us to discuss our business while walking," I told her. "A restaurant might not be safe."

We walked across to the Hippodrome and strolled up the quiet and not very well lit North End Road.

At the second street light I stopped and faced her. "Did you bring your half of the photograph?"

She opened her handbag and took it out. I took my half out of my wallet and put the two together, making the head of the centre boy whole again to reveal a smiling face.

"Does that satisfy you, madam?"

"Oh yes," she said, hardly glancing at the photograph. "I know George sent you." She spoke with a slightly foreign accent but her English was perfect.

We walked slowly on.

"Well, Mrs. Blake, I'll get straight to the point. George has asked me to help him escape."

She registered no surprise. "I thought that was what he was trying to tell me when I visited him. How can I help?"

"Something like this costs money," I told her. "George is asking you to lend him that money. We'll need seven hundred pounds."

We walked on in silence for a moment. "George asked me to say that it is only a loan," I continued. "Later he will be in a position to write his story and will be able to repay you."

"But how could *I* give you the money?" Mrs. Blake asked, and her voice was still nervous. "You see, I lead a very quiet existence in Radlett. It's only a little village and everybody knows everybody else's business. I never draw more than a few pounds out of the bank at a time, just enough to do my shopping. If I were to draw out seven hundred pounds my bank manager would be suspicious. He knows who I am, you see."

We walked to the end of North End Road and back, discussing the problem of handing over the money. I agreed that it would be impossible for her to give me the money without the fact of her having drawn it out becoming known to the police after the escape. I hinted as gently as I could that as her son's freedom was at stake, this was a hazard that she might be prepared to face.

"After all, madam, this is a free country, and you don't *have* to tell the police why you drew the money out. You can tell them to mind their own business. They can't put you in jail for that. And you would have bought your son's freedom for a mere seven hundred pounds. It might be worth the inconvenience."

Mrs. Blake looked at the ground and shook her head slowly. "I've been through so much before, when George was arrested. All those reporters . . ."

We reached the Hippodrome again and stopped on the corner. "I really do wish, Mrs. Blake, that you could find some way of handing over the cash. George is counting on it. There's a lot at stake for him."

"I'll have to think about it," she said. "Can we meet again?"

"How about next Friday? Here at the same time."

"Very well."

I walked her across to her bus and we said good night.

The following Friday I was again waiting outside the Hippodrome at a quarter to eight. I let Mrs. Blake stand on the pavement outside the tube station for ten minutes while I watched for any other watchers. Then I approached her. Again we walked across towards North End Road.

"Let's not walk tonight," she said wearily. "I'd rather sit down somewhere and have a cup of coffee."

"As you wish, madam."

We turned back and went to a café in Finchley Road.

"Well," I began as we sipped our coffee, "have you decided on anything?"

"Yes. I've thought about it a lot during the past week, and I've come to the conclusion that this is not something I can decide about alone. I'm an old woman, and I can't face this by myself. I shall have to ask my daughter."

I looked at her sharply. "But George has not authorized me to discuss this matter with anyone else. I would have to get in touch with him again before I could do that."

"Oh, don't worry," she said. "My daughter Adele is a good girl and very clever, and she'll know the right thing to do. And she's very fond of George too."

"Where does Adele live?"

"She's married to a scientist who works for the United Nations, and they are both living in Bangkok at the moment. I'll write to her tomorrow."

"Isn't that dangerous?"

"Oh, I don't think so. We write to each other all the time, so why should anyone think this letter is different? And we write in Dutch, you see."

"How will I know when you've had a reply from her?"

"Can I phone you?"

"No, I'm afraid not," I said. "But you could write to me at the Hostel. Our letters don't get opened." Then a thought occurred to me. "You write to George often," I went on, "and his letters come in for very special attention. Your handwriting is known at Wormwood Scrubs." I took an envelope out of my pocket, wrote my address on it, and stamped it. "You had better use this when writing to me." I handed her the envelope. "And sign the letter *Jean*."

She became nervous again. "I'm frightened of all this. If anything goes wrong I hate to think of poor George being sent to that dreadful Parkhurst prison with all those Train Robbers. At least where he is now he is fairly comfortable and I can visit him regularly."

"But, Mrs. Blake, he's bound to be sent to a top-security prison sooner or later anyway. It's amazing he hasn't been transferred already, especially since those two Train Robbers escaped. After all, he is serving twelve years longer than the Train Robbers, and because of his circumstances his escape would be much more embarrassing for the British Government than the escape of anyone else. Indeed, this operation of ours is a race against time."

My words seemed to distress her even more, and ten minutes later we parted company.

"I look forward to hearing from you," I called after her as she got on the bus.

This was a complication that neither Blake nor I had allowed for. Now I realized how crude was our means of communication and how inadequate were the simple signals we had agreed upon before I left the cell block. I would have to let him know about this new development, and the only way to do that was by writing him a letter. Back in the Hostel I went straight to my room to do this. I devised a simple code built around the idea of the escape operation being represented by the building of a house. I wrote:

As you know, I am very anxious to buy this house as soon as possible, certainly within the next couple of months. Unfortunately, this lady from whom I had been hoping to borrow the deposit for the mortgage is reluctant to part with the funds. She says she is too old to make decisions like this and insists that she should consult her daughter, who is abroad at the moment. As you know this old lady, perhaps you could put in a good word for me when next you see her. I would appreciate it very much.

Of course, this letter was neither addressed nor signed. I put it in an envelope and sealed the envelope. I then wrote a very brief note on another piece of paper: "Please pass this envelope to our mutual friend." I put the envelope and this note into a second envelope and sealed it in turn. Next day I gave the envelope to a trusty and casually asked him to pass it on to Peter Martin for me. This sort of traffic between the Hostel and the cell block was fairly common. If the letter fell into the hands of a screw he would assume that it was just another routine fiddle between a prisoner and a friend on the outside. And everybody accepted that such fiddles went on.

Blake replied a couple of days later. On reflection he was in sympathy with the "old lady" and said he could perfectly understand her nervousness. But he thought there was no need to worry as he felt the daughter would be cooperative. "There is no doubt in my mind," he wrote, "that the young lady will agree that you should have the loan for the mortgage." I was interested to note that Blake used the most common paper available in the prison, a type of paper that could not possibly be traced to a single individual. And he wrote in small neat block capitals that effectively disguised his distinctive handwriting.

A few days before Christmas I received a letter from Mrs. Blake. It was waiting for me in my slot in the hostellers' rack in the gatehouse as I came in from work. I recognized my own handwriting on the envelope and was a little worried to notice how clearly the postmark *Radlett* stood out on the white envelope. But, as with all hostellers' letters, it was unopened. I waited to read it until I got to my room. It was very brief and said that Adele would be coming to London in February and that I would have to wait until then for a decision. The decision would be made by the daughter.

I spent Christmas with some friends in Sussex. Every Saturday night in January I carefully studied the movements of traffic and people in the vicinity of Wormwood Scrubs. By four-thirty Artillery Road was in darkness, and a person passing along Du Cane Road could not see more than a few yards up Artillery Road towards the park. The visitors to Hammersmith Hospital did not begin to arrive much before a quarter to seven. By beginning the operation at six I would have half an hour at the very least to get Blake over the wall without interference. Things looked very promising. All I needed now was the money.

At the beginning of February I wrote Mrs. Blake again and enclosed a stamped addressed envelope. A week later, as I came in from work, the gatekeeper said, "Good evening, Sean. There's a letter for you in there." He grinned as he walked behind his desk to book me in his thick ledger.

"Thanks," I said, taking the letter out of the rack and glancing at my own handwriting. My God, I thought to myself, looking at the screw's friendly face, if you only knew what this letter was all about you wouldn't be grinning like that.

In the letter Mrs. Blake asked me to meet her and her daughter for dinner at the Cumberland Hotel on the following Friday evening at eight.

On the Friday, after I had handed in my pay packet to the Hostel Warden and received my three pounds pocket money, I booked out at the main gate and caught a tube from East Acton to Marble Arch. At Marble Arch I ran across the street through the rain to the Cumberland Hotel. Mrs. Blake and her daughter were waiting for me in the lounge. Mrs. Blake introduced us. Adele Boswinkle bore a very strong family likeness to her brother and had the same sudden brilliant smile. I estimated she was about five years younger than George. We found a quiet table in a corner, and Adele called the waiter over.

"What would you like to drink?" she asked.

"A whisky," I said.

I knew that her mother would have told her that I was on the prison Hostel and that an agreement would have been made between them that I would not be required to pay for anything this evening. It made me feel uncomfortable.

Mrs. Blake and Adele ordered brandies. When the waiter had brought our drinks and gone, Adele flashed me that brilliant smile again. "Well"—she raised her glass—"to the right decision."

"To the right decision," I said.

It was obvious to me from the start that this woman was very much in command of the situation and would do most of the talking.

"Well, Mrs. Boswinkle—" I began.

"Oh, please call me Adele," she interrupted.

"Very well. Now, do you want me to start at the beginning or has Mrs. Blake told you what it's all about?"

"Oh yes, she's told me. But there are some details, of course, that I would like to discuss with you."

"Of course," I said. "Let's begin with my credentials." I took my half of the photograph out of my wallet and asked Mrs. Blake to produce hers. I handed both halves to Adele. "Compare them yourself."

She put the two halves together and studied the completed picture very carefully. "Yes, this is all right. In fact, I already accept that you are acting for George. You see, we went to visit him on Tuesday, and he left me in no doubt that you were to be trusted."

"Just as a matter of curiosity," I said, "how did he go about that with a prison officer in the room?"

Adele smiled. "Very simple. We just talk about an uncle of ours who lives in Holland, and all the time we're really talking about you. We discuss this uncle's desire to buy a house and the problem of raising a mortgage. In this way we can go into the most extraordinary detail about you and your plans. To the officer it's a perfectly innocent conversation."

"Not bad," I said, "not bad at all. Let's just hope that the room isn't bugged. But even if it is, your conversation would probably mean nothing to them until *after* the escape."

Though there was no one within listening distance of us, we spoke in very low tones.

Adele held up my half of the photograph. "Would you mind if I keep this?"

"No. If you want it, keep it."

"Thank you." She put it in her handbag. "I have a friend who's clairvoyant, and she can tell me a lot about a person by holding something that that person has also held."

I looked at her sharply. "Thanks," I said dryly.

"Oh, it's nothing like that," she went on quickly. "I trust you completely. This is just an old habit of mine."

"I see."

She finished her drink. "Well, shall we eat?"

"Why not?" I finished my whiskey in one gulp.

We went to the dining-room and asked the head waiter for a quiet table. He gave us one in a corner well away from everyone else. We all opted for steak.

Adele ordered the meal, then beckoned the wine waiter. "With meat," she said, "something red and dry, I think." She studied the list and gave the order. A minute later the wine waiter, resplendent in his chain of office, came back with the bottle. Adele sipped the small drop poured out for her. "Thank you, that's all right."

She gave me that brilliant smile again. "Well, what do you think of it?" She held her arms out as though embracing the dining-room.

My eyes swept over our plush surroundings. "A little overawed. My usual limit is the pub on the corner."

"Well, don't let it worry you. Remember, these people are working for their living just like the rest of us."

I felt I was being patronized. Her gaze came to rest on my wrist, and when she said, "That's a nice watch you have," I knew beyond all doubt that I was being patronized. I also felt, and knew that I was, at a distinct disadvantage with this woman paying the bill. I had never been in such a position before, and I felt a little humiliated. The poor prisoner on the Hostel was being given a treat.

"Right," I said, trying to assert some degree of independence, "let's get down to business." I explained how her brother and I had met and the circumstances leading up to his approach to me. "So you see," I concluded, "all he wants from you is the seven hundred pounds necessary to finance the operation. I'll do all the work."

Adele was now smiling a lot less. "But before I could consider that," she said, "I would have to know all your plans in detail."

I looked at her in surprise. "George didn't say anything about discussing the details of our plans with you. On the contrary, he feels— and I agree with him—that it would not be in your interests to know these details, quite apart from any consideration of our own security. Obviously, the fewer people who know these details the better. I'm sure you must appreciate that."

"I'm sorry," she said, "but I must insist on knowing all the details."

"Now, look here, am I going to be trusted or not?" I tried to speak in a level voice. "It was your brother who asked me to get him out of prison, not the other way about. If he didn't think I was capable of doing the job he wouldn't have asked me. All you have to do is part with a few hundred pounds to buy your brother's freedom. I'll do all the work and take all the risks. And remember, it is your brother who is asking you for the money, not me."

"Oh, I appreciate that," she said, sipping her wine, "but I must have all the details. You see, I feel responsible, and I would not want to be the cause of George jumping out of the frying pan into the fire. You do see my position, don't you?"

I looked at Mrs. Blake, but she was obviously determined to leave all the talking to her daughter.

My feeling of humiliation was growing. I had been put in the position of a beggar, and I wasn't even begging on my own behalf. "Very well, if you insist on knowing the details you can have them." I explained how Blake proposed to escape from the cinema while the other prisoners watched the film, and how I would be waiting for him with a rope ladder at the wall. She listened in silence, carefully weighing my every word. "Naturally," I concluded, "George and I know Wormwood Scrubs like the backs of our hands, and we both feel we have a very good chance of success."

"And what happens after he escapes—if he does escape?" Adele asked brusquely.

I explained patiently how George would hide out for a while and then leave the country with a false passport.

"And where will you get the passport?" she asked.

I deliberately paused for a moment before speaking. "I haven't spent five years in prison for nothing. I know where to get a passport all right. This is a mere formality."

"Well now, I'll be frank with you," she said. "I really do not have very much faith in your plans. It all seems so very vague. I honestly do not think that you have any chance of succeeding. I mean, it all seems too easy to be true. Throwing a rope ladder over the prison wall, just like that. I mean, really!" She shrugged impatiently.

"The execution of the escape is my responsibility," I said coldly, "and obviously I am more qualified than you to judge the merit of my plans—plans, incidentally, that your brother helped to draw up."

"That may be so, but it is my mother and I who are being asked to finance the project, and I would have to be satisfied that you were going to succeed before I would agree to help."

I felt the anger well up inside me. "We are talking about a jailbreak, about breaking the most important prisoner in Britain out of his prison cell! It is not going to be handed to us on a platter. The prison Governor is not going to throw the gates open and invite me to help myself. It is going to require a certain amount of effort and involve a certain element of risk. Nothing is for nothing in this world. I cannot give you a hundred-per-cent guarantee that I am going to succeed. Nobody can ever do that before the event, except, of course, in fiction. And this is no James Bond adventure with the happy ending preordained from the start. This is real life. We won't know if we are going to succeed until we try—and I would like to try."

She put her glass down. "Hm . . . yes . . . but I would still have to have confidence in your plans, and I certainly don't have that."

"What exactly do you want of me?" I asked flatly.

"There are a number of things I would require," she said. "I would want to inspect the accommodation where you intend hiding George after the escape. I would want to see the false passport. I would want precise details of how you intend getting George out of the country, and I would have to be satisfied that these arrangements are foolproof. I would also want a detailed list of the expenses to see where the seven hundred pounds is going. I don't see how you could possibly need so much money."

I felt my temper rising again but suppressed it with an effort. She had assumed control of the operation, and I had become a mere assistant. To have to take all this from a man would have been bad enough, but from a woman it was almost unbearable.

"You cannot inspect the accommodation and the passport until they have been bought, and they cannot be bought until I get the money. And I can assure you that seven hundred pounds is the very minimum that would be required to carry out the operation. This figure, in fact, was suggested by your brother."

She thought for a moment and appeared to be trying to make a decision, but I knew it was a pretence. She had made her decision even before we met.

"I'm still not happy," she said. "I feel I ought to discuss this again with George. We're going to see him next Thursday."

"As you wish," I said resignedly. "George has already indicated to you that he wants to escape, and he has told you that I can be trusted. I honestly don't see how you can expect him to accept your advice on the technical aspects of the operation. He and I know more about this than you do, and we are better qualified to judge. However, if that's how you want it."

"Yes, that's how I want it."

"All right. But I hope you make up your mind as soon as possible after Thursday. March is nearly upon us, and our present plans are geared to carrying out the escape under cover of darkness. Even if the money is forthcoming it's going to take another month to make the final preparations. There is no time to lose."

"Mr. Bourke could telephone us next Saturday, couldn't he?" Mrs. Blake suggested.

"Yes, that's an idea," her daughter agreed. "By then we will have seen George and will have had a couple of days to think about it."

Mrs. Blake gave me the number, which I memorized.

"And now, what about some coffee?" Adele was once more smiling her brilliant smile.

"I could do with some," I said, making no attempt to return the smile.

She beckoned the waiter and ordered the coffee. "Let's have something with the coffee," she said, crooking her finger at the young man in charge of the dessert trolley. He wheeled his trolley across, and we selected a variety of tiny sweet pastries no larger than biscuits.

A quarter of an hour later I started to get to my feet.

"Oh, please don't go until you've finished these little cakes," Adele pleaded.

I glanced at the plate. There were about half a dozen of the pastries left. "But I'm quite full."

"Oh, but surely you can finish them. They're not very big."

I sat down again and slowly worked my way through four of them. "Well, I really have had enough," I said then.

"Oh, do finish them, do, please."

Reluctantly I ate the other two.

"Oh, that's better!" Adele beamed. "Such a pity to waste them."

I was being indulged, like a schoolboy being given an enormous treat. But the word *waste* had registered. It gave me an insight into Adele's attitude to money. And a few moments later, when I saw the extremely small tip she gave the waiter, I knew I had not been mistaken. The evening's events, at first perplexing, were now beginning to fall into some sort of perspective.

We said good night in the lobby.

"And remember one thing," Adele said, "regardless of how this thing works out, you have at least tried to help George, and if there is anything we can do for you, please get in touch with us."

It was still raining. I ran across to Marble Arch station and caught a tube back to East Acton. I strolled dejectedly along Du Cane Road towards the prison gate, my hands buried deep in the pockets of my mac, my hat pulled down over my face, my eyes on the wet pavement. "If there is anything we can do for you, please get in touch with us." I could feel the anger rising inside me again. "Dear Mrs. Boswinkle, as you will remember, I once offered to help your brother escape from prison and you told me if I needed help to look you up. I am very hard up at the moment and could you please lend me a hundred pounds?" I cursed myself for having allowed myself to be put in such a humiliating position. Still, I would have to see it through. I had promised Blake.

Next day I sent a note to Blake, telling him about his sister's reluctance to help:

> The daughter appears to be completely dissatisfied with my plans for the house and says she would not be prepared to help financially unless she could be given a guarantee that the house would be a success. She is, in effect, trying to take over the running of the business. I hope that you will succeed in making her see sense. All that is holding me up now is the money. Give me the tools and I will finish the job.

The following Tuesday I received a reply, saying that he would talk to "the young lady" and reassure her.

On Friday I received another letter:

> I met the two ladies yesterday and was very much concerned at their nervous state. They are obviously very worried about all this, and I have reluctantly come to the conclusion that they should no longer be involved, for their own sakes as well as ours. I have told them that they will not be troubled further. I appreciate that this will be a great disappointment to you, especially as you have tried so hard. Can you think of any other way in which the funds might be raised?

My heart sank. My feelings were a mixture of anger and acute disappointment. This, I thought, must surely be the end of our hopes. But I had become so used to living with a belief in our success that I decided not to let Mrs. Blake and her daughter off the hook as easily as that, despite Blake's letter. The following evening I booked out at the main gate and went to the telephone kiosk near the entrance to Hammersmith Hospital. Mrs. Blake herself answered the phone.

"Oh, hello, Mr. Bourke. One moment. I'll get Adele."

Adele came on the line. "Hello."

"Hello," I said. "What decision have you come to?"

"Oh, didn't George tell you?"

"Yes, he did. I got a letter from him."

"Well?"

"Well, I think George is being extremely generous and understanding, but I was wondering if, despite his generosity, you might not still be prepared to help him."

"Has the situation changed, then, since we last met? Have your plans improved sufficiently to merit further consideration?"

"Of course the situation hasn't changed." I tried to keep my voice level. "And the plans are the best possible plans in the present circumstances. Nothing can be done before we get the money."

There was a short silence at the other end. Then, in a cool, businesslike voice, she said, "In view of all the circumstances, I think a full stop should now be written to this matter."

"Very well," I said. "Good-bye." I put the phone down and went back to the Hostel.

A few days later I decided to appeal directly to Mrs. Blake once more and give her one last chance to help. I wrote her a long letter, ten pages, going over the details of my plans to effect her son's escape, and concluded:

> Unless he is helped, your son is doomed to languish for forty-two years in a prison cell. This is a slow death. He now has an opportunity to escape, an opportunity which will never present itself again. You can help him escape. For a mere seven hundred pounds you can buy your son's freedom, his life. I am writing this letter in my own hand and signing it in my own name in order to provide you with an indisputable guarantee of my sincerity in this matter. If at any time in the future you feel that I have not treated you fairly, you need only take this letter to the nearest police station and have me arrested.

All I got for my trouble was a severe reprimand for "putting other people's security at risk."

Contact by Radio

During the remainder of March, Blake and I exchanged several notes.
In one he asked whether I thought it was now worth while pursuing
the matter. I replied that I would do my best to provide the tools as
well as finish the job.

It had become clear to me that Blake's escape could not take place
while I was on the Hostel. Somehow between now and next winter I
would have to raise the money myself, but I was not very hopeful.
There was also the strong possibility that Blake would be transferred
long before then or that Wormwood Scrubs itself might change considerably. And, indeed, the process of change was to begin sooner than
I expected.

There were two escapes from the prison towards the end of March
—one from D-Rec and the other from D-Hall itself. The authorities
did a little hasty research and discovered that most escapes in the past
had involved men going over the east wall behind D-Hall, facing
Hammersmith Hospital. The second favourite was the north wall, on
the park. The authorities took a measure that was as effective as it was
simple. They stationed a screw permanently at the corner where the
north and east walls met, commanding a clear view of both. A screw
was to stand or sit there all day and all the evening. Thus, at one
stroke, the authorities rendered Plans A and B completely useless.
Standing in that corner, the screw would be a mere thirty yards from
the spot where the rope ladder was supposed to come over for Blake.
There was still Plan C, but this had really been an emergency stand-

by plan. It involved carrying out the escape in the full view of the screws and any people who might be near the wall on the park. It would be hazardous. If a better plan, something like our original Plan A, could be worked out (in which there would be a chance of getting away without causing the alarm to be raised immediately), it would be infinitely preferable.

I exchanged several notes with Blake on the subject during April. He agreed that Plans A and B were out. As things stood at the moment, the only alternative he saw was Plan C:

> I envisage a house nicely situated where, towards three o'clock on a sunny Sunday afternoon, you can serve champagne to your guests on a spacious lawn and later invite them to join you for a walk in the park nearby.

But without funds nothing could be done anyway, and until these funds materialized we were at the mercy of sheer luck. We could only keep our fingers crossed and hope that Blake would not be transferred. (We were to learn later from the Mountbatten Report that at that moment the prison Governor had already urged the Home Office to move Blake to a maximum-security prison. It was perhaps fortunate for us that we did not know of this at the time, for if we had we would surely have resorted to some panic measure resulting in complete failure.)

I was due to be discharged from the Hostel on July 4. From now until then it was going to be a nervous game of waiting and watching. In the meantime I was getting acclimatized to civilian life again. The men I worked with in the factory stores were, as the foreman had told me, nice people. It isn't until a criminal has spent a number of years in prison with people like himself that he comes to realize how decent most law-abiding citizens are. The contrast in attitude and outlook is at first very noticeable. The fact that for the first month or so you are a little awe-struck by people saying "excuse me" and "thank you," without being afraid of being thought *soft*, is a stark reminder of the way of life you have just left behind. And if you accidentally bump into someone he will insist on accepting the blame rather than look upon it as a challenge to his manhood. (" 'Ere, are you trying to have a fuckin' go at me, you cunt?") Law-abiding citizens, you conclude, seem to have a greater feeling of security and self-confidence.

Nobody in the factory (except the personnel manager and the general foreman) knew that I was in prison. This at times caused me a little nervousness. Once or twice a headline in the newspapers started off a tea-break discussion on the subject of crime and criminals. Unlike the professional penologist, the average workingman, I discovered, had little sympathy to spare for the criminal. The criminal should not be feather-bedded. If he chose to go about robbing people and hitting them with iron bars he had no right to consideration. He should be thrown into a prison cell and left there. To hell with all this nonsense of rehabilitation and psychoanalysis and prison hostels. Treat a criminal soft and he'll think *you're* soft. Society doesn't owe these thugs anything. We have to work overtime to keep our wives and families, and we also have to keep these bastards who rob us and beat us and rape our children. What do you think, Sean?

"Well"—nervously fingering that prison pass in my pocket which would get me through the main gate of Wormwood Scrubs a couple of hours later—"I seem to remember reading somewhere that it's supposed to be in society's own interests to rehabilitate the criminal. I think these prison people do it not just to make things easier for the criminal but to try and make sure that he won't beat and rob people again after he's released. I read somewhere that that's the official attitude. Whether it's right or wrong, of course, I'm not in a position to judge."

I was always at pains to guard against using slang words that might be even remotely associated with prisons or criminals. During our discussions I would be careful to say "prison" and "prison officers" and would be surprised and relieved to hear my fellow workers talk of "the nick" and "the screws." One day I was quite taken aback when one of my fellow storemen, a big, boisterous, good-natured Cockney, came marching through the stores shouting at the top of his voice, "Slop out!" He had, of course, seen it in a film or on television.

By mid-April I had completely resigned myself to the fact that the escape could not take place for at least several months after my release from the Hostel. By then I would have about a hundred pounds in my savings and would have to try to borrow the remainder, though where I would borrow it from I as yet had no idea. But in the meantime I would have to take certain steps to ensure that after my departure from the Hostel I would still have some channel of communication with the prison. This was of vital importance. Accordingly, I cultivated the friendship of a recent arrival on the Hostel who I knew would not be discharged until December. His name was Barry Richards. We went for a drink together several times at the Western pub, and I told him that after I left prison I would still be interested to hear about life in Wormwood Scrubs, as I intended writing about it. We agreed to meet in the Western from time to time after my release.

By the end of April I was quite sure of Barry's cooperation. He would carry notes for me into the prison after my discharge. But I was still uneasy. Just a small last-minute change in prison routine could upset the most carefully laid plans, and if I were no longer in the prison it would be impossible to know of such a change. For instance, the film show was occasionally switched from Saturday night to Sunday night to make way for a concert or other entertainment brought in by civilians. Admittedly Plan A was out, but there was still the possibility that Blake might want to escape from D-Hall while the majority of the prisoners were at the cinema and there were only two screws in D-Hall. Those two hours were the real Achilles' heel. I could not expect Barry to keep me informed of such last-minute changes, even if he were aware of them, which he probably would not be. There was no reason at all why a hosteller should know everything that was going on in D-Hall. Of course, Blake could send me notes, but a note would take several days to travel from D-Hall, through the Hostel, to the Western. Blake would not be able to inform me of changes decided on at the last moment or, for that matter, decided on even a couple of days before.

I was preoccupied with this problem for days. I considered, among other possible solutions, the idea of arranging with Blake to give me prearranged signals from a cell window on the Fours as I stood in the park or even on the roof of Hammersmith Hospital. Then suddenly it came to me, like a flash of light. Why not? It was daring, very daring. It had never been done before in the history of English prisons. But why not? Why not avail ourselves of the benefits of modern science? I would communicate with Blake direct as he sat in his cell. This was the era of the transistor, and you could get a two-way radio that would fit in your pocket.

I sat down and wrote a note for the P.O. in charge of the Hostel:

Sir,

Now that I have accumulated a substantial sum of money in my savings I would appreciate it if you would allow me to draw out twenty-five pounds this week for the purpose of buying a new suit.

Yours faithfully, Sean Bourke

I gave this note to the red-band who would pass it on to the P.O. while I was out at work.

On Friday night at pay-in, I handed over my wage packet and was given my usual three pounds plus twenty-five. I signed for the money and thanked the P.O.

Next morning I was standing on the pavement in Piccadilly looking into the window of McDonald's radio and electrical shop. I saw what I wanted: a pair of Japanese two-way radios in black leather cases small enough to fit inconspicuously into a man's inside pocket. The ticket said the maximum range was five miles. That, of course, would apply only from hilltop to hilltop or on a plain or on the open sea. Half a mile, or even quarter of a mile, would be sufficient for my purpose. I went into the shop and bought the sets. They normally cost thirty-five pounds, but as there was a sale on they were going for twenty-five. The salesman explained what I already knew about the range varying according to the geographical features of the area in which the sets were used. He then took one of the sets out into Piccadilly while I stayed in the shop with the other, and we tested them. They worked beautifully. A passing police constable smiled indulgently at the spectacle of two grown men apparently trying to amuse themselves by playing cops and robbers.

"Where will you actually be using them?" asked the salesman as he wrapped up the sets.

"Oh, down in the country," I said. "Communications can be difficult on a large farm."

"Here's a spare set of batteries," said the salesman, "and if you have any difficulty with the sets, or they're not suited to your purpose, bring them back and you can try something else."

I walked in the prison gate with the parcel under my arm. A hosteller could go in with a suitcase at that time and not be searched.

"Been shopping, Sean?" The gatekeeper smiled.

"Yes. All the way to Piccadilly and back."

Next day was Sunday. Before tackling the problem of getting Blake's set in to him I would have to satisfy myself that it was strong enough to penetrate the prison walls. "Two-Way Family Favourites" is a request programme to be heard on the BBC between midday and one-thirty every Sunday. That could help. I tied a piece of string round one of the sets to keep the transmitting button depressed. I then placed it on the floor of my tall locker and extended the telescopic aerial. The aerial's full length was six feet, but the locker would allow it to extend only five feet. I looked at my watch. Twelve o'clock. "Family Favourites" would be just beginning. I picked up my ordinary wireless, tuned it into the BBC Light Programme, and placed it close to the two-way radio in the bottom of the locker. I then switched on the two-way radio, locked the locker, and left the room, with the second two-way radio in my inside pocket.

I booked out at the main gate, turned left, walked along Du Cane Road, past the Governor's house, and turned left again into Artillery Road. I walked up Artillery Road to the park at the back of the prison, occasionally playfully touching the prison's east wall as I walked.

It was now the middle of May, and there were quite a few people strolling about the park or sitting down reading or just enjoying the sun. I went to the centre of the park and sat down. I took out the two-way radio, extended the aerial fully, and switched on. The BBC programme came over loud and clear, transmitted from my bedside locker in the Hostel. Nobody was near me, but even if they had been they would have taken my two-way radio for an ordinary receiver, especially with "Two-Way Family Favourites" blaring out of it. I was more interested in the girl announcer's voice than in the music, and, to my great delight, it came over clear as a bell. What added to my satisfaction was the fact that the Hostel, being at the front of the prison, was much farther away from where I sat than D-Hall. If I could receive so clearly from the Hostel I would have no difficulty at all receiving from Blake's cell in D-Hall.

I looked across at the prison wall and D-Hall and then looked at my small radio nestling in the grass, its chrome aerial glinting in the midday sun, and I smiled at the simplicity of it all. How easily I had breached those thick, forbidding walls! And it had never been done before! I folded the aerial back into the set and switched off. I stood up and looked at the prison wall again. "My friend," I said, patting the radio affectionately, "between us, you and I are going to make a little bit of jailbreak history."

That evening I wrote another note to Blake. I explained that I was due to move fairly soon to a new address, on a temporary basis, and that one of the problems arising from this move was that the building site would then be much farther away. As I was anxious to be in constant touch with the people on the site I had decided to start using two-way radio. Letters took too long.

Blake finally replied that he thought the idea was a brilliant one.

I then set about working out our call signs and an identifying code. For the call signs I decided to use the initials of two of the best-known characters in Irish mythology: Fionn MacCuhaill, leader of the Fenians, and Baldy Canaan, his lieutenant. Thus, rendered into the phonetic alphabet, I would be "Fox Michael" and Blake would be "Baker Charlie." As for the identifying code, that too could be on a literary theme. The first term of the extramural course Blake and I had done in the prison college had covered "Chaucer to the Stuarts," a period that embraced the seventeenth-century poets. One of these poets, I remembered, had written something rather appropriate. It was Richard Lovelace.

> Stone walls do not a prison make,
> Nor iron bars a cage;
> Minds innocent and quiet take
> That for a hermitage;
> If I have freedom in my love
> And in my soul am free,
> Angels alone, that soar above,
> enjoy such liberty.

The identifying code would be as follows:

ME: Stone walls do not a prison make,
nor iron bars a cage.
BLAKE: Minds innocent and quiet take
that for a hermitage.
ME: Richard Lovelace must have been a fool.
BLAKE: Or just a dreamer.

I drew up a copy of this operating procedure and sent it to Blake. I also told him that I would let him have the radio within a week through Peter Martin ("our mutual friend P."). There was still no reason, I suggested, for Peter to be brought into the scheme fully.

The business discussed in this note could not be woven into the fiction of buying a house, but as it was to be the last note and as Blake had to know the operating procedure, I decided the risk had to be taken. And, anyway, none of the other notes had gone astray, so why should this one?

In his reply Blake assured me that he fully understood the operating procedure. He wondered, however, whether Peter Martin should any longer be kept in the dark, particularly as he was now going to be asked to play such an active role. "I will leave that decision to you," he concluded. I gave it further thought and decided that, after all, it might be best to confide in Peter. In any case, the moment he saw the radio he would know what we were up to. And, most important of all, Peter could be trusted completely.

The prison drama group's spring production had begun its week's run. The old lags and the Borstal boys had seen the play on Wednesday and Thursday, C-Hall had seen it on Friday and Saturday, and D-Hall were seeing it this evening, Monday. Outside visitors would see it on Tuesday, Wednesday, and Thursday. These outsiders were prison visitors and their friends, the families and friends of the prison staff, prominent local citizens, Home Office officials, and so on. On the three evenings that the play was shown to the civilians there would be about a dozen Leaders on duty all along the route from the main gate to the theatre in D-Rec to show the civilians the way. These Leaders usually stood or sat at the back of the theatre during the play and performed their guide duty again as the visitors were leaving.

On my way to the Hostel after work I met Peter Martin. He had recently been made a Leader. We walked together for a few yards between C-Hall and the Officers' Mess.

"Peter," I whispered, without looking at him, "I've got something to give you, but we must have a little chat too. How can we arrange it?"

"I could find some excuse for calling at the Hostel," he replied.

"Too dangerous. How about the prison play? For the next three evenings it will be for civilians. Can you arrange to be detailed for Leaders' duty?"

"I've already arranged it," he said.

"Okay. I'll get the A.G.'s permission to attend tomorrow night's performance. I'll sit in the back row and keep you a seat."

"Right. See you."

"See you."

Back in the Hostel I wrote a note to the A.G. and gave it to the red-band to be passed on the following morning. When I got in from work next evening the written permission was waiting for me.

There was one more small chore to be done before going to the theatre. If I were going to communicate with the cell block later in the evening I would have to have a room to myself. The first floor of the building had recently been taken over from the Officers' Mess to extend the Hostel and increase its capacity. There were still several empty rooms upstairs, and I decided I would move into one of them by myself. I put all my belongings in a blanket and carried them upstairs. I took the first room past the stairs on the left. The window looked out over the roofs of the Reception and the gymnasium beyond it to command a clear view of the front end of D-Hall. The large gothic window at the end of the Hall was clearly visible, though the door beneath it was hidden from view by the roof of the gymnasium. Also visible from my new room were some of the cell windows on the Threes and Fours; the Ones and Twos, like the door, were out of view.

I had a quick shave and went down to the sitting-room for dinner. It was minced meat again. I was pleased to discover that no other hosteller was going to the play.

Back in my room I put one of the radios in my inside pocket and examined the effect in the mirror. No suspicious bulge. I had also recently acquired a miniature camera that was so small it could be concealed in the palm of the hand. I put this in another pocket with three tiny rolls of film. And in yet another pocket I put half-a-dozen cigars. Peter, I knew, liked a cigar.

At seven-fifteen I was sitting in the back row of the theatre in D-Rec. I kept one arm stretched over the back of the chair on my right. Just beyond it sat three girls with whom I chatted briefly. They were regular supporters of the Wormwood Scrubs drama group and knew me from the plays I had been in. On my left sat a prison visitor and his wife and daughter. As always on the civilian nights, the prison theatre was going to be packed to capacity. This was understandable. A play performed in a prison by prisoners is bound to have a special attraction to members of the public, and not solely for the quality of the performance. These decent, law-abiding citizens sitting all around me this evening would experience the same feeling of elation as they walked unhindered through the prison gate in a few hours' time as I myself had felt when I stood in the park for the first time and looked up at the barred windows of D-Hall peering at me over the top of the perimeter wall—except that their elation could never be quite as intense, never quite so appreciatively savoured as my own.

The lights went out, the curtain went back, and the play commenced. One or two late arrivals continued to drift in, and finally Peter Martin arrived, his duty done. He came over and sat beside me. The back row of chairs on which we sat actually touched the back wall of the theatre, which was ideal for our purpose.

"Hello, Sean."

"Hello, Peter."

"You're looking well."

"Thanks."

We watched the play in silence for about fifteen minutes and then I leaned a little closer to Peter and spoke out of the corner of my mouth without turning my head. He, knowing the drill, also kept his eyes straight ahead on the stage.

"Peter, I have to tell you something very important that I feel you're entitled to know. I'm going to spring George Blake."

Peter did not turn his head. "Glad you told me that. If you hadn't I'd have been very annoyed."

"Yes, and you would've been entitled to be annoyed. A man like you doesn't allow himself to be used, I can understand that. Up to this point there was no need to tell you, not because you couldn't be trusted but because I didn't want to involve you unnecessarily. However, now I have to ask you to do something that will involve you, and so you've every right to know what's going on."

"What do you want me to do?"

"I have here in my pocket a small two-way radio that I would like you to give to George. It's complete with leather case and earphone as well as an instruction booklet. I also have a miniature camera and three rolls of film. I would like you to take some head and shoulder photographs of George for possible use on a passport and get the films back to me while I'm still in the Hostel."

"Okay, I've got all that."

"Are you sure you don't mind?"

"Sean, I've told you before, you're a friend of mine. Anything you want done, just let me know. Anything at any time."

"Thanks, Peter. By the time you get back into the Hall tonight everybody will be locked up so you won't be able to give George the radio until tomorrow. In the meantime, do you mind if you and I make contact tonight, just to test the sets?"

"Not at all. That's a good idea."

"I'll contact you after lights-out, just after ten o'clock. I can see the lights being switched off in D-Hall from my window in the Hostel." I looked round the nearby seats. Everybody was intently watching the play. "Are you ready, Peter?"

"Okay."

He slowly unbuttoned his jacket to give easier access to his inside pocket. I took the radio out of my own pocket and, still keeping it under my jacket, I lowered it to my lap. Very carefully I moved it towards Peter. His left hand came over to meet me halfway; he kept the set in his lap for a few seconds, and then slowly his hand went up under his jacket, reversing my own action of a few seconds before. When his hand came out from under his jacket it held a handkerchief. Peter pretended to blow his nose and replaced the handkerchief in his inside pocket. The camera and films were handed over in like manner, and then I explained the operating procedure agreed to with George. Finally I gave him the cigars.

At the end of the play a couple of white-coated hotplate workers from the dining-room next door wheeled in a tea trolley, and after a few minutes the actors and civilian visitors were scattered about in little groups chatting and sipping cups of tea and nibbling at biscuits. The Governor himself was leading a discussion in one of the groups. As I was going out the door the Assistant Governor, Mr. Rham, was standing near the collection box with a couple of Leaders. I dropped two half crowns into the slit.

"Thank you, sir," he said with a smile.

"You're welcome, my good man," I said, and we both laughed.

Outside the door I met a visitor with his wife and decided to walk to the main gate with them. There were a few women and girls walking just ahead of us and another group of civilians behind. As we approached C-Hall the prisoners were waiting at their windows, as I knew they would be. "Girahrovit, you fahking lesbians!" they screamed at the women in front of us. "Wot a right couple of fahking queers!" they greeted me and the visitor, much to the amusement of the latter's wife. The people behind us fared no better, nor the people behind them. All you could see of the prisoners were their wide-open, screaming mouths framed in the tiny ventilating panels of their windows.

Back in the Hostel I went straight to my new room. I had chosen the bed near the window, and now I sat on it with my eyes on D-Hall and waited. It was ten o'clock, but the lights were still on on the Fours. This meant that the night watchman had started his rounds on the Ones. It would be another half-hour before he had put out the light on the Fours, and Peter Martin was on the Fours. Sure enough, after about twenty minutes they started to go out, one after the other, at four-second intervals—the time it took the night watchman to move from one cell door to the next.

I waited another five minutes and then lay comfortably back on my bed, my radio resting on my chest. I switched on but kept the volume control low in case Peter should unexpectedly come in. I pressed the transmitting button and started to call him.

"This is Fox Michael calling Baker Charlie. Fox Michael calling Baker Charlie. Come in, please. Over."

Peter had already been switched on and answered immediately. "This is Baker Charlie to Fox Michael, Baker Charlie to Fox Michael. Receiving you loud and clear. Over."

"*Stone walls do not a prison make, nor iron bars a cage. Over.*"

"*Minds innocent and quiet take that for a hermitage. Over.*"

"*Richard Lovelace must have been a fool. Over.*"

"*Or just a dreamer. Over.*"

"Boy, am I glad to hear you!" I said. "This reception is great. It sounds like you're right here in the room with me, and the volume isn't even halfway up. This is very encouraging. Over."

"I can hear you loud and clear too. Over."

"By the way," I said, "there's hardly any need to remind you that we mustn't use any names over the air. You never know who might be listening. Over."

"Quite right, Fox Michael," Peter replied. "It's not my first time using one of these things. I know the drill. Over."

"Well, my friend, it really is very good of you to help like this. You're taking a hell of a chance, and it's very much appreciated by our mutual friend and myself. Over."

"Oh, don't worry about that. I keep telling you you're a friend of mine. Anything I can do, just let me know. You realize, of course, that the original plans are out. We shall have to think of something new. You may have heard that there is a gentleman sitting on a chair in that corner all day long, keeping an eye on things. We'll have to find a way round it. But you can leave that to me. I'll think of something. Over."

"Thanks, Baker Charlie. If you can just arrange somehow for our friend to move those few vital yards from the inside of the building to the outside, I'll do the rest. Over."

"Okay, I'll work on it. Now listen, there's something you should know, so that you can take precautions. There's a gang of six men here in the Hall who are going to have it away very soon. They have already cut the bars of a cell window on the Ones and stuck them together again with Bostik. There's only one thing holding them back, and that's the man sitting in that corner. Over."

This was disturbing news. "And how are they going to overcome that problem?" I asked. "Over."

"Very simple. When it rains, this man has to go and shelter in the porch at that end of the Hall. When he does this he can no longer see along both walls. He can still keep an eye on the north wall, but not on the wall facing the hospital. That's the weakness, you see. Well, there it is. As soon as it rains, these six men are away. Everything is ready. The bars have been cut now for a week, and the rope and hook are hidden in D-Hall. I just thought I should warn you so you won't leave anything incriminating lying about in case of a search. From now on you'll have to be very careful, especially on rainy days. Over."

"All right. Thanks again for telling me. I'll take all the necessary precautions. There's nothing we can do about it. We must just sit tight and hope that the repercussions won't be so drastic as to make our effort pointless. Does himself know about this? Over."

"Yes, I've already told him. Over."

"And how is he taking it? Over."

"He's very disturbed, of course, but as I pointed out to him, other people are entitled to have a go too. Over."

"Okay, do what you can to find a way out of the Hall for our friend and I'll take care of the rest. There's no great hurry. The job can't be done until some time after I leave here. Will you give the radio to him tomorrow? Over."

"Yes, tomorrow. And I'll find a way out of the Hall, don't worry. Over."

I heard the firm tread of the night patrol's footsteps as he passed the Hostel. I sat up on the bed and looked out the window. The patrol was walking past the Reception. In half a minute he would be at the corner where the front wall of the prison joined the east wall facing the hospital. He would then turn left and stroll past the prison college and then walk the full length of D-Hall to the other corner where the east wall met the north wall. There he would turn left again and patrol the north wall.

I pressed the transmitting button. "Baker Charlie, is your window open? Over."

"Yes. Why? Over."

"There's a man in blue approaching on his rounds. He's turning left by the college just now, and he should be under your window in about two minutes. Is he likely to hear you? Over."

"No, I'm too high up, and anyway I'm only talking in a whisper. Still, I'll shut the window just as a precaution. My only worry is the people in the next—er—*rooms* hearing me. But even if they do they'll probably think I'm either talking in my sleep or listening to a programme on the wireless. Over."

"Okay, my friend, that seems to be about all for now. Tell *himself* that I'll contact him at the same time tomorrow night. Over."

"Right, I'll do that. Over."

I pressed the transmitting button for the last time. "This is Fox Michael to Baker Charlie. Over and out. Good night."

"Baker Charlie to Fox Michael. Over and out. Good night."

I pushed the aerial back into the set and placed it in the locker. From now on that radio, that precious link between the two different worlds, would have to be kept in my locker at the factory. I would bring it to the prison only on the evenings I had to make contact.

The thought of those six men escaping made me nervous. There was bound to be a furious outcry. But what could I do about it? Nothing. Of course the obvious thought occurred to me. An anonymous call would put an end to the plot. But then one would have to be a grass to do a thing like that. No, I would have to stand impotently by and watch other people do their best to destroy my own plans. There was nothing else for it.

The next evening the night watchman in D-Hall began turning out the lights on the Fours, instead of the Ones, so I again waited until ten thirty before trying to make contact, as Blake's cell was on the Ones. I could not actually see the lights going out on the Ones and Twos because of the intervening roofs of the Reception and the gym. At ten-thirty I lay on my bed, extended the aerial to the full, rested the radio on my chest, and switched on.

I pressed the transmitting button. "This is Fox Michael calling Baker Charlie, Fox Michael calling Baker Charlie. Come in, please. Over." I released the transmitting button and listened. There was a short pause and then, to my delight, I heard the hum induced by the pressing of the other set's transmitting button. Then Blake's unmistakable voice came over the air and seemed to fill the room.

"This is Baker Charlie to Fox Michael, Baker Charlie to Fox Michael. Receiving you loud and clear. Over."

"Stone walls do not a prison make, nor iron bars a cage. Over."

"Minds innocent and quiet take that for a hermitage. Over."

"Richard Lovelace must have been a fool. Over."

"Or just a dreamer. Over."

"Well, my friend," I said, "how are you? Over."

"Very well indeed. And I can hardly tell you how delighted and thrilled I am to be talking to you like this. This is my first free and unrestricted contact with the outside world in five years—it really is a wonderful feeling. Over." Blake really did sound excited.

"It's quite interesting for me too. It isn't every day one finds oneself in a situation like this. It does relieve the tedium somewhat. Over."

"Yes, I agree." Blake laughed. "I mean, even if we did not ultimately succeed, this business with the radios would be quite an adventure in itself, something to remember. Over."

"Quite. And you can hear me quite distinctly, can you? Reception is okay? Over."

"Oh yes, quite distinctly. It's as if you were sitting beside me. Indeed, I have to keep the volume turned down quite low. And how do you hear me? Over."

"The same," I said. "And what is the position with you, technically? I mean, is your aerial fully extended? And are you standing up or sitting down or what? Over."

"I'm lying very comfortably in my bed with the aerial fully extended. I have shut my window as a precaution against being heard by any passing night patrol outside. I also have my ordinary wireless switched on and tuned into a musical programme to drown my voice in case it might be heard by my neighbours on either side of me or by hidden listening devices. If I should hear the night watchman approaching I can have the aerial folded and this small set hidden under the blankets in a matter of seconds. But, as you know, the watchman rarely looks through a spy-hole between lights-out and six o'clock in the morning. He will only do so if he thinks there's something wrong or if somebody rings his bell. And since there's nothing wrong with me and I have no intention of ringing my bell, I don't expect to be disturbed. In fact, I feel very secure indeed. Over."

"I'm pleased to hear that," I told him. "And, of course, I myself have even less worries in my present position. Over."

"Good," said Blake, "and now to business. Our original plans cannot be implemented. Our mutual friend and I are trying to work something out, and I shall keep you informed of progress. In the meantime there is this question of finance. I take it you have now severed all relations with the two ladies? Over."

"Yes, I have. I won't pretend that I am not disappointed, but there it is. So far as the ladies are concerned, you know best. Over."

"I'm glad you see it that way. I know it must be a great disappointment to you, but I think it will probably be all for the best. I do think the ladies were altogether too nervous and that in itself could constitute a danger. Over."

"Anyway," I said, "it doesn't matter now. I've thought of a possible source of help which I intend to explore this weekend. An old friend of mine, very sympathetic usually to a cause like this and completely reliable. He loves the police just as much as I do. And don't let that observation trouble you. He is not a criminal. If he were I wouldn't touch him with a barge-pole. You know what my attitude is to all these self-justifying myths like 'honour among thieves' and all the rest of that phony malarky. With very rare exceptions I wouldn't trust a fellow criminal literally as far as I could throw him. No, my friend, this man that I have in mind is of the highest integrity. He is the sort of man that if he found a five-pound note in the street he would hand it to the nearest policeman. And that, by the way, is about the only time he would be seen talking to a policeman. I think this man will be the answer to some of our problems. Over."

"That sounds very promising," said Blake. "Needless to say, I am not in the least bit worried about this man. If you say he can be trusted, that is good enough for me. I have complete faith in your judgement. How soon will you be able to let me know the result? Over."

"Well, as I said, I shall be seeing him this weekend. I will contact you at the same time on Monday night. Over."

Blake pressed his transmitting button and paused a moment before speaking. "If this man does agree to help with money, it will still not be possible to carry out the operation before you leave, will it? Over."

"No, I'm afraid not. It is now the middle of May. I shall be moving from here in about six weeks, hardly enough time to do all that has to be done. I'm afraid we will have to accept that it will be a month or so after I go from here before the job gets done. In the meantime I will keep in regular touch and keep you informed of progress. And, of course, you yourself will be busy trying to work out a way of getting out of the Hall. Over."

"That's true," said Blake. "An idea has already occurred to us, as a matter of fact, but we will have to do a little more exploration before making up our minds finally. You know, I take it, about those other six men? Over."

"Yes, I do. It's a hell of a bloody nuisance but there's nothing we can do about it. Over."

"A nuisance is putting it mildly." Blake sounded a little upset by the thought. "It could mean measures being taken afterwards that might make our own operation impossible. But, as you say, there's nothing we can do about it. Over."

"By the way, did you get the miniature camera and the films all right? Over."

"Yes, I've got them. I doubt, though, whether they'll be of much practical use. I have, as you can imagine, a certain amount of experience with miniature cameras and microfilms. They're not really much good for taking the sort of photographs you have in mind. Anyway, we'll try, and if they don't come out it doesn't really matter. We will, presumably, have better facilities after the event. Over."

Blake and I then started to gossip about many different things unconnected with the escape. He was very curious to know all about my new life in the outside world, and I told him. He also told me that he had now got a very good job, that of prisoner in charge of the canteen. Of course, he added with a laugh, there was no danger of his being given the blue-band that normally went with the job. He would be the first prisoner ever to do the job without a blue-band. One of the greatest advantages of the job was that one had to work for only about three days of the week and the rest of the time one could spend in one's cell reading or studying. And the authorities themselves were happy with the arrangement since it meant that a prisoner who was a bit of a headache to them was now under lock and key all the time, as it were, in the Hall. They didn't have to worry about his escaping while on his way to and from the Mailbag Shop.

It was well after midnight before we decided to say good night, and the remarkable thing about our two-hour conversation was that we were able to go into such great detail without giving away our identities.

"Well, that's about it," I said finally. "I had better let you get some sleep. And I will contact you again on Monday night and let you know how I get on with my friend. Over."

"Very well, my friend," said Blake. "There is no sense in trying to press our luck too far. Two hours on the air is really far too long. We must be much more brief in future. Over."

"I agree with you," I said. "This is Fox Michael to Baker Charlie. Over and out. Good night."

"Baker Charlie to Fox Michael. Over and out. Good night."

5
My Friends
Are Brought In

My police-loving friend was named Michael Reynolds, and on Saturday I called him and arranged to visit that evening.

I made my way by tube to Camden Town and walked for about twenty minutes from the station.

It was a modest house for a man with a modest income. Michael was the sort of man who scorned riches and the rich. He would never himself be materially well off for he was too concerned with the needs of others for that. He was a Socialist at heart. But he was not a Communist, any more than I was, and I wondered as I approached the house whether this would influence his decision. His background was Irish Catholic, though he himself was only half Irish—his mother was a Dublin woman and his father a Londoner.

I rang the bell, and almost immediately the door opened.

Michael shook my hand vigorously. "Come in, Sean, come in." As we went to the sitting room he said over his shoulder, "Did you know that I've got married?"

"Yes, I heard about it."

"This is my wife, Anne," he said, introducing me to an attractive girl of about twenty-five. "This is Sean, Anne."

"These are ours," Michael said, nodding at the two small children playing on the floor. "One is four and the other is two and a half."

"I'll make some coffee," Anne announced and went to the kitchen.

"Well, Michael," I began, "congratulations on your degree. I read the results in *The Times*. What does it feel like to be a highly educated man?"

Michael smiled wryly. "I don't feel any different now to what I felt before I got my B.A. It hasn't helped to pay the rent yet. In fact, I'm finding it difficult to get a suitable post, like an assistant lectureship in a college. At the moment I'm working in an office, fourteen pounds a week. It keeps us from starving." He threw a glance round the sitting-room, not exactly luxuriously furnished. "This place costs us six pounds a week in mortgage payments," he said. "I don't know where I'd be without Anne. She's a great girl. She's been the breadwinner in this house for the past few years while I've been at university. She's been slaving in an office all day, and the children've been in a kinder-garten."

I looked intently at my friend for a moment. He was about thirty years of age, very slightly built, and his face was rather pale and drawn, reflecting the struggles of the past few years. It certainly had not been easy for him, with a wife and family to think about while he was at university. There really seemed little point in discussing the business which had brought me. This family had enough troubles of their own, and in any case they obviously could not help with money. Still, I would mention it, if only to see how Michael reacted. Even if he could not help, what I said to him this evening would not go outside these walls. This man's honesty and sincerity were stamped all over him.

"Michael," I said, "what I want to discuss with you is dangerous. Just talking about it is dangerous, and probably constitutes a conspir-acy. I don't know what you feel about Anne's being present while we talk. Perhaps you would prefer that she were not involved at all?"

Michael looked at me sharply. "Oh, don't worry about that, Anne is completely reliable. Anything you have to say you can say in front of her."

Anne herself had heard these last remarks as she brought in the coffee. She handed the cups round and then sat down to join us. The decision had been made. I took a sip of the coffee and sat back.

"Well," I began, "you all know where I have been for the last few years. There is no need to go into all that again. At the moment I'm on the prison Hostel, and won't be finally discharged until the fourth of July, about six weeks' time. While in the prison I became a close friend of a man called Blake, George Blake. He's a former Foreign Office man serving forty-two years for spying for the Russians. You may remember the case. It made the headlines. It was the longest sentence ever passed in a British court of law."

Michael nodded. "Of course, I remember the case quite well. Blake was tried in 1961, wasn't he?"

"Yes—which means that he has now served five years. Thirty-seven years to go. But not really. A prisoner normally serves two-thirds of his sentence, which means that Blake has to serve a total of twenty-eight years. He can't even hope to be released before he's sixty-six."

Michael whistled a long, low whistle. "What an awful prospect! If only there was something one could do for a man like that."

"That," I said, "is precisely why I'm here."

"Eh?"

"Yes. I have agreed to break him out of jail."

Michael's mouth opened silently, and Anne's cup, halfway to her lips, was brought back to the saucer with a little clatter.

"Anne, do you still want to stay and listen?" I asked.

"I certainly do. I wouldn't want to miss this for anything."

I then explained the situation in detail, beginning with Blake's first approach and ending with my radio conversation of a few days before. Michael and his wife showed great interest, interrupting me now and then with a question or an exclamation.

"And so," I concluded, "everything is now ready at the prison end, and we have this vital radio link so that we can keep in touch right up to the last moment. The only thing that's holding us up is the money. Seven hundred pounds. Just enough for an old car, some clothes and other odds and ends, and, of course, the rent for a flat."

Michael shook his head. "If only *we* had some money," he said, looking at Anne, "but, we're broke."

"Broke is right," Anne nodded a little sadly.

I glanced at my watch. Nine o'clock.

"Do you have to be back there at a certain time?" Michael asked.

"Yes, at a quarter to eleven. I should leave here at about nine-thirty to be on the safe side. This is no time to start losing the Hostel, with so much at stake."

"Well, Sean," said Michael, "as we've told you, we've got no money, but we agree to help in every way we can, and I think I can speak for Anne here."

"Yes indeed," Anne agreed. "If there is anything at all we can do we'll do it. I'm quite prepared to have him hide here in this house. It would save the cost of renting a flat."

"I appreciate that," I said, "but it wouldn't be a good idea. It would be a bit of a risk, both for you and for Blake. It would be impossible to conceal him from the children, and the children talk to other children, and other children talk to their parents. And also we can't be sure how long he will have to hide before trying to leave the country. It would be too much of a strain on you and Michael, and your friends might begin to wonder why they're not encouraged to visit you."

"That's a point," Michael said. "Anyway, we'll do everything we can. I know some people who might be prepared to lend me the money. I think I will be able to raise the seven hundred pounds all right. It will take a little time, but I'll start work on it next week." He paused a moment, looked across at Anne, and then looked back at me again. "There's just one thing I'd like to know," he said slowly. "What is the penalty for helping someone to escape from prison?"

"The maximum penalty for aiding the escape of a prisoner from legal custody is five years' imprisonment. And out of five years you serve three years and four months."

He looked at Anne again, but she just shrugged. He stood up and looked down thoughtfully at the two children playing on the floor. Then he turned to me, a look of resolution on his face. "Very well, Sean," he said, "we're with you."

I stood up too, and we shook hands.

"Thank you, Michael," I said. "Thank you very much indeed." I turned to Anne. "And thank you, Anne. This is very generous of you, in the circumstances."

We agreed to meet again the following Saturday and then I said good night to them and walked slowly back to the tube station. My admiration for Michael had increased considerably in the past couple of hours. And what a wife! If any couple were entitled to refuse to get involved in such a dangerous mission it was surely Michael and Anne Reynolds. And politics had not once entered into the discussion. Blake's class or creed made no difference. They saw him simply as a man in need of help.

On Monday night at ten-thirty I was again lying on my bed in the prison Hostel. By crossing the Hostel red-band's palm with a couple of ounces of Old Holborn tobacco I had ensured that new arrivals to the Hostel would be allocated to the other empty rooms and that I would have my room all to myself for the remainder of my stay in Wormwood Scrubs.

I pressed the transmitting button. We went through the Lovelace passwords. Blake sounded exuberant.

"Well, how have you been keeping?" I asked. "Over."

"Oh, not bad, thank you. Much happier these days. Much, much happier. At last I can see the light at the end of the tunnel. I must say, these radios were a brilliant idea, quite brilliant. I feel a new man. And I am also beginning to realize just how crude our original method of communication was. Over."

"What surprises me," I said, "is that the idea had not occurred to us in the first place. But then, of course, we had no means of knowing how small these radios had got in the past five years. Quite a few things have changed in the world since you were last out here. These days, everything is miniaturized. The science-fiction writers have a job keeping abreast of developments, let alone keeping ahead of them. Over."

I heard Blake laugh.

"Well, let's hope that soon I shall have an opportunity of seeing all these changes at first hand. By the way, can you hear my radio in the background? Over."

"I can hear it all right. I always did dig Beethoven. Over."

"I think it's probably just a little bit too loud," he said. "I don't want the night watchman coming along and asking me to turn it down. Can you excuse me for a moment? I'll go and reduce the volume a bit. The radio is over on the table so I must get out of bed. I'll call you back. Over."

"Okay," I said, "carry on."

In a moment he was back. "What does that sound like?" he asked. "Not too loud, is it? Over."

"No, that sounds fine from here." Then I told him all about my visit to Michael Reynolds. "I think," I said finally, "you can now rest assured that the necessary help will be forthcoming. There is no longer a problem. It is now just a matter of time. Over."

"Well, that is really excellent news, my friend. It's almost unbelievable that there are people who are prepared to risk everything to help a complete stranger. It restores one's faith in the human race. If nothing else were to come of all this, if we were to fail, it would still have been worth while for the sake of getting to know people like your friends. Meeting them—if I ever do meet them—is going to be a great pleasure for me. Over."

"They're old friends of mine," I said. "They know I'm not trying to con them, and that's all that matters. After that, the decision is a clearcut one. They are just that sort of people. As you say, it restores your faith in the human race. When you spend a long time in a place like this you tend to forget that such people exist. Over."

"I agree with you," he said. "And now I'll tell you what has been happening at this end. I mentioned last time that an idea for getting out of the Hall had occurred to us. Well, we have carefully investigated it, and we are now convinced that this is the answer. You know that the Hall is dominated at each end by a large gothic window. These windows are for natural lighting, the only ones allowing light to enter the body of the Hall itself as distinct from the cells. As you may remember, these windows are broken up into cast-iron frames measuring about eighteen inches high by six inches across. There are no bars on these windows as the cast-iron frames are considered to be secure in themselves. But, in fact, they are not secure. By breaking the upright separating any two of these frames you will then have one large opening measuring eighteen inches by twelve. This is more than enough for a man of my build to go through. In fact, I have experimented in my cell with a mock-up frame made from some old bits of wood. These large gothic windows begin at the level of the slate slabs on Three landing and extend right up to about halfway between the Fours and the roof of the Hall. Now, there is also a door at each end of the Hall, immediately under the gothic windows. Leading into each door there is a porch with a sloping roof. Rather conveniently, the apex of this sloping roof just reaches the level of Three landing, where the window begins. Now, as you know, the window at the north end of the Hall is just yards from the corner where that man in blue is now permanently on guard. The window we have in mind, therefore, is at the south end, towards the front of the prison. At that end, the porch roof slopes down to a covered way that leads to C-Hall. Having removed the glass from two adjoining frames, I can break the strut separating them, climb out of the large opening onto the roof of the porch, slide down this roof to the covered way, and then drop to the ground. All this time I will be out of sight of the man sitting in the corner up near the other end of the Hall. The perimeter wall, facing the hospital, will be a mere fifteen yards away from where I land on the ground. We will be in radio contact, and at a signal from me you can throw over the rope ladder and I will dash across and climb up. Naturally, the moment I emerge from behind the end of the Hall the man sitting on his chair up at the other end will see me. But by then it will be too late. He will be a hundred yards from the ladder while I will be only fifteen yards from it. Well, Fox Michael, that's it. What do you think of it? Over."

I had already moved to a sitting position on the bed and was studying the window that Blake had been describing in such great detail. Though the cell lights were out, the lights in the body of the Hall stayed on and the large gothic window glowed dimly just beyond the roof of the gymnasium, in the darkened interior of the prison. Beyond the Hall I could see part of the east perimeter wall silhouetted against the night. That would be the very spot at which Blake would go over.

I pressed my transmitting button. "I think you've hit on an excellent idea there, Baker Charlie. As you point out, the man in blue will be a hundred yards away and you will already be virtually at the ladder. You would have such an advantage that you could just stand there and laugh at him as he ran towards you, and you could let him get halfway before you climbed up. An excellent idea. Over."

"I'm glad you approve," said Blake. "It's the weakest spot in the Hall. Indeed, why they haven't ever done something about it I can't understand. The alternative would have been one of the recess [lavatory] windows on that side of the Hall facing the wall, but that's now out of the question. Recently the bars on the recess windows were changed from ordinary ones to ones made of tungsten steel. They are virtually indestructible. They certainly cannot be cut or filed. Of course, the bars on the cell windows are still of the ordinary type, but then my cell is not on that side of the Hall facing the wall. Even if it were, the bars would have to be cut some time before, which, for me, would be quite a risk. And if one did make one's exit from a cell window on that side of the Hall, the trouble is that one would immediately be seen by that man on guard down at the corner. If he was alert he'd start running before one was halfway out the window. Now, with this big gothic window at the end of the Hall, none of these disadvantages apply. For one thing, the window frame can be broken at the last minute, and for another, as I have already mentioned, one is out of sight of the man on duty throughout. Over."

"Yes, I can see all these advantages. And another one is that if I have any difficulty getting the ladder over after you have emerged from the Hall, you can hide near the porch for quite some time. The man on duty won't be able to see you. But, of course, there is the patrol to think about. You can count on his passing by about every twenty minutes. This danger can be avoided by your emerging from the Hall immediately after he has passed, and then you can be sure of being undisturbed for twenty minutes. I think I'll send a stop-watch in to you so that you can satisfy yourself about timing. Just one question: how is the window frame to be broken? Over."

"I'm advised that that's not difficult," Blake answered. "One blow from some heavy instrument, such as piece of iron or a stone, will suffice. It appears that cast iron doesn't have to be cut. It just snaps. Over."

"Quite right," I said. "You're very lucky to have the services of a professional in there. P. knows his job. Over."

"Yes, he does. He's quite an extraordinary man. His help is invaluable. Over."

"We must try to pay him back someday for his help. I haven't mentioned anything like this to him, so you see he is not doing it in the hope of getting any reward. A very good man, Baker Charlie, a very good man indeed. Incidentally, I'd like to talk to him once more, say next Monday night, to discuss some technicalities. Over."

"Very well, I'll tell him, and give him the radio. And when you speak to him you can arrange the date of our own next meeting. Over."

"Okay," I said. "Well, that seems to be all the business for tonight. It's getting on for midnight. Have you any further points to make? Over."

"No," said Blake, "nothing further. I think we can call it a day. Over."

After we signed off I continued to stare at D-Hall for a few minutes, my eyes on the ghostly glow of that gothic window, the Achilles' heel of that armoured sarcophagus of stone and steel. Three hundred men entombed. I could imagine Blake in Tomb Number Eight on the ground floor at this moment. He would fold the telescopic aerial, place the radio out of sight under his bed, turn over on his side to face the brick wall, and sleep peacefully in the comforting belief that he was one step nearer freedom, and life.

Now that we had finally agreed on the escape route to the wall I felt much happier. The rope ladder would go over in Artillery Road at a point directly opposite the near end of D-Hall. My research and reconnaissance, already thorough, could now become more specific.

During the next couple of days I let everybody on the Hostel know that as I was due to be discharged into the free world within a matter of weeks I considered it was time I did something about my weight. I would buy a track-suit and boots and spend some time running about the park at the back of the prison. Everybody thought this was an excellent idea and encouraged me to do it.

On Thursday I bought the track-suit and boots, and also a stop-watch. Back in the Hostel I changed and told the red-band I'd be back in an hour for dinner.

At the gatehouse, as I collected my pass, the screw on duty joked about my belated interest in physical culture.

"Blimey! What's this, then?"

I grinned and patted my stomach. "Must get rid of it," I said. "Five years of porridge and potatoes is no joke."

I was about to put the pass in the top pocket of the track-suit when I felt the stop-watch there. I took the watch out and put it in a trouser pocket instead. The screw saw the watch.

"Oh," he said, "you're taking this business quite seriously, then?"

"Believe me," I said, patting the watch, "I have never been more serious about anything in my life."

He unlocked the gate and let me out. I paused for a moment in the forecourt, just outside the Officers' Club, and set the watch. Then I started to run. Out to the street gate, left turn, along the pavement, past the screws' flats and the Governor's and P.M.O.'s houses, and left again into Artillery Road. I stopped at a point opposite the end of D-Hall and pretended to be tying a bootlace so that I could look at the stop-watch: well over a minute. It would take the average screw at least a minute to run from the main gate to Artillery Road. In fact, it would take him longer. Screws were not athletes—their unstrenuous work tended to make them unfit. Nevertheless, our policy must be that if we were to err, it should be on the side of caution. We must give the opposition every advantage in our calculations.

One minute from the main gate to Artillery Road. But a screw would not be conveniently waiting at the gate with a telephone in his hand, ready for somebody to say "Go!"

I walked up to the end of Artillery Road to the park. Here the east wall met the north wall. A few yards from me as I passed, on the other side of the wall, a screw would be sitting on a chair in that corner, keeping an eye on both walls and the back of D-Hall. This man would see Blake dart across to the rope ladder down at the other end of the Hall. What would he do? If he was foolish enough he would run down and try to catch Blake—but he would never get there in time. And he could not climb up the ladder after Blake had gone over because I would no longer be holding it on the outside. If he did try to catch Blake it would, in fact, give us an added advantage. But, in keeping with my policy, I would assume that he would not do this. No, I would allow that he would first press the nearest alarm button. And this button was fixed to the end of D-Hall, just left of the porch, about twenty yards from where the screw sat.

What would happen after that was well known to me. The man on duty in the Orderly Room would have to phone to the different Halls for help. Some of the screws would space themselves out along the wall on the inside, and others would be instructed to go outside the prison. All this would take time, several minutes. And even after the first screw reached the main gate it would, as I had just discovered, take him at least another full minute to get to Artillery Road. Blake could be over the wall in less than a minute. The spot at which he came over would be very near the front end of Artillery Road. With the car, we could be in Du Cane Road in less than half a minute. From the moment Blake gave the signal to throw the rope ladder over, it would take us less than two minutes to be lost in the traffic in Du Cane Road. The screws wouldn't arrive in time to see the car, let alone to stop us.

I did a couple of laps of the park, just for appearances, and went back to the prison.

"How did it go?" asked the gatekeeper as I booked in.

"Very satisfactory," I told him. "You can do things in a track-suit that you wouldn't be able to do otherwise."

Since Peter Martin had told me about the impending mass break-out by those six men, I had looked at the sky apprehensively every day on my way to and from the factory. An overcast sky caused me as much distress as it must have caused expectant pleasure to those six men. The first downpour and they would be away, while the screw sheltered in the porch out of the rain. Such a mass escape *must* have serious repercussions. Those men were going to use *our* wall. They would probably go over within yards of the spot where Blake hoped to climb my rope ladder. Surely the authorities would do something to ensure that it did not happen again. It was a disturbing thought.

The following Monday was June 6, 1966. At four-thirty in the afternoon I took the two-way radio out of my locker, said good night to my fellow workers, and left. At the factory gate the young boy was standing as usual selling the evening papers. I bought the *Evening News* and started to walk up Warple Way towards The Vale and East Acton Lane. I unfolded the paper and stopped dead in my tracks. The huge black headline screamed out at me from the front page: BIG MANHUNT IN LONDON. Under the headline was a large photograph showing D-Hall and the east wall of Wormwood Scrubs Prison. There were the usual dotted line and arrows showing the escape route from a cell window on the Ones, across to the east wall, and along Artillery Road. *Our* route. A subhead said: "WORSE THAN ANIMALS" PRISONERS ESCAPE. I read on. Four of the escapees had been involved in a particularly bad case of rape, and the judge had told them that they were "worse than animals." The other two were serving long sentences for crimes involving grievous bodily harm. The photographs of the escaped prisoners were also published. The mass break-out had taken place early that morning and already the indignant comments of several M.P.s were quoted. There were to be questions in Parliament. The public had to be protected from such vicious thugs. Britain's prisons would have to be made escape-proof.

I walked on, crossed The Vale, and headed up East Acton Lane, reading the story over and over again, hardly aware of where I was going. Suddenly I thought of the two-way radio in my pocket. Too late to take it back to the factory; I would not be allowed in. And yet I could not risk taking it to the prison. There was bound to be the usual flap with a lot of routine searching, and there was a strong possibility that the hostellers themselves would be searched on their way in from work. To walk in the gate with the radio would be folly. But where could I hide it? I made my way slowly to the top of East Acton Lane, turned left into Old Oak Road, crossed the Western roundabout to Old Oak Common Lane, and turned right into Du Cane Road. I still had not got rid of the radio.

I walked along Du Cane Road and stopped at the corner of Wulfstan Street. This was the last turning before the prison gate. I stood there for a moment and then walked up Wulfstan Street. At the corner of Wulfstan and Erconwald there was a telephone kiosk. It had, like most other telephone kiosks in Britain, been smashed by vandals. At the moment I felt grateful to the vandals who had smashed this particular kiosk. I went into the kiosk and pretended to be looking up a number in the directory. The five volumes of the directory, which miraculously had escaped the wrath of the vandals, were neatly housed in a boxlike compartment under the shelf which had once held a telephone. I noticed that although these volumes filled the compartment from left to right they did not fill it completely in depth. Even when they were flush with the front edge of the compartment there was still a considerable gap at the back. When I re-emerged from the kiosk the radio was hidden in this gap behind the London telephone directory.

In the prison forecourt there were still a few reporters and photographers hanging about in the hope of getting something for the next morning's papers. In the gatehouse there were several screws laughing and joking. The escape had not dampened their spirits. After all, it was the Governor's responsibility, not theirs, and everybody likes to see the mighty get a kick in the pants from time to time. I was not searched, nor was any other hosteller that evening.

Fifteen minutes later I was back at the main gate in my track-suit. The screws made some humorous remarks about my appearance, and you would never have guessed from their manner that six dangerous prisoners had slipped through their fingers that day and put Wormwood Scrubs Prison on the front page.

I walked slowly up Artillery Road to the park. The place was deserted—not a policeman or a screw in sight, no signs of any special precautions having been taken. At that moment, within hours of a mass break-out, I myself might have been an accomplice in another escape. There was nothing to prevent me from throwing a rope ladder over the wall.

At the corner where the east wall met the north wall I set my stop-watch and started to run across the half-mile stretch of park towards Scrubs Lane, its eastern boundary. I came back to the prison wall and then ran in the other direction to Braybrook Street. Undoubtedly the quickest and safest route would be along Artillery Road and straight into Du Cane Road. There would be no advantage at all in running to Scrubs Lane or Braybrook Street.

After dinner I again booked out at the gate and made my way to the telephone kiosk in Wulfstan Street. I spent five minutes flicking through the pages of the directory before groping for the radio and putting it in my pocket. There were council houses all round me, and the nearest sitting-room window was only yards away from the kiosk.

I went for a walk for an hour so as not to arouse suspicion by going back to the prison too quickly. I still felt uneasy going through the prison gate with a two-way radio in my pocket on the same day that a mass break-out had occurred. But again the screws were smiling and friendly and I was not searched.

At ten-thirty that evening I shut my window tightly, put out the light, and lay on my bed. I did not have any real hope of making contact. An escape such as had taken place that morning would auto-matically be followed by a thorough search of D-Hall. Of course, I realized that Blake's radio would have a secure hiding place and that it would be taken to his cell only minutes before lock-up time on the nights we had agreed to make contact. But I could not imagine Blake taking even that small risk on a day like this. He would have seen pictures of D-Hall and the east wall on the television news that eve-ning, and he would be a very worried man. But tonight I was due to contact Peter Martin, and he was audacious enough to do almost any-thing. But would he go so far as to take a two-way radio to his cell on a night like this? If a screw walked in on him there would be no hiding place in the cell—cells were deliberately designed that way.

I pressed the transmitting button. "This is Fox Michael calling Baker Charlie, Fox Michael calling Baker Charlie. Come in please. Over." I released the transmitting button and listened.

No response.

I was just about to try again when I heard the hum from my speaker. He had pressed his button. He? If the set ever fell into the wrong hands they would, of course, try to trap the accomplice. But I had two advantages. First of all, both Blake's and Peter's voices were distinctive and unmistakable, and second, there was the identifying code.

"This is Baker Charlie to Fox Michael, Baker Charlie to Fox Michael. Receiving you loud and clear. Over."

It was Peter Martin all right.

"*Stone walls do not a prison make*," I said with heavy irony, "*nor iron bars a cage*. Over."

When we had finished the code I asked, "Do you think you are safe, my friend? Over."

"Oh yes, I think so," he answered. "The excitement has all died down. Everything is back to normal already, see. And I didn't collect the radio until the very last minute. Nothing to worry about. Over."

"Well," I said, "I've read the evening papers and I've seen the television. We haven't heard the end of it yet, by a long chalk. There are still tomorrow morning's front pages and all those questions in the House. I hope our own chances haven't been ruined. By the way, how did it go in there this morning? I thought those fellows were supposed to be waiting for rain. Today we had brilliant sunshine. What happened? Over."

"Well, what happened was this, see. These fellows *were* waiting for the rain, but then they discovered another loophole. The screw on duty in that corner all night finishes at seven o'clock in the morning, and the day-shift man doesn't start until eight, so you see the east wall is unguarded for a whole hour. Well, that's when they had it away. Of course, that loophole will be plugged now. It was very exciting here this morning between slop-out and breakfast-time. Everybody in the Hall knew that these fellows were going to have it away. Every prisoner on the east side was standing on his chair and looking out his window to enjoy the spectacle. It was very entertaining. The alarm was raised straight away, and the last fellow didn't have a chance to climb the rope before the screws pounced on him. Another one was caught just outside the wall in Artillery Road. The others got away. If they'd had a rope ladder instead of just a rope they would all have got away. It took them ages to climb that rope. It's not an easy thing to do, you know, climb a single rope for eighteen or twenty feet. These fellows were all young and strong and they only just made it. I hope that you and our friend won't be relying on a single rope. Over."

"No, we won't be relying on a single rope. Now I have some questions for you. How exactly is it intended that the two panes of glass should be broken on that gothic window without attracting attention? And, also, how is it proposed to smash the cast-iron bar separating the two frames? Will you need any instruments smuggled in? Over."

"The glass is dead easy," Peter replied. "Professionally I do it with brown paper and gum. I stick the gummed paper all over the glass and the frame and then hit it. The shattered glass doesn't fall on the ground with a clatter but stays stuck to the paper. Then I very carefully remove the paper from the frame, the broken glass coming away with it. No noise, see. The frame is done in a similar way. If I wrap some adhesive tape around the strut that we're going to break, it will deaden the sound of the blow and at the same time hold the broken bar in position so that it doesn't fall with a bang on the landing or on the roof of the porch outside. But I'd prefer not to have to hit the cast-iron strut with something heavy. It's possible that only a piece of it might break off first time and I'd have to hit it again, see, and that's messy. I'd prefer to do it scientifically. A small jack placed in the right position would do the trick, no bother. So I'd like you to get me a car jack, the smallest you can get. When it's right down at its lowest it must not be more than six inches high. When I've removed the glass I'll put this jack in the frame sideways and lever away until the bar snaps. Try and get a hydraulic jack if you can because it doesn't have to have such a long lever. I think that's all we'll need. Over."

"Okay, Baker Charlie," I said, "I'll get the jack. But I don't think I should send it in to you until shortly before the event. That would be a dangerous thing to have in D-Hall even if it was very well hidden. Do you agree that I should not send it in for the time being? Over."

"Yes, I agree with that. But will you be able to get it in after you leave? Over."

"Yes," I said. "I don't think I'll have any difficulty there. I've made one or two useful contacts in this place, and there will definitely be a channel of communication. Well, I think that's about all for now. I may not have an opportunity of speaking to you again but we can exchange messages through himself. In the meantime I would like to repeat that I am extremely grateful to you for all your help. And I think that taking that radio to your cell tonight was a hell of a thing to do. Thanks, my friend. Thanks a lot. And tell himself that I'll contact him at the same time next Monday. Over."

"Okay," said Peter, "I'll tell himself. And don't mention about the help. Over."

After we signed off in code I left the set switched on for a full minute and lay in the dark listening to the gentle buzz of the atmosphere coming from the tiny speaker. It occurred to me that we might be monitored, and I hoped, without much conviction, that the man on the monitoring set might give himself away by accidentally pressing his transmitting switch or even by deliberately communicating with someone else on the same frequency in the mistaken belief that I had gone off the air. But I heard nothing. I switched off, folded the aerial, and put the set in the locker. Our two-way radios were on a fixed frequency of 28 megacycles, and I was aware that most civilian walky-talky sets were on this same frequency. However, the chances of someone else operating a walky-talky set between ten-thirty and midnight on a Monday night, close enough to Wormwood Scrubs Prison to pick up our signals, were very remote indeed.

I had, of course, done a certain amount of research and had established that the channels used by the Metropolitan Police were so far removed from 28 megacycles that a patrol car could not accidentally tune in to us even if it was parked in Artillery Road. Similarly, the citizens of the neighbourhood, groping for the BBC or Radio Luxembourg or for the numerous off-shore pirate stations, could not accidentally pick us up. Of course, a monitoring unit set up for the purpose in the prison could hear us, but such a deliberate act would mean that the game was already up. If the authorities did their job properly I would know nothing of such a trap until I was caught in it.

I lay back on the bed and thought about that mass break-out again. So everybody had known about the escape except the screws? It was a miracle, then, that no one had grassed. (To my utter amazement I was to learn later in Moscow from the Mountbatten Report that these six men had, in fact, been grassed and that the screws had been given the precise day and time of the impending escape. The informant had made an anonymous call to Scotland Yard and had erred only in saying that the escape would be effected by overpowering one of the landing screws and taking his keys. Presumably the screws kept a slightly more firm grip on their keys that morning, but it is almost unbelievable that it did not occur to the authorities to watch the six men more closely—certainly closely enough so that all six of them could not casually make their way to the same cell and then climb out a window whose bars were already cut. The least that might have been expected after such a precise warning had been received was that the prison would have been surrounded on the inside by screws and on the outside by the police. As it was, the one officer sitting on his chair in that corner had been allowed to go home at the usual time, thus leaving the north and east walls completely unguarded during the hour of the *expected* escape.)

If this record of incredible carelessness could be maintained a few months longer, we would have a good chance of success. And, incredibly, it was.

6

Freedom

Next day the mass break-out was on the front pages and there were
some indignant editorial comments. Some of the men I worked with at
the factory were as angry as the editorial writers. Among the things
they suggested as a remedy for the situation were that the wall at
Wormwood Scrubs should be twice as high as it was and should be
patrolled by armed guards; that convicts should be kept locked in their
cells twenty-four hours a day and their doors opened only long enough
to allow their food to be thrown at them; that violent criminals should
be regularly flogged; that sentences should be even longer and
remission abolished. These views were sincerely held and articulately
expressed.

The indignation of these ordinary workingmen was genuine and
could not be compared with the phony moral indignation expressed by
one criminal towards another whom he likes to regard as being worse
than himself. These men in the factory had no guilt complexes to com-
pensate for; they had no need to seek out scapegoats to purge their
own feelings of unworthiness, for they were not, of course, unworthy
people. Many of their remarks were addressed to me in the belief that
I was one of them, that I was an ordinary, hard-working man who had
never seen and was never likely to see the inside of a prison, that I was
one of those "minds innocent and quiet" that "take this for a hermitage." My own remarks in these debates had to be judiciously weighed
for I knew that one day soon they would be recalled and discussed by
my former fellow workers. My seven months in that social limbo, half-

way between prison and freedom, were an eye-opener. All those editorials in the prison magazine pleading for understanding for the criminal seemed pointless now. And the difficulties facing the reformers were brought home to me forcefully.

That day Mr. Roy Jenkins, the Home Secretary, personally visited Wormwood Scrubs, and the evening papers showed pictures of him coming through the prison's main gate. He also appeared on the television news later in the evening, and in response to questions from the interviewer he assured the public that there was no need for any immediate drastic action. The escape, he said, was the result of a loophole in the security system, which had now been plugged. He did not, of course, say what the loophole had been, but I knew it was the one-hour gap between the departure of the night-shift screw from that vital corner and the arrival of the day-shift screw.

A couple of days later in the House of Commons the Home Secretary assured questioners that plans were afoot to make Wormwood Scrubs, and other prisons, much more secure. He was not, he said, prepared to put the clock back by locking prisoners in their cells all day. Instead the policy would be maximum perimeter security, allowing maximum freedom of movement within the prison walls. Modern methods would be employed, including closed-circuit television. It was only right, he said, that men who had to spend a very long time in prison should be given living conditions that were as humane as it was possible to be in keeping with the requirements of security.

I was considerably relieved by the Home Secretary's statement in the House but was still somewhat worried on two counts. How soon would the television cameras be mounted on the prison walls? Even if they were *not* put there before I was ready for the escape, could Blake survive at Wormwood Scrubs that long? The Home Office must now be more acutely aware than ever of the length of Blake's sentence and of his presence in a cell block whose weakness had been so dramatically demonstrated. These thoughts must also be uppermost in Blake's mind.

(It was just as well for both of us that we did not know that as these thoughts were occurring to us, the Governor of Wormwood Scrubs Prison was sitting at his desk writing an urgent request to the Home Office that George Blake be transferred without delay to a top-security prison. And this, we learned later from the Mountbatten Report, was his *second* request that Blake be moved. Incredibly, the Home Office decided to ignore the Governor's worried plea.)

On Saturday morning I went to Sussex again to collect the remainder of my belongings, including my letters, from the house where I had lived before going to prison. Again there was the staring and the pointing, and one man whom I had known came up to me with his wife and told me that he had since been elected to the Town Council and was now on the National Assistance Board Committee and if I wanted any help to let him know.

That evening I visited Michael Reynolds for the third time. I took a small bundle out of my pocket and handed it to him.

"Your letters," I told him. "I've collected every letter I've ever received from you and I would like you to destroy them personally. That way you can be sure that you will never be connected with me if anything goes wrong."

"That's a wise precaution, Sean," he said. "I'd better go and dig out yours. Excuse me."

He went upstairs. Anne and I were alone in the sitting-room.

"Anne," I said, "you're an extraordinary girl. There can't be many wives who would agree to get involved in a thing like this. Why did you accept it so readily?"

"That's very simple. Because Michael accepted it. He's my husband, and I know from experience that once he makes up his mind to do something he will do it regardless of what anybody thinks. I like to be on Michael's side. And, anyway, we hold the same views in matters like this. Our attitudes don't differ very much."

"In that case," I assured her, "you have nothing to worry about. Michael's a great fellow. I've known him a long time. He's one of the most unselfish people I've ever met."

She looked at me thoughtfully. "And why are you doing all this? Taking all these risks?"

I sipped my coffee. "I don't think," I said slowly, "that it is an altogether good idea to delve too deeply into people's motives. None of us are simple people. We're all inclined to be a bit complex, and our motives can be complex too. Blake, of course, is a friend of mine, but I still don't deceive myself that my motivation is one-hundred-per-cent altruistic. Perhaps I'm bitter. Perhaps I'm after some sort of revenge.

But one thing I do know in my heart: I'd hate to see any man serving a sentence like that. When you see someone lying on the pavement your first instinct is to help him to his feet, isn't it? Well, that doesn't necessarily make you good, but the instinct is there just the same. You can do an act of charity like that half an hour after hurting someone else. Often, Anne, we don't even know our own motives, or don't want to know them, let alone anybody else's. I reserve the right to be confused and uncertain."

"So do I," said Michael, entering from the hall and placing a number of letters and cards on the coffee table. "There is far too much cynicism in this world," he went on. "Whatever the philosophical considerations might be, I think we are all entitled to give ourselves some little credit for honesty of purpose. What does it matter if we happen to derive some personal satisfaction from doing something for somebody else? If the other person benefits, that's sufficient justification. To hell with cynicism!"

Michael had not yet got any hard cash but he had been promised some. Within a couple of weeks he would have the first two hundred pounds. That should be enough for the second-hand car. We agreed that it might not after all be necessary to have the full sum of money before the escape actually occurred. Living expenses after the escape could be taken care of as the need arose.

I said good night to Michael and his wife and caught a tube back to East Acton.

On Monday night I contacted Blake again. After going through the identifying code he asked me if I could hear him clearly.

"Perfectly clearly," I told him.

"Good," he said, "because I have hit on another idea which makes things even safer for me here. You may remember that the aerial on my ordinary wireless is a long piece of copper wire stretching from one end of the cell to the other. I now disconnect this wire and tie it to the cap of the telescopic aerial on this two-way radio. This way I can keep the telescopic aerial folded down and can talk to you with the radio held in any position, even under the blankets. Previously one had to hold the radio so that the aerial was always perpendicular. Now, if the watchman should look in the spy-hole unexpectedly he won't notice anything even if I'm actually talking to you. And it makes no difference to the reception. I too can hear you quite clearly. Over."

I asked him about the repercussions of Monday's escape.

"So far," said Blake slowly, "nothing very drastic has happened, though there are the inevitable wild rumours—all lifers to be moved to other prisons, all association to be abolished, that sort of thing. These sort of rumours originate from the prisoners themselves. However, as for my own position, I rather expected to be transferred. This is still possible, and all we can do is hope that it will not happen or that no decision will be taken before the date of our operation. We must also hope that there will be no further escapes or attempts at escape within the next few months. I doubt very much if I could survive another incident like last Monday's.

"There has been one small change," Blake continued. "The officer on duty in that corner has now been provided with a telephone kiosk, and he sits in there all day. It will no longer be necessary for him to leave his post to seek shelter from the rain. Over."

"And does he actually have a telephone or an alarm button in this kiosk? Over."

"That's something I'm not sure about," Blake answered. "However, I shall arrange for some discreet observations to be made during this week and let you know next Monday. Over."

"Thank you," I said. "It will, of course, be a factor. And what night of the week do you favour most for the operation—Saturday, I suppose? Over."

"Without a doubt. All the advantages of Saturday evening which we have discussed in detail still apply—skeleton staff and so on. And now there is another advantage. If I am to make my exit through that window it is important that there should be as few people as possible in the Hall and particularly on the landings. And on Saturday evenings most of the men are at the cinema and there are only two officers in the Hall. Yes, Saturday is the night all right. Over."

"Okay, Baker Charlie. Well, I have been to see my friend twice since I last spoke to you, and I am pleased to be able to tell you that the first part of the funds will be forthcoming in a matter of weeks. I have also taken the precaution of eliminating all previous links with this man. I have given him back all his letters to destroy and he has given me mine. Over."

"That's a good idea," said Blake. "I hope you will all maintain the highest standards of security-mindedness throughout. Remember one thing, my friend, and have no illusions about this: the moment I go from here we will be up against their best people, their top brains. The forces deployed against us will be formidable. Getting out of here will not be the end of the story, by any means. *Staying* out is not going to be easy. You are an amateur and you are going to be fighting this country's top professionals. Please bear that in mind at all times. Over."

"I will," I said, "and I am more flattered than overawed at the prospect. Which, by the way, brings me to a delicate subject. The possibility of a direct confrontation on the night of the operation must have occurred to you. I would just like you to know now that as a matter of deliberate policy I shall not be armed. If any public-spirited individual decides to have a go at us it will be a case of 'may the best man win.' But there will be no weapons. Over."

"I agree wholeheartedly with this policy," said Blake quickly. "I mean, it would be quite inconsistent to think along any other lines. After all, our aim is to put right what we regard as an injustice, and we could hardly, in all conscience, set out to remedy this injustice by doing another injustice to someone else. Over."

"Right, my friend," I said. "I'm glad you see it that way. I think that's it for tonight and I'll call you up again next Monday. Anything further to add yourself? Over."

"No, I think we've covered everything. Over."

After we had signed off, I again listened in to the radio for a couple of minutes before switching off. And again I heard nothing more than the atmospheric buzz.

A week later I was talking to Blake again. He told me he had established that there had been no telephone or alarm button installed in the telephone kiosk in the corner. The kiosk had apparently been provided only as a shelter. We agreed to talk again the following Monday, for the last time before my departure from the Hostel.

On Saturday I strolled to the shopping centre in Old Oak Common Lane and looked carefully over the cards on the noticeboard outside the news-agent's shop. I was looking for a bed-sitting-room as near as possible to the prison, with a view to making radio contact direct between this room and Blake's cell. There was such a room on offer, at 26 Perryn Road, just off the Western Avenue and halfway between the prison and the factory where I worked. I spent half an hour going carefully over the route between the prison and Perryn Road. I was looking for intervening obstacles to good radio reception. The terrain looked favourable. There were no very tall buildings or industry employing heavy machinery or anything of that nature. The area was entirely residential save for the shops in Old Oak Common Lane and the Western Garage next to the Western Avenue roundabout. This garage was about halfway between the prison and Perryn Road, but I considered it extremely unlikely that they would be using heavy electrical plant late at night. Another encouraging feature was that the stretch of Western Avenue between the roundabout and Perryn Road sloped slightly upwards, thus putting Perryn Road on a higher level than Wormwood Scrubs Prison. My maps showed that the distance from the prison to 26 Perryn Road (halfway along) was a mile. I doubted if we could communicate over that distance in a built-up area, with our radios, regardless of how favourable the conditions appeared to be. Still, I would try. And, anyway, this was the nearest room available.

I phoned the landlord and made an appointment for that afternoon. The room, to my great satisfaction, was at the top of the house and its window faced in the general direction of Du Cane Road, though the prison was not visible at that distance. I took the room, paid two weeks' rent in advance, and was given a key to the front door of the house and another one to the room itself. I told the landlord that I was moving from Sussex to London in a couple of weeks and was taking a temporary job at a local factory while I "finished my book." Did I have a passport? Certainly not! An Irish citizen cannot and must not be asked to produce a passport in Great Britain! The landlord was a foreigner and could not be expected to understand the special relationship that existed between Britain and the Irish Republic.

Next day I moved in half my luggage. The remainder I would take with me on the morning of my release from prison.

On Monday night I contacted Blake again.

"Well," I told him, "this is the last time I shall talk to you from here. Next Monday is D-for-Discharge-Day. The fourth of July, appropriately enough. I have secured a room within a mile of here and I shall try to contact you from there at the usual time next Monday. I doubt if I shall succeed, but there's no harm in trying. If we fail to make contact from that distance I shall come back here to the park at the same time the following week. I know for certain that I can contact you from the park. Over."

"I've got all that," said Blake. "There is just one small alteration I would like to suggest. If we fail to make contact from your new home next Monday, can we then change our day to Saturday? The reason is this: one never knows, these days, when there's going to be a spot check, an unexpected search. It might happen even first thing in the morning. If it did, this radio would be found before I had time to take it to its hiding place. But if we make contact on Saturday nights this danger will not exist because there is only a skeleton staff on duty on Sundays, as on Saturdays. Skeleton staffs cannot carry out searches. Is this agreeable to you? Over."

"Yes, quite agreeable. It really makes no difference to me at all. So, then: I shall try to contact you next Monday night from my new apartment. If this fails I shall contact you on the following Saturday, the ninth of July, from the park. I too have a small alteration to suggest. Obviously it is important that I should be alone in the park and have the cover of complete darkness. I would therefore like to change our time of contact from ten-thirty to eleven o'clock. Is this all right with you? Over."

"Yes," Blake agreed, "that's all right with me. And I think that's all the business for tonight, isn't it? Over."

"Yes."

During the week I bought some bamboo canes in a hardware shop in Old Oak Common Lane.

"I hope you're not going to beat anyone with those," the salesman joked.

"Not in the way you imagine," I told him with a smile. "I am not about to join the Christian Brothers."

He was an Englishman, and I don't think he understood the last remark.

At the factory I secured some copper cable. Both the cable and the bamboo canes I deposited in my new room at 26 Perryn Road. I arranged with the factory to have the following Monday off from work as I was "changing houses." On the Sunday I telephoned a car-hire firm and arranged to have a chauffeur-driven car waiting outside the prison at nine o'clock next morning to take a "Mr. O'Brien and his luggage" to Perryn Road. I packed my luggage in the Hostel that night, and next morning at breakfast said good-bye to those hostellers that I bothered to talk to.

At eight-thirty I was in the Chief's office.

"Right, Bourke," he said, "here you are. Your Hostel savings. One hundred pounds. Sign here, after you have counted it, of course."

"That won't be necessary, Chief." I signed and stuffed the bundle of notes into my pocket.

"Just one more formality," said the Chief. "You are required by law to sign the Firearms Act." He handed me a printed card about six inches square. "That," he said, "contains the relevant passage of the Act."

It was a warning to the effect that it was a criminal offence to possess a firearm or any form of explosive within five years of leaving prison. A prisoner actually convicted of an offence involving firearms or explosives was banned for life from such possession. This seemed a pointless exercise to me since it was a criminal offence for *any* member of the public to go about armed, whether he had been to prison or not. And, obviously, the only reason an ex-prisoner would want to have a gun or a stick of dynamite would be to commit a crime that he hoped to get away with anyway. Signing this Act would be no deterrent. I handed the card back to the Chief and signed my name in the book.

"And that," he said with a grin, "includes home-made bombs."

At the gate the shiny limousine was waiting for me, the chauffeur standing at the door. I walked up to him, and he touched his cap.

"Mr. O'Brien?"

"That's me," I said.

"Good morning, sir. Let me take your bag."

He put the bag in the boot and held the rear door open for me.

We engaged in light conversation during the ten-minute journey to Perryn Road, and I knew that nothing would have pleased him more than to know who or what this strange man was who had walked out of the prison gate and stepped into a hired car. Was he a prison Governor or a gangster? At 26 Perryn Road he offered to carry the bag into the house for me, but I declined his offer and paid him off with a ten-shilling tip.

I spent the next hour constructing an aerial from the bamboo canes and the copper cable. I tied the two longer canes together to give a total of about ten feet and fixed a short piece across about two feet from one of the ends. I hammered some small nails into this cross about one inch apart and wound the cable round them to form a diamond-shaped frame aerial. There was still about twenty feet of cable left—enough to allow me to lie comfortably on the bed with the radio while the aerial protruded from the window. Next I fixed a couple of brackets to the window frame as a housing for the cane. I tried the cane in this housing and it was quite successful; the aerial protruded upwards past the level of the roof gutter. I pulled it back into the room and stood it in a corner.

There were three other bed-sitters on my floor besides my own. Some discreet observation that day revealed that two of these rooms were occupied by Pakistanis (two men to a room) and the third by a married English couple. On the ground floor there were three more bed-sitters, each occupied by an English couple. I would have to keep my voice down when talking into that radio.

My room was a single one and very simply furnished. There was an old wardrobe, an old chest of drawers, an old table and chair, a washstand with a yellow plastic bowl, and a divan-type bed. The cooking facilities consisted solely of a gas ring on the floor. It was going to be a hard few months.

I went out and bought a kettle, a frying pan, a mug, a knife, fork, and spoon, and some provisions. For lunch I would have a couple of pork chops, followed by an apple pie and a mug of tea.

At eleven o'clock that night I was sitting on the bed repeating Blake's call sign into the two-way radio but without success. I kept it up for half an hour and then abandoned it. Though only a mile apart, with radios as small as ours, we were out of range in a built-up area.

All that week I accustomed myself to eating only fried food and cooking it on my knees. The flexible tube leading from the gas pipe to the ring was so short that the ring could not be put even on a low chair. To do my washing up I had to take the yellow plastic bowl to the bathroom on the landing, insert a sixpence in the gas heater, light the gas, fill the bowl, and take it back into the room. I washed and shaved in the same way, in the same bowl.

On Saturday night at ten o'clock I went to the Western pub near the Western Avenue roundabout. During the next half-hour I drank six double whiskies and had a friendly chat with the barmaid. My radio was in my mac pocket. At ten-thirty I left the pub, crossed the round-about, made my way along by the shops in Old Oak Common Lane, and turned right into Erconwald Street.

I walked up to the park and then turned left away from the prison towards that fence separating the park from the railway lines. I chose a spot in line with D-Hall, now a faint shadow in the distance. I was feeling quite relaxed, thanks to the whisky. The fence was about five feet high and consisted of spiked vertical bars about six inches apart, with a horizontal bar near the bottom and another one near the top. I caught hold of two of the spikes and heaved myself up until I could rest one foot on the top crossbar, between another two spikes.

I balanced precariously in that position for a moment, looking down at the sharp spikes pointing threateningly at my unprotected vital regions, and I suddenly became very aware of those six double whiskies. "Christ," I muttered aloud, "if I slip now, my only pastime in the future *will* be whisky."

I let go the spikes and jumped. This spot on the railway embankment was a short uncultivated stretch between two allotments and was overgrown with tall grass. I lay on my back in this grass, my hat tilted forward over my forehead, and took the radio out of my pocket. I also took out a small torch that I had brought with me for the purpose and glanced at my watch: two minutes to eleven. I listened for a moment. Not a sound to be heard from the park or the nearby railway lines. I extended the aerial and switched on.

"This is Fox Michael calling Baker Charlie. Come in please. Over."

I listened. Blake was trying to call me but the signal was so faint that it was almost non-existent. I tried for a few more minutes but the reception did not improve. And I could not know if he was receiving me.

"Listen, Baker Charlie," I said, "I don't know whether you can hear me but I certainly can't hear you. I shall have to come closer. Just in case you *can* hear me, please stay tuned in and I shall begin to walk across in your direction. Over."

I climbed back over the fence and started to walk slowly across the park towards the prison, alternately calling on Blake to come in and then listening for the strength of his signal. Halfway across the park the reception was still bad and I began to worry. Finally I reached those Irish goalposts, and I could hear Blake quite distinctly. He could also hear me. But I was only yards from the prison's perimeter wall and also dangerously close to the park end of Artillery Road, slightly to my left. Although it was a private road, anybody deciding to enter the park from Du Cane Road (for whatever reason) would do so at that point, and I would not see them until they were actually in the park and capable of seeing me. I was in an extremely dangerous position.

I lay flat on my stomach and rested the radio on the grass in front of me, the aerial fully extended upwards. If a policeman came round the corner of the prison wall out of Artillery Road there would be no escape for me.

"Listen, Baker Charlie," I whispered urgently into the radio, my chin resting on the grass, "I'm in an extremely vulnerable position. I'm so close to the bloody wall that we could shout across at each other without using the radios at all. We must be brief, my friend, very brief. Over."

"I agree we must be brief," Blake said. "Anything to report? Over." He sounded as worried as I was.

"No," I told him, "nothing to report. I just wanted to establish contact. I tried on Monday from my new address and I assume you were also trying. Over."

"Yes, I was trying too, as agreed. We were out of range. Our present precarious position would seem to confirm that. I have just one piece of information for you. About that kiosk in the corner: a phone has now been installed and the authorities are confident that the whole place can be surrounded within four minutes of the alarm being raised. How does this affect you? Over."

"It leaves me quite unperturbed. All *we* need is two minutes at the very most. If four minutes is the best they can do, then they've already lost the contest. Actually, I'm even relieved that they're so confident. This will make them smugly self-satisfied and they will become complacent about further measures. This is all to the good. As you know, there is nothing much I can do at the moment; I am waiting for the funds. I shall be seeing my friend again in a few days. Can we talk again next Saturday night at the same time? Over."

"Yes," said Blake, "and I think we had better go now. You are, as you said, in a very dangerous position. Over."

"Right," I said. "This is Fox Michael to Baker Charlie. Over and out. Good night."

"Baker Charlie to Fox Michael," said Blake quickly. "Over and out. Good night."

I folded the aerial, stuck the radio in my pocket, and stood up. I turned my back on the prison wall and walked quickly towards the centre of the darkened park. I wanted to put as much distance as possible between myself and the prison before turning towards Braybrook Street. That way, a casual observer might think that I was simply taking a short-cut from Scrubs Lane. There was, in fact, a footpath leading from Scrubs Lane to Braybrook Street just in front of that spiked fence at the other side of the park. It was as well that I took this precaution for as I stepped from the park onto the street a police patrol car approached. It slowed down, the driver and his observer stared at me, and I thought for one awful moment that the car was going to stop. I clutched the radio nervously in my pocket and wondered if I would be able to drop it on the edge of the park as they got out of the car. But they seemed to be satisfied that I had just walked from Scrubs Lane, and the car sped off and turned into Erconwald Street.

How much easier it is, I mused, to use a two-way radio inside a prison than outside! And how much safer!

7

Braybrook Street Murders

During the week I met a Hostel acquaintance, Barry Richards, in the Western pub. I bought him a few whiskies and we chatted amiably for an hour. Inevitably the talk centred on the prison and the people we both knew there. Then quite casually, and with a little laugh, he gave me some quite startling news.

"By the way," he said, "did you know that they've started monitoring the prison?"

"Monitoring the prison? What do you mean?"

"Well, they think somebody's in radio contact with the nick [the prison] and they're going to monitor the gaff. At least that's the rumour I've heard, see. And the radio shop—you know, the place where they mend all the radios and TV sets—they've closed it down."

I had to try very hard to conceal my amazement. "But why," I asked, for want of something more sensible to say, "should anybody want to be in radio contact with the nick?"

"Dunno." Barry shrugged. "It's just the rumour I've heard, see. They're tightening up on the hostellers too. They've started reading our mail and searching us sometimes coming in the gate."

On Saturday night I made my way to the park again, a very worried man. It might be just wild rumour resulting from the mass breakout (all the men, incidentally, had now been recaptured), or there might be some substance in it. The new restrictions imposed on the hostellers would seem to suggest that there *was* something in the air. Could one of my fellow hostellers have overheard me talking in my room late at night? It was certainly possible. But what could I do? I had to maintain contact with Blake. The alternative was to call the operation off. If there was going to be a chase, or even capture, it was as well that it should happen *before* the night of the operation. That way only I was vulnerable, and Blake might still find a way of escaping after I was arrested. It would also be in my own interests, if I *had* to be arrested, that the identity of the other man was not known. The arguments, I told myself, were in favour of making contact tonight.

If they were, in fact, monitoring the prison they would hardly have a man listening twenty-four hours a day from one end of the week to the other. They would more likely have a tape recorder fixed up near a receiver and play the tape back daily at high speed. Whichever way it was done, I did not think the showdown would come tonight. They would simply note the time of my next visit and the police would be waiting then.

I walked along the footpath near the spiked fence, then turned sharply to the right and headed across the park towards the prison. The park was so dark I would have to be very close to another nocturnal prowler before I saw him. I stopped at the white H-shaped goalposts and again lay flat on my stomach. At most, I was thirty yards from the prison wall and just a little to the right of D-Hall, in line with the exercise yard.

I held the radio in my right hand and rested my chin in the clenched fist of my left hand on the grass.

"This is Fox Michael calling Baker Charlie, Fox Michael calling Baker Charlie. Come in please. Over."

"Baker Charlie to Fox Michael. Receiving you loud and clear. Over."

We went through the identifying code.

"Now listen very carefully, Baker Charlie," I said. "Special instructions. If I should suddenly go off the air and fail to call you back within five minutes, you must destroy your radio and get rid of the pieces. Throw them as far away from your own window as possible. Is this understood? Over."

Blake pressed his transmitting button but paused before speaking.

"Yes," he said presently, "your instructions are understood. Is everything all right? Over."

"Yes, everything is all right. Just an extra precaution because of my vulnerable position. There is nothing new to report from this side. Anything special happening in there? Over."

"No," said Blake, "nothing remarkable to report."

He had obviously not heard the rumour about the prison being monitored.

"I would just like to ask you," he went on, "when you think the operation might be carried out. Can you make even a rough guess? Over."

"About two months. I shall be buying the car within a couple of weeks, and then I shall start searching for a flat and making all the other necessary arrangements. Over."

"Thank you," Blake said. "I just like to have something to set my sights on, as it were. I think that's all. I feel uncomfortable with the thought of you in that exposed position out there. Over."

"I feel uncomfortable too," I assured him. And then, for the benefit of anyone who might be listening in, I added slowly and distinctly, "I shall contact you at the same time next Saturday. This is Fox Michael to Baker Charlie. Over and out. Good night."

I put the radio in my pocket and looked around cautiously before standing up—first towards Artillery Road, then along the wall to the right before looking over my shoulder at the park behind me. I peered into the darkness for a moment and then lay rigid, without breathing, the blood pounding through my veins. About twenty yards away a shadowy figure was approaching me with a dog on a lead. Almost in the same instant that I saw him he turned and moved off in another direction, pulled along by the dog straining at the lead. As soon as he disappeared into the darkness I stood up and headed obliquely towards Braybrook Street. I remembered that I was wearing a white shirt and turned up the collar of my mac to hide it, at the same time pulling my hat down over my face. Such stage-villain tactics could, after all, have a practical application.

If I had not said good night to Blake when I did that man would surely have heard me. And if his dog had not been a dumb mongrel it would have led him straight to me. It was a narrow escape.

On the following Saturday night I put the radio in my pocket, left my room in Perryn Road, and headed once more towards the prison. I called in at the Western pub and had my usual six whiskies. If the prison had indeed been monitored the previous Saturday they would be waiting for me tonight. And if I was going to be arrested it was as well to have a drink beforehand. I would not get another for a long time.

At half-past ten I was walking up Erconwald Street. I was deliberately early so that I could do a little reconnaissance. I walked slowly along the full length of Braybrook Street, carefully scrutinizing the parked cars in search of a police undercover vehicle, or "Q-car." I was also looking for a Post Office detector van, though I really believed that if the prison was monitored the Post Office equipment could more conveniently be housed *inside* the prison than outside it. I saw nothing suspicious but at the same time realized that this was no real cause for satisfaction. They could be hiding anywhere. The whole area could be surrounded at this moment—and I would know nothing about it.

I made my way along the footpath and at the usual spot turned right and headed across the park towards the shadowy bulk in the distance that was Wormwood Scrubs Prison. I stopped at the goalposts and once again lay flat on my stomach. I glanced across at the entrance to Artillery Road. If a police car suddenly screeched round that corner into the park I would not be unduly surprised, and they, having heard my warning to Blake the previous Saturday, would know that I was not surprised.

I put my ear close to the ground and listened, but the park was still. If they were lying in wait they were doing it very efficiently. I took out the radio, extended the aerial, and switched on.

"This is Fox Michael calling Baker Charlie, Fox Michael calling Baker Charlie. Come in please. Over."

He answered without delay. "This is Baker Charlie to Fox Michael. Receiving you loud and clear. Over."

If they were going to make their move this was surely the moment to do it. I kept my gaze on the entrance to Artillery Road as I spoke. We went through the identifying code, though there was no mistaking Blake's voice.

"There is still nothing concrete to report," I told him. "Anything of interest on your side? Over."

"No, nothing to report. There have been no further developments, no improvements on that telephone in the kiosk and the four-minute warning. In view of the present unavoidably slow pace, do you think it is necessary to make contact so often? Couldn't we have our next contact in, say, a fortnight from now, on August the sixth? What do you think? Over."

"I agree wholeheartedly," I said. "Lying here like this is an unnerving experience. It gives me the bloody creeps. If there's no further business I'll sign off and clear out of here. Over."

"Yes, I think you should," said Blake. "I have nothing further to contribute. Over."

"Okay, then." We signed off.

My eyes were still on Artillery Road as I folded the aerial and stuffed the radio into my pocket. I stood up. As usual, I would not walk straight from the prison wall to the street. It would take me about five minutes to reach the fence near the railway lines and another five to walk along the path to Braybrook Street. They had ten minutes in which to make their move. I was waiting for a whistle blast and then an invasion of the park from every direction. Nothing came.

I reached the footpath and walked slowly through the darkness to Braybrook Street. I was still nervous as I made my way down Erconwald Street towards Old Oak Common Lane. I did not relax until I reached the Western Avenue.

Back in my untidy, ill-furnished bed-sitting-room I knelt on one knee by the gas ring on the floor to fry a supper of sausages and eggs. The smell of grease and gas filled the small room, forcing me to open the window wide. As I ate my simple meal in these very humble surroundings, I thought for a moment about the current popularity of the spy thrillers and the glamour surrounding them, and I smiled at the contrast between that popular fictional image and the reality of my own singularly unglamorous situation. Not a fast car or a gun or a devastating blonde anywhere in sight. Sausages and eggs in a smoke-filled bed-sitter in Acton.

Next day I went to see Michael Reynolds again. He had raised the first hundred pounds, which he handed over to me. The hundred pounds I had saved on the prison Hostel had since been spent on a badly needed suit and other clothing. I knew of a shopkeeper in North London who had a 1955 Humber Hawk for sale. It was being offered for sixty pounds. I bought this car a couple of days later and drove it back to Perryn Road. It had a good engine and good brakes. I could now at last rehearse the getaway under realistic conditions.

I had made up my mind that the getaway would be along Du Cane Road, and the only remaining question was whether we should turn left or right after leaving Artillery Road. The precise location of the hideout would have a bearing on this, but in the meantime I would thoroughly familiarize myself with both routes. I decided that provisionally the terminal point of both routes should be an Underground station. If I turned left in Du Cane Road I would drive to Notting Hill Gate station, and if I turned right I would go to Stamford Brook, just off Chiswick High Road.

At six o'clock on the Saturday evening I was parked in Artillery Road close to the prison wall at a point directly opposite the end of D-Hall. As far as parking was concerned, this was an ideal time for the escape. The hospital employees who parked in Artillery Road during the day were always gone by five o'clock, and the visitors to the hospital (some of whom also parked in Artillery Road) did not begin to arrive until shortly before seven. I allowed ten minutes for all the business preceding Blake's dash to the wall—enough time for me to contact him and for him to get from his cell to the gothic window, to break it and climb down to the ground.

At ten minutes past six I put the stop-watch in motion and started the engine of the car. I allowed a minute and a half for Blake's ascent of the rope ladder, his drop into Artillery Road, and his entry into the car. Then I moved off.

I had no difficulty turning right in Du Cane Road. As I turned left into Old Oak Common Lane I glanced at the watch again. Only three minutes had elapsed from the moment at which I would have thrown the rope ladder over the wall. I did not carry straight on from Old Oak Common Lane into Old Oak Road. This would have been the easiest way to Stamford Brook, but it was also one of the two shortest routes between Shepherd's Bush police station and the prison. Instead I turned right on the Western Avenue and turned left again into Glendon Road. I would travel parallel to the police cars (but at a safe distance from them) as they raced to the prison. I crossed East Acton Lane and entered Bromyard Avenue. There is a church on an island in the middle of the road halfway along this avenue that creates a blind spot and forces motorists to slow down. I made a mental note of this hazard. At the bottom of Bromyard Avenue I turned right in The Vale and left again into Larden Road. It was a straight run through Larden Road, Emlyn Road, and Prebend Gardens. Just before the bridge carrying the District Line of the Underground over Prebend Gardens, I turned left into Vaughan Avenue. I parked halfway along and walked round the corner to Stamford Brook Underground station in Goldhawk Road.

Seven minutes had elapsed from the moment at which the ladder would have gone over and the alarm been raised, and I was already more than two miles from the prison. In the weeks that followed I was to reduce this time to six minutes. But the important thing was that within three minutes I was already out of Du Cane Road. A whole minute to spare before the prison was surrounded.

The following Saturday, August 6, was a busy one. I was due to contact Blake again that night in the park. At six o'clock I was again parked in Artillery Road. I would try the other route, to Notting Hill Gate. It was, of course, even easier to turn left in Du Cane Road than to turn right. I turned left into Wood Lane, right into North Pole Road, right again into Latimer Road, and left into Oxford Gardens. I turned right in Ladbroke Grove and drove down almost to the bottom, parking the car in a side street just short of the main road, Holland Park Avenue. Notting Hill Gate station was just round the corner, a couple of minutes' walk.

That night at eleven o'clock I was again lying in the darkened park near the prison wall talking to George Blake. I told him in guarded language about the car and the trial runs, and this encouraged him. We agreed to make contact again on the following Saturday, August 13. But something was to occur on Friday, August 12, that would have made such a contact suicidal.

I got my first hint that something was wrong almost immediately I walked out the factory gate at the end of work that day. As I walked up East Acton Lane towards Perryn Road I passed two police motorcyclists, a police van, and two patrol cars with blue lights flashing on their roofs. The vehicles were going very slowly, and the grim-faced policemen seemed to be scrutinizing every pedestrian and motorist they passed. In Perryn Road I passed two more motorcyclists and another car. Something was very wrong. My first thought was that there had been another mass break-out from the prison. If this had happened Blake would most certainly already be on his way to another prison.

In my room I turned on the wireless. After about fifteen minutes the music programme was interrupted and the announcer said, "And now the latest news on the murder of three policemen in West London today . . ." He went on to talk of the three policemen in a Q-car who had been shot dead in Braybrook Street "within sight of Wormwood Scrubs Prison." The motive for the killings was not yet known, nor was the identity of the killers.

My first reaction was one of great concern. Who had done the killings? Was it escaping prisoners? Or men on the outside attempting to rescue their friends on the inside? I was convinced that if these killings were in any way connected with Wormwood Scrubs Prison, Blake's chance of freedom had disappeared. The papers next day were, of course, full of the police murders, and it was to go on like that for four months. It was the beginning of one of the biggest manhunts ever launched in Britain.

Saturday morning I bought several newspapers in Old Oak Common Lane and made my way slowly up Erconwald Street, reading them as I walked. The three policemen, plainclothes men, had got out of their Q-car to question some men in another car. The other men shot them dead. I was relieved to read the comment of a prison spokesman to the effect that none of the prisoners was missing and that there appeared to be no connection between the shootings and the prison.

Long before I reached Braybrook Street I saw the police. There were at least two hundred men in uniform. Some were standing in small groups talking in low voices. Others sat on the grass. A long line of about forty constables, their jackets and helmets discarded, were down on their hands and knees moving slowly along the park near the street, their eyes on the grass. Scotland Yard had set up a mobile headquarters, bristling with aerials, not far from the prison wall. There were a lot of spectators and newsmen. One of the papers in my hand had a picture of the three policemen lying dead in the street. The Home Secretary and the Metropolitan Police Commissioner were talking to senior detectives near the mobile headquarters. There was tension and anger and shock in the air. And I was due to lie in the park tonight, virtually in the middle of this scene, a two-way radio in my hand, and plot the escape of George Blake from prison! It was one appointment that was not going to be kept.

By the middle of the following week the police had completed their investigations on the spot, and the mobile headquarters was towed away on the Friday. The next night, within one week of the murders, I was lying in the park. Blake and I had agreed in the beginning that if for any reason we failed to make contact on any occasion we would try again at the same time one week later. I was extremely nervous. I could see no reason why the police would want to patrol the area any more intensely after the murders than before, but there was always the element of curiosity. A police driver might be drawn to Braybrook Street for no other reason than that three of his colleagues had been murdered there a short while before. I felt more exposed than ever.

"This is Fox Michael calling Baker Charlie, Fox Michael calling Baker Charlie. Come in please. Over." I whispered the words.

"This is Baker Charlie to Fox Michael. Receiving you loud and clear. Over."

We went quickly through the code.

"Sorry I couldn't contact you last week," I said. "I don't have to tell you the reason. Over."

"You're quite right," said Blake. "I didn't even bother to take this radio to my cell last Saturday because I knew it would be impossible. We here could see everything out there from the upper windows. It was quite a frightening sight."

I suggested that since I would have to contact him from the car later on anyway, why not start now? And since the operation would be commencing at six o'clock, perhaps we should get used to contacting each other at that time.

He concurred and we signed off.

On Wednesday I took a tube to Camden Town to see Michael Reynolds. He told me he had a friend who, he felt, would be willing to help us in a practical way, though, like Michael, he had no money. The man's name was Pat Porter. His mother too was Irish and his father English.

"He's calling here this evening," Michael said. "I haven't discussed it with him because I didn't know if you'd agree."

"If he's a friend of yours, Michael," I said, "that's good enough for me. We'll need all the help we can get."

Pat arrived half an hour later and when told of the project agreed without hesitation to help in every way he could. He was a couple of years younger than Michael, about twenty-eight, and generally much more robust. From the outset he showed great enthusiasm.

"Im only sorry I've got no money to give," he said. "I started a little business with a couple of other fellows a year ago and everything we've got is on hire purchase. Half of what we make every week belongs to the finance company, and that's how it will be for the next three years. But if there's anything else I can do I'll be only too pleased. George Blake can even hide in my flat if necessary."

We discussed all aspects of the escape and paid special attention to the question of whether we should try to get Blake out of the country on the night of the escape or hide him for a while.

"It would be a big risk trying to get him out the same night," Pat said. "Every exit from the country will be closely guarded."

We agreed that I should get Blake's own views on the subject when I next spoke to him.

On Saturday I bought a bunch of chrysanthemums in the florist's in Old Oak Common Lane. At five minutes to six I pulled up in Du Cane Road directly opposite the entrance to Artillery Road. The chrysanthemums were on the seat next to me. There was another car parked a little bit ahead of me and about six behind me opposite the hospital. This was an advantage; I would not look conspicuous. I was just one of many parked cars.

I wound the window shut and then put my hand under the seat and picked the two-way radio up off the floor. I unplugged the aerial lead from the car radio and with the aid of a small clamp specially bought for the purpose I attached it to the cap of the folded-down aerial of the two-way radio. This way I could communicate through the car's own aerial and no passer-by would be any the wiser. Next I inserted the two-way radio into the middle of the bunch of flowers so that it was completely hidden and proceeded to smell the flowers appreciatively for the benefit of anyone who might throw a glance in my direction. What could be more natural than a man sitting in his car holding a bunch of flowers outside Hammersmith Hospital as he waited for the visiting hour to begin so that he could go and see his loved one?

I stuck my thumb through the stems of the flowers and found the transmitting button. I glanced at my watch: six o'clock.

"This is Fox Michael calling Baker Charlie, Fox Michael calling Baker Charlie. Come in please. Over."

I glanced across at the prison. The cell windows of D-Hall on the Threes and Fours were clearly visible over the top of the east wall.

"This is Baker Charlie to Fox Michael. Receiving you loud and clear. Over."

Reception was perfect—so much so that I was caught unawares with the volume turned full up and gave a startled look round me to see if anybody was nearby. Blake's voice boomed deafeningly out of the small radio. I quickly turned the volume down about two-thirds. We went through the identifying code.

"Baker Charlie," I said, "this reception is fantastic. It is not just as if you were right here in the car with me; it is as if you were shouting at the top of your voice into my ear. You are not, I imagine, in your own cell on the ground floor at the other side of the Hall. You must surely be behind one of those windows on the Fours which I can see from where I'm parked. Over."

"As a matter of fact, I am," Blake answered. "And I can hear you perfectly too. My volume is turned down to the minimum. It would be much too dangerous for me to attempt to talk to you from my own cell at this time of the day. Anybody might just walk in on me, as you know. It's quite safe up here on the Fours. Most of the others are at the cinema, and the two officers are down on the Ones chatting and drinking tea. Over."

I laughed. "Yes, I can see the scene quite vividly. It's a great advantage for someone in my position to know exactly what's happening on *both* sides of the wall at any moment. It's like having X-ray eyes. Anyway, I can now tell you that the job will be done in about six weeks. I'm sorry about the delay, it can't be helped. But, on the other hand, in six weeks' time we shall have the advantage of darkness again. My God, imagine that! It's almost a year since we first discussed the project. Over."

"Yes," said Blake, "a year. It is amazing that either of us has survived this long, considering the hazards on both sides. Over."

All the time we were talking I was keeping a careful watch on Du Cane Road. From where I was parked I could see right down to Old

Oak Common Lane, and through the rear-view mirror I could see to Wood Lane. The traffic was moderately heavy. Now and then screws would enter or leave the prison forecourt, but they were too far away to notice me. Long ago I had established, to my satisfaction, that nearly every screw who left the prison turned right and went towards Old Oak Common Lane. The married quarters were on that side of the forecourt, and even those screws who lived some distance from the prison all, without exception, had their houses located in that direction. Suddenly a police patrol car turned into Du Cane Road from Old Oak Common Lane and raced towards me.

I pressed my transmitting button. "Baker Charlie, this is urgent. A patrol car is approaching. I'll sign off until it goes by—if it does go by. Keep your fingers crossed and wait for me to call you back. Over and out."

I switched off the radio and started nonchalantly to examine, arrange, and smell the chrysanthemums, making sure that they were clearly visible from outside the car. The patrol car slowed down as it passed the prison gate and approached the hospital. Out of the corners of my eyes I could see the two policemen glancing at me as they came abreast. They were so close I could see the chrome numbers on their shoulders. I pretended not to notice them. The moment they passed I put the car in gear and placed my thumb over the starting button. If they stopped and started to walk back towards me I would make a dash for it. With the Braybrook Street murders still in the headlines, police patrols were likely to be more sensitive than usual to men sitting in parked cars. I kept my eyes glued to the rear-view mirror. I did not look around, for I allowed for the policemen to be looking in their own mirrors, and if they saw me taking such an interest in them they would be suspicious. The patrol car cruised slowly past the hospital entrance and carried straight on to Wood Lane, where it turned left and went out of sight.

I put the car back in neutral and switched on my radio again. "Fox Michael calling Baker Charlie. Come in please. Over."

"Baker Charlie to Fox Michael. Receiving you loud and clear. Over."

I said, "Phew! Over."

"That's exactly how I feel," said Blake. "I was holding my breath here. No trouble? Over."

"No, no trouble. They've gone. And now there's something I've got to ask you. What are your views about leaving the country on the night of the event? One possible route I have in mind is to travel to Ireland immediately, either in disguise or hidden in a vehicle on the car ferry, and catch a plane for the Continent next morning from Shannon Airport, having driven south through Ireland during the night. I have studied all the relevant timetables and I know that it is just possible. What do you think? Over."

Blake had obviously thought about this already, for he gave me his answer straightaway. "I'm not in favour of this," he said firmly. "It is fraught with danger. It is infinitely preferable that we go into hiding immediately and plan the second stage of the operation, the exit, at our leisure. Over."

"Okay," I said. "Actually this makes things easier. Over."

We agreed to make contact again in a fortnight and then signed off. I did not want to have to contact Blake on the following Saturday, the first Saturday in September, for on that day I wanted to devote my attention to Shepherd's Bush police station. This was the prison's *local* station, the one to which the emergency phone call would be made by the orderly officer on duty at Wormwood Scrubs, on the night of Blake's escape.

I plugged the aerial lead back into the car radio and wound down the window. The sun was shining brilliantly, and the sweat was pouring down my face in the stifling hot car. I drove past the prison gate and back to Perryn Road.

On Monday I went shopping in Old Oak Common Lane. In Woolworth's they were selling clotheslines that measured exactly thirty-six feet in length. You'd think they were made specially to dangle down on both sides of an eighteen-foot-high prison wall. I bought three of these lines. Two would serve as the uprights and the third I would cut up for the rungs. I also bought a ball of twine and a strong needle with which to fix on the rungs. It occurred to me that when you stepped on the first rung of a ladder made entirely of rope, the two uprights would immediately be dragged together and it would be extremely difficult to ascend the ladder thereafter. Conventional rope ladders had wooden rungs but such a ladder would not be suitable for my purpose. For one thing it would be very bulky and too heavy to throw over the prison wall; and for another, even if it could be thrown, the wooden rungs would make too much noise striking against the brick wall.

I went into another shop a couple of doors away from Woolworth's.

Here they sold women's underwear, all sorts of fabrics, wools, and knitting needles. It was a woman's shop, and I was the only male in there. At the knitting-needle counter I chose a No. 13 needle. It was made of steel, covered in grey plastic, and measured fourteen inches in length. Ideal in every way. Steel for strength; plastic to deaden the noise; fourteen inches to give a generous margin on either side of a twelve-inch-wide rope ladder.

"I'll have thirty," I told the woman.

She visibly raised her eyebrows. "Your wife must be doing a lot of knitting." She smiled.

"They're not really for knitting," I told her in my best English accent. "They're for my pupils at school. It's amazing the abstracts that these young art students can produce from simple things like knitting needles."

"Oh, well," said the woman in a much more refined voice, "I'm *quaite* sure these *needolls* will be ideal for your purpose."

I spent the next three evenings after work carefully constructing the ladder, using the knitting needles to reinforce and stiffen the rungs. Once or twice I was interrupted—by the landlord coming to empty my gas meter or by his resident representative, a Mrs. Smith, telling me something or other of interest—and on these occasions I would hastily throw the unfinished ladder under the bed before answering the door.

On Saturday I did not get out of bed until ten o'clock. I cooked my lunch of pork chops. Then at five-fifteen I got into the car and headed down Perryn Road towards East Acton Lane and The Vale. The Vale is the Acton section of the Uxbridge Road, a road that begins at Shepherd's Bush. The Shepherd's Bush police station is at the corner where Loftus Road, a mere side street, joins the Uxbridge Road. I drove about Acton for half an hour and then, at ten minutes to six, I cruised slowly along the Uxbridge Road towards Shepherd's Bush.

At two minutes to six I pulled up at the kerb outside the front door of the police station. It was a modern building with lots of glass and black, shiny, synthetic-looking materials. It was also a police station that was, at this moment, on the lips of every man, woman, and child in Britain. The three policemen murdered in Braybrook Street had belonged to this station. Two of the killers had already been apprehended and now a big manhunt was on for the third, a man named Harry Roberts.

I glanced up at the windows. Behind one of them, as I sat in my car outside, some of Scotland Yard's top detectives were directing the manhunt. If they took a moment off from their maps and their plans to look out of their window they would see a light-green Humber Hawk motorcar parked at their door, and they would not give it a second thought. How could they know that the presence of this car, the width of the pavement away from their very door, was part of a carefully laid plot that within a few weeks was going to cause them to launch a second huge manhunt even while the first one was still in progress? I smiled grimly at the thought.

At six o'clock I pressed the button of the stop-watch and moved off. Past Tunis Road, Stanslake Road, Frithville Gardens, and under the bridge carrying the Metropolitan Line of the Underground from Shepherd's Bush to Goldhawk Road. One more side street on the left, Macfarlane Road, before reaching the junction with Wood Lane and Shepherd's Bush Road. Here I encountered the first set of traffic lights. They were at green. I turned left into Wood Lane. Past the BBC television studios on the left, White City Underground station on the right and White City Stadium a little farther on on the left. Next came the Westway, a wide road parallel to Du Cane Road and extending from Wood Lane to the Western Avenue roundabout, where the second set of traffic lights were, and again they were at green. Finally to Du Cane Road and the third and last set of lights. They were at red, and I had to wait almost a minute. I turned left into Du Cane Road and put my foot down. Nothing on the left but private houses. On the right, the sports ground at the corner, the grammar school, and then Hammersmith Hospital.

I pulled up opposite Artillery Road. I looked at the watch. Five minutes. And that had been in favourable conditions with two of the three sets of traffic lights in my favour. I had satisfied myself also that it would be extremely difficult for the police to jump the lights even if they wanted to. I did the run three more times that evening but could not get the time down to less than five minutes. Indeed, with any two of the lights against me the run took six minutes. This was very encouraging. The police cars would not begin the run until the desk sergeant had taken the phone call and alerted the available men. And the orderly officer at the prison would not make his phone call until he was quite sure of his facts. Even allowing them every advantage, as I was determined to do, we could pull it off with a comfortable margin.

Within three minutes of throwing the rope ladder, Blake and I would be out of Du Cane Road. Even if the police started for the prison at the *same moment* that I threw the ladder (which, of course, was impossible) we would still make it.

8
Ireland

Next evening I was again in Camden Town, discussing the operation
with Michael and Anne Reynolds and Pat Porter. They listened en-
thusiastically to my latest report, frequently interrupting to ask questions or make suggestions. Pat was inclined to be more vocal than
Michael. Michael was a deep thinker while Pat was impetuous and a
little excitable. He would sometimes talk with glee of the scandal that
Blake's escape was likely to cause. Anne was by far the least complicated of the team. Her approach was practical and workmanlike.
Whatever private satisfactions Michael, Pat, and myself were likely to
derive from Blake's escape, Anne saw it only as a means of bringing
satisfaction to Blake himself. She never speculated on the possible consequences of our actions and confined herself to questions and suggestions designed to improve our chances of success.

This evening we decided to fix a date for the escape. It would take
place the following month, on Saturday, October 22, 1966. Then my
position came up for discussion. How likely was it that the police
would connect me with the escape? Would it be safe for me to stay on
at the factory and Perryn Road?

"What do you think your chances would be, Sean?" Michael asked.

"Well," I said, "there isn't the slightest doubt that I would be investigated as a matter of routine. In cases like this they draw up a long
list of possibles and then whittle it down systematically. Naturally, the
innocent will have no difficulty establishing their innocence."

"Why are you so sure you'll be on the list?" Pat asked.

"First of all," I said, "I was known to be a friend of Blake's in D-Hall. During my last couple of months there I was seen walking up and down with him almost every day. And then, as editor of the prison magazine, I once wrote an editorial in defence of spies that found its way into a national newspaper, where it was severely criticized. This paper even suggested that I had conspired with Blake and another man to whitewash Blake's crimes. 'Strange New Friends of Traitor Blake,' the story was headed. The Home Office kicked up a hell of a stink, and I think the Governor regretted having allowed me to publish the editorial. And, of the many people Blake has known in Wormwood Scrubs, I am the one most recently discharged. To crown it all, it is known that I have stayed on in East Acton instead of going back to Sussex. I honestly don't think I would have much of a chance once they suspected me."

"Suspecting you is one thing," said Anne, "but how could they prove it?"

"That wouldn't be difficult. This is the age of the science cop. Nowadays an ordinary policeman is merely a gatherer of evidence, not an assessor. They have a forensic science laboratory at Scotland Yard, and the rule with these forensic people is simple: 'Where there is contact there is trace.' A fibre from the rope ladder deeply embedded in a crack in the floorboards at Perryn Road, other fibres in the boot of the car, fibres from Blake's prison uniform on the seat of the car, tire marks in Artillery Road, and so on. It's virtually impossible to eliminate all these traces. If I were not a suspect it wouldn't matter about the traces, but I will be a suspect."

"Yes, it looks like it," said Michael. "And even if you had not left any traces and the police were convinced you were involved, they might be inclined to, shall we say, *help* the scientists a little."

"Such a thing is not without precedent," I said. "I know for a fact that it happened to one of the Great Train Robbers."

"But quite apart from this scientific evidence," said Pat, "we don't know what's going to happen at the scene of the escape itself. You may be seen, and there might even be a chase. There is certainly a good chance that your car number will be taken."

"It would be too risky to stay in Perryn Road and try and brazen it out," said Anne. "I think you should move."

"We could get the hideout flat straightaway," Michael suggested, "and you could move in there."

"Getting the flat might not be so easy," Pat pointed out. Then his face broke into a smile. "I've got an idea. Why not move into my place? I've got a three-bedroom flat with only myself living there. It would also save us the expense of renting a flat so early."

We discussed this further and in the end agreed that I should give two weeks' notice at the factory and move to Pat's towards the end of September. I should make it known to my fellow workers and to my neighbours in Perryn Road that I was returning to Ireland for good. I should then actually go to Ireland for a week and come back under a different name and get the hideout flat. That would make things more difficult for the police.

On Friday I gave two weeks' notice at the factory. Next day I was again sitting in my car opposite Artillery Road at a few minutes to six, ostensibly admiring a large bunch of chrysanthemums. These flowers, because of the largeness of the blossom, were ideal for concealing the two-way radio. Blake was very pleased to hear that a definite date had been fixed.

As I was disconnecting the car's aerial lead from the two-way radio at the end of our conversation, I accidentally bent the top (and therefore the thinnest) section of the telescopic aerial on the two-way radio. When I tried to straighten it, it snapped off. This top section contained the cap, without which it was extremely difficult to pull out the aerial.

On Monday I took the radio to the factory and got one of the men on the production line to solder the aerial for me.

"What do you want a walky-talky for?" he asked curiously.

"Oh, just a hobby of mine," I told him. "I have always been interested in radio."

Then the inspector from the Ministry of Defence came up to us. He had his own office in the factory, and his job was to ensure that the Ministry's contracts were properly carried out. He looked at the radio that the man was soldering.

"What's this then?" he said with a grin. "Part of some new fighting vehicle?"

We all three laughed.

During the week I met Barry Richards in the Western pub. He gave me some very disturbing news.

"Did you know, Sean," he said quite casually between swigs of whisky, "that a couple of geezers tried to have it away out of D-Hall the other day?"

"No, I didn't know. How did they try to get out?"

"Through that big window at the end," said Barry with a laugh. "They were caught trying to do the frame with a hacksaw blade. They're on special watch now."

On Saturday I was talking to Blake again from my car in Du Cane Road.

"You remember that we've asked you to get a car jack?" he said. "Over."

"Yes," I said, "I remember. Over."

"Well," he went on, "we may now need a wire cutters as well. They have started putting grids on the gothic windows in the four halls. They are already up on A-Hall, and it is only a matter of time, perhaps a week or so, before they reach D-Hall. I am told that the mesh is a quarter-inch gauge. Over."

"Okay," I said, "I'll send you in a cutters with the jack in a couple of weeks' time. No point in getting them in to you too soon. Over."

We signed off, and I drove slowly past the prison. Yes, A-Hall already had the grid. It was fresh from the engineer's compound and still rusty and unpainted. I drove to Braybrook Street and stopped the car not far from the spot where the three policemen had been shot. I looked up at the four cell blocks in turn. Only A-Hall had the grid. Today was September 17: another five weeks to go before the escape. They would reach D-Hall long before then. The surprising thing was that they had not started with D-Hall, considering that that was where the attempted escape had occurred. But that was typical of the prison works department. Everything had to be done in a ponderous fashion according to some obvious and easily understood sequence. A, B, C, D—that was easy and uncomplicated. D, C, B, A was unthinkable, or even D, A, B, C. The works department didn't have to concern themselves with subtle considerations like security. That was a matter for "ordinary screws," not for skilled craftsmen. Still, even the prison works department, I felt, could hardly be so inefficient as to fail to install another six grids in five weeks.

A few days later at the factory I was having another chat with the man who had repaired my aerial. I started casually to discuss wire cutters and asked him which make he thought was best.

He looked at me and frowned briefly. "Wire cutters?" he said.

"What are you planning to do—break out of a prison? Or into one?"

I laughed uneasily. "You've been watching too much television," I said.

That was too close, and it reminded me of the folly of overconfidence. At the same time I realized that the basic reason for my carelessness was that I had already become convinced that the police would be able to establish my guilt within a short while of the escape. A concerted effort to cover my tracks therefore seemed pointless to me. Nevertheless, I would have to be more careful in future if the plot was not to be exposed before it had a chance to come to fruition.

On Friday, September 23, I collected my cards and money and left the factory for the last time. I had done my packing the night before, and within a few minutes of arrival at Perryn Road I had all my belongings in the boot of the car, including my rope ladder. I drove to Pat Porter's flat, which was in Hampstead.

Pat, I soon discovered, was a very undomesticated character. He was inclined not to notice that the flat was a little untidy. The concrete floor of the kitchen was uncovered, as was the floor of one of the rooms, though there were a couple of rolls of linoleum standing in a corner. The kitchen lacked an electric outlet, and the lead from the refrigerator snaked dangerously across the centre of the damp concrete floor and disappeared into another room where there was an outlet. Putting these things right would help me while away a few hours later on.

Next day I contacted Blake again from the car. "I think," I said, "it's about time I sent in the car jack and the wire cutters. I can easily arrange it through one of the hostellers, unless you have some other suggestion to make. Over."

"As a matter of fact I do have a suggestion," Blake said. "Do you know the large house in the prison forecourt which used to be occupied by the Chaplain? It's on the right as you come in from the street. Well, at the moment it is unoccupied and is being renovated by the works department. Just inside the front door, to the left, there is a toilet. Directly in front of that there's a loose floorboard. If you lift this up you will find a cavity underneath about twelve inches deep. If you can put the tools in there they will be brought in by a member of the working party. You will have no difficulty entering the house because the door has been removed. Have you got all that? Over."

"Yes," I answered. "I've got it. Walking into that forecourt is a bit risky. I could get one of the hostellers to put the stuff there, but I think I'd better do it myself. I'll think of an excuse in case I'm seen. Over."

"What day will you deposit the tools?" Blake asked. "Over."

"Today is Saturday," I said. "I shall buy them on Monday and deposit them on Wednesday evening. I think that's a safe day. By Wednesday the screws are broke and there shouldn't be very much activity in the Officers' Club. Over."

"Very well," said Blake, "I'll get our friend to alert his contact on the working party. Over."

On Monday I bought the car jack and the wire cutters. It was a small jack, measuring the required six inches in height when folded right down. The handle, however, was much too long, almost thirty-six inches. I took it to the Western Garage, next to the Western pub, and got it reduced to twelve inches. That would be plenty of leverage to break a not very thick cast-iron frame. It would also make it easier to smuggle the tools in. I very carefully parcelled the jack, the wire cutters, and the stop-watch, squaring the parcel off and padding it with rags to disguise the shapes of the contents. It may be that the man taking it through the gate was not necessarily supposed to know what the parcel contained.

On Wednesday evening I caught a tube to East Acton and walked round to the prison. I paused for a moment outside the street gate. I could hear voices in the Officers' Club on the left of the forecourt, but they sounded few. I looked at my watch: ten o'clock. There should not be very much movement in and out of the prison at this time of the night, just the occasional hosteller coming back. If I were seen in the forecourt I would say that I had come back to inquire if any mail had arrived for me which the censor had failed to forward. I went in and walked quickly across the forecourt to the gaping doorway of the old Chaplain's house. It was totally dark inside, but I had brought a torch and found the loose floorboard immediately. Sure enough, there was a cavity underneath about twelve inches deep. I put the parcel there and replaced the board. I listened. No sound of footsteps on the gravelled forecourt. I hurried back to the street.

The following Saturday was October 1, and I again parked the car opposite Artillery Road.

"Well," I said after we had hurried through the identifying code, "did the goods arrive?"

"Yes." Blake sounded pleased. "It is as well you sent the cutters because the grids have now been fitted to the other three Halls. With three more weeks to go before the event, our own window simply *must* be fitted with a grid. Over."

We signed off. I drove past the prison and could see the rusty wire mesh on the gothic windows of the other three Halls. I went to Braybrook Street. It was the same picture at the back. Only D-Hall remained to be serviced.

I spent all of the next week searching for a flat, but without success. Paradoxically, the more I was prepared to pay in rent the more difficult it was to secure the accommodation, for the grander the flat the more demanding the owner was when it came to references. If I learned nothing else during that week I learned what a handicap it was to be an ex-convict. I went to one or two rather better-class agencies, which were staffed entirely by lovely girls in miniskirts with debs' accents. How much was I prepared to pay? Oh, anything from ten to fifteen pounds a week. The girl would make a phone call to the prospective landlord or landlady. These calls were usually quite revealing. "Oh yes, madam, he's British all right. Pardon? Oh, of course, white. He's English, in fact. Well, he's a journalist. I see. That's a pity. I can assure you he looks quite respectable. Well, perhaps you wouldn't mind interviewing him yourself? Oh, good. I'll send him along."

Journalists, I found out, are not generally regarded as solid citizens, especially free-lance journalists. And I, having decided on this pose, had to be a "free lance," otherwise I would be asked for my employer's name and address. Two of the prospective landladies reluctantly accepted me as a journalist but then went on to demand references. "But the position with me is that I have just come back to Britain after ten years in Australia," I would say. "I have not yet had time to establish myself or to open a bank account. But I can pay you a month's rent now in advance—in cash." But it was no good. One had to have references. Once I thought I had made it. The miniskirted deb had sent me to see a woman who had a comfortable flat in a very select area. She was a woman of means who always spent her winters abroad in sunnier lands.

"I'll be away for about six months," she said with a pleasant smile. "Will that be long enough for you?"

"Oh yes, madam," I assured her. "Quite long enough."

She had no objection to my being a journalist. She even conceded that I looked "quite nice, in fact." She never once mentioned references. But there was a snag. Apart from the agency which had sent me, she employed another agency to attend to business matters for her. That dampened my spirits. She gave me the address, and I went along there. I was shown into an office where a very severe-looking woman with pointed features, and dressed all in black, sat behind a desk strewn with documents that had lots of dotted lines on them.

"Good afternoon," she said. She didn't smile and she didn't get up. "You are Mr. . . ."

"Renshaw," I said, "David Renshaw."

"Oh yes, of course, Mr. Renshaw. I have just had a telephone call about you from Mrs. Broadbent. You are interested in leasing her flat for six months. Please sit down."

She picked up a large form and started writing in it. *Full name? Occupation?* (A frown when I said "journalist.") *Nationality?* With this woman, I felt sure that any answer but British would have meant an abrupt end to the interview. I daren't say Irish. She looked like the sort of woman whose father might have been a Black and Tan. I was careful to sound very English. *Present address?* I told her I had just got back from Australia and was staying at a hotel temporarily. And then, of course, it came. *References?* Well, as I had said, I had just come back from Australia.

"Oh, well, you see, I must have references," she said firmly. "And, indeed, I shall have to take them up. I must have a banker's reference and at least two social references." She held her pen poised threateningly over the form and gave me a piercing look.

There was an awkward silence. I rubbed my chin thoughtfully. "Well, now," I said, "I can naturally provide you with these references, but as a matter of courtesy I feel I should consult the people concerned first before giving their names. I'll go and make a couple of calls. I'll be back in an hour."

"Very well, Mr. Renshaw, I shall be waiting."

She's still waiting.

By the end of the week I was still without a hideout. I decided that I would go home to Limerick on the Monday, spend a week there, and try again for accommodations when I got back. On the Saturday I spoke to Blake and told him I would contact him again on Tuesday, October 18, four days before the escape.

On Monday I flew to Shannon Airport, buying a one-way ticket at the Aer Lingus office in Regent Street. I gave my correct name. I was glad to be going home. I had not seen my mother for five years, and there was no telling how long it would be before I was in a position to visit Limerick again. I paid special attention to the ease with which people could enter the Irish Republic from Great Britain. There were no immigration formalities. It was like flying to Scotland, except for the customs check. The hostess made a number of announcements in Irish, which none of the Irish people on board could understand, and then she made them in English, which they could.

I caught a bus from Shannon Airport to Limerick and got off at O'Connell Street. I would not catch a taxi. After five years I wanted to see if there were any changes. Limerick had always been a dump, but now it was dirtier and more dismal than ever. I walked up William Street and went into the red-brick public lavatory in the middle of the road. The doors were hanging off the cubicles and the plumbing was out of action, but people went on using them, and they were piled high with excrement. I went to the urinal. The same glass-fronted panel that was there when I was going to school was still fixed to the wall at eye level. On it, printed in an immaculate copperplate, there was a prayer to God beseeching Him to protect the beholder from all temptation. Years before, some anonymous ecclesiastic in an inspired moment had hit on the idea that a man's immortal soul was in greatest danger while he held his penis in his hand. At the top of the panel, painted in large letters, were the words: "Not for ourselves but for our country." The panel and the neatly printed prayer seemed incongruous in the surrounding squalor. I found this difference of approach between the Irish lavatory authorities and the English rather interesting. The Irish exhorted you to avoid sin, while the English assumed that you had already sinned and gave you the address of the place where you could get treatment for venereal disease. But both tried to make you feel guilty for having a piss.

Outside the lavatory I was accosted by one of the gypsies who always hung around there. He wanted the price of a pint, and I gave it to him.

I walked up Mulgrave Street and The Pyke to the Munster Fair Tavern. It was one of the few pubs in Ireland which did not sell Guinness; it sold Murphy's instead. It had an entrance both in the Ballysimon Road and in the Cork Road, and the latter was almost directly opposite the entrance to a cemetery. (In Ireland you will always find a pub not far from a cemetery.) As I approached the tavern I saw a man standing there facing down The Pyke. He seemed to be waiting for someone. A few minutes later I discovered that he was waiting for me. At first I did not recognize him. But when we shook hands and spoke I remembered. It was Ger Carey, a fellow I had gone to school with.

"Hello, Sean," he said. "Your mother told me you were coming home today. God, 'tis a long time since I saw you, now. It must be fifteen years."

"Is it as long as that, Ger?" I said.

"Indeed it is. Sure you left Limerick when you were only seventeen. I wasn't long after you myself. And since then we were never home on holiday at the same time, sure."

"When are you going back?" I asked.

"I'm off on Wednesday," he said.

"Will you come in for a pint?"

"Indeed I will." Then, lowering his voice confidentially, he said, "Can you lend me a pound before we go in and I'll send it to you when I go back?"

"I will, Ger." I gave him a pound and we went into the pub.

"Well, good look," he said, raising his pint of stout.

"Good luck, Ger." We drank.

"So you've been in England yourself all this time," I said presently.

"I have," said Ger. "In Birmingham. I'm with Birmingham Corporation."

"Birmingham Corporation?"

"Yes." He took six gulps of stout in quick succession. "I've been a dustman these ten years."

"What's it like?"

"Ah, 'tis not bad. The work is easy enough and the money is good. The only crux is that you're out in all weathers. Still an' all, the work might be dirty but the money is clean, says the fella. And what are you doing yourself, Sean?"

"Oh, I'm unemployed at the moment."

"Is that so?" He took another six gulps, and I found myself hoping that he had been wise enough to buy a return ticket before leaving Birmingham. But then every Irishman took that precaution.

I wanted to know if my neighbours in Limerick knew I had been to jail. Ger, I felt sure, could tell me. I was wondering how to bring the subject up when he himself gave me the opening.

"So you're not working," he went on. "Well, now, I thought you'd be on the stage or in the films by this time."

"Why's that?"

"Didn't I read about you having a romance with some actress in London when the two of ye were in the one play? You were playing the part of a doctor, the paper said. 'Twas on the front page, sure."

That incident had been a misunderstanding in the drama group at Wormwood Scrubs. There had been a photograph on the front page, right enough, with a caption that said: "Proposed in Jail." It had all been very embarrassing.

"And do the English daily papers get sold in Ireland these days?" I asked.

"They do indeed. They've been sold here this many a year, sure."

"So you all know where I was when that incident occurred?"

Ger hesitated, a little embarrassed. "Well," he said, looking into his pint, "I heard you got into a little bit of trouble all right. But, sure, that could happen to anyone."

We started to talk about our schooldays. Despite his absence in England, Ger knew everyone who had been born, got married, or died in our district during the past fifteen years. The *Limerick Leader*, I thought, must be sold in Birmingham.

"Old Ma Murphy is dead too, the Lord have mercy on her soul," he said presently.

"Who's Old Ma Murphy?"

"Don't you remember?" Ger was surprised.

"I'm sorry, I don't. I've been away a long time."

"She's the old woman with the shawl," he said, "who used to come in the road with a donkey and cart selling sour milk at a penny a quart an' we going to school. Don't you remember her, Sean?"

"Oh, of course," I said. "Isn't that the woman who was passing underneath when a gang of us were up on the railway bridge that day?"

"That's her," said Ger, draining his second pint. "And didn't my brother Fonsy destroy the poor woman!"

I ordered another couple of pints. "Destroy" the woman was putting it very politely, but then Ger had never been one for vulgarity or bad language. He was a better Christian than any of the rest of us in the gang could ever hope to be. I remembered the incident as if it had happened yesterday. The gang of us were up on the railway bridge just beyond Bengal Terrace where the countryside abruptly began. Old Ma Murphy was coming in from the country where she had a cottage and half an acre near Ballyneety village. She was sitting up on the little cart next to the tank of sour milk and the jaded donkey was pulling her towards the town at the rate of about two miles an hour. We all saw her coming. There was a hurried conference, as there usually is when there are a few very young boys on a bridge and a likely target comes into view. But we had no missiles handy. Stones were out of the question, and there was no water nearby. "I have it!" said Fonsy, Ger's brother. "I have it!" He dropped his trousers, placed one foot on either side of a wide gap in the boards, and squatted down. His rectum was poised with precision over the centre of the opening. "Give me the signal, Sean," he said, looking up at me with a grin. "And you better allow a couple of yards because 'tis a high bridge."

I took up a strategic position and raised my hand in the manner of a battery commander, as I had seen it done in the films. Ma Murphy came closer, her eyes fixed permanently about halfway along the donkey's burdened back, completely oblivious to the impending danger. The rest of the boys were all down on their hands and knees peering through other gaps in the boards. She was under the bridge. A couple of yards to go. "Now!" I said, dropping my hand suddenly. The first one, tapered just like a bomb, landed dead centre between the donkey's ears, exploding on impact to splash all over the animal's neck.

Ma Murphy stared disbelievingly for a moment at the brown mess. She was sixty years old and had never before seen shit falling from the sky. Hail, rain, and snow, yes; but shit, never. She looked up, her eyes and her mouth wide open in an expression of shocked incredulity. But the second one was already on its way. It might have missed her if it weren't for the donkey. Even that docile creature was so taken aback it stopped dead in its tracks. And by now Ma Murphy was staring straight up at Fonsy's bare arse. She saw it coming but couldn't believe it. She just stared at it, mesmerized. Then it landed, right on her forehead, and splashed smoothly all over her face. "Jesus, Mary, and Joseph," she screamed, "I'm destroyed! Holy Mother of God, what's happening at all!" A dozen pairs of eyes, like cats in the night, were staring down at her through the gaps in the boards, and Fonsy's arse was still poised there menacingly. "Ye dirty blaggards!" she screamed. "Ye dirty blaggards! May God forgive ye!" And her face was brown all over.

"My God, Ger," I said, "that was a long time ago. We were only ten or eleven then, weren't we?"

"That's all, sure."

I wondered how Ma Murphy had related the incident to other people. How did you retain your dignity when telling someone that you had literally been shit upon? How would she have worded it? "I was up on the donkey and cart and driving into town with the sour milk as I have been doing these twenty years and minding my own business, God knows, when suddenly the heavens opened up and we were showered with shit. There was a little boy up there, sure, with his trousers down and shitting away to his heart's content through a crack in the planks. Wouldn't you think, now, that he'd be inclined to use a lavatory instead of getting up on top of a railway bridge and shitting down on God-fearing people below? Sure that's awful depredation altogether. I've never seen the likes of it in all my born days and I'm gone sixty, thank God."

"And how's life treating you in Birmingham, Ger?" I asked.

"Ah, not too bad, Sean. The digs are all right, that's the main thing. So long as a man has enough for a pint, what more does he want?"

"You're not married then?"

"Indeed I'm not," he said. "I don't think I'll ever get married. And I'll never commit adultery either."

For a brief moment I was taken aback by this expression. It was straight from the children's catechism that we had had to learn by heart at school and was meant to imply *all* sex outside of the bonds of holy matrimony, whether between married or single people. Since leaving school this was the first time I had heard the term used in this context. But it was characteristic of Ger. He could never use any other mode of speech. I remembered that when we had played together in the street years ago and Ger accidentally uttered a swear word, he would promptly bless himself and say an act of contrition on the spot. The game would have to wait.

I ordered another couple of pints. There were half-a-dozen or so other men at the far end of the bar. Some I recognized immediately, and Ger reminded me who the others were. These were men about the same age as ourselves who had not emigrated to England. They had found work in Limerick, usually alongside their fathers, who had put in a good word for them. They had all said hello to Ger as we came into the bar, but they ignored me completely. They were hard-working, law-abiding citizens. They knew I was a criminal and they would no more be seen drinking with me than they would be seen with a leper.

It is an interesting sociological fact that an Irishman who has been in an English jail is more readily acceptable afterwards to the English themselves than he is to his fellow countrymen. The Irish approach to the criminal is not as sophisticated as is the English. In Ireland a young criminal is not referred to as a juvenile delinquent. If a boy of twelve steals he is called, simply, a robber. Later he will be expected to leave Ireland. If an adult offends he must leave the country straight-away, unless he is prepared to spend the rest of his life as an outcast. There is no room for a criminal in the "island of saints and scholars." I couldn't bring myself to resent this, for I knew that if Ireland were to become as sophisticated as England it would lose a lot of its Irishness in the process.

Ger and I finished our pints and made for the door.

"Good look, byes," the barman called after us. (This means, of course, "Good luck, boys." In some parts of Ireland "good luck" has exactly the same meaning as "good-bye.")

"Good look," Ger replied, and we went out. He looked across at the cemetery gate. "Will we go and have a look at the graves, Sean?"

"Why not?"

We crossed the road and went in.

"Your father's grave is just around here on the left, isn't it, Sean?"

"It is," I said. But we couldn't find it. The area was overgrown with weeds.

We found the grave of Ger's father easily enough. Ger, I felt sure, attended to it every time he came home on holiday. He knelt and said a few prayers over the grave.

On the way back to the road we saw a man standing in a freshly dug grave trimming off the sides with a spade.

"Don't you know who that is?" Ger whispered as we approached.

"I don't," I said.

"That's Timmy O'Keefe. He's been a gravedigger this many a year."

I had been to school with Timmy O'Keefe. We went over and had a chat with him. It was a strange reunion in that consecrated place. Three former schoolfriends: a dustman, a gravedigger, and an ex-convict. The unaccomplished.

"How's things?" said Timmy with a grin.

"Not bad, Timmy," I answered. "Not bad at all."

He was completely unself-conscious about being in the grave. Ger and I stood on the piled-up earth and looked down at him. He wielded the spade with skill.

"And whose final resting place is that? God be with him," asked Ger.

"Ah, sure I don't fucken know," Timmy answered. " 'Tis all equal to me. I only have to dig the shaggen thing."

It was the first time I had heard a man swearing in a grave. The whole scene reminded me a little bit of the graveyard scene in *Hamlet*.

"Good look, lads," said Timmy as we started to move away.

"Good look," said Ger.

"Good-bye, Timmy," I said.

I had lost my Limerick accent a long time ago and I wasn't going to make a fool of myself by trying to assume one for the occasion of my brief visit. Ger's accent had remained intact over the years, but then he lived in an Irish community in England and worked with Irish people.

Outside the cemetery gate Ger said he had to go into town, and we agreed to meet later in the evening in the pub.

"Good look, Sean. I'll see you after."

"Cheerio, Ger. See you later."

I walked up the road. Bengal Terrace was a row of fifty houses, at the side of the main road, built by the British Government for ex-soldiers of the First World War. Now most of the soldiers were dead and their children emigrated, and only the elderly widows remained. At the near end on the right was a grotto to the Blessed Virgin built on subscriptions from the residents of the Terrace. It was by now a firmly established practice in Limerick that every outlying district should have a grotto to the Blessed Virgin. As I passed the grotto I noticed that there was an abundance of fresh flowers at the foot of the statue inside the wrought-iron railing. A number of people gathered there to say the rosary at seven o'clock every night.

Halfway up the Terrace I saw Mrs. Rooney coming towards me.

There was no mistaking her. She was about the last woman in Limerick to persist in wearing a shawl, which was characteristic of her. She had absolutely no pretensions and laughed at those who did. She was the sort of woman who would tell you exactly what she thought of you. She had great character. Her sons too had long since emigrated.

"Hello, Mrs. Rooney," I said.

She stopped. "God, Sean, is it yourself?"

"It is."

" 'Tis a long time since you were here, now."

"Yes," I said, "a long time."

We chatted for about ten minutes about the people we knew.

"My Tommy was home a year ago," she said, "after being ten years away. And I don't think I got more than three letters from him in all that time. But sure as you know yourself, he can't read or write. He do be asking the fellas at work to write for him. He wouldn't go to school for love or money and now he's paying for his blaggardism."

"How was he, Mrs. Rooney?"

"How was he? Well, now you're asking me one. After ten years in London he walked in the door without a lowry. He didn't have a make, not a penny to bless himself with. I had to borry the price of his fare back to England. And while he was here he was eating me out of house and home. You'd want a dog with a copper arse to keep him going."

I laughed.

"Did you hear about your man Toddy?" she said, changing the subject.

"Toddy O'Connor, is it?"

"Yes. He got married."

That surprised me. "Well, now, Mrs. Rooney," I said, "I didn't think he was the marrying kind."

"Nor did anyone else," she said. "We all got a great surprise. Everybody was saying he'd have to take in a lodger after a while."

"A lodger? Why's that?"

"Why's that?" Mrs. Rooney laughed. "Sure he couldn't tell his prick from his t'umb only for there's a nail on one of them."

Then I decided to broach a delicate subject. "I have heard a strange report," I said, "that some nonsense appeared in the papers some time ago about me sending a bomb to a policeman. Did you hear anything like that, Mrs. Rooney?"

She gave me an old-fashioned look. "Nonsense, how are you! Is it codden me, you are? 'Twas in all the papers, sure, English and Irish. Everyone in the Terrace read it."

"Now, really, Mrs. Rooney! Can you imagine me doing a thing like that?"

She stopped smiling and looked at me intently for a moment. "Why wouldn't you? The biggest hoor that ever walked!"

We said good-bye, and I walked up the Terrace. At Number 32 I opened the gate and walked in the short path to the door. There would be just one person in there, my mother, and she would be expecting me. I had written to say I was coming. Would she, like all the neighbours, know about Wormwood Scrubs? Or would those occasional letters, posted by a brother from a different part of the country, really have deceived her? She was sitting in front of the open grate when I entered the front room. She looked up as I came in.

"God, Sean, you were a long time gone."

"I was, Mother, but as I explained in my letters I was all the time away on business trips for my firm."

"Business trips, how are you!"

"It's true, Mother."

"All right so."

"Anyway," I said, "I'm glad to be home. Apart from wanting to see you, there's one good reason why I like to visit Limerick—your bacon and cabbage. Nobody can cook it like you. I smelled it coming in the gate."

" 'Tis on the hob, sure, waiting for you."

"Thanks."

I went out to the scullery to get a plate and a knife and fork. There were four large ribs of bacon in the pot and lots of white cabbage boiled with it. I put one of the ribs on the plate.

" 'Tis no use eating one, Sean, that wouldn't feed a sparrow. Take the whole four, there's plenty more where they came from."

"But what about yourself?" I asked.

"Don't mind me. I'm just after eating my dinner, sure."

I piled the other three rib cages onto the plate and topped them with a heap of cabbage. They were done just right, the meat falling cleanly away from the bones.

"You wouldn't get the likes of that in London, Sean, sure you wouldn't?"

"That you wouldn't, Mother." I started to eat.

"I'll put down the kettle and we'll have a cup of tea after." She went and filled the kettle in the scullery and put it on the coal fire. "Come here 'till I tell you, Sean," she said after a while. "Wasn't your photo in one of the English papers one time? Yourself and an actress, or something like that. I didn't read it myself. I haven't read a paper this many a year. The eyes are getting too bad. I was out at Mrs. O'Neill's one night and she had the paper. She read it out to me."

"What did she read?" I asked. The newspaper article had given full details of my seven-year sentence.

"Oh, she just said that you were in this play somewhere in London. She didn't say the name of the theatre."

That, I thought, was very decent of Mrs. O'Neill.

"And there was a rumour going around here another time, Sean, that you were supposed to have sent a bomb to a policeman in England. A bomb, mind you! Picture that, Sean! Heart o' God! But sure they blame you for everything. One of the neighbours told me after that they caught the fellas who did it. I suppose they got a long sentence, wouldn't you think so, Sean?"

"Oh yes, Mother. At least seven years, I'd say." My neighbours were indeed decent people. It was almost as if there had been a neighbourhood conspiracy to shield my mother from the truth.

"A bomb, if you don't mind. Heart o' God! I've never heard the likes of it since the days of the Tans. Anyone would think you were one of the lads, one of the boyos, a member of the IRA—an *illegal organization*, as the papers have it." She frowned. "Sean, take care fear you'd have anything to do with that crowd, that's your mother's advice to you now, and you have only one mother. If I was depending on the heroes up in the Dail I'd be starved long ago. 'Tis John Bull that keeps your mother, don't ever forget that, let you. I have a good pension from the British Government because your father fought for the Bull in the First World War. And 'tis the Bull that provides me with this roof over my head rent free. The widow's pension that I get from the Irish Government wouldn't be enough to feed me, sure, not to mind anything else. And even that they tried to rob from me last year when I spent a couple of months in Canada with your brother Gerry and his wife. They tried to tell me I wasn't entitled to my widow's pension for them two months. Picture that, Sean! And if it wasn't for John Bull I wouldn't have been able to afford the holiday at all. Anyway, the robbers didn't get away with it. Gerry wrote them a stiff letter."

I poured out the tea and joined my mother at the fireplace, putting a cup on each hob.

"A bomb, Sean, picture that! Sure that's awful depredation altogether. Sending-an-infernal-machine-through-Her-Majesty's-mail-with-intent-to-maim. God, that's a peculiar way to word a summons. Have you ever heard tell of a thing like that before, Sean, clever as you are?"

"No, Mother, I haven't."

"Nor have I."

Serious crime is virtually non-existent in Ireland, but petty offences, I learned, tended to be on the increase.

"But sure there's no shortage of depredation in Limerick, either," my mother went on. "This town is gone to the dogs lately. Mrs. Fitz and her spinster daughter who lives with her just along the Terrace there were raided a couple of weeks back. The boyos went up the stairs and into their room at dead of night, an' they lying there in the bed! That's an awful cheek now, Sean, isn't it? Into their room, an' they lying in bed! Heart o' God! I've never heard the likes of it. There isn't a gas meter safe in the Terrace these days. And the Garda Siochana are no good at all. Mrs. Fitz reported to them, sure, and they came up and parked in a squad car in the middle of the Terrace. But sure them squad cars have a big notice up on top of the roof saying 'Garda,' and the fellas inside of them do be dressed up in uniform. The boyos aren't going to do their raids through the front door with them fellas parked out there in the street. They're going to creep up along the back of the houses, sure. Wouldn't you think they'd send the plain-clothes fellas up to hide down the back and jump out and catch the boyos in the act? Mrs. Fitz and her daughter could have been got dead. Their bodies could be rotting there for weeks and nobody would be any the wiser. We wouldn't know they were dead at all 'till we could smell the putrefying corpses an' we passing their door. They could be taken in the height of their sins, God forbid, and 'twould be all equal to the fellas abroad in the street sitting in their squad car, like male models. But sure I could be done for myself if it comes to that. If I got a blow on the pole an' I coming in the path, I was finished, sure. Have you me, Sean?"

"I have, Mother."

"God, Sean, you're awful quiet altogether. What ails you at all?"

"Nothing, Mother. I was just—just thinking, that's all."

"All right so." She might have been protected once by the neighbours, but even their extreme generosity would not shield her from the consequences of Blake's escape. Within a few weeks this small room would be filled with Special Branch men, English and Irish. They would be infinitely more subtle than the fellows in the squad car marked "Garda."

I looked across the room. In a corner there was a table which had been made into an altar. Standing in the centre of it was a two-foot-high statue of the Blessed Virgin. The statue was surrounded by pictures of the Sacred Heart, the Madonna and Child, and various saints. There were at least four rosaries scattered about the table top. In this household, as in nearly every household in Ireland, communism was the ultimate evil, the final sin. Communist was synonymous with Devil. When I was going to school I had actually seen a house in Limerick stoned because the family within were suspected of having Communist sympathies. The Irish found it difficult to accept fellow Christians of a different faith, let alone non-Christians or anti-Christians. Jehovah's Witnssses had been beaten up in Limerick more than once, sometimes by a mob led by a priest. Hanging on the wall to the left of the altar was a picture of the late President Kennedy—the personification of the Western, Christian, Catholic, Irish struggle against the evil of Communist atheism.

My mother was poking the fire and singing something like, "I See Diamonds in Amsterdam." She had been singing this since before I was born. It was the first song I had ever heard. I looked at her intently. She was seventy years old and her sight was nearly gone. Her eyes were glazed. Despite her age her hair was still mainly black with just a few streaks of grey. Her face was deeply lined. For the first time in my life, at the age of thirty-two, I found myself loving her as a son should love a mother. Love was so easily stifled in youth. The poverty and degradation of those days provided a soil far too barren for the survival of anything more than a somewhat tenuous family loyalty. Who or what are you supposed to love as you walk to school barefooted through the snow on a breakfast of tea and bread and margarine? In the sermons we were told that it was God's divine will and that far from complaining, which was sinful anyway, we should actually give thanks to God for our poverty. "Blessed are the poor," they reminded us, "for theirs is the Kingdom of Heaven." But the man up in the pulpit was well fed, wore a good pair of shoes, and lived in a big house next to the church. He was fed and clothed by the poor of the parish who were bound under the Precepts of the Church to support their pastors. Of course it wasn't the priests who made us poor: their fault lay in telling us that poverty was a virtue, a blessing from God, a means to sanctifying grace; that we should emulate Our Lord and Saviour Jesus Christ. But then Jesus had never been very badly off. He was never short of a few shillings, and he didn't have to work hard either. And why complain about his being crucified? That was exactly what he wanted, wasn't it? He would have fared no better in this day and age. If witch-hunters didn't get him, the Irish Hierarchy would. Just as they got the courageous Minister of Health who advocated the very Christian policy of giving free maternity treatment to *all* women, whether they were married or not. Perhaps the Archbishop of Dublin had never heard of Mary Magdalen.

I knew as I looked at my mother that my love had come too late. It was born of the knowledge that the final parting was at hand. Could I ever step over this threshold again? Even if one day I should be free to do so, would I be welcome? Most important of all, would there be anyone here? She was seventy. No matter what happened next week, a long time was going to pass before I set foot in Limerick again.

At seven o'clock my mother said she was going to visit a friend in the new housing estate in Rathbane. I said I would take her there. We walked down Bengal Terrace together. As we passed the grotto to the Blessed Virgin there were about a dozen elderly men and women saying the rosary. It was being led by a retired bus conductor, the man who had organized the collection to build the grotto. Ger Carey was in the midst of the gathering, his rosary beads dangling from his fingers.

We walked on. We were passing the cemetery gate when an old woman of about sixty in a long black coat staggered out of the Munster Fair Tavern and made her way across the road, narrowly missing death from a passing car.

"Jesus, Mary, and Joseph," my mother whispered, " 'tis Mrs. O'Toole! Pretend you don't see her, Sean. In the name of God, pretend you don't see her."

But it was too late. Mrs. O'Toole saw us.

"Hello there, Agnes," she greeted my mother. "Who's the fella you have with you at all?"

"Heart o' God," my mother whispered under her breath, "what'll we do at all? She'll make a holy show of us." Then in a very loud voice she said, " 'Tis one of my sons home on holiday. Sean is his name."

"God, he's a grand bye," Mrs. O'Toole said, breathing John Jameson's whisky all over me. "A grand bye, God bless him."

"He's looking well, right enough," my mother said, shouting again.

"Why are you shouting, Mother?" I whispered.

"She's nearly deaf, sure, God help us. She can't hear you at all unless you shout in her ear."

"I know your brother Kevin," Mrs. O'Toole said, swaying uncertainly on her feet. "He was here last year. He's a fine bye too, God bless him."

"They're twins," my mother shouted. "Sean and Kevin are twins."

Mrs. O'Toole's glazed eyes opened wide and her mouth fell open in an expression of surprise that was out of all proportion to the information just imparted to her. "Go on!" she said. "Is that so? Well, I'd never have taken them for twins, now. Sure they don't look a bit like each other, sure they don't, Agnes."

"Kevin is fair," my mother said; then, lowering her voice, she said, "Sean, in the name of God, give the poor misfortune a couple of shillings for a drink or we'll be here all night."

"But won't she be insulted?" I asked.

"Insulted, how are you! Is it codden me you are, Sean? Sure the only reason she came across to us is because she knew you were home from England. She had you spotted, sure."

I gave Mrs. O'Toole ten shillings.

"God bless you, Sean," she said. "I'll say a prayer for you at Mass. I'll offer it up for your intentions."

Just then a girl in her early twenties was passing, wearing a smart red coat. She looked very respectable. "Come here, little girl," Mrs. O'Toole said, grasping her unsteadily by the arm. "Would you ever give me a hand up the road at all, God bless you?"

"Well, good-bye now, Mrs. O'Toole," my mother said.

"Good look, Agnes," she replied.

"Good-bye, Mrs. O'Toole," I said.

"Good look, Sean."

I smiled and nodded to the captured girl as we moved away. She blushed crimson. I looked back over my shoulder—Mrs. O'Toole was dragging the girl all over the pavement as they made their way towards Bengal Terrace.

My mother was highly amused. " 'Tis terrible to be laffen, Sean, I know, but that little girl is very stuck up, that's the funny part of it. She wouldn't talk to you at all, sure. She's too grand altogether to be living in a place like Limerick. All airs like a new fiddle. God, how is she going to walk up the Terrace at all? Mrs. O'Toole will make a holy show of her."

"Does Mrs. O'Toole often get drunk?" I asked.

My mother looked at me. "Is it codden me you are, Sean? She's never sober, sure. The poor misfortunate woman!"

We caught a bus just past the Munster Fair Tavern. It stopped again a couple of hundred yards farther on. "Anyone for the lunatic asylum?" the conductor shouted.

"Not yet, thanks be to God," said a woman up front.

"God between us and all harm," responded my mother.

We got off at the next stop and turned into the Jail Boreen, leading to Janesboro and Rathbane. I noticed a policeman standing at the corner, watching the jail. Up at the other end of the boreen there was another policeman.

"Why are the Garda watching the prison?" I asked.

"Because a fella escaped from there a few months ago," my mother told me.

"And how long was he serving?"

"Six months."

"Is that all?" I said. "And they've been guarding the prison ever since?"

"Ah yes, but he was one of the boyos," my mother said, "and there's still a few more of them inside there. They wouldn't mind so much if he was an ordinary prisoner, but he's one of the lads, one of the IRA. But sure they'll never catch him. 'Twas his own men who came along and got him out, and now they're hiding him up in the mountains, don't you know. Them fellas do be training with guns up in the mountains all the time, sure. The Garda are afraid that your man will come back with a detachment and get the other fellas out. They're in dread of their lives of it, sure."

"And what did the lads do to get in there in the first place?" I asked.

"Well, now, Sean, that's the comical part of it. An English ship came into Waterford harbour on a courtesy visit and the boyos were waiting for it with guns. One of them fired a revolver at it, if you don't mind. A revolver, Sean! Picture that! Heart o' God! But sure what good is a revolver against a battleship? They fired a revolver, I'm telling you. And the Englishmen inside in the ship laffen at them, don't you know. Isn't that a good one, now, Sean? But sure them battleships do have big guns. If they were to aim one of them at the boyos, they were finished. One shot and they were all gone to meet their Maker. 'Tisn't firing a revolver they'd be then, the ould eejets."

"And what was supposed to be the purpose of the operation, Mother?"

"The purpose? Sure they wanted to die for Ireland, don't you know."

I laughed. " 'Wrap the green flag around me, byes,' " my mother went on. "And sure if a war broke out tomorrow, 'tisn't firing guns they'd be, but hiding under the bloody bed. Ah, now, don't be talken. Enough said, says the fella."

The asylum wall was on our left as we walked up the boreen, and on our right another, lower, wall. Between this low wall and the prison wall itself there was a short stretch of no-man's-land. I remembered that in one corner of this weed-covered area there used to be a stagnant pond. I had spent many a day in there mitching from school, usually with some other fellow of like mind. We would catch roach in the pond with a piece of bread stuck on a bent pin at the end of a piece of string. The float would be a cork from a Guinness bottle. As soon as it dipped, one quick jerk and you had a roach. We would fill a bucket with them and then later throw them all back into the pond. It was more interesting than school, and anyway I hated the Christian Brothers. I was delighted when they eventually threw me out and I had to go to St. John the Baptist's, a four-room little school in Garryowen, staffed entirely by lay teachers. To be deprived of the teaching skills of the Christian Brothers and handed over to laymen was supposed to be the ultimate disgrace for a schoolboy, but I wouldn't have swapped one of those decent lay teachers for all the cassocked snobs in Sexton Street.

I remembered that when I was ten the Irish Government decided to issue clogs (boots with wooden soles) to the barefooted children of the poor. But you had to have a ticket issued to you by the head brother of the school. It was the middle of winter, and I approached the head brother at Sexton Street. "I won't give you a ticket for a pair of clogs, Bourke," he said haughtily, "because your school attendance isn't good enough. You can go home and tell your mother that from me."

"Well, now, isn't that a disgrace," my mother said when I told her. "Are you supposed to feel the cold less than a boy who goes to school every day?" She decided to bypass the Christian Brothers. The people charged with distributing the clogs in Limerick were St. Vincent de Paul's, and she took me there herself. The man in charge that evening was of medium height, about forty-five years old, and had red hair. When I told him what the head brother had said he shook his head and gave me the Government clogs. He also threw in a pair of stockings from his own organization.

"If you have any other sons who need clogs, Mrs. Bourke, bring them along and we'll fix them up," he told my mother.

A year later when the Christian Brothers threw me out of Sexton Street and I had to suffer the "disgrace" of going to a lay school, I discovered that the kind-hearted man from St. Vincent de Paul's was the headmaster of St. John the Baptist's. His name was Sean Walsh. Mr. Walsh died some years ago. He and the other three teachers at the school worked ten times harder than any Christian Brother. The four of them had to teach eight classes. The first teacher wasn't too badly off; he taught only the First Form. The next two taught Second and Third, and Fourth and Fifth Forms respectively. One class would be sitting down doing sums while the other would be standing up around the wall reading their English books. But Sean Walsh was the hardest-working of all. He taught three forms simultaneously, Sixth, Seventh, and Eighth. He would have one class seated and the other two standing along both walls and the back partition, each studying a different subject. And when he went home at night he would take the notebooks of all three classes with him to be corrected for next day. He was very popular. A gang of us would be waiting outside the school gate in the morning, and when we would see him coming down the road we would race up to him to see who could get there first and carry his bag. He had no time for the Christian Brothers and he didn't care who knew it.

We got to the top of the Jail Boreen and turned left into the Roxboro Road. We caught another bus and got off a quarter of an hour later at the grotto to the Blessed Virgin in Rathbane. My mother introduced me to her friend, Mrs. Whelton, and her young children, and I stayed for a cup of tea. I discovered that my mother spent most of her spare time in this house. Later Mrs. Whelton saw me to the door. We talked for a moment in the path.

"Mrs. Whelton," I said hesitantly, "I don't know quite how to put this, but if I were ever to get involved in something a little, shall we say, irregular, would you be kind enough to do your best to minimize the effects on my mother?"

"Your mother is always sure of a welcome here, Sean, you needn't worry about that."

"Thank you, Mrs. Whelton. Thank you very much indeed."

An hour later I met Ger in the Munster Fair Tavern. Afterwards we went to Kirby's in William Street. By eleven o'clock we were both very drunk, and I had lent Ger another couple of pounds. We staggered up Parnell Street to one of those dirty, smelly little "shops" that sell boiled pig's toes. These "shops" are little more than private houses with a tray of steaming toes in the window and other toes still boiling in a big black pot in the kitchen/sitting-room that is separated from the hall by a small counter.

Parnell Street is a dingy place with a smell all of its own, comprising a mixture of pig's toes, fish-and-chips, and Guinness. We made our way up Mulgrave Street and The Pyke, contentedly eating our pig's toes from their newspaper wrappings, and Ger was all the time singing,

> " 'Twas down by the glenside I met an old woman;
> A-plucking young nettles, she ne'er saw me coming;
> I listened a while to the song she was humming,
> Glory O! Glory O! to the bold Fenian men."

I remembered him singing that up on the railway bridge that day when the heavens opened up on poor Ma Murphy.

There were a couple of Garda standing near the prison gate as we passed, and they gave Ger and me a suspicious look. It occurred to me at that moment that if the English were to put just one constable on patrol around Wormwood Scrubs nobody could escape, including George Blake.

At the grotto to the Blessed Virgin, Ger fell on his knees at the railing and said three Hail Marys and three Our Fathers.

Next morning I was walking down the Terrace with my mother. As we approached the cemetery I saw Ger. He was sitting on the steps of the monument to Allen, Larkin, and O'Brien, which is just inside the cemetery wall at the Bengal Terrace end and separated from the road by a high railing. Resting on the step next to Ger was a spade, pieces of clay still clinging to it. I stopped to talk to him.

"I'll leave ye two together," my mother said. "I must hurry on. I want to catch Mass at the Augustinians'. Mind yeerselves now, byes."

"What's the spade for, Ger?" I asked.

"Ah, I thought I'd clean up your father's grave a bit, that's all." He was quite self-effacing about it, almost apologetic.

"God, that's very kind of you. But how did you do it? We couldn't find the grave yesterday."

"Ah, sure I got the caretaker to look it up in his book and then we measured it out together." Ger's shoes were also covered in clay.

"And where did you get the spade, Ger?"

"Timmy O'Keefe lent me that. I must go back and give it to him now."

"I'll come with you."

We walked down towards the main entrance to the cemetery. I glanced sideways at my friend. He was wearing an old suit and an open-necked shirt. To look at him you would think he had never been to England at all. His weather-beaten face was open, honest, and sincere. I suspected that part of the reason for the extraordinary thing he had just done was that he wanted to be sure of paying me back in some way for the few pounds I had given him. Sure enough, the grave was clearly marked out from the surrounding wilderness and freshly dug all over. I blessed myself to say a prayer and noticed that Ger did the same.

Next day I saw him off at the railway station. He had, after all, bought a return ticket in Birmingham.

"You're going by boat then, Ger," I observed.

"Ah, yes. Sure I come and go by boat every year. I was never up in a plane yet."

We shook hands, and Ger's eyes suddenly shone bright with pleasure. He looked down at his palm. "Thanks, Sean," he said without looking up.

"You're welcome, Ger. I hope we meet in Limerick again."

"We will, sure, with the help of God."

Ger went through the barrier to the boat train. In a day or two he would be riding on a dustcart through the streets of Birmingham, singing "The Bold Fenian Men." One thing was certain. He would never see the inside of an English jail.

I left the station and walked down Parnell Street, sickened at the sight and smell of those pig's toes in the windows. For the next three days I would have to drink by myself. Emigration was a curse. Born to be scattered. No wonder we were such a melancholy race.

> Lonely is the house now
>   And lonely the moorland,
> The children are scattered,
>   The old folks are gone.
>
> Why stand I here
>   Like a ghost and a shadow?
> 'Tis time I was moving,
>   'Tis time I passed on.

On Saturday morning it was time to go. I had bought a plane ticket for London in O'Connell Street the day before, giving the name of Sullivan.

"Well, Mother, I'm off to Dublin now. I shall spend the next few months writing. A friend of mine has placed his house at my disposal. I won't be going back to England until next year sometime." That was all for the benefit of the Special Branch later on. I did not enjoy it but it had to be done.

"All right, Sean," she said, "but don't be too long away this time."

"I'll do my best, Mother."

"And come here 'till I tell you, Sean. Don't forget your mother's advice to you. Don't ever do anything against John Bull, for when the Bull falls, there's many another will fall with him. Don't forget that, let you. God bless John Bull anyway." She picked up a medal from the altar to the Blessed Virgin. "Take this medal with you, Sean," she said. " 'Tis Our Lady of Knock. She was seen there in a vision some years ago. I was there myself on a pilgrimage last year."

I took the medal and put it in my pocket.

"She'll intercede for your intentions," my mother went on. Then she picked up a bottle of holy water from the altar and tilted it a couple of times into her palm. She shook her hand at me and the holy water splashed all over my face and chest.

I embraced her. "Good-bye, Mother, good-bye." I wanted to say something else but I couldn't. It had been stifled beyond recall a long time ago. Anyway, it was too late.

I drank a lot of whisky at Shannon Airport to try and cheer myself up, and a couple of hours later I was back in London.

9
Final Preparations

Next day was Sunday, October 16, the first day of the week in which ⚑⚑
the escape would take place. That evening we had a meeting at Pat ⚑⚑
Porter's flat. We agreed that we would have to abandon the search for
a good-quality flat. Such a flat could not be got without references, and
it was easier for an ex-convict to break a spy out of jail than to acquire
a reference. We would have to lower our sights and be content with
some more modest form of accommodation.

On Monday I went to a more working-class agency in Paddington.
There were no debs in miniskirts but I got what I was after.

"What area did you have in mind?" I was asked.

"Oh, anything West," I said. "Acton, Hammersmith, Kensington." I
had now come to favour a hideout as near as possible to Wormwood
Scrubs. What I got could hardly have been nearer. There was a flatlet
available at 28 Highlever Road, W. 10.

"The rent is four pounds fifteen a week. Does that suit you?"

It suited me fine. I filled in the form in the name of Mr. Sigsworth,
giving a false address in Croydon. There was no mention of references, banker's or otherwise. The fee was a sum equal to one week's
rent, to be given to the houseowner who would pass it on to the
agency.

Out in the street I flicked quickly through the "A to Z" of London
that I had made a point of carrying with me when flat-hunting. Highlever Road was virtually round the corner from Du Cane Road and the
prison, and it was directly on the route to Notting Hill Gate Under-

ground station, over which I had already driven many times. From Du
Cane Road I would turn left into Wood Lane, and two hundred yards
farther on, right again into North Pole Road; another two hundred
yards along North Pole Road and right once more into Latimer Road;
a quarter of the way down Latimer Road and left into Oxford Gardens. Highlever Road was at this end of Oxford Gardens, a mere
thirty yards along on the left. As I looked at the map I estimated that
it would take about three minutes by car from the prison to Highlever
Road.

I was relieved to discover that the owner of the house did not live
there but in another street some little distance away. I was accepted
without question and paid a month's rent in advance, plus the agency
fee. I was given three keys: one to the front door of the house and one
to each of the two rooms comprising the flatlet. These rooms were a
bed-sitting-room and, next door, a kitchen-bathroom. This was the
only flatlet in the house, and so I was the only resident with my
own kitchen and bathroom. All the other rooms were bed-sitters and
the occupants shared a communal bathroom. This was an ideal arrangement; there would be no danger of Blake being disturbed after
he had reached the flatlet.

The bed-sitting-room had a French window leading onto the back
yard, and beyond the yard were the back gardens of the houses in the
next street, Balliol Road. Highlever Road was quite a long road, about
half a mile, stretching from Dalgarno Gardens to Oxford Gardens.
Our house, however, was only half a minute's walk from the Oxford
Gardens end. We could be in the flatlet in less than four minutes after
leaving Artillery Road.

With a little feeling of pride and achievement I locked the doors of
my new, temporary home and walked to the junction of Du Cane Road
and Wood Lane. I stood there for half an hour, leaning against the
railing of the sports ground on the corner. When I left I was pleased.
The traffic lights at that junction included a filter light to allow motorists coming from Du Cane Road to turn left while those who wanted to
turn right had to wait for the main lights to change to green. I had
established during my half-hour vigil that when the lights facing Du
Cane Road changed to red, the filter light changed back to green again
twice as quickly as the main lights. Thus, a motorist wanting to turn
left into Wood Lane would have to wait only half as long as a motorist

who wanted to turn right, when the lights were against him. And I would be turning left.

Next morning I moved my belongings from Pat Porter's flat to Highlever Road.

That evening at six o'clock I was parked opposite Artillery Road holding a bunch of chrysanthemums. The lead from the car aerial was trailing out from the base of the flower stems, unseen by the occasional passer-by. My thumb groped through the flowers and found the transmitting button.

We went through the routine code identification. "Listen carefully, Baker Charlie," I said. "I have some detailed instructions to give you for the night of the operation. Are you in a position to listen to me without interruption for several minutes? Over."

"One moment," Blake said, "I'll just make sure. Over."

He was back in about a quarter of a minute. "Very well, Fox Michael," he said, "I'm ready to listen. Carry on. Over."

"Right," I said, "here goes. The operation will take place this Saturday, the twenty-second, as planned. All is ready. I will make contact with you by radio at six o'clock precisely. I shall be parked in Artillery Road directly opposite the end of D-Hall. Assuming the coast is clear, I shall give you the signal to proceed to that window and attend to the frame. When this has been done you will call me back and tell me so. I shall then give you your second signal, instructing you to climb out the window and down to the ground. When you have done this you will call me again to let me know. Finally, I shall give you the third signal, which will be, 'The ladder is coming over now.' I shall then get out of the car and throw the rope ladder over the wall. The moment you see the ladder you will run to it and climb up. There will be no need for any further signals. You must not delay as we must assume that the man on guard will see the ladder at the same moment. We must both keep our radios turned on throughout and each of us must be prepared to give the other an immediate warning if anything goes wrong. For example, if my capture appears to be imminent I shall warn you so that you can cover your tracks in there. And if you, for your part, suddenly have reason to believe that you are going to be caught, you will warn me so that I can clear out of here. Have you got all that so far? Over."

"Yes, that's perfectly clear. Please proceed. Over."

A young couple approached on the pavement and I started to arrange and smell the flowers. They went by without looking at me. As I watched their receding backs in the rear-view mirror a police motorcyclist came roaring along Du Cane Road from the direction of Wood Lane. I kept my eyes glued to the mirror but the policeman sped past without a glance and turned left in Old Oak Common Lane.

I pressed the button. "Right, then, Baker Charlie," I said. "Now for the second leg of the operation. You will sit in the back seat of the car as we drive away. On the seat beside you, you will find a mac and hat. You will put these on. In the right-hand pocket of the mac you will find a brown envelope. In this envelope there will be a sum of money including threepenny and sixpenny pieces for phone calls. There will also be a slip of paper containing seven figures. This will be a telephone number written in code. I shall not give you the key to this code now. I shall do so as we drive away in the car. If an emergency should arise during the getaway and we are forced to separate, this telephone number will put you in contact with my two friends. If I am apprehended they will immediately take over. We have only a short way to go in the car. Again, I shall not give you the address over the air. I shall do so when we are on our way. I shall stop the car round the corner from the house and you will make your way to the house on your own. In the left-hand pocket of the mac you will find three keys on a ring. There will be one Yale-type key and two ordinary latch keys. The Yale-type key will let you in the front door and the other keys will unlock the doors of the flatlet. When you go through the front door you will find yourself in a long, narrow passage with a stairs on the right leading to the first floor. Our flatlet is on the ground floor. Go right down to the end of the passage, until you can go no farther, and you will find yourself facing a door. That is the door to the flatlet. It has the figure five screwed to it. In the room you will find a bed and on the bed will be some new clothing. You should change into this immediately. On the table you will find an "A to Z" of London and an Underground guide. In an emergency you will need these to get to the home of one of my friends. As soon as you have decoded the telephone number, memorize it and then eat the paper. It will only be a small piece. I'm afraid I *must* ask you to eat it, for there is no other safe way of disposing of it in this flatlet. In the room you will also find a television set and a transistor radio. The radio will be already tuned into the BBC Home Service, so you only have to switch it on to hear the news. You will also get a news bulletin on television at about nine o'clock. By that time you will be able to hear all about your own escape. While you are settling-in in the flatlet I shall be getting rid of the car. I shall drive it as far away as possible. If I am chased I shall do my best to shake them off, but failing this I shall make a run for it. If I am not back in the flatlet within two hours I want you to assume that I have been caught. You will then make the emergency telephone call. You will find a pay telephone in the passage near the foot of the stairs. If you should subsequently hear an announcement to the effect that 'a man is helping the police with their inquiries,' don't believe it. I shall definitely *not* be helping the bastards. Well, Baker Charlie, that is all. Is everything understood, and do you have any questions? Over."

I sat back and relaxed, sniffing the chrysanthemums. That little speech had been quite an effort, with cars and pedestrians constantly going by and my gaze alternating between the road ahead and the rear-view mirror. The car windows were tightly shut and the sweat stood out on my forehead.

"Well, my friend," said Blake, "all that is perfectly clear, so much so that I have no questions. Everything still looks quite favourable in here too. You will be pleased to hear that we have not yet got our wire grids on this Hall. Today being Tuesday, there is a strong possibility that we still will not have them by Saturday. Over."

I glanced quickly across at D-Hall. The gothic window was clearly visible, and, sure enough, there was no grid. "My God," I said, "I can hardly believe it! What's the matter with those bloody people? They finished with the other Halls weeks ago. Suddenly we've got new allies. Somebody in there likes us. Over."

I heard Blake laugh. "Yes," he said. "That grid would be quite a nuisance. Let's keep our fingers crossed that nothing will change before Saturday. By the way, will I hear from you again before then? Over."

"Yes, I shall contact you at the same time on Thursday for a final review before the day of the operation. Over."

"Very well, Fox Michael," Blake said. He hesitated a moment, then went on, "Are you absolutely certain that everything is ready for Saturday, that nothing remains to be done? Over."

I pressed my transmitting button. "My friend," I said, "have no fear. All is ready. In four more days it will be just like the words of the old Irish song." And I sang, loud and clear:

"I'll walk beside you through the world today,
While dreams and songs and flowers bless your way,
I'll look into your eyes and hold your hand,
I'll walk beside you through this golden land.

Over." I released the transmitting button and listened but there was silence at the other end.

Blake must have been quite taken aback, and I could well understand why. There he was, the most important Communist spy in captivity in the Western world, a former Foreign Office man and British secret agent, sitting in a cell under lock and key in Wormwood Scrubs Prison, and I, an Irishman, was sitting in my car outside in the street, a few yards from the prison Governor's front door, serenading this spy with an Irish song by means of a two-way radio hidden in a bunch of pink chrysanthemums. By any standards, it was an extraordinary situation.

Blake got over his surprise. "Well, my friend," he said, "I hope that in a few days I shall have the opportunity and the pleasure of hearing you sing that direct. Over."

"I'm sure you will," I said. "And I think that's about all for now. Have you any further comments? Over."

"No," said Blake, "I have nothing to add. Over."

We signed off, and I disconnected the aerial lead and plugged it back into the car radio. I put the two-way radio under the seat. I looked at the flowers. They were still fresh. I had bought them in Old Oak Common Lane at the last moment, just before the shops shut. Previously I had been throwing them away, but what a pity to waste them, I thought.

I was in a jubilant mood. I got out of the car and went across to the hospital. It was half-past six, and in the foyer there were several people sitting about waiting for the visiting hour to begin at seven. I walked across the foyer and went through the door leading to the wards. Near the bottom of the corridor, on the left, I entered a ward. Just inside the door there was a good-looking young nurse sitting at a desk, writing.

"Good evening, Nurse," I said.

She looked up. Her gaze went quickly from me to the flowers. She smiled and stood up. "Oh, good evening," she said. "I'll get you a vase. Who have you come to see?"

"There's no need to get me a vase, Nurse. I've come to see you."

She looked at me blankly.

"I came into this hospital," I went on, "determined to give these flowers to the most beautiful girl I could find. *You* are the most beautiful girl. I would deem it a great favour if you would accept this small offering from an ardent admirer." I handed her the flowers.

"But—but—who . . . ?" She looked confused and incredulous.

I laid a hand on her shoulder. "Good-bye, Nurse," I said. "Good-bye, and thank you very much." I turned and left the ward.

She came running after me. "But who are you? Please, tell me," she pleaded.

But I just walked on down the corridor without looking back. My God, I thought, what a pity I can't make a date with her! The hazards of a criminal life!

I drove the car to Old Oak Common Lane and parked it there. I would walk back to Highlever Road. The car must never be seen anywhere near the hideout, I decided. If it were identified at the scene of the escape its description and number would be widely broadcast.

That evening we had another meeting in Hampstead. We agreed to hold our final meeting on Friday night when Michael, Anne, and Pat would each bring a piece of paper containing questions to be fired at me in a last determined effort to ensure that nothing had been forgotten. With the escape now an imminent reality the light-hearted enthusiasm of the early days had given way to a nervous excitement. None of us mentioned it, but we all realized that whatever happened on Saturday would be big, such was the nature of the thing we were planning to do. If we succeeded, it would be a big achievement; if we failed and were caught, it would be an almost equally big disaster. With the central figure a man like Blake, there could be no middle course. And, having done the thing, we would have set in motion a chain of events over which we would have no further control. We were pitting ourselves against forces whose power was unlimited.

Next day I went to Tottenham Court Road to do some shopping. In Jackson's the Tailors I bought a dark green Harris Tweed sports coat and trousers to match. The salesman began to put his tape-measure around my waist. "They're not for me," I told him. "They're for a friend of mine. He's just about your size. If they fit you they'll fit him. Would you mind trying them on?"

"Certainly, sir."

He tried them, they fit, and I took them. In another shop I bought some shirts and underwear. I took the purchases back to Highlever Road.

The following morning, Thursday, I bought a second-hand television set for fifteen pounds up in Seven Sisters Road. I brought it back to Kensington by taxi, paying the driver off in Oxford Gardens and carrying the set round the corner to the house when he had gone. I cooked myself a lunch of sausages and eggs and washed these down with a bottle of Guinness. Having a gas cooker was a great comfort after all that kneeling on the floor in Perryn Road.

At five o'clock I left the house and walked to Old Oak Common Lane, passing the prison on the way. I sat in the car for a while and then drove down Westway to Wood Lane and entered Du Cane Road from the opposite end. I had to do it this way in order to park at the opposite side of the road to the prison, facing towards Old Oak Common Lane. I pulled up at the usual spot, just opposite Artillery Road. I looked up at D-Hall. There was still no grid on the window.

Blake was waiting and answered immediately. There was really nothing further to discuss, and we agreed to make contact at midday on Saturday. This was a final precaution against any last-minute changes in the prison routine that might make the escape at six o'clock impracticable.

I was tempted to take the flowers to that nurse again but decided against it. It might lead to complications, and this was no time for taking chances. I dropped them in a waste bin instead. Again I parked the car in Old Oak Common Lane and walked back to Highlever Road.

Our final pre-escape meeting began in Pat's flat at eight o'clock on Friday evening and went on until eleven. Anne kept making pot after pot of coffee as we talked. We went over every detail of the operation until we were satisfied that we had done everything to ensure success.

"What about that guard in the telephone box?" said Michael, glancing at his list of questions. "We have already allowed that he will see the rope ladder coming over the wall. Do you really think he has no chance at all of reaching the spot in time to stop Blake?"

"No," I answered, "no chance at all. He would have to run more than a hundred yards, while Blake has to cover a mere fifteen yards. And even if the screw does run to the spot he cannot follow Blake up the ladder, for the moment Blake reaches the top of the wall I shall, of course, let go of the ladder on the outside."

"And what about the patrol?" Pat asked, looking at his list.

"Well," I said, "Blake will be able to hide in the shadows under that gothic window for quite some time. He won't give me the all-clear to throw the ladder until he's satisfied that that stretch of wall is free. But even if the patrol should come round the corner as Blake runs for the ladder he will be in no better position than the screw in the phone box."

"Let's assume then," said Anne, "that the man in the phone box immediately alerts the Orderly Room. Will you have time to get out of Artillery Road before the reinforcements arrive?"

"Yes, Anne," I assured her. "Not only will we be out of Artillery Road, but we should even be clear of Du Cane Road before reinforcements have time to reach the spot. Within three minutes of my throwing the rope ladder we should be in Wood Lane. I have timed all this. And now that the hideout is in that direction it means that we turn left when we leave Artillery Road and so only have to break into one lane of traffic. And again, at Wood Lane, we have the advantage of that filter light."

"And what about the people going to and from the hospital?" Michael asked next. "I have often seen cars parked around there, in Artillery Road too. What are the chances of some of these people seeing you?"

"That has also been carefully studied," I told him. "There is a car park in the hospital grounds, behind the main buildings, for the exclusive use of the hospital staff. During the day, access to this car park is gained through a side gate in Artillery Road, facing the prison wall— almost directly opposite the spot where Blake is going to come over, in fact. From Monday to Friday the hospital staff working the normal day-shift finish at five o'clock and those with cars leave the hospital grounds through that side gate in Artillery Road. But even on these weekdays they have all gone within about twenty minutes and that side gate is securely locked for the night at five-thirty. Anyone leaving the hospital after five-thirty must do so through the main gate in Du Cane Road. Anyway, that is all on weekdays, Monday to Friday. Now, on Saturdays, the day-shift finish work at midday and the side gate in Artillery Road is locked for the weekend by half-past twelve. The few cars that you see parked in Artillery Road itself always belong to the day-shift. The hospital staff naturally prefer the security of their own car park when they are working late."

"And the visitors to the hospital?" Pat put in.

"They park mainly in Du Cane Road," I said. "Only a few of them leave their cars in Artillery Road. But this is no problem. The visiting hour begins at seven and so the visitors don't begin to arrive much before a quarter to seven. A few very early ones arrive at six-thirty. This means that, from Monday to Friday, Artillery Road is clear of cars between five-thirty and six-thirty—the vital hour that concerns us. And on Saturdays it is clear of cars from shortly after midday until, again, six-thirty. The operation, of course, begins at six, so we have a very generous margin. Remember, throughout all this planning it has been the policy to allow the other side *every* advantage. We allow for the Orderly Room being alerted immediately by the screw in the phone box, and we allow for the police at Shepherd's Bush being alerted immediately by the Orderly Room. We take nothing for granted."

The map of Hammersmith and surrounding districts lay open on the table before us. Michael glanced down at it. Number 28 Highlever Road was marked with an X in red ink, and a red line traced the route of the car from the prison to the hideout.

"How long will the run take?" Michael asked.

"Within four minutes Blake will be safely in the flatlet."

"And he'll have the phone number to be used in an emergency?" asked Anne.

"Yes, he will."

"And, of course, it is in code?" Pat added quickly.

"Yes," I said, "it is."

"What is this dotted line running down the middle of Latimer Road?" Michael asked, glancing at the map.

"That line gives us yet another slight advantage. It marks the boundary between Hammersmith and Kensington. The hideout is just over the border from the borough in which the prison is situated and therefore just outside the *manor* of the prison's local police station, at Shepherd's Bush. Since it is the Shepherd's Bush police who will be alerted in the first place, the initial police activity will be confined to the area west of that dotted line in Latimer Road. We are just outside the line by a matter of yards."

Pat spoke next. "What do you think the chances are of the houses around there, including Highlever Road, coming under suspicion?"

"Not a hope," I told him. "These streets are really dismal. One row of terraced houses after another spread over a wide area in monotonous uniformity. It could hardly be a more unlikely place for a spy to hide. And, anyway, it is much too close to the prison. No policeman would dare suggest it for fear of being laughed at. No, Pat, the police will be in too much of a hurry to get to London Airport and the docks and the Iron Curtain embassies to be able to afford the luxury of speculating on such novel ideas. And later, when they begin to suspect me of being involved, their thoughts will naturally turn to Ireland and the possibility of Blake's hiding there."

"If they haven't already convinced themselves that Blake left the British Isles immediately," Ann pointed out.

We were all silent for a moment. Michael took a mouthful of coffee, put his cup down on the map of Hammersmith, and looked across at me, a serious expression on his face.

"Sean," he said, "what happens if, despite the careful planning, at the last moment you are seen by some member of the public who decides to tackle you? Or, for that matter, if a prison officer manages to reach you before you have time to leave Artillery Road? What will your attitude be?"

I had been waiting for this question. Michael, Anne, and Pat had no doubts about the rightness of rescuing Blake from a forty-two-year prison sentence; but these three people were not criminals and they could never reconcile their consciences to an act of violence against an innocent citizen, in whatever cause. All three of them, in fact, were devout pacifists. They knew that I knew this, and it must have occurred to them that if I had decided to carry a gun I would keep the fact concealed from them. Preying on their minds was the shooting of those three policemen in August. The Braybrook Street murders were still in the news, and the third killer, Harry Roberts, had not yet been apprehended.

"Michael, Anne, and Pat," I said, looking at each of them in turn, "if an emergency like that should arise it will be a case of may the best man win. I shall not give up our prize without a struggle. But I shall not be armed. Indeed, I am so determined to be *un*armed that I shall not even have a wrench in the car. I won't even carry my fountain pen."

They all looked visibly relieved.

At eleven o'clock we had a ceremonial bonfire. The map of Hammersmith, the "A to Z" of London, the various notes we had made for the meeting, and all other paper evidence of our plans were piled into the open grate and set alight.

"Well, Sean, it's all yours now," Pat said.

"Yes, it's all mine."

He shook hands with me. "Good luck."

"Thanks."

I walked to Hampstead Underground station with Michael and Anne. They were going to Camden Town so any train would suit them. I was going to Latimer Road and therefore had to wait for a train going via King's Cross, where I could change to the Metropolitan Line. The indicator showed that the first train in was going via Charing Cross. Not for me. Presently we heard the train rumbling deep down in the tunnel.

"Well, Sean," Michael said without smiling, "this is it. I wish you success."

We shook hands firmly. "Thank you, Michael."

Anne took a step closer and extended her hand. "Good luck, Sean."

I grasped her hand appreciatively. "Thank you, Anne."

The doors of the train rattled open, and Michael and Anne went in. Out of courtesy they went to the opposite side and sat down facing me as I stood alone on the platform. As the train started to move away they both raised a hand in a half-hearted little wave, but they didn't try to smile. I imitated their action and I didn't smile either. None of us had smiled very much this evening. The smiling would have to wait. The train bore them away towards the gaping hole at the end of the platform and the darkness of the tunnel closed in behind them and they were gone.

I was alone. That was how it had to be. Michael and Pat were not the sort of people to throw rope ladders over prison walls, and that was their greatest merit. They had been deliberately sought out because they were the sort of poeple that they were. You could not have it both ways. The emptiness and silence of the platform added to my feeling of loneliness.

The train to Latimer Road was almost empty too, and later the flatlet itself seemed oppressive. I went to bed immediately but sleep was slow in coming, and when it did come it was shallow and troubled. The feeling of being outside of oneself and watching one's own actions from a distance—a feeling that was to last all of next day—had already begun. There was still time to turn back, but I knew that was now unthinkable. Failure and imprisonment would be infinitely more bearable than the look in the eyes of my friends and the thought in their minds if I said, "No, I cannot do it."

I would be glad when it was over.

10
The Escape

On Saturday morning I cooked myself a breakfast of sausages and
eggs but I could hardly taste it. At ten o'clock I went shopping for
food. For the next few days I would need enough supplies to feed two
men. All this week I had been doing my shopping locally so that the
people of the neighbourhood would get used to seeing me before the
escape hit the headlines. I bought chops and eggs and a lot of tinned
fruit and vegetables.

Back in the flatlet I put on a clean shirt and changed my underwear
and socks. There was always the possibility of my being arrested, and
anyone who has been through the degrading process of being re-
manded in custody for weeks will appreciate the need for starting off
with a clean shirt and underwear. I also put on my best suit, made for
me a couple of months before in Regent Street. A clean handkerchief
in the breast pocket, and I looked quite presentable. Finally I checked
through my pockets to make sure that I was carrying nothing that
could incriminate anyone else. I put on my hat and mac, stuck the two-
way radio in my pocket, and left the flatlet.

I walked down Du Cane Road to Old Oak Common Lane. It was
eleven-thirty. Half an hour to go before the midday contact. I bought a
bunch of chrysanthemums in the florist's, and a few doors along, in
Clark's the confectioner's, I bought a large apple pie for three shillings. This would be my lunch today. The car was parked a few hundred yards up the road from the shops. I went and sat in it, placing the
flowers on the seat beside me and turned on the car radio to listen to

some pop music. I ate the apple pie slowly and enjoyed it. It was fresh and crisp.

At ten to twelve I moved off; down Westway, along Wood Lane and into Du Cane Road from the far end. When I stopped opposite Artillery Road it was two minutes to twelve. I switched off the car radio, unplugged the aerial lead and fixed it to the two-way radio. At midday my thumb groped through the chrysanthemums and found the transmitting button.

"Well," I said after we had gone quickly through the code, "this is it then. This is the day. Everything is okay out here. How are things with you? Over."

"Fine," said Blake, "fine. Everything is ready here for this evening. I am all prepared to make my move. The conditions are perfect. Most of the others will be at the cinema and there will be only two officers in the Hall. And, by the way, I don't know if you can see it from where you are, but our window has still not been fitted with a grid. Over."

I looked across at the gothic window. There was no grid. "My God, Baker Charlie," I exclaimed, unable to conceal my delight, "I never thought the day would come when I would be grateful for the incompetence of those overalled layabouts. All those cold winters without proper central heating now seem worth it. Over."

"Yes, it's quite incredible that this obstacle has not yet been put in our way. And it would indeed have been quite an obstacle. Over."

It certainly would have. Cutting a wire grid whose gauge was a quarter inch would involve a lot of noise.

"Well," I said, "I'd better go now. I'll contact you at six o'clock precisely. Over."

"Very well," said Blake. "I take it all is definitely ready for tonight? Over."

"My friend, in just six hours I shall walk beside you through this world today. Oh, and by the way, it's chops for tea, followed by strawberries and cream. Does that suit you? Over."

"My mouth is already watering." Blake laughed. "Over."

"Okay," I said. "Till tonight, then, this is Fox Michael to Baker Charlie. Over and out."

"This is Baker Charlie to Fox Michael. Over and out." It was the first time we had concluded a radio contact without saying good night.

I parked the car in Old Oak Common Lane and went back to the flatlet, walking along Du Cane Road past the prison. I met a screw on the way who knew me.

"Hello there," he said with a grin. "How are you then?"

"Oh, not too bad, you know," I said. "And yourself?"

"Can't complain, Sean. I'm as happy as a man can be, working over the weekend. Still, you can't have it both ways. I've got to pay off the old hire-purchase somehow. Are you working yourself?"

"Oh yes," I told him. "I'm a local now. Living and working in Acton." I spread my arms out in an all-embracing gesture and looked around on either side of me. "This is now my *manor*, as they say."

It occurred to me as I made my way along Du Cane Road towards Wood Lane that that screw, if he was interested in the psychology of the criminal, might suspect that I belonged to that category of ex-prisoners who were subconsciously drawn back towards the environment of that closed, secure little world where one had no responsibility and where all one's bodily needs were taken care of. Perhaps he would discuss the discovery with his colleagues. But he had only a short while in which to do so before the real reason for my presence in the vicinity would come to light.

I was in the flatlet by one o'clock. I made a pot of tea and sat back to relax. I would not set out on my mission until four-thirty.

At two o'clock I started an hour's practice of throwing the rope ladder. It must go over the wall first time. If it failed to do so and the screw in the phone box saw the first attempt, he could well reach the spot before the ladder finally went over the wall in a satisfactory manner. I stood in one corner of the room and threw the rope ladder up at the ceiling in the diagonally opposite corner. The ladder was very light and throwing it was easy. The important thing was to devise the best way of folding it prior to the throw in order to minimize the risk of its becoming tangled. This is the way it would also be folded in the boot of the car so that I could pick it up and throw it immediately. By three o'clock I had worked out the best way of folding the rope ladder. I had already tested it for strength but decided to give it one final test just to make sure. The rungs were exactly twelve inches apart and twelve inches wide. There were two coat hooks fixed to the room door, which by coincidence were also about twelve inches apart. The sixth rung of the ladder I fixed over these hooks so that the bottom rung was just clear of the floor. I then stepped on the bottom rung, grasping the coat hooks above. It sagged a couple of inches but held me, and I was relieved to see that despite my weight the second rung and all those above it were kept perfectly straight by the steel knitting needles, which reinforced them. I was a couple of stones heavier than Blake. If the ladder held me it would hold him.

I laid Blake's new clothes out on the bed, including underwear, shoes, and socks. I placed a new copy of the "A to Z" of London in the centre of the table with an Underground guide. I wrote Michael's telephone number in code on a small piece of paper and put it in a brown envelope with some banknotes and coins. I tuned the radio into the Home Service and then switched it off. I turned on the television set, adjusted the indoor aerial until the picture was right, and turned it off again. I carefully folded the rope ladder and put it in a large paper carrier bag marked "Jackson's the Tailors." It was the bag they had given me to carry Blake's new clothes. I put on my mac and hat, put the brown envelope in the right-hand pocket and the two-way radio in the left. I picked up the paper carrier bag, took one last look around the room, and left, locking the door behind me and putting the keys in the left-hand pocket of my mac. I had decided that Blake should use *my* hat and mac for the short journey. That would make things easier.

In the passage I made a phone call. The voice at the other end said, "Yes?" and recited his phone number. It was Michael. We had decided weeks ago not to identify each other over the phone but to rely on recognizing each other's voices.

"Hello there," I said. "How are you?"

"Oh, hello. Not bad, thank you," he answered, "and you?"

"Well," I said, "I've known days when I've felt better. I just called to say that I'm now on my way."

"Good luck," said Michael.

"Thank you," I said. "I'll need it. Good-bye."

I walked slowly along Du Cane Road. The sky was overcast and a very light drizzle was falling. I looked at my watch: quarter to five. If that drizzle would develop into a downpour during the next hour it would suit me fine. Heavy rain would not encourage people to loiter in the street, and it would not help visibility on a prison perimeter that was already inadequately lit. It would also obscure the view from a phone box at a distance of a hundred yards. I walked past the prison, keeping to the opposite pavement, and passed several screws who did not seem to notice me.

I went into the florist's in Old Oak Common Lane. They were sold out of cut chrysanthemums so I had to settle for a potted one. It was pink. I went to the car, put the paper bag containing the rope ladder into the boot, and climbed in behind the wheel, placing the flower pot beside me on the driving seat. I turned on the car radio to try and steady my nerves. It was five-fifteen. Plenty of time.

I drove down East Acton Lane to The Vale and sat in the car just a short distance from the King's Arms pub. I thought of the very attractive young barmaid in there who used to serve me my pint of Guinness at lunchtime every day when I was working just across the road. The rain was getting heavier. That was good. I wound up the window. My nerves had got worse. People said that a cigarette helped, but I was a non-smoker. Still, I could do with something to moisten my throat. I got out of the car and walked across to the sweet shop at the corner of Larden Road. I bought two Rollos and went back and sat in the car. I undid the paper wrapping at one end and removed two of the chocolate sweets. I put them both in my mouth together.

I looked at my watch: quarter to six. It could not be put off any longer. I drove slowly up East Acton Lane towards Old Oak Road and the Western Avenue roundabout. There was a traffic jam at the roundabout—a nerve-racking hazard I had not anticipated. The cars stretched in all directions: along Old Oak Common Lane directly opposite me on the other side of the roundabout; to the right in Westway; to the left in the Western Avenue itself; and in front of me and behind me where I was stuck in Old Oak Road. There were traffic lights at the junction, but the traffic was so bad that a couple of policemen were on duty to help things along. In fact, the lights had been abandoned and the two policemen had taken over complete control of the traffic.

By the time I had edged forward to the roundabout it was already six o'clock. I cursed myself for not waiting nearer the prison. Blake had by now already switched on his radio and was calling me, and here I was in a traffic jam at the mercy of a policeman. Suddenly the policeman turned round to face Old Oak Road. I was at the head of my particular queue of cars and he was looking me straight in the face. The rain was dripping down over the rim of his helmet onto his cape. He signalled me to proceed.

I was going straight across, and as I passed him I leaned out of the window and said, "Thank you, officer."

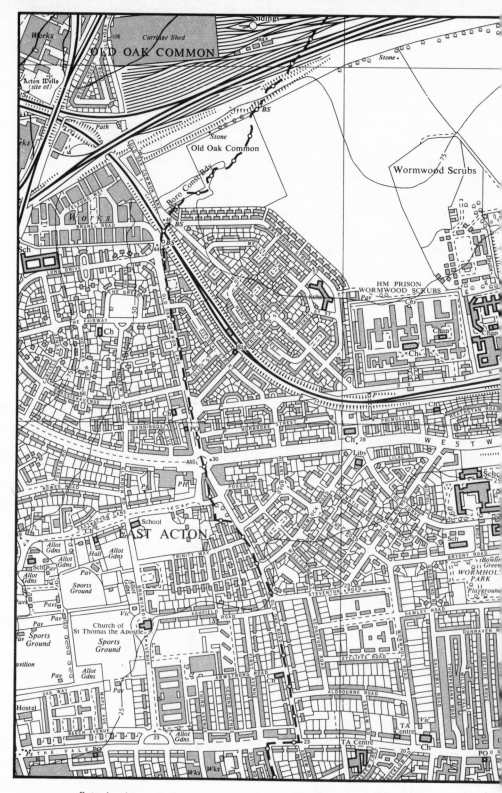

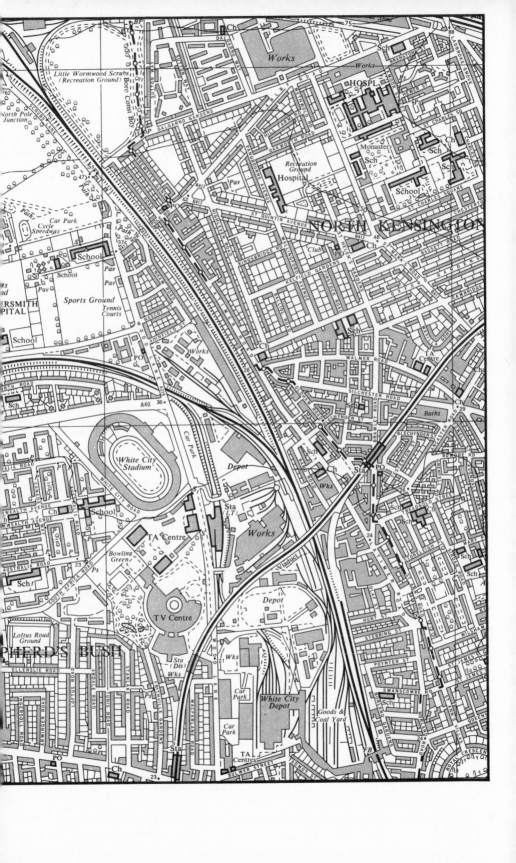

"You're welcome, sir," he replied.

I went along Old Oak Common Lane and was relieved to find a gap in the queue of cars at the mouth of Du Cane Road. English drivers are the most courteous in the world. This evening, for the first time, I had to approach the prison from the East Acton end. I drove slowly past the prison gate, turned left into Artillery Road, and drove to the top, where I did a three-point turn. I cruised slowly back and pulled up on the prison side just past that side entrance leading into the hospital car park. I knew exactly where to stop so that the car would be closest to the end of D-Hall. To the right of the hospital's side entrance there was a traffic sign fixed to the boundary wall. That was my marker.

I quickly took off my hat and mac and placed them on the back seat. I fixed the car's aerial lead to the two-way radio. There was no need to conceal the radio in the flowers, for Artillery Road was dark and deserted. I would use the flowers as a pose if the need arose. I was only inches from the prison wall as I sat in the car facing Du Cane Road. I glanced at my watch: six minutes past six. I pressed the button.   ⁕

"This is Fox Michael calling Baker Charlie, Fox Michael calling Baker Charlie. Come in please. Over."

"This is Baker Charlie to Fox Michael, Baker Charlie to Fox Michael. Receiving you loud and clear. Over."

"*Stone walls do not a prison make, nor iron bars a cage.* Over."

"*Minds innocent and quiet take that for a hermitage.* Over." Blake sounded impatient.

"*Richard Lovelace must have been a fool.* Over."

"*Or just a dreamer.* Over."

"Sorry for the delay," I said, "I got caught in a traffic jam. But everything is okay out here now. Are you all ready to proceed? Over."

"Yes. I'm all ready. Our mutual friend has very kindly agreed to attend to the window for me. He's standing here beside me at the moment with the jack in his hand. Can I tell him to go ahead? Over."

I glanced at my watch: ten past six. "Yes, tell him to proceed— *now.* Over."

"He's on his way down. Over."

"It would be a wise precaution," I said, "if you were to go out onto the landing and lean over the rail so that you can watch what he's doing. That way, if he gets into trouble we will both be warned. Over."

"Very well. I'll call you back. Over."

I turned round in the seat and looked through the rear window of the car towards the park at the top of Artillery Road. It was pitch-black. I faced Du Cane Road again. There were quite a few cars flashing by, about one every ten seconds. It occurred to me in that moment how vulnerable I was. If a police car suddenly turned into Artillery Road I would be caught in its headlights and trapped. There could be no escape, since one single car could completely block this narrow road. The rain was now quite heavy, beating down on the roof of the car and lashing the windows and almost completely obscuring the outside world. Once that gothic window was broken it would have to be used this evening, for it would be very quickly discovered. Any postponement, for whatever reason, and we would have to start all over again on a new plan of exit—if indeed another way *could* be found and if Blake could survive at Wormwood Scrubs that long.

Blake's voice came back over the radio. "Baker Charlie calling Fox Michael. Come in please. Over."

"Fox Michael to Baker Charlie. Receiving you loud and clear. Over."

"The window has been taken care of," said Blake. "I'm ready to make my exit. Over."

That had been quick: three minutes exactly. This, then, was the crucial moment. As soon as Blake went through that window and down to the ground he would have reached the point of no return. If I failed to get him over the wall he would be in Parkhurst, England's Alcatraz, tomorrow. At this moment he was still safe. Either way his future was at stake. It was a hell of a responsibility.

He was waiting for me to speak. I pressed my transmitting button, and in the same instant a pair of brilliant headlights swung into Artillery Road and lit up the whole area, dazzling me. I had been holding the radio down low as a precaution against just such an emergency. Now I dropped it into my lap and picked up the potted chrysanthemum and proceeded to smell it.

The headlights stayed full on, blinding me, as the vehicle came towards me, making it impossible for me to see anything else. It kept on coming and then passed me very slowly, and I noticed it was a van. I hadn't looked at the driver, not wanting to appear curious. In the rear-view mirror I followed the red tail-lights of the van as it made its way to the top of Artillery Road. That was unusual. Why should a van be going up there? Where Artillery Road touches the park, the left half is blocked by four short concrete posts to prevent traffic going onto the park itself. The right half, however, joins straight onto a narrow track leading to the sports pavilion way off to the right. Where the track begins there is a low barrier, about two feet high, which swings open like a gate. The barrier was open now, and the van carried straight onto the track and disappeared from view to the right in the direction of the pavilion.

I pressed the transmitting button. "Are you still there?" I said. "Over."

"Yes," Blake answered. "What happened? Over."

"A van has just gone onto the park. I think it's a groundsman or a patrolman or something like that gone to check on the sports pavilion. He will be coming back, of course, so I cannot let you climb out of that window yet. As soon as he's gone I'll give you the signal to proceed. Over."

"All right, I'll be waiting. Over."

Five minutes later the van's headlights reappeared at the top of Artillery Road. Even at that distance they lit up the inside of my car. I was again holding the flower pot. The van stopped just outside the barrier and the driver got out. I couldn't see him but I heard the van's door slam. He was, I concluded, locking the barrier for the night. During my months of reconnaissance I had noticed the padlock and chain. The door slammed again and the van started to move. It approached very, very slowly, at a mere crawling pace, its lights full on, and I knew immediately that I was under scrutiny—which meant that I was also under suspicion. A parks patrolman was paid to be suspicious.

The van crept past me and stopped about two yards ahead, close to the hospital wall. Nothing happened for about a minute. I was now definitely suspect. I couldn't pick up the radio to talk to Blake because the van was too close, and I knew the driver was watching me through his mirror. Then the door opened and a man got out. He had *Security* stamped all over him. He was tall, wore a flat cloth cap, a dark donkey jacket, and turned-down rubber boots. He stood there by his vehicle just staring at me, making no attempt to conceal his suspicions.

I still held the flower pot in my hands. I glanced at my watch, hoping to convey to him that I was impatient for the visiting hour to begin at the hospital. It made no difference. He stood his ground. There was absolutely no pretence here: it was a direct confrontation. If there had been a policeman nearby this man would have called him. Perhaps if I were to get out of the car with the flowers and walk towards the hospital that would satisfy him. Just as I was about to do so, the man turned his back on me, leaned in over the driving seat of the van, and muttered something. I heard the rattling of a chain and then a huge Alsatian jumped out onto the road. The man turned to face me once more, holding the dog on a short, tight lead as if to imply that it was a dangerous animal. We were no more than four yards apart, the patrolman and his suspect, and each knew what the other was thinking. There was no pretence. That dog was meant to be used against me if the need arose.

Finally I decided I would have to leave. This man had more time at his disposal than I did. For me and for Blake time was fast running out. Every minute spent in this game of cat and mouse was a minute wasted, a minute nearer to failure. My God! I thought to myself, what I would give to be on legitimate business at this moment. I would get out of the car, walk up to that bloke, and ask him who the fucking hell he thought he was staring at.

Reluctantly I started the car and moved off. This in itself, I felt sure, must be taken by the patrolman as an admission of guilt. Why should an innocent man run away? As I turned left in Du Cane Road I felt sure the escape had failed—not just for tonight but for all time. And I didn't even have an opportunity to give Blake an explanation. He would now be calling urgently into a mute, unheeding radio set and wondering bitterly why he had been abandoned at the very moment when freedom was within his grasp. Never to have had any hope at all would be better than this. I could imagine Blake's feelings. But what else was there to do? That patrolman must now surely call the police, or at least lie in wait in case I came back. How could I explain it to Michael, Anne, and Pat? Would they believe me? Wood Lane lay ahead and the lights were at green. Left to Highlever Road and the desolation of that flatlet? Or right to Westway and back once more to Du Cane Road?

I turned right. The rain was beating against the windscreen. Right again into Westway. I looked at my watch: nearly half-past six. The D-Hall men were always back from the cinema by seven, sometimes earlier. That meant crowded landings and another half-a-dozen screws going round unlocking the doors. If Blake was not out before then he would not get out at all. Right into Old Oak Common Lane and right again into Du Cane Road. I cruised past the prison gate and stopped outside the Governor's front door. I got out of the car and walked slowly past Artillery Road.

The van was gone, but there was a car parked where the van had stopped. Could it be a police car? A Q-car? I glanced at my watch: twenty-five minutes to seven. Either the job must be done now or abandoned altogether. I went back to the car. I started up and moved off. I turned left into Artillery Road and drove once more to the top, where I did a three-point turn. I cruised slowly back and stopped at the same spot. I glanced across at the other car. My God! A courting couple!

Unlike the van, this car was facing away from Du Cane Road, towards the park, and I could see the young couple in the front seat as clearly as they could see me. Only a few yards separated us. I had to get rid of them. One way or another, I just *had* to get rid of them. I glanced at my watch: twenty minutes to seven. I got out of the car, leaned against the door, and just stood there in the rain staring deliberately at the young couple. The girl removed her head from the man's shoulder and sat upright. The man glanced across at me and then started to fidget nervously with the steering wheel. They exchanged a furtive glance and smiled at each other self-consciously. I stood my ground and kept staring. They stuck it out for a full minute and then the girl turned and said something to the man and he started up the car. He backed away from me, did a three-point turn, and left Artillery Road.

I had successfully reversed the position of half an hour before. Perhaps they thought *I* was a policeman. I jumped back into the car and picked up the radio. Half an hour had elapsed. Would Blake still be waiting?

"Fox Michael calling Baker Charlie. Come in please. Over." I rattled the words off.

He *was* waiting. "Baker Charlie to Fox Michael. Receiving you loud and clear. I cannot delay here any longer. They're on their way back from the cinema. I must come out now. No time for explanations. Over."

"Okay. Go ahead. Over."

"Right. I'm coming now. I'll contact you when I'm outside. Over and out."

At that moment another pair of headlights swept in off Du Cane Road. The car stopped about thirty yards away, close to the prison wall, facing me. The headlights remained on, drowning me in light. Blake's voice came back over the radio.

"Baker Charlie to Fox Michael. I'm out. Throw the ladder. Over."

My eyes were blinded by the light, my ears deafened by Blake's booming voice reverberating through the sealed, airless car. My head was spinning. For the benefit of the people in the other car, whom I could not see, I picked up the flowers and started to smell them. The headlights stayed on.

"Fox Michael, are you still there? Come in, please. Over." There was impatience in Blake's voice.

I picked the radio up off the seat and held it below the windscreen, lowering my face to it. I held up the flowers in my left hand. "Fox Michael to Baker Charlie. Hang on just a minute. There are some people here. I must wait for them to go. Over."

"Well, I'm already out of the Hall and waiting for that ladder! The men are back from the cinema. The patrol might come along any minute! Hurry! Over."

Blake's voice reflected the great anxiety he was going through as he crouched there in the rain, a mere fifteen yards away, waiting for the lifeline that would pluck him to freedom. He knew too that he had reached the point of no return.

The headlights of the other car were switched off and the occupants started to get out—two men and two women. They walked toward Du Cane Road. I looked at my watch: quarter to seven. Those people would be visiting the hospital, and from now until seven there would be a constant stream of traffic.

Just as I was about to call Blake another car swung into Artillery Road. It stopped across from the first one, close to the hospital's boundary wall. The headlights stayed on, and I once again picked up the flowers. The radio was lying on the seat beside me, switched on.

"Fox Michael! Fox Michael! Come in, please! I cannot wait much longer! Come in, please! Come in!"

Those headlights were still on, and the people were not moving. I got out of the car and started to walk towards them, holding the flower pot in my hands. As I passed the car the headlights were switched off and a man and woman got out. They walked behind me. On the pavement in Du Cane Road I slowed down to let them pass and then hurried back to the car. I jerked the door open.

Blake's voice was still blaring from the radio on the seat. "Fox Michael! Fox Michael! Come in, please! Come in! Come in! There's no more time! Come in!"

As I pulled the car door shut behind me another pair of headlights swept in from the main road and lit up the whole area, right up to the park, picking out that white-painted barrier and the stone posts at the top of Artillery Road. The car pulled up in front of the last arrival, near the hospital wall. I picked up the flowers once more and got out of the car. As I did so Blake's voice came over the radio again. "Fox Michael! Fox Mi—" I slammed the door shut and hoped the other people had not heard.

The headlights went off and a man and two women climbed out of the car. I waited until they had rounded the corner into Du Cane Road. I looked at my watch: five minutes to seven. It was now or never. Blake could not go back into the cell block. He would never see the inside of D-Hall again. For him it was either freedom, or Parkhurst. The comparative ease of Wormwood Scrubs was already lost to him forever. And it was *I* who had told him to climb out of that window. The ladder would go over now, regardless of interruptions. If there had to be a fight, that was too bad. I placed the flower pot against the prison wall—I would have no further use for that.

I climbed back into the car. Blake's voice was still blaring from the radio, now close to panic. "Fox Michael! You *must* throw the ladder now, you simply *must*! There's no more time! Throw it now, Fox Michael! Throw it! Are you still there? Come in, please!"

I already had the radio in my hand. I let him finish and then pressed the transmitting button. "Fox Michael to Baker Charlie. The ladder is coming over now. No matter what the consequences, the ladder is coming over now. Over." I spoke slowly, deliberately.

"All right, Fox Michael, all right! But you must hurry! There's no more time! I expect to be taken at any moment! Throw it now! Over."

"It's coming over now," I said. "Just watch the wall. Over and out."

I got out of the car and went round to the boot. I lifted up the lid and very carefully took the rope ladder out of the paper bag, gripping it in the manner I had so painstakingly practiced. I shut the boot quietly. The ladder had twenty rungs; they would hang down on the inside. The other half of the ladder, my half, consisted of the two uprights wound together to make one thick rope, terminating in a loop. At the twentieth rung, the one that would be nearest the top of the wall on the inside, I had wound two large knots of rope, one around each upright. These knots would keep the ladder a couple of inches out from the wall as it hung down and so make it easier for Blake to grip the rungs as he climbed up.

I put my left arm through the loop, gripping the thick rope with my left hand. I held the folded rungs in my right hand. I looked up at the wall and started to swing. Then I hesitated. That wall seemed a lot higher when you stood directly underneath it. I wanted the ladder to go over first time, one clean throw. I doubted if I could do it. I looked at the car; it was only inches from the wall. The number plate was on the middle of the boot and above it the number-plate light was contained in a protective metal housing that projected outwards a couple of inches. I placed my left foot on this projection and sprang forward and upwards onto the roof of the car. I glanced quickly towards Du Cane Road. This, then, was the showdown. A car turning into Artillery Road now would catch me full in its headlights standing on the roof of my car swinging a rope ladder. Now *I* had reached the point of no return. There was no more posing.

I looked up at the wall. The combined height of the car and my own body had brought the stone coping at the top very much nearer. I swung the folded ladder three times and threw it. I was *too* careful; it went several feet higher than necessary—but dropped neatly down on the inside. I jumped down off the car and jerked the ladder a couple of yards to the right. I did not want Blake to land on the car; he would probably go through the roof. At the same time I pulled the ladder towards me until I could feel the resistance of those two knots of rope touching the stone coping. That meant that the twentieth rung was now near the top of the wall and so the first one would be actually on the ground. The loop was still wound round my left arm, and now I held firmly onto the thick rope with both hands. I would not have to take all of Blake's weight; because of the sharp angle, the wall would take most of it.

I stood very close to the wall to make this angle as acute as possible. My forehead was actually touching the brickwork as I waited to feel the pressure on the rope. At first nothing happened, and I wondered if Blake had been caught. It seemed ages since I had thrown the ladder. "Come on, come on, come on!" I muttered through my teeth, and I was beating my forehead painfully against the brick wall. There had been no more cars for several minutes, but this luck could not last. My own car shielded me from view, since it was between me and the main road, but it could not conceal the upper half of the rope. Blake himself, the moment he appeared, would be exposed, and there was now no means of giving any further warning.

I kicked the wall. "For God's sake, man, hurry up!" I said, almost shouting. The rain was pouring down my face and neck and my clothes were saturated right down to my underwear. Then I heard the wall being kicked directly in front of me and low down, near the ground—then another kick, a little higher up, and then another. Somebody was climbing the ladder, but I could feel hardly any pressure. The wall was taking more of the weight than I had expected. But was it Blake who was climbing? Or a screw? The regular impact of stout shoe leather against solid brickwork was now occurring halfway up the wall. Who was it? Who was approaching me, unseen, less than twelve inches from where I stood? Who was it that was climbing relentlessly upwards towards the top of that wall with the ladder that I had provided? Was I helping Blake? Or was I at this moment unknowingly playing an active role in my own destruction?

I looked up at the wall, keeping my eyes fixed firmly to the spot where the rope disappeared over the coping. If the wrong face appeared I would let go. The kicking against the brickwork was now very high up. Any moment, I thought, any moment. Then a pair of hands slapped loudly over the stone coping, fingers wide apart and desperately rigid. A moment later a face appeared.

It was Blake.

He looked down at me, wide-eyed, bewildered. It was nearly a year since we had seen each other, and it took him a few seconds to recognize me in the dark road. It often occurred to me afterwards that Blake might have had last-minute doubts about who or what might be waiting for him on the other side of the prison wall. The British Secret Service? The KGB? In Blake's profession you could never be sure of anything—or anyone. That was the price you paid. Was that why he hesitated for those few seconds, while he was still in a position to drop back into the prison?

"Come on, man, come on!" I shouted.

He heaved himself up onto the wall, sat astride the coping for a second, then lowered himself down on the outside, hanging by his hands from the top of the wall. He was in his shirt sleeves. He looked down at me over his shoulder, questioningly.

"Jump," I said. "Jump!"

He let go the wall, at the same time throwing himself outwards. I moved forward in a mistaken attempt to break his fall. He brushed against me and sprawled at my feet. His head hit the gravelled road with a thud. He lay still.

At that moment Artillery Road exploded into light. Another car had arrived, its headlights full on. The rope was dangling from the wall. Blake lay on the ground. Fortunately we were both shielded by my car. I straightened up and looked through the rear window and the windscreen towards Du Cane Road. The car was coming slowly towards us, its headlights still on. I looked down at Blake. He didn't move. I looked at the dangling rope; too late to remove it. The other car stopped about ten yards short of us and then backed away again and came to a halt just in front of the car parked close to the prison wall. I waited but the headlights stayed on. Our only hope was to get into the car and start moving; nobody could stop us then.

I straightened up and walked round to the side of the car. I was now in full view of the other people, whoever they might be. I pulled open the rear door, left it open, and went round behind the car again. Blake still lay where he had fallen. I grasped him under the arms. "George! Are you all right? For Christ's sake, what's the matter with you?" It was not a very intelligent thing to say in the circumstances, but I couldn't think of anything else. Blake just groaned; at least he was not completely unconscious.

I began to drag him towards the car, and just then the headlights of the other car went out. But we would still have been seen were it not for the protection of the open rear door of our own car. I pushed Blake in onto the back seat and he lay there, still groaning. I slammed the door shut and then very quickly got in behind the wheel. I pressed the starter and the engine jumped to life. As I reached for the gear lever the other people got out of their car—a man, a woman, and a girl. The two females stood in the middle of the road, chatting, while the man locked the car. I moved off, grinding noisily into second gear even before I reached them. This gave them a fright and they jumped out of the way. Out of the corners of my eyes I could see the man giving me a startled look as I passed. There was a gap in the traffic and I was able to turn into Du Cane Road without delay.

Blake was by now sitting up in the back seat, recovered.

"Are you all right, George?" I asked without looking round.

"Not bad, not bad," he answered, his voice trembling.

"There's a hat and a mac on the seat beside you. Put them on."

The rain was really heavy now, beating noisily against the windscreen. The car windows, which I had tightly shut earlier while we were in radio contact, were still shut, and the windscreen was almost completely steamed up. I could hardly see the road ahead. I started to wipe the screen with my hand and then saw the car in front of me. But it was too late. We were at the zebra crossing near the hospital gate and the other car pulled up to let some people cross the road. I slammed on the brakes. The wheels stopped all right, but the tires skidded forward on the wet road. Our bumpers met with a loud crash and my engine stopped.

I continued to wipe the windscreen and peered forward through the rain. The last person had crossed the road, but the car in front made no attempt to move. I glanced to my left. There was a long queue, about forty people, standing on the pavement, waiting for a Number Seven bus. They were less than two yards away and staring straight at us. The nearest ones were leaning forward, peering in at Blake and me. We had provided them with an interesting diversion as they huddled together in the torrential rain.

I started the engine again. "For Christ's sake, why doesn't that bastard move!" I shouted.

Blake leaned forward over the back of the seat. "Take it easy, Sean," he urged me. "Keep calm. Whatever happens, we mustn't lose our heads."

That was easier said than done. There was now a small queue of cars behind us. At last the car in front started to move. It went slowly forward to get clear of the zebra crossing and then pulled into the kerb. The driver was signalling me to pull in in front of him. "You've got some bloody hope!" I muttered. I slammed my foot on the accelerator, changed noisily into second and third, and screeched away towards Wood Lane.

I could see from a distance that the lights were at red. "Bollocks to the lights!" I said.

"Sean, for heaven's sake, take it easy!"

But there was no need for me to jump the lights after all. They changed to green before I reached them. Left into Wood Lane. The lights ahead at North Pole Road were also at green. I turned right. No more lights before the hideout. Right once more into Latimer Road. I glanced in the rear-view mirror: we were not being followed. Then I remembered my instructions for Blake.

"George," I said, keeping my eyes firmly on the road ahead, "the keys are in the left-hand pocket of the mac, as agreed, and the envelope is in the right. The phone number is written on a small piece of paper in the envelope. The code is simple. You just subtract *one* from each figure. Thus five means four and eight means seven. The first three figures correspond to the exchange letters on the telephone dial. Have you got that?"

"Yes," Blake answered, "that's perfectly clear."

"The address is Twenty-eight Highlever Road. I'm taking you there anyway."

I turned left into Oxford Gardens and stopped the car about twenty yards past Highlever Road. I turned round in my seat to look at Blake and got a shock. His face was covered with blood. It was streaming down from a lacerated forehead. He could not go into the house on his own in that condition.

"On second thought, George, I'd better come with you. I'll get rid of the car later. Let's go."

We climbed out of the car. The rain was still pouring down. The street was deserted. "You'd better give me the keys," I said. He made as if to put his left hand in his pocket but he couldn't. Then I noticed that it was limp. "Looks like you've sprained it," I said.

"I'm afraid it's not just sprained. It's broken." He held his hand up. The wrist was bent at an ugly angle just above the joint.

"That looks broken all right." I reached into his pocket and took the keys out. "Does it pain much?"

"Very little. It's more numb than anything else."

We turned into Highlever Road and walked in silence for a moment. Then Blake looked at me. "Sean, you're a great fellow." His voice was charged with emotion.

I laughed. "We'll discuss all that later. First things first."

We reached the flatlet without meeting anyone.

"Well," I said, "here we are. It isn't much, but it's the best we could do. And anyway, it's only temporary. Your clothes are on the bed. I hope you'll be able to change into them. There's a sink there in the corner with running water so you can wash your face without having to go next door to the bathroom." I lit the gas fire. "This place will be nice and warm in a few minutes."

Blake had taken off the hat and mac and stood there in the middle of the room in his prison-grey trousers and striped shirt.

I shook my head. "George, I can hardly believe that you're standing here in this room. Free. It's going to take me a long time to get used to the idea. It's rather like seeing a double-decker bus on top of Nelson's Column."

Blake laughed. "I cannot believe it myself."

I removed the front-door key from the ring and handed him the other two. "I'll get rid of the car now," I said. "Lock this room after me. When I come back I'll knock three times."

"Will you be long away?"

"About an hour. I want to put as much distance as possible between this house and that car out there. Even without the escape that car has already made a formidable reputation for itself in West London tonight. Everybody in Hammersmith must have my number by now. See you later." I put on the hat and mac.

Blake crossed to the door to lock it after me. "Can you bring a drink back with you?" he said.

"Sure. Sorry about that—it's the one thing I forgot."

I went out into the passage and heard the key turning in the lock behind me. I flicked on the hall light and looked at my watch: twenty minutes past seven. Even if Blake had not actually been seen climbing the wall by that screw in the phone box, he would have been missed by now. Lock-up time was at seven o'clock on weekends, and every prisoner had to be in his cell when the screws went round looking through the spy-holes. This was the final—and the most foolproof—roll-call of the day. At lock-up time nothing could hide the fact that a prisoner was missing. My God, they were in for a shock at Wormwood Scrubs tonight!

I went to the telephone at the foot of the stairs and dialled Michael's number. He and Pat had agreed to provide themselves with cast-iron alibis by surrounding themselves with very respectable people this evening. (There was always a vague possibility that Michael might be connected to me.) They had also decided to be close to a television set to follow the news. It was not part of the plan for me to call Michael, but I decided to give him a pleasant surprise. He answered the phone himself.

"Hello there," I said.

He knew it was me. "Oh, hello, my friend." His voice was questioning, expectant. He knew that by this time the whole thing was over. We had either succeeded or failed.

"How are you?" I went on.

"Oh, not too bad, you know. And you?"

"Could be worse." I could hear many voices in the background. Yes, he had got some friends in all right. I said nothing for a moment. I could just imagine him biting his lip. "Oh, by the way," I said then, as if a thought had suddenly occurred to me, "the operation has been successfully completed."

"Oh, really? I—" He checked himself. "I'm very pleased to hear that. How did it go?"

"Well," I said, "I went to the party, as arranged, and contacted our friend. I threw him the bait and he took it, hook, line, and sinker. And now he's on my side. In fact, he's right here with me."

Michael was silent for a moment. I knew he was finding it difficult to be restrained in the presence of his friends.

"Well, I don't have to tell you how delighted I am," he said, and his voice was trembling a little.

"I've got to go now," I told him. "I'll come and see you tomorrow morning. A little problem has arisen and we're going to need some help."

"All right," Michael said. "I'll see you in the morning. I must go back and watch television now."

"Do that," I said. "There should be some interesting programmes later on. Good night."

I left the house and walked back to the car. At first I thought I was in trouble: the engine wouldn't start. It was five minutes before it finally came to life. I drove to the bottom of Oxford Gardens and turned right into Ladbroke Grove. At the bottom of Ladbroke Grove I turned left and cruised past Notting Hill Gate Underground station and along the Bayswater Road. After that I drove aimlessly through the streets of London for half an hour. Finally I entered a long street with houses on one side and a railway line on the other. I stopped the car halfway along and got out and locked it. I walked back to the end of the street and looked at the nameplate. Harvist Road N.W. 6. (Later when I looked at the map I concluded that I hadn't really been putting as much distance as possible between myself and Highlever Road, but simply circling round the district.)

I turned left and started to walk down Kingswood Avenue. I noticed a pub on the right and I crossed over. Outside the door I was accosted by a couple of little girls who wanted a penny for the Guy. They had a large, roughly made rag doll propped up in an equally roughly made wooden cart with two pram wheels.

"A penny for the Guy, mister? A penny for the Guy?"

I searched my pockets but had no coins. I was feeling very happy—much too happy to disappoint a couple of nine-year-old girls looking for pennies in the rain. I took out my wallet and handed them a ten-shilling note. "Children," I said, "you will never know to what great events you owe this gesture."

But they weren't listening. They were staring wide-eyed at the note, both of them holding it at once. Then they looked up at me. "Cor, thank you, mister! Thank you, mister! Thank you!"

A moment later I learned something of the economics of the Guy Fawkes business. The two children grabbed their cart and started running down the street, squealing with delight. "Thank you, mister!" they kept shouting back at me. "Thank you, mister!" No more standing in the rain for them. I had often wondered what sort of money was to be made at that game. Ten shillings was obviously considered to be more than enough for one day.

I went into the pub and downed four double whiskies in fifteen minutes. When I left I had a bottle of whisky in one pocket and a bottle of brandy in the other.

I walked to the end of Kingswood Avenue and caught a taxi. "Oxford Gardens," I said, "top end." I paid the cabbie off round the corner from Highlever Road and walked to the house. I let myself in, walked to the end of the darkened passage, and knocked three times on the door.

Blake opened it cautiously, and again I thought I detected that shadow of doubt in his eyes. What tormented thoughts had gone through his mind during my absence? Was I really just getting rid of the car? Or reporting to some sinister figures in the background that their prey was now safely delivered? His was indeed a strange profession.

I went in and locked the door behind me. Blake had changed into his new clothes and was looking very smart. His prison clothes were in a bundle on the bed, which I helped him tie.

"Well, George, it's the first time I've seen you in civvies. I'd hardly know you."

He smiled. "I must say, they feel quite comfortable."

He had washed his face, but the blood kept oozing out of that cut forehead. I took a closer look at it. There was no specific gush, just a lot of small indentations made by the rough gravel, and concentrated over the right eyebrow. It looked rather as though he had been sprayed with pellets. The right eye was already beginning to close. The left arm hung limply by his side.

"Well," I said, "that eye will be closed tomorrow, but it's not serious. Those cuts on the forehead are only superficial. About the wrist —there's nothing we can do tonight, but tomorrow we'll get a doctor. My friends have got lots of other friends. In the meantime I'll make you a sling."

We made the sling by tearing up Blake's prison shirt. I made a cold compress and wrapped it round the broken wrist before putting it in the sling. "How does it feel?" I asked.

"Oh, not too bad," said Blake with a grin. "The compress helps. I'll be all right until tomorrow."

I held up the two bottles. "Whisky or brandy?"

"Brandy for me if you don't mind."

"Right. I'll have a drop of the hard stuff." I filled a couple of tumblers and handed him his brandy. I held my drink up. "Well," I began, "to—"

"To this great moment," Blake interjected. "And to you, Sean."

We touched glasses and drank.

"I needed that," said Blake. "It's a long time since I had a—er—a drop of the hard stuff, as you say."

I filled the glasses again and then turned on the television. Blake sat on the bed and I sat in the armchair. I looked at my watch: quarter to nine. "The news will be on at nine," I said. Then, with an air of elaborate nonchalance, I added, "I wonder if there'll be anything interesting?"

He laughed. "I wonder," he said.

The programme ended. The screen was blank for just a second and then the news signature tune began. At the same time a photograph of Blake filled the whole screen. The photograph stayed there until the signature tune ended and then the announcer appeared. "High drama in West London tonight!" he began. "George Blake, the double agent who was serving forty-two years' imprisonment for spying for the Russians, escaped from Wormwood Scrubs Prison in London this evening. Blake was tried at the Central Criminal Court in May 1961. His sentence was the longest ever imposed in a British court of law. He had been convicted on five counts of passing information to the Russians while working for British Intelligence in Berlin. A Home Office statement says that Blake was missed from his cell at the seven o'clock roll-call, when all the prisoners were being locked away for the night. A search was made of the prison grounds but no trace of Blake could be found. He is, therefore, presumed to have escaped. A huge manhunt has been launched under the direction of Scotland Yard's Special Branch. Careful watch is being kept at all airports and harbours, and East European embassies are also being kept under observation. News is still coming in of this dramatic escape, and we will keep you informed."

I turned to Blake and raised my glass. " 'Mischief, thou art afoot; take thou what course thou wilt.' "

We touched glasses and drank.

Sean Bourke

George Blake   (*Central Press*)

One of the cell blocks at Wormwood Scrubs Prison   (*Central Press*)

The entrance to Wormwood Scrubs Prison   (*Wide World Photos*)

George Blake with his mother, when he returned from Korea in 1953
(*Central Press*)

Prisoners in the yard at Wormwood Scrubs Prison   (*Central Press*)

BOUGHT OF

N⁰ 10041

McDONALD STORES
(COVENTRY STREET) LTD.

RADIOS · RECORDS · CAMERAS · TYPEWRITERS

26, PICCADILLY, LONDON, W.1.
REGent 4442

66, SHAFTESBURY AVE.,
LONDON, W.I

34, COVENTRY ST.,
LONDON, W.I

30 - 11 19

M_____

	Tuf itu W/Talkie			
		£25-0-0		

Cash	✓				
Cheque					
Account		Stock No.			

The receipt for the two-way radio

Wormwood Scrubs Prison. The installation of arc lamps was part of the security arrangements made *after* the escape of George Blake   (*Central Press*)

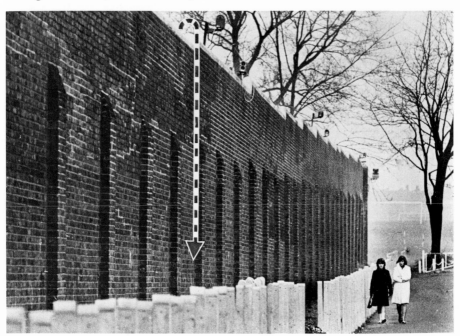

Wormwood Scrubs Prison. The dotted line shows George Blake's escape route   (*Central Press*)

Two pages from the original manuscript, showing the extent of the alterations made in Moscow

Sean Bourke at Shannon airport, after his return from Moscow (*London Daily Express*)

BOOK TWO

BOOK TWO

11

The Doctor

Neither Blake nor I got any sleep that night. He had the bed, and I lay
on the floor in front of the gas fire on a couple of spare blankets. The
compress had to be removed from his wrist every hour and soaked
again in cold water to ease the pain. But it was not this task that kept
me awake; I would not have been able to sleep anyway. I kept reliving
that nightmare hour between six o'clock and seven, and every ten minutes or so, at the thought of how close we had come to disaster, I
would exclaim aloud, "Jesus Christ!"

Earlier in the evening, as I had promised Blake, we had a tea
of chops followed by strawberries and cream. We could hear the
mumble of voices coming from the other bed-sitters, and even from the
house next door, and we knew that they would be discussing the dramatic escape of the master spy George Blake.

"Just imagine," I said, "there are six other persons or groups of
persons in those other rooms, and as they follow the story of the escape
on television they are completely unaware that they are sharing the
same house with you, that you are actually listening to their voices at
this moment and that they are listening to yours."

"And what's more," Blake said with a smile, "by their presence here
in this house they are, in a way, helping to hide us."

Next morning, after a breakfast of sausages and eggs, I went out to
buy the newspapers. I went to the news-agent's in North Pole Road.
There was no sign of any police activity, which did not surprise me.
The police, as I had expected, would be concentrating their efforts on

all the points of exit from the country. They would not expect Blake to be hiding in a house a few minutes' walk from the prison, nor would they expect his rescuer to be strolling unconcerned through the neighbouring streets within hours of the crime. I bought a copy of every paper and walked slowly down Latimer Road, reading them. The escape was in big black headlines on every front page, and each paper carried a photograph of Blake. I went back to the flatlet.

"What news?" asked Blake.

I read out the first paragraph from the newspaper on top of the pile: " 'George Blake, the master spy serving forty-two years' imprisonment for passing secrets to the Russians, made a dramatic escape from Wormwood Scrubs Prison in London last night. The Prime Minister was immediately informed at Chequers.' " I threw the papers on the bed. "The Prime Minister, if you don't mind! They're going to be very angry with us, George, very angry indeed."

"I think you're right," said Blake, "but you can hardly blame them, can you?"

"Hardly," I agreed.

We spent the next half-hour going through the papers.

Then it was time to do something about that broken wrist. "I'll have to go to Camden Town," I told Blake. "I'll be back in a couple of hours. Don't open the door to anyone."

I walked to Latimer Road Underground station and caught a tube. Everybody seemed to be reading about the escape. Blake's photograph was staring at me from all directions. I got out at Camden Town and walked to the house.

Michael answered the door. He was so overcome with joy at our success that he threw his arms around me. "Well done, Sean! My God, well done! A magnificent bloody job!"

Anne came downstairs and we kissed quite spontaneously. The newspapers were spread all over the settee, Blake's banner headlines uppermost.

"How did it go?" Anne asked. "For heaven's sake tell us how you did it, in detail."

I explained all about the agony of the night before, that nerve-racking hour between six and seven. "That was the longest hour of my bloody life," I concluded. "I wouldn't want to go through that again for a million bloody pounds." Then I told them about the broken wrist.

"We must get a doctor," I said, "we just *must*. If we don't I'll have to take George to a hospital tonight and say that he's a brother of mine who has just fallen down the stairs, or something."

Michael frowned. "That would be dangerous, wouldn't it? I mean, with his photograph on every front page?"

"These official prison photographs can be very deceptive," I said. "There's a good chance he wouldn't be recognized, and anyway nobody would be expecting him to walk into a hospital."

Michael looked thoughtful. "I think I can in fact get a doctor," he said. "I know of someone who might be sympathetic. He's not a friend of mine personally but a friend of a friend. I'll make a phone call."

He was gone for five minutes. When he came back he said, "Well, I think we've got a chance. I have arranged to go see this friend later today, and he'll take me to the doctor. We must now hope that the doctor will be available, and that if he is available he will be prepared to help."

"I hope so," I said. "I hope so. Otherwise it's the hospital. We don't know how long George is going to have to hide in London, and he can't just sit there with a broken wrist for weeks, or perhaps months. That would be a security hazard in itself." I was determined to lay it on so that if there was the slightest chance of getting a doctor, he would be got.

"If the doctor is not at home we may have to chase about London a bit," said Michael. "It may take some time, and I'd like to keep you informed of progress. But I think we should have as few trails as possible leading back to Highlever Road. I suggest that I phone Anne every hour, and then when you want a report on progress you can phone here too. Let's work out a little code."

We worked out a simple code and then said good-bye. I went back to Highlever Road.

Blake was considerably happier when I told him the news. He was in pain but pretended not to be. He put on a brave face. We had a lunch of bacon, peas, and more sausages, followed by tinned pears. We spent most of the day going over the events of the night before and wincing at the near-failures. When I had been forced to leave the vicinity of the prison by that patrolman and his dog, Blake had continued calling me. Finally he had ·reluctantly concluded that I had called off the attempt. He was actually folding his aerial when I came back over the air. And even then he thought it might already be too late. The other prisoners were coming in the side gate of D-Hall from the cinema. Once they had started filing up the narrow iron stairs to the landings it would have been impossible to squeeze past them on the way down. And Blake had to get down from the Fours to the Threes to reach the broken window.

"I reached the bottom of the flight of stairs connecting the Threes and Fours at exactly the same moment as that long line of prisoners coming up. A second later and I would have been trapped on the Fours for ten or fifteen minutes, and by then the landings would have been so full of prisoners and officers that it would have been impossible to climb out that window without being seen."

"And that, of course, was not the end of the agony."

"The end of it?" Blake looked at me through his one open eye. "It was only the beginning! I was standing there under that window, in the pouring rain, with a radio in my hand, for twenty minutes. There again I concluded that you had called the attempt off. I was literally just waiting for the patrol to come along and take me. I was as much surprised as pleased when your voice came back over the air. It was the last thing I expected."

"I had my moments of despair too," I told him. "We had more luck than anyone has a right to expect. I still cannot understand why that patrolman did not call the police. I mean, if he was suspicious enough actually to threaten me with his dog, you'd think the least he would do afterwards is phone for the police. We shall probably never know the answer to that little mystery."

Blake sighed audibly. "My goodness," he said, "it's just as well I didn't know what you were going through on the other side of the wall, otherwise I would have given up hope altogether."

I phoned Michael's house every hour throughout the day. Michael was indeed having difficulty. His messages to Anne indicated that he was dashing about all over London in search of a doctor. The first doctor was out of town and could not be got hold of. The second doctor on the list was proving elusive. It was seven o'clock in the evening before he was tracked down. I was told on the phone that I could expect a visit "within an hour or so."

At eight-thirty the doorbell rang three times, a very definite and uniform gap between each ring. I opened the French windows leading onto the back yard. "You never know," I said to Blake. "It might give you just a little chance. Lock the door after me, and if you hear a commotion out in the passage, make a dash for it."

I heard the key turning in the lock behind me as I walked down the darkened passage to the front door. It was Michael all right, and with him on the doorstep stood a man of about forty-five holding the familiar black bag. I led them back along the passage and knocked three times on the room door. The key turned in the lock and we went in. We shook hands all round but there were no introductions.

The doctor lifted Blake's arm and looked thoughtfully at his wrist. "Well," he said without raising his eyes, "it's definitely broken. There's no doubt about that." He looked at me and then back at Blake. "The position with me," he said, "is this. You have a broken wrist. The normal procedure is that you should go to a hospital to have it set. However, I understand that for some reason or other you are allergic to hospitals. You refuse, in fact, to go to a hospital. Now, obviously, you cannot go about with a broken wrist, and therefore I, as a doctor, consider it my duty to help you. This, I take it, is understood?" The doctor was still looking at Blake.

"Yes, that is perfectly understood," said Blake. "And I appreciate it very much."

"Good," said the doctor. He went to the table and opened his bag. "I think it only fair to tell you," he went on, "that it's at least ten years since I performed this particular operation."

This was a patently honest man. He looked you straight in the face when he spoke. His manner and appearance were highly intelligent and sober. He was obviously no back-street quack, otherwise he would not have been known to Michael and Pat.

He turned to me. "I shall need some hot water for the plaster, and if you've got some newspapers we can use them to cover this table."

The only papers we had were that morning's. I spread them on the table and completely forgot about what they contained. Four front-page photographs of Blake were staring up at us. I glanced at the doctor but he did not appear to notice anything. I half filled a bucket with hot water in the bathroom and brought it in and placed it in the centre of the table.

Then the phone rang out in the passage and I went to answer it. It was Pat Porter. "Congratulations," he said. "This is the first opportunity I've had to call. I know that I shouldn't be, but I couldn't resist it."

"That's all right," I assured him, "we've all done some odd things today."

"Do you mind if I come over?" he asked. "I'm not very far away."

"Okay, why not?"

"Thanks, Sean. See you in about fifteen minutes."

I went back into the room.

"You'll have to take off your shirt," the doctor was saying to Blake. Blake did so. The equipment was laid out on the table but very little in fact was required. A hypodermic needle, anaesthetic, bandages, a tin of plaster. "I shall give you a local anaesthetic," the doctor said. "It may not kill all the pain but it will help." Then he turned to me. "Is there somewhere I can wash my hands?"

"Yes, Doctor. Follow me." I took him next door to the bathroom and handed him a bar of soap. I was very impressed by the care with which he washed. He spent at least fifteen minutes doing the job. He rolled his sleeves up high and washed thoroughly from the elbows downwards, scrubbing each finger individually and cleaning every speck of dirt from under his nails. Then he held his forearms outwards as doctors do in operating theatres, and I placed the clean towel in his hands. He was obviously determined not to touch anything else before handling his instruments, and so I held the bathroom door open for him and then the door to the room.

There were three rings at the front door and I went to answer it. It was Pat. He came in and stood quietly in the background. Since I appeared to have been cast in the role of chairman of the proceedings, I decided that the introductions should wait until the doctor had departed. It would have been unfair to him to do otherwise.

I went over to the table. "Can I help in any way?"

"I think you may have to hold his arm steady," the doctor said.

Blake was sitting on a chair, his forearm stretched out on the table, palm of the hand downwards. I gripped the forearm firmly in both hands, and the doctor stuck the hypodermic needle into the centre of the fracture between the broken ends of the bone. He allowed about ten minutes to elapse and then caught hold of the wrist on either side of the fracture and started to manoeuvre the broken ends of the bone back into line. To do this he had first to pull the ends well apart. The anaesthetic only partially killed the pain, and the sweat was pouring down Blake's face. He was writhing in the chair. If I had not held his arm on the table the operation would have been impossible.

Pat and Michael couldn't stand it; they moved away to the farthest corner of the room. This struggling and manoeuvring with the broken bone went on for about five minutes.

"I think that's back in position all right now," the doctor said finally.

That ugly lump was certainly gone and the wrist looked straight again. Next the doctor opened the plaster tin and emptied some of the white powder into the warm water in the bucket, stirring it well as he did so. Finally he dipped the bandages into the liquid plaster and wound them round the injured wrist and the forearm and hand, leaving only the fingers free. We used the same sling as before, made from Blake's prison shirt.

"That should be all right now," the doctor said. "The plaster will be hard in a couple of hours." He took another needle from his bag and a small bottle containing a transparent liquid. "You had better have a shot of penicillin to make sure there will be no infection."

Blake held out his good arm.

"Not there"—the doctor smiled—"you'll have to drop your trousers."

Blake started to fumble hesitantly with his fly buttons, and at the same time Michael, Pat, and myself turned away and started chatting together.

"That's all, I think," said the doctor and started to put his equipment back into the bag.

"There's just one more thing, Doctor," I said. "Have you got anything for inducing sleep?"

"Of course." He dipped his hand into the bag once more and gave me some small plastic phials containing a greyish powder. "One per person per night," he said.

I thanked him.

Michael glanced at his watch and turned on the television, just in time for the news. The escape was the first item again. Blake's photograph was flashed onto the screen, followed by photographs of Wormwood Scrubs and diagrams showing the escape route from the gothic window to the wall and along Artillery Road.

The doctor glanced briefly at the screen, smiled faintly, said nothing. Then he turned to me once more. "Is there a toilet?" he asked.

"Yes, Doctor, third door on the right."

He went out.

I looked at Michael. "Would it be all right to offer a fee?" I asked.

He thought for a moment. "I don't think so," he said slowly. "It might be misinterpreted, and he's not that sort of doctor."

The escape item came to an end on the news. "Anybody want to watch the rest?" I asked. Nobody did, so I switched off.

The doctor came back in and picked up his bag. I shook him by the hand. "Good-bye, Doctor, and thank you very much."

"You're welcome," he said.

Blake shook hands with him next. "Good-bye," he said. "I am very grateful to you for your help."

"That's all right," the doctor replied.

I walked with him and Michael to the door. There was a car parked in the street and the doctor got into it.

"There's no need for you to come with me," he said, turning to Michael.

"All right," said Michael. "Good night."

The doctor drove off and turned left into Oxford Gardens. We went back to the room.

"Well," I said to Blake, "by this time there is hardly any need for introductions. This is Michael Reynolds and this is Pat Porter. As I've already told you, I knew Michael before I went to prison. Pat I met only a few months ago. He's an old friend of Michael's."

They shook hands warmly.

"Well," Blake began, "it is difficult for me to know what to say. I honestly didn't know there *were* people like you. I shall never be able to express my deep gratitude for what you've done."

Michael and Pat assured him that he was welcome and that his thanks were not necessary. Then the phone rang and I went out to answer it. It was Anne.

"Is Michael still there?" she asked.

I told her he was.

"Would you mind very much if I came over, Sean?"

"Please do. You're the only one missing. Come over and we'll have a party."

"All right, I'll be there in half an hour."

I went back to the room. "Anne is on her way," I announced. "We might as well have a little celebration. I'll go and buy a couple of bottles and let you people get acquainted. I'll be back in about twenty minutes. Lock the door after me. Three knocks, as usual."

I went to a nearby pub and bought another two bottles, whisky and brandy. By the time I got back Blake was chatting with Michael and Pat as though they were old friends. Shortly afterwards the doorbell rang again. It was Anne. I brought her in and introduced her to George.

"Well, gentlemen," I announced, "since this little gathering was not part of the plan of operation, I have been caught unawares. I bought only two glasses. Anne, of course, must now have one of them, and the other one, I think, for our distinguished guest. The rest of us will have to drink out of cups." I poured out the drinks.

"Got anything to eat, have you, Sean?" Pat asked. "I'm bloody starving. I've had nothing since lunchtime."

"We're very low on rations at the moment. I've got to go shopping in the morning. But we've got plenty of bread and butter."

And so the five of us sat there, four men and a woman, in a shabby bed-sitter in West London, eating bread and butter and washing it down with whisky and brandy, and three of us drinking out of tea-cups. George and Pat sat on the narrow bed, Anne sat in the one arm-chair, and Michael and myself sat on a couple of straight-back chairs. We formed a rough circle, and on the floor in the centre of this circle were two plates, one piled high with chunks of roughly cut bread and the other containing a slab of butter. There was one knife on the butter plate, which we passed round from one to the other as the need arose. Everybody was in high spirits as we relived the dramatic events of the previous day.

"I didn't want to admit this before the job was done, Sean," said Pat presently, "but I could never have done what you did. It would have been physically and emotionally impossible for me to go to the prison wall and throw a rope ladder over." He shook his head vigorously to rid himself of the image. "I just couldn't. I simply couldn't. I'd be absolutely terrified."

"Neither could I," Michael said. He gave a mock shudder. "My God, I don't know how you did it, Sean! I couldn't do it to save my life."

Most men would think twice before making admissions like these, especially in front of a woman, but it was characteristic of Michael and Pat to do so. They were incapable of dishonesty.

"Don't kid yourselves that *I* wasn't terrified," I assured them. "It's just that I felt instinctively that if it wasn't done last night it would never be done. And, of course, once that window was broken there was no turning back."

We all got a little drunk, and Pat got drunkest of all. "My God," he declared, "I'm so delighted that I'd like to get up on the roof and tell the whole world we've done it."

"I hope you don't," Anne said, and we all laughed.

"I think," said Michael, "that it's the best thing any of us is ever likely to do in his lifetime. If we never did anything else we can always say we did something useful while we were on earth."

Then we discussed the future. Highlever Road was never meant to be anything more than a temporary hiding place, somewhere to go straight from the prison in order to get out of sight as quickly as possible. Some more secure accommodation would have to be found as soon as possible. I pointed out that this flatlet was cleaned once a week, on Wednesdays, by the owners of the house. That left us only two days. Michael and Pat started discussing the possibility of approaching some of their mutual friends who had houses with spare rooms.

"It's important," Blake reminded us, "that as few people as possible should know. The more people involved, the greater the risk of a leak."

Michael and Pat said they would only approach those friends who were completely reliable and trustworthy.

This was sufficient assurance for Blake and me. If the friends in question were only half as reliable and trustworthy as Michael and Pat we would have no need to worry.

It was nearly midnight when I showed our guests to the door. "We are very lucky men," I said to Blake when they had gone, "to know people like them."

"My friend," he replied, "you don't have to remind me."

12

On the Run

Monday was a quiet leisurely day in the flatlet at Highlever Road. I ⚜⚜ did the shopping in the morning and brought back a copy of every ⚜⚜ paper. The escape was still on the front pages in banner headlines, and it was to continue like this for most of the week. It was also to be a great week for the cartoonists. No other prisoner in Britain could have given Fleet Street so much copy as Blake did. And at this time there was also something of a spy cult in the cinema and on television, inspired by the adventures of James Bond. The "experts" and the commentators were going to be busy during the next few months with their fantastic theories of international intrigue.

I glanced through the headlines. That little pot of pink chrysanthemums, so casually abandoned at the scene of the escape, was already being endowed with a mysterious significance far removed from its true, simple purpose. THE CLUE OF THE PINK CHRYSANTHEMUM, one huge headline said. It was just a foretaste of what was to come. At lunchtime, on a BBC radio programme called "The World at One," a Canadian journalist who had been interned with Blake in Korea came out with the first of the fantastic theories. Over the transatlantic cable he told a BBC man that Blake could not have escaped from prison for the simple reason that he had never *been* to prison. It was all, he claimed, part of a huge plot by the British Secret Service to fool the Russian KGB. Blake's trial had been a mock one designed to convince the Russians that Blake really had been their faithful servant, whereas all the time he had really been carrying out the instructions of MI6.

After the mock trial Blake went to live somewhere in comfort under a false name, and a substitute went to Wormwood Scrubs in his place. Now MI6 had arranged an equally mock escape. The substitute would be paid off for his services and the real George Blake would reappear and find his way to Russia, where the KBG would welcome him as a hero and faithful servant. Blake, of course, would then work for the KGB full-time and send back regular reports to his real masters in London. Thus, MI6 would have succeeded in planting one of their very own men in the KGB Headquarters in Moscow.

At the end of the broadcast I said to Blake, "So that's your little game, is it? I've been working for MI6 all the time, have I? Well, I wish they had made it a little easier for me on Saturday. Or did they specially lay on that patrolman and the courting couple and all the other heart-stoppers just to make it look convincing? Very clever. Diabolically clever. It's more subtle than *The Spy Who Came in from the Cold*. I've got to hand it to you, George. Or should I be calling you George at all?"

Blake laughed. "Can you imagine the British Secret Service daring to make pawns of the Home Secretary, the Attorney General, and the Lord Chief Justice?"

No, I couldn't imagine it.

In the House of Commons that afternoon the Home Secretary announced that he had already appointed Admiral of the Fleet, the Earl Mountbatten of Burma, to head a Government inquiry into prison security, with particular reference to the escape of George Blake. But this gesture was not enough to satisfy the Opposition, who introduced a censure motion. It was agreed that the motion should be debated on the following Monday. Mischief was indeed afoot.

About four o'clock I went next door to the kitchen-bathroom to have a bath. Blake was in the bed-sitting-room reading. I had been in the bath about fifteen minutes when the doorbell started ringing. The ringing followed an ordinary haphazard pattern and so I decided to ignore it. The caller would soon get tired of ringing and go away, I thought. But I was wrong. The ringing persisted. Presently Blake started banging on the wall separating the two rooms. He wanted to draw my attention to the doorbell.

"Ignore it," I shouted through the wall. "They'll soon go away."

But they didn't. The ringing went on. Then Blake left the other room and came and knocked on the bathroom door.

"For heaven's sake, Sean," he said anxiously, "go and answer the door. You never know what complications it might lead to if you don't."

"All right," I answered. "I'll go." Reluctantly I heaved myself out of the bath. I wrapped a towel around my middle and made my way to the front door, leaving a trail of little puddles behind me in the passage. I opened it and stood aside.

A schoolgirl of about fourteen walked in, her satchel under her arm. She was Indian or Pakistani. She gave me a pleasant smile and was not at all embarrassed. "Thank you," she said and made her way up the stairs to the bed-sitter that was home for her and her father and mother, and perhaps for a brother and sister too—wide-eyed witnesses to their parents' copulation.

"Who was it?" Blake asked when I went back to the room.

"A fourteen-year-old schoolgirl," I told him. "And me standing there almost bollock naked. If that towel had slipped I could have been had up for indecent exposure. Christ Almighty, just imagine that! What a way to get caught! What an ignominious way to end this adventure! Indecent bloody exposure! Jesus! I'd have to spend my whole sentence making toys for orphans and going to church every morning, like all those other sex cases."

On the television news that evening it was announced that all the other spies in Britain's jails had been switched to new locations during the day. They were all now under special guard in top-security prisons.

The following afternoon, Tuesday, Michael phoned and said he had found alternative accommodations. Blake and I packed our belongings. At eight o'clock in the evening the doorbell rang three times. It was Michael and Anne. On the road outside was a car they had borrowed for the evening.

Michael looked at the two cases standing in the middle of the floor. "I'm afraid I've got bad news for you, Sean," he said. "These people have got only one small spare room and they can take only one of you."

"Well, how is that bad news?" I asked. "I'm safe here for a little while yet. After all, the owners and some of the tenants have seen me. I'm quite safe until they start printing my photograph and flashing it on the television screen and all that sort of business. But George, here, must go. This flatlet will be invaded tomorrow when they come to clean it and change the linen."

Michael and Anne looked relieved, but Blake appeared to be anxious about something.

"It's a pity, Sean, you can't come too," he said.

"We'll try and find another place for Sean, of course," Anne said.

Michael looked at me quizzically. "How can you be so sure that the police *will* get onto you?" he asked.

"That," I answered, "is a foregone conclusion, for the reasons we have already discussed. And since then there have been all those witnesses at the scene of the escape, including that patrolman. No, it is just a matter of time. Indeed, I wouldn't be surprised if they were already actively searching for me."

"But if that's the case, why don't they issue your name and photograph straightaway?" Anne asked.

"That would be bad strategy," I told her. "They don't want to warn me that they're looking for me, and in this way they think they can catch me off guard. They will only issue my photograph when they're convinced that *I* know they're looking for me."

"Well, anyway, Sean, we'll do our best to find you somewhere to go to," Michael said. Then he turned to Blake, a troubled expression on his pale face. The laughter and merrymaking of Sunday night had now gone. "These people you're going to," he said quietly, "know, of course, who you are. They are worried about one thing. They are no more anxious than the rest of us to help Russian Intelligence and they'd like some sort of assurance that you're not going to pass on any more information."

I was taken aback by this demand, and Michael himself had obviously not found it easy to make it. There was an awkward silence. I looked at Blake. It was something he had not expected either, though, of course, he realized that none of his helpers was a Communist.

"Well," he began hesitantly, "I can assure you this question does not arise. Even if I wanted to pass on any more information, I couldn't, because I possess none. Any scraps of intelligence I might have still known at the time of my arrest would now be quite useless anyway. So, you see, you need have no worries on that score."

Michael nodded. "Very well," he said.

I was a little puzzled. The exchange I had just witnessed was, I thought, naïve in the extreme. Obviously Blake would have to give the answer he gave. And equally obviously, as a dedicated Communist and spy, he would not hesitate to tell the KGB everything he knew at the earliest opportunity. None of us wanted to help the Russians or to harm Britain, but we could console ourselves that by helping Blake we were not putting other people in danger, since the British would have taken all the necessary precautions from the moment of Blake's escape. Michael, Anne, Pat and the others, I imagined, wanted to satisfy their consciences insofar as it was possible to do so in the circumstances. On the one hañd they wanted to help to put right what they considered to be an injustice, but on the other hand they would be revolted at the idea that they were harming their country.

"Well," I said, "let's go then."

All four of us went out to the car, I leading the way to ensure the coast was clear. Michael and Anne got into the front seat, and Blake climbed in behind with the small suitcase I had bought for him. He would never be a front-seat passenger this side of Moscow. I shook hands with all three of them and stood back on the pavement to try to assess how suspicious they looked. They didn't look suspicious at all. With his arm in a sling and still sporting a black eye, and with a hat on his head that Michael had brought for him, Blake did not look at all like his photographs. He could have walked up to a policeman and asked him the time. The car moved off and turned left into Oxford Gardens and headed for the centre of the town.

I went back to the room and lay on the bed, staring up at the ceiling. I had to think. This was an unexpected development. Although Blake could obviously not stay here in Highlever Road, I felt uncomfortable with him out of my sight. On the other hand it was only a matter of time—perhaps days—before Scotland Yard issued my name and photograph. As soon as they became convinced that I was the one responsible for the escape they would concentrate their efforts on searching for me. This would make Blake's new hiding place even more secure. That being the case, the sooner they became convinced of my guilt the better. It was only a matter of days anyway, so why not speed the process up a little? Yes, why not?

I jumped off the bed, put on my hat and mac, and left the flat. I walked to Latimer Road Underground station and caught a tube to Paddington. On the platform at Paddington I passed a police constable and a man in civvies who was obviously a detective. They gave me a searching look and then turned their attention to the other people leaving the train. They were looking for someone. Me? It was possible. Those prison photographs were a greater help to the fugitive than to his pursuers. I walked to the main line station and found a row of telephone booths. I put on my gloves and entered the first one. I dialled Whitehall 1212.

"New Scotland Yard," a voice said.

"I've got a message for you."

"I'm sorry," the voice said, "we're not allowed to take messages on the switchboard."

"In that case put me through to a policeman," I said.

"Which policeman?"

"Any policeman."

"One moment, please."

There was a short pause, then another voice, cooler, more self-assured, came on the line. He announced his extension number and then said, "Can I help you?"

"Are you a policeman?"

"Yes."

"Have you got a pencil and paper handy?"

"Yes."

"Very well, start writing. The getaway car . . ."

"The-get-a-way-car . . ." he repeated slowly.

". . . which took George Blake from Wormwood Scrubs Prison . . ."

There was a moment's hesitation. "The get-a-way-car . . ." the policeman repeated.

God, I thought, he's got a bloody cheek! I could just see him reaching for that other telephone as he tried to stall me. I felt angry at this insult to my intelligence.

"Now, look here," I said. "I know you're trying to trace this call but you're wasting your time. The car is parked in Harvist Road, N.W.6."

"Any identification?" the policeman asked.

"Yes," I said, "117GMX. Good night." I put the phone down and left the booth.

I caught a tube back to Latimer Road. That, I thought, apart from leading them away from Blake, should cause a great deal of confusion at Scotland Yard. They would now conclude that I had done the job with the help of the underworld and that one of the hired criminals had betrayed me in order to settle some grievance or other. Perhaps he hadn't got a fair share of the loot? And, furthermore, before there could be any loot there had to be someone who was prepared to pay for Blake's release. That could only be the Russians. Back in the room I poured myself a large whisky. I felt very pleased with myself. Yes, I thought, a good evening's work. The Special Branch were now well and truly on a fool's errand.

On Thursday the car number was announced on television and the police were quoted as saying that they were anxious to trace the owner. They did not, however, mention the owner's name, though, of course, they knew by now it was me.

On Friday, Michael phoned and said he had found a place for me to go. I packed my bag once more. That evening he and Anne called again in the same borrowed car. We drove to a house in Cromwell Road, not far from Gloucester Road Underground station.

"The owner," Michael told me on the way, "is away for the week-end. He'll be back late Sunday night. I've talked to him on the phone and he says it's all right. George will be coming to join you tomorrow night. He is very anxious, by the way, that you should be together. He's not very happy where he is at the moment."

Michael had a key to the house and we let ourselves in. We went upstairs to a spare bedroom. "There's an old lady living here too," Michael said. "She's this man's mother. She's expecting you and George but she has no idea who you are. She doesn't read and doesn't watch television. You are just friends of her son and his wife."

"Okay," I said. "So far so good."

Anne put a paper carrier bag on the floor. "Some food for you, Sean. It should keep you going until your hosts come back."

I thanked her. Michael handed me the key to the front door and then we said good night.

Next to the bedroom was a spacious, comfortable sitting-room complete with television. I went in there, turned on the electric fire, and sat back to watch television. The escape was still in the news. They were showing photographs of the car and saying that Scotland Yard knew the identity of the owner but were not yet prepared to divulge his name. He was, however, believed to be a thirty-two-year-old Irishman.

I heard footsteps on the stairs and presently the old lady came in. She was about seventy, tall and thin, dressed all in black. She had an old-fashioned air about her.

I stood up. "Good evening, madam."

"Oh, good evening," she said in a shaky but cultured voice. "Has the other person arrived yet?"

"No, madam. He'll be here tomorrow."

"I see. Very well. You know where everything is, do you?"

"Yes, I think so."

"Good. The bathroom is on the next landing. I hope you will be comfortable. Good night."

"Good night, madam."

She went out and made her way slowly down the stairs.

Next morning she invited me to join her for breakfast—coffee, bread and butter, and a couple of boiled eggs. Later I went out to buy the papers. By this time, I knew, every policeman in Britain would be carrying a photograph of me in his pocket—but it was a photograph that would not be of much use. Apart from anything else, it had been taken five years before, when I first went to Wormwood Scrubs.

On my way to the news-agent's I passed two policemen. All the papers had photographs of the car. Later in the day the evening papers were talking openly of a wanted Irishman. I walked along Cromwell Road reading my own description. It was accurate enough but quite a pointless exercise. Any one man's description will fit millions of others. When a member of the public reads a thing like that he promptly forgets it. He has other things to think about.

Blake arrived at about eight o'clock with Michael and Anne. They came into the sitting-room.

Blake extended his hand. "My friend, am I glad to see you!"

"Glad you could make it," I said.

We all sat down and chatted for a while and then I turned on the television. The escape was there again, seven days after it had happened. Two senior Special Branch officers from Scotland Yard had flown to Ireland, the announcer told us. They would visit the home of the wanted Irishman's mother in Limerick and talk to her about her son. It was believed that Blake himself might be hiding in Ireland.

"Let us hope they go on thinking that," Blake commented.

Michael stood up to go. "Well," he said, "you should both be safe here for a while." He and Anne then left.

"And where have you been all this week?" I asked Blake with a smile.

He pulled a face. "What an experience! I haven't the faintest idea where I was but I'll never forget it. My hosts were quite terrified. They locked me in a room and refused to let me out. My meals were brought to me, and I had to perform my natural functions into a bucket. They would not allow me to go to the bathroom to empty this bucket until one o'clock in the morning. And during the day they insisted that I should not only be confined to the room but that I should stay in bed! As if my walking about the room would make the neighbours suspicious!"

I laughed. "Just like solitary confinement, eh?"

"Worse than that. At least when you're in solitary you're allowed out for an hour's exercise each day. And you don't have to stay in bed."

"Have you had something to eat?" I asked.

"Oh yes, I had some supper before I left. And you? What are the arrangements here?"

"Well, I had breakfast with the old lady this morning but I had my lunch out of that carrier bag Anne brought. I expect she'll invite us both to join her for breakfast in the morning."

"I heard footsteps on the stairs and went to the door to greet the old lady.

"Oh, good evening," she said. "Has the other person arrived?"

"Yes, madam, he's already here."

She came in and said good evening to Blake. Then she invited us to join her in the kitchen for a little supper.

We followed her down the stairs to the kitchen.

"Please be seated," she said in her dowager-like manner.

We sat.

She placed a knife and fork in front of each of us and then a glass. Ah, I thought, a drop of the hard stuff. She then went to the cupboard and came back with several slices of black bread which she placed on a plate in the centre of the table. Next she went to the electric cooker and took the lid off a pot and looked in at the contents. "Hm," she said, "that looks satisfactory." She came back to the table, picked up a large wooden spoon, and proceeded to ladle the contents of the pot onto our plates. It was boiled cauliflower—just that, on its own.

I looked at Blake and he looked at me. Ah well, there are still the glasses, I thought.

"Oh, your glasses," said the old lady, as if reading my thoughts. She picked up a jug, went to the sink, and came back and filled our glasses with cold water. "I think I'll join you," she announced. She put some cauliflower on a plate for herself and sat down at the end of the table.

Blake put a forkful of the lukewarm cauliflower in his mouth and chewed it thoughtfully. He made an approving face, turned to the old lady with a smile, and said, "But how delicious!"

The old lady allowed the faintest hint of a smile to touch the corners of her mouth. She nodded benignly. "Yes, it is quite fresh," she conceded.

I was first up next morning, Sunday. Blake and I shared the room —he had the bed and I used a sleeping bag on the floor. On the way to the bathroom to have a shave I met the old lady.

"Oh, good morning," she said. "Has the other person got up yet?"

Blake was fast asleep. "Yes, madam, he's just getting dressed."

"Oh, good. If you would both care to join me in about half an hour there will be some breakfast."

I thanked her and went and had my shave. Then I woke Blake up. "Time for breakfast," I told him.

In contrast to the supper of the night before, the breakfast was quite substantial. We had plenty of bread and butter and marmalade, two boiled eggs each, and lots of coffee.

Later I wanted to go out and buy the papers, but Blake was alarmed at the idea. He pleaded with me not to leave the house.

"You don't seem to realize," he said, "that every policeman in the country is looking for you, even more than they're looking for me. The ordinary policeman doesn't regard me as being any of his business. He leaves that to the Special Branch and the Secret Service. But he regards *you* as his business. And by now they must all be carrying photographs of you."

"Very well," I said, "I won't go."

But half an hour later the old lady came into the sitting-room. "Oh, excuse me," she said. "Would you mind very much going down to the delicatessen and buying some frozen fish for Claudia?"

Blake and I exchanged a nervous glance. "Claudia?"

"My cat," said the old lady. "The poor thing is starving."

"Oh, I see. Well, of course, madam, of course."

"Thank you. You're very kind." She left the room.

I shrugged. "Well, I can't very well refuse, can I?"

"No," he admitted, "you can't."

On the way to the shop I passed a sergeant and a constable standing at a corner, chatting. I knew what to do if I was recognized. I would just lead them as far away as possible from the hideout. I took the opportunity of visiting the news-agent's. The escape was still on the front pages. Two Special Branch men from Scotland Yard had spoken to my mother. She was quoted as saying that I had been to Limerick from the tenth to the fifteenth of October and had then gone to Dublin on business. "But I can't understand it," she was quoted in one paper. "My son is a good boy. He wouldn't do a thing like that."

I gave the old lady the frozen fish for Claudia and took the papers upstairs.

Blake was peering out at Cromwell Road through a chink in the venetian blinds. He looked over his shoulder as I came in. "You know, it's rather interesting," he said.

"What is?"

"When I was with MI6 my office was in this street, not very far from where we are now."

"Very interesting indeed," I agreed. "They're probably all over there right now, scratching their heads and wondering where you are, and you're in the same bloody street."

We ate lunch and supper from the paper carrier bag. On television, during a police information programme called "Police Five" (it lasted five minutes), there was an appeal for witnesses who might be able to help the police in their inquiries into the escape. The man on the screen held up a pot of flowers and a No. 13 knitting needle and asked shopkeepers who might have sold them just before the escape to come forward. "The needles should be easy to remember," he urged. "There were twenty of them used on the rope ladder, and any shopkeeper selling such a large quantity at once to the same person would be bound to think it a little remarkable." On the news later in the evening the two Special Branch men were shown leaving a Limerick hotel.

It was eleven o'clock before our host arrived. We heard the front door open and shut and then the footsteps on the stairs. He came into the sitting-room. He was a man of about forty, tall and thin, and very flamboyantly dressed. He wore tight-fitting plaid trousers that clung precariously from very low down on his hips. The bottoms were slightly belled. At the top of the trousers, but not really supporting them, was a leather belt about four inches wide with a huge brass buckle. He wore a check shirt and a sports jacket. His hair was almost shoulder length. In his hand he held a large transistor radio.

Blake and I stood up and said good evening.

"Where's Michael?" he asked, ignoring our greeting.

I knew immediately that this sanctuary was going to be very temporary indeed. "Well, he isn't here," I said.

"I'd better phone him." He put the radio on the coffee table. On his way out he paused. "Should I use this phone?"

"I think it would be wiser not to," I said.

"I'll go use a public call box." He left the house.

I said to Blake, "I have the distinct impression that we're not altogether welcome here. I think there's been a misunderstanding, a breakdown in communications."

"You may be right," Blake said, "but let's wait and see."

Our host came back about fifteen minutes later, still frowning. "Michael's on his way," he announced.

Then a young woman came in. I judged her to be in her late twenties.

"This is my wife," our host announced. She looked as worried as her husband. "Well, while we're waiting shall we have something to eat?" he suggested. "The dear old lady has prepared a meal for us, which I think is rather gracious of her."

We all trooped down to the kitchen.

During the meal our host began to thaw out a little. We talked along general lines about the excitement of the past week without going into details of how the escape was done or what our future plans might be.

It was midnight when Michael and Anne arrived. We all gathered in the sitting-room for a conference. It soon became clear that Michael's nerve was going. There was panic in the air. Our host had not realized that he was being asked to harbour the most wanted men in Britain. Of course, he would like to help, but there were dangers. This house was not really very secure. Our host was a writer and had many visitors calling on him in connection with his work. He also employed a secretary who was in this house with him seven hours a day. She would be bound to notice that there were two grown men in the house who never seemed to go outside the door. And there were relatives who sometimes called.

"I think," I said at last, "that the problem would be halved if I went back to the other place. The rent is paid up for a month. As long as my photograph isn't published I'll be quite safe there."

"Yes, that might be the best idea," Michael agreed. He turned to Blake. "I've thought of one way out for you," he said. "You could go to the Russian Embassy."

Blake's mouth fell open. "The Russian Embassy!"

"Yes," Michael urged. "I've been doing some reconnaissance and it would be quite easy. I could drive you there in the boot of the car and say that I'm going in to apply for a visa. There's a yard round the back where you could get out of the boot without being seen by the Special Branch people, and you could then enter the Embassy by the back door. I can assure you it can be done. I've studied it closely."

Blake was quite amazed at the suggestion. "But that would be utter folly! Even if I could get in there under the noses of the Special Branch—which I don't for one moment believe—what would that solve? I would have to come out again to escape from this country. Why go and hide in a building that is being specially watched by the police and which I could not hope to leave again without being caught? I have no desire to spend the rest of my life in an Embassy. I don't want to do a Cardinal Mindszenty. I would rather go back to Wormwood Scrubs tomorrow than to do that. In prison I could lead a much more comfortable life than in an Embassy. I would have a lot more space and a lot more facilities, and, vague though it may be, some little hope of eventual release. But to go to the Russian Embassy would be tantamount to volunteering for solitary confinement for life. And remember, the Russians wouldn't thank me for it. Indeed, they might well feel obliged to hand me back to the British."

"But nobody would know you were there," Michael protested, "and later on the Russians would be able to smuggle you out."

"Don't believe it," Blake said emphatically. "Even if I could get in there, I can assure you it would be known to the British Secret Service within hours."

"I still think you should try," Michael persisted. "It may not be as bad as you say."

"Michael," Blake said decisively, "that is a counsel of despair."

We were all silent for a moment. Then Michael had another idea. "Supposing," he said, "that I were to go along to the Embassy and ask them for help? I could tell them where you are and let them take over."

"That would be extremely dangerous," Blake replied. "There would be a very strong chance that you would be followed by the Special Branch after such a visit, even if you did say that you were just inquiring about a visa."

At this point I felt obliged to intervene. "Michael, the moment you went to the Russian Embassy this whole affair would take on a completely different complexion. We would immediately become Russian agents, with all that that implies."

Michael looked at me thoughtfully. "Yes, you're right. And I certainly don't want to be branded a Soviet agent."

"Not to mention the imprisonment involved," I went on. "Fifteen years for treason instead of five years for springing a prisoner." My last remark, though necessary, only added to the tension in the room and to the feeling of panic and hopelessness.

"Well, anyway," our host said finally, "I think the most you can count on being safe in this house is three or four days."

"At least that gives us a little breathing space." Michael sighed. It was two o'clock in the morning by now. We agreed to have another conference the following night.

Next day, Monday, October 31, the House of Commons debated the motion of censure against the Home Secretary, Mr. Roy Jenkins. But Mr. Jenkins acquitted himself so well that he emerged from the debate with a greatly increased stature, both in the Commons and in the country. There were even hints that he might be the next Prime Minister. The Prime Minister himself stood up and assured the House that Blake no longer constituted a threat to Britain's security.

"Well," I remarked to Blake, "we haven't done *him* any harm, have we?"

"On the contrary." Blake laughed.

Throughout the day we could hear the faint tapping of the type-writer as our host and his secretary worked together in the study downstairs. His wife went out to buy the papers that day. From the evening papers we learned that the police had already been to my old bed-sitter in Perryn Road. This was not surprising since that address was never meant to be secret. Indeed, the prison authorities had forwarded my mail to Perryn Road. The papers had photographs of the house, with Mrs. Smith, the resident representative, standing at the door, smiling. There was a report of a ten-foot aerial having been taken away by the police. That was the aerial I had made from bamboo canes and then abandoned when I failed to contact Blake from Perryn Road.

Michael and Anne arrived just before six, and we all sat round the television to watch the news before beginning our discussions. What we saw on the news might, after all, affect our talks. The censure debate was reported, and, of course, the Government had a large majority. Then the house in Perryn Road was shown, and the camera was even taken into my old room. Mrs. Smith was questioned about me in the front garden; the interviewer was holding a microphone in front of her face.

"What was he like?" the man asked.

"Well, he kept himself very much to himself. He was really quite a nice man. He was always smartly dressed and he was very well spoken. Oh yes, very well spoken indeed. Not the sort of person you'd expect to get mixed up in anything like this. He left here and said he was going to Ireland. Later on I got a card from him."

"She thought well of you." Michael grinned.

"I think she liked him," Anne said with a smile.

The atmosphere was not nearly as tense as it had been the night before. The panic appeared to have receded. Michael said he felt confident that he could find a hideout for Blake. During the course of our discussions we drifted next door to the bedroom that Blake and I occupied. The talk was going along quite smoothly and calmly, and everybody's confidence appeared to have been mainly restored. There was a short silence, and then our host, in a supremely urbane manner, began to make a pronouncement. So cool and unconcerned was his tone that we expected nothing very startling to be said.

"So far as my wife and I are concerned," he began, "there is just one small aspect of our private lives which might, shall we say, impinge upon your position in this house. My wife is at the moment undergoing psychiatric treatment. Now it is an essential ingredient of this treatment that my wife should be completely frank with her analyst at all times, otherwise her treatment loses its value. She must be quite honest about all the various domestic pressures, and so on, which might have any bearing at all upon her state of mind and her mood." He looked from me to Blake. "This is where you two come in."

There was an awkward silence. All eyes were on our host and his wife.

"You mean," Blake began uncertainly, "that she might feel obliged to tell her—er—analyst about us?"

"Oh, but she has already done so," our host replied. The words were thrown away, a mere afterthought.

Michael and Anne were frozen to the spot. Blake's mouth fell wide open but he couldn't speak. The mistress of the house, pale and drawn, stood close to her husband, nodding her head in agreement.

Blake turned to her, a mixture of confusion and incredulity on his face. "So, your—er—your analyst—er—*knows* that we are here in this house?" he stammered.

"Well, not exactly," the woman replied. "I didn't actually give him your names. I just told him that the reason I'm nervous is because we're hiding two men who are on the run from the police, that's all."

Nobody moved, nobody breathed. Blake was staring at her, wide-eyed. "And—er—what did your—er—analyst say?"

"Oh, he just thought I was exaggerating," she said in a hurt voice. "He told me that I was being influenced by all the publicity in the papers and on television about this spy George Blake who escaped from prison. He said I'll get over it."

There was complete silence. Nobody knew what to *say*. The situation was so bizarre that if the liberty of every person in the room had not been at stake, it would have been funny.

Blake was visibly shaken. "Well," he said, striving desperately to remain calm, "in view of what you have just said I think we might now be well advised to return immediately to High"—he stopped himself just in time—"to our former address."

My own comment was mute but no less pointed. I had started packing my case even before Blake spoke. I fully expected the front door to be smashed in at any moment.

After some further discussion Blake was persuaded to remain in Cromwell Road another night and then move to his new hideout direct instead of going immediately to Highlever Road. I was relieved that nobody had been foolish enough to mention Highlever Road by name in the presence of our host's wife, since there was no reason to suppose that the lady would be any less frank with her psychoanalyst in the future than she had been in the past.

Michael and Anne went home, and then our host offered to drive me back to my former address. I was not keen on the idea but it was difficult to refuse. The fact that his wife insisted on coming along made me even more nervous. I said good-bye to Blake once more and left the house. I climbed into the back of the car with my case. The host's wife sat beside him in the front.

The host turned round. "Well, where to?" he asked.

"Ladbroke Grove Underground station," I said. "That will do me very nicely. I live next door to it."

Half an hour later they dropped me off in Ladbroke Grove. I walked the half-mile up Oxford Gardens to Highlever Road, stopping to buy a bottle of whisky on the way. In the flatlet I lit the gas fire, poured myself a drink, and sat back to relax in the armchair. I felt a lot more secure, but I also felt a little frustrated. It was not pleasant or satisfactory to be entirely dependent on other people. Michael, Anne, and Pat were excellent people, daily risking their liberty for our sakes, but that did not make it any easier to have to depend on them for every penny. I would have much preferred to have had sufficient funds to remain on my own, independent, free to make my own decisions. But, on the other hand, no amount of money could buy the practical help that these people were giving. You could buy the services of professional criminals and put yourself in the hands of ruthless people who would not hesitate to sell you to the highest bidder, but you could not buy people like Michael, Anne, and Pat. That was the essential difference. With these people you could feel safe, for you knew that they were on your side only because they wanted to be, only because they agreed with your cause.

I spent that week quietly in the flatlet, going out daily to do my shopping and to buy the papers. On Wednesday morning when the landlady and her assistant came to do the cleaning I had a foolscap sheet of paper in my typewriter and was banging away furiously at the keys. This was designed to support the pose of journalist. I started the typing the moment they entered the house and continued while they cleaned all the other bed-sitters. In all, I was typing non-stop for about two hours. (Later in Moscow I was to read a newspaper report in which the landlady was quoted as saying of her former tenant that he was "always at his typewriter.")

On Thursday, Michael phoned and we arranged to meet outside Great Portland Street Underground station. We walked along Albany Street, by the side of Regent's Park, as we talked. He told me that Blake was now installed in a very safe hideout—in Pat Porter's flat. We agreed that I should move there on Monday, which also happened to be Blake's birthday. We would have a party. Everybody was now much more relaxed, and the future once more looked bright.

13

Two Exits from Britain

On Monday afternoon, November 7, I arrived in Hampstead with a 🏴🏴
suitcase. I had not given up the Highlever Road flatlet. That would 🏴🏴
be retained for emergencies. In fact, I had left some of my luggage
there, as well as the typewriter and the television set. The rent could
be posted on as it fell due. I walked from the Underground station to
Pat's flat. Michael had told me the signal that had been agreed upon. I
pressed the doorbell twice in quick succession, paused for a couple of
seconds, and pressed it twice more.

Blake let me in. "Hello there," he said, "hello." He was smiling
broadly, a lot happier than when I last saw him.

"Where's Pat?" I asked.

"He's at work," Blake said. "He won't be home until about five."

"Oh, of course. Well, many happy returns on your birthday."

"Thank you."

Pat arrived just after five laden with provisions, and Michael and
Anne rang the doorbell at seven o'clock. We had a very pleasant
dinner party with plenty of wine. By the time we reached the dessert
course we had moved on from reliving the exciting adventures of the
past fortnight to a discussion on human motivation. The wine flowed
freely and inhibitions melted away. *Why had we done it?* We all
agreed on the obvious answer. We had been anxious to rescue a man
from what we believed to be a cruel and unjust prison sentence. But
that, of course, was not the whole answer. Human motivation was not
as simple as that. Human beings were complex animals. We all had

our deep-rooted, private motives for everything we did, and these motives were often wholly unrelated to our outward actions. Though we might sometimes strive to display our honesty by admitting to such motives, we were never wholly frank about their true nature. They remained buried, jealously guarded secrets, and in discussing them we rarely did more than touch the surface. Which was how it had to be. If everybody could look into everybody else's soul, life would be impossible, society as we know it could not exist. Of course, many of us knew, or believed we knew, the true motivation of others, but to discuss it openly would be disastrous.

"But I think we would all agree that there is no such thing as absolute purity of motive," Michael suggested. "In this particular case, for instance, we cannot isolate our indignation at George's harsh sentence and say that that is why we did what we did. We must first ask ourselves *why* we are indignant. After all, not *everybody* is indignant. Why should *we* be? Because we are the sort of people we are. And why are we so? Well, then we've got to start considering our whole lives, all our past experiences, our private fears and hopes. In the end it becomes too deep, the exercise is hardly worth while."

"I agree with you entirely," Blake said, "because it doesn't end just with ourselves. What is it that has given rise to our various hopes and fears, our attitudes and inhibitions, our relationships with other people? And why did these people affect us in a particular way? Because of *their* relationships with other people still. And so it goes on *ad infinitum*. It is quite true that no human being is an island. We are influenced by people and events, and in turn we influence people and events without being even remotely aware of it. Everything we do and say and think is part of the totality. It is an indisputable fact, for instance, that if the Archduke Ferdinand had not been shot I would not have been born."

"This is all very acceptable," I said, "but the fact remains that our immediate passions and prejudices are still individually identifiable."

"Very well then," said Pat. "Accepting that we all wanted to help George, here, what was *your* private motive for throwing that rope ladder over the prison wall?"

I drained my glass. "That's very simple. I hate policemen. I despise policemen with every fibre of my being. In my eyes, policemen are vermin, the garbage of human society. The fact that they're necessary doesn't make them any less verminous. Believe me, when George, here, asked me to spring him, *he* was doing *me* a favour. I was delighted with the opportunity of striking a blow against those dirty bastards."

"And what is your attitude to the shooting of those three policemen in Braybrook Street?" Michael asked.

"I have no sympathy for policemen, dead or alive. And all that phony emotionalism worked up by the popular press makes me sick. There are more ordinary, decent, harmless citizens slaughtered on the roads in Britain in one day than there are policemen killed on duty in a century. *Three heroic policemen!* As if they would have gone near that other car if they had known that the people in it were armed! They were actually running away when they were shot. Not that I blame them for that. If somebody was pointing a gun at me I'd run away too. But I'll bet you the papers wouldn't call me a hero."

"What I don't like," said Pat, "is their habit of framing people. That's diabolical."

"And that wholesale framing racket that was exposed at West End Central was only the tip of the iceberg," Michael added.

Michael and Anne left at eleven. Since there were three bedrooms in Pat's flat I at last could have a room to myself instead of having to share with Blake.

Our weeks in Hampstead were uneventful. Pat was out at work daily from nine to five, and when he came home in the evening he would be laden with provisions for the one big meal we had each day. I was usually up before Blake in the mornings and I would take him a mug of tea. "But how extremely kind of you," he would say, struggling to a sitting position.

The first half-hour of each day we devoted to physical training. Blake, being something of an enthusiast, acted as instructor. We considered this training very necessary because of our otherwise inactive way of life.

One day while doing these exercises I got an abrupt insight into a side of Blake's character that I had never known before. I was sitting on the floor with my legs stretched straight out in front of me and close together. I had to lean forward, grasp my ankles, and force my head down to touch my knees without bending them. I was having a little difficulty doing this at first. "Let me help you," said Blake. He stood behind me, placed his hands on my neck and his knee in my back and started to force my head and shoulders down.

Then he seemed to lose control of himself. "Get down, get down, get down!" he muttered through clenched teeth. His knee dug painfully into my back, and he forced me viciously downwards till my head touched my knees, and he kept me in that position for several seconds. "Get down, get down, get down!" he repeated, and his tension transmitted itself to me through his fingers as they dug like claws into my neck. Suddenly he let go and stood back.

I looked up at him in surprise. He was flushed and excited. Then he started to laugh. But it was a forced, nervous laugh, and I felt sure that even he must realize that he had gone too far and given something away. There was only one word to describe what he had just done: ruthless.

For the first week I remained confined to the flat but after that I went out regularly on shopping expeditions or to take our washing to the launderette in Hampstead High Street. To get to the launderette I had to pass the police station, and I would often pause to read the WANTED notices on the board outside. I was constantly passing policemen on the pavement. They didn't recognize me because they were not looking for me. No policeman expects a wanted man to walk brazenly past him in the street.

The appointment of the Mountbatten Inquiry started off a spate of escapes up and down the country, and this provided Blake and me with considerable entertainment as we read the papers and watched television. There appeared to be a fear among the inmates of Britain's jails that if they did not escape now it would be impossible later on. Another source of entertainment was the constant stream of "experts" who appeared on television to give their theories on the escape of the master spy George Blake. People always prefer a complicated answer to a simple one. It is much more interesting. And the television theorists were no exceptions. One man said that I had done it with the help of the IRA and that both Blake and I were now hiding in Ireland with the help of that organization. And why had the IRA done it? It was not that they were pro-Communist but that they were anti-British.

But the most interesting theory was put forward by some foreign journalist with a heavy Central European accent. According to him, the whole thing had been planned like a military operation under the direction of the KGB. Blake had left Britain on the night of the escape and made his way across Europe by plane, helicopter, and car with an escort of Czech secret agents. Diagrams of the route were shown, and the hotels where Blake was supposed to have stayed were named. Where had this journalist got his information? Eastern European sources, which, for obvious reasons, could not be named. Blake and I considered the possibility that the KGB had leaked this false story in order to put the British off their guard and so make it easier for Blake to get to Russia. (In Moscow we later discovered that this was not so.)

In the second week of our stay I acquired a false passport for myself in case it should be needed. This was not difficult. I had the photographs taken quite openly in a studio in Hampstead, giving my name as Kennedy. I then went to a pub just off Tottenham Court Road and made contact with a man whom I had met through a fellow hosteller before my discharge from prison. I had the passport within twenty-four hours, made out in the name of James Richardson, British subject, architect, of Oxford Gardens, London, W.10.

Blake examined the passport with interest. "Speaking as a former British vice-consul, one of whose tasks it was to issue these things, I can assure you it is an excellent job."

We had a number of callers from time to time while Pat was out at work and we never hesitated to answer the door. But we always took some precaution. Blake would go into his room and lock the door on the inside. He would have the window wide open in readiness to make a dash across the back garden to the next street. We realized, of course, that if the Special Branch suspected this flat the whole area would be sealed off and there would be little chance of escape, but we felt that we should do something.

On Saturdays the milkman would have to be paid, and now and then a neighbour would ring the bell and inquire about something. As Christmas approached, the carol singers started to call. When the doorbell rang we would take all the necessary dramatic precautions, and when Blake was securely locked in his room I would cautiously open the front door to find a five-year-old looking up at me with angelic innocence as he sang "Oh, Come All Ye Faithful."

But one day we had a visitor who was not so innocent. He was an official from the company that owned the flats. He showed me his card.

I had to invite him in. He had come to inspect. While he was in the kitchen I tapped on Blake's door. A bedroom door locked on the inside might look suspicious. I told Blake in a whisper who the man was. "Just keep your back turned and be making your bed," I suggested. And this is what he did. The man came out of the kitchen and looked around the sitting-room. He glanced in at Blake, who was bending down over the bed tucking in the blankets, his back to us.

"Well, everything seems all right. If you have any complaints, please get in touch with me."

"Yes, I'll do that," I told him. I showed him to the door and watched him walk down the long path to the street.

Blake was a little anxious. "I wonder if he really is what he says he is?"

"Well, he showed me his card," I reminded him.

"That means nothing," Blake said authoritatively. "The Special Branch have a wide selection of such cards. They can pose as anything from the borough architect to the gas-meter man. I ought to know."

"Yes, indeed you ought," I agreed. But we need not have worried. The man really had been what he claimed to be.

On another occasion a police constable walked up the path and disappeared through the front door of our block of flats. But, though Blake and I both saw him coming, neither of us was very worried. "We have nothing to fear from a single policeman in uniform," I said. "If Scotland Yard had the slightest suspicion that we were here, this place would be invaded from all directions by a couple of hundred plainclothes men with guns. We wouldn't have a chance."

Blake nodded his agreement.

I kept my vigil at the window, and presently the constable emerged through the front door and walked down the path. "That fellow will never know how close he came today to being a sergeant."

Every three or four days Michael and Anne came for dinner. During these meals we would discuss Blake's exit from Britain. Blake had no great desire to go behind the Iron Curtain. He preferred to go to some neutral country that would be unlikely to hand him back to the British. Egypt was his favourite choice. He offered no explanation for this, but I suspected that he felt unsure of the sort of reception that might be awaiting him in Russia. The spying game was a treacherous business in which no one could ever be sure who his friends were. However, in view of our extremely limited funds, it soon became clear to all of us that Blake would have no choice but to cross into Eastern Europe at the nearest possible point. Germany seemed to be the obvious choice, especially as Blake happened to be fluent in that language.

The only question to be decided was method. There were two ways in which Blake could leave Britain: he could travel openly with a false passport; or he could leave the country concealed in a vehicle driven by someone else. We had long arguments about the merits and demerits of each method.

"As I see it," I said finally, "if George travels openly, no matter how well disguised, he must come face to face with immigration officials at every frontier. There is, therefore, the possibility of his being recognized. On the other hand, if he travels in a hidden compartment in a vehicle of some kind, he will not come face to face with anyone unless the vehicle itself comes under suspicion."

After further argument we settled for a vehicle.

The question then arose as to who should drive the vehicle. I had no objections to driving it, but Michael was quick to point out the dangers that would involve. "If you're recognized, Sean, George's discovery will be automatic, because the vehicle will be torn apart."

"But if he got away with it," Pat put in, "we would be killing two birds with one stone. They would both be escaping at the same time."

"That's true," Michael countered, "but the risk would be too great. We would be giving Scotland Yard the chance of nabbing the two most wanted men in Britain at one fell swoop. We would be handing it to them on a platter."

"But what's the alternative?" Blake asked.

Michael looked at Anne, paused for a moment, then said, "The vehicle should be driven by someone who is not being sought by the police. I'll drive it myself."

"And I'll come with you," Anne added quickly. "That will make you look even more respectable."

"Well, that's extremely generous of you both," Blake said. "You are taking an enormous risk."

Michael shrugged. "It's the only way it can be done."

Within two weeks Michael had bought a second-hand Dormobile, which was fitted with a small kitchen unit and a bed. The bed consisted of a wooden flap hinged to the top of a drawer unit about two feet high and containing one big drawer. The drawer measured about five and a half feet in length by about thirty inches in width and was designed to be used for storing blankets and linen. We cut off the back half of the drawer, reducing it to fifteen inches in width, and replaced the back board. With the modified drawer pushed fully in there was now a cavity at the back just barely large enough to hold Blake in a cramped position. On the floor of the cavity we placed a sheet of foam rubber to make Blake's journey a little less uncomfortable.

We settled on Saturday, December 17, 1966, as the date for Blake's departure. Michael and Anne drove up in the Dormobile at six o'clock that evening. Pat had spent a couple of hours preparing a very tasty dinner of fish baked in thinly sliced potatoes and milk. Michael, Anne, and Blake himself drank very little wine, but Pat and I helped ourselves liberally. The atmosphere was one of controlled nervousness. We had agreed that the van should make the crossing from Dover to Ostend, travel across Belgium and West Germany to the East German border, and then join the Autobahn leading to Berlin. Blake was to be dropped off just outside Berlin on East German territory, and Michael and Anne were to continue into the city. They would stay there a day and then travel back to England over the same route.

My own eventual departure had also been discussed during the past few weeks. I had argued in favour of going to Ireland and fighting extradition on the grounds that by helping Blake escape I had committed a political offence, in the same way as if I had aided the escape of a member of the IRA. My friends, however, were alarmed at this suggestion and argued that as Blake was a Communist who had spied for Russia against Britain, I could not expect a sympathetic hearing in a Catholic Ireland that was economically dependent on Great Britain. Reluctantly, I had agreed that I too would go to Eastern Europe, but only for a short while. I had no intention of staying there.

"So you will definitely be following me to East Germany?" Blake asked after a while.

"Yes, I will," I said.

"Can we settle on a definite date so that I can tell them you're coming and they can be waiting for you?"

I pulled a piece of paper out of my pocket and looked at the notes I had made. "Yes," I said, sipping the red wine, "I shall leave here in exactly two weeks, on Saturday, the thirty-first, New Year's Eve. I shall board the London-Paris train at Victoria Station at eight-thirty in the evening. The train leaves at nine o'clock and arrives at the Gare du Nord in Paris at eight o'clock the following morning, New Year's Day. I shall go straight to Orly Airport and catch a plane to West Berlin. I shall spend one night in West Berlin and cross over into East Berlin through Checkpoint Charlie at ten o'clock on Monday morning, the second of January."

Blake leaned back and smiled. "Well, that sounds easy enough. Provided you've got a good passport, you should have no difficulty. I know from my own experience that crossing from West Berlin to East Berlin is not a problem. In fact, any person holding the passport of any of the occupying nations is entitled to move freely between the two Berlins. Any Briton, Frenchman, or American is legally entitled to cross into East Berlin at any time. That's the Potsdam Agreement."

"And any Russian can cross into West Berlin?" Michael asked.

"Quite so." Blake nodded.

Anne looked at her watch. "Ten to eight," she announced. "The ferry sails at midnight and we have to be on board by eleven."

"That's right," Michael agreed. "We'd better get moving."

Pat filled all our glasses with wine and then raised his own. "Well," he said, without smiling, "to a successful trip."

We all stood up and touched glasses. "To a successful trip," we chorused.

Michael produced a small brown parcel, unwrapped the paper, and held up a rubber hot-water bottle. "You will be hidden in that compartment a long time," he said to Blake, "from here to Dover and certainly all the way across in the ferry to Ostend. Nine or ten hours in all. Just in case nature should make an untimely demand, it will be useful to have this." He unscrewed the cork and inserted his forefinger into the hole. "I hope it's the right size."

Anne laughed, and Blake blushed.

We went into the street. The van was parked about twenty yards away. It was quite dark and there was nobody about. Michael and Anne got into the back of the van with Blake. I shut the doors firmly behind them, then climbed into the driver's seat to keep an eye on the street ahead, while Pat stood on the pavement to keep watch in the other direction. I glanced over my shoulder. Michael lifted up the hinged flap that formed the bed platform, and Blake climbed into the cavity behind the drawer with his hot-water bottle. He sat upright on the foam-rubber sheet. Pat got into the seat beside me and reached into the back of the van. Blake stretched out his arm and they shook hands.

"Good-bye, George," Pat said solemnly. "I hope we meet again."

"I hope so," Blake replied, "and I feel sure we will. Thank you for everything, Pat."

"You're welcome," Pat said.

Then I shook hands with Blake, leaning back over the driver's seat. "*Au revoir*," he said simply.

"*Au revoir*," I said. "See you in a fortnight."

Blake looked around at all four of us in turn, taking one last long look at our unsmiling faces, an anxious expression on his own, then very slowly—reluctantly, it seemed—he lowered himself into a lying position in the coffinlike compartment. Michael closed the flap and Anne spread a mattress over it and made up the bed with sheets and blankets and a pillow. It looked the picture of innocence. We were silent for a moment, thinking about the significance of Blake's hesitation. Michael and Anne would be travelling in the passenger lounge of the ferry, while the van with its precious cargo would be down in the depths of the hold with all the other vehicles. If anything went wrong, this tiny space in which Blake now lay might indeed become his coffin in a watery grave.

We said good-bye, Michael got in behind the wheel, and Anne sat beside him. Then the van started up and moved slowly down the street, disappearing out of sight round a corner, on its way to Dover.

I set the alarm clock for seven o'clock next morning, Sunday. "There's a news bulletin at eight," I told Pat. "If they're caught at Dover it'll be on that news." We were both up at seven, and at eight we were huddled anxiously over the small transistor radio. But there was no mention of Blake.

"Phew! So far so good." Pat heaved a sigh of relief.

"So far so good. At least they've got past Dover." I looked at my watch. "They're in Ostend by now, and if they've been caught there we should know by about midday."

We listened to every news bulletin throughout the day, but Blake was not mentioned. After the six o'clock news Pat allowed himself a faint smile, the first time either of us had smiled that day.

"We can now take it, Sean, that they got through Ostend without trouble."

"We can. And if there's nothing on the nine o'clock television news it will mean that they're safely into West Germany and well on their way to the East German border."

On the nine o'clock television news there was no mention of Blake.

"What time are they due to cross into East Germany?" I asked.

Pat looked at his watch. "About an hour from now."

"The last frontier, eh?" I smiled grimly.

"Yes." Pat nodded.

"And we won't know if they've succeeded before tomorrow."

"That's right. The eight o'clock news in the morning, at the earliest."

Again I set the alarm clock for seven, and at eight we were once more crouched over the radio. Blake's name was not mentioned.

"Looks like they've made it," Pat said, turning off the radio.

I thought for a moment. "Maybe."

"What do you mean, *maybe*? They were due to cross into East Germany at ten o'clock last night. If they'd been caught the BBC would know by now."

"Unless," I said, "Scotland Yard deliberately held back the news for a few hours to give them a better chance of checking on Michael's friends."

Pat left for work half an hour later.

All that Monday, I listened in to every news broadcast, and there was still no mention of Blake. At six o'clock that evening Pat came bounding in from work and threw the shopping bag into an armchair. "They've made it, Sean! They've actually bloody made it! Michael phoned this afternoon from West Berlin."

"Jesus, that's great!" All the worry and anxiety of the past few days, the past few months, drained out of me.

"They're staying in Berlin until Wednesday in order not to look suspicious. They'll be back in London on Thursday evening." He produced a bottle of whisky from his shopping bag and filled two large glasses. "To a great success!"

"To a great success," I said, "and to Michael and Anne."

"To Michael and Anne."

"You know, Pat, Michael and Anne are a tremendous asset. They look so honest and respectable because they *are* honest and respectable. Nobody would dream of suspecting them. You couldn't buy a cover like that for any price. That's the great thing about them, they are so obviously the sort of people that cannot be bought. That's why they were not suspected, that's why they got through."

On Friday morning Michael phoned Pat at work and told him that they had got back the night before. It was now two days before Christmas, and as they were going down the country to spend Christmas Eve and Christmas Day with friends, they would not be able to see us until Boxing Day.

Pat and I spent Christmas Day quietly in the flat. We ate too much turkey and Christmas pudding and afterwards could do nothing but sleep.

Michael and Anne called on Boxing Day. They were still very excited about their trip and relived the whole thing in detail for Pat and me. It had gone without a hitch. Blake didn't have to remain in his cramped hiding place for the entire journey. He went in there about half an hour before each frontier and emerged again half an hour later. "The real ordeal for him," Michael explained with a shudder, "was the first leg of the journey, from here to Ostend. He got into his hiding place, as you know, here in this street at eight o'clock on Saturday night. The ferry was a couple of hours late in leaving, and when we got to Ostend there was another hour's delay before we were able to drive the van off. Then we decided to wait until we were well clear of the city before letting George get out, and this took another hour. In the end he didn't emerge until nine o'clock on Sunday morning. He had spent thirteen whole hours in that tiny space."

Anne gave a little shudder. "God! We thought when we lifted that flap that we were going to find a dead body. We felt sure George must have suffocated. God, it was an ordeal!" She shook her head to rid herself of the memory.

"And no trouble with any of the frontier guards or customs people?" I asked.

"None at all," Michael said. "It was amazing. Just a brief glance at our passports and we were waved on. The van was not inspected once. It was never even opened. We could have had half-a-dozen spies in there."

"But what about the East Germans?" Pat asked.

"Even they didn't look in the van. We thought they were bound to, and it didn't worry us because we were then in effect behind the Iron Curtain. But they didn't look. We drove on and dropped George off on the Autobahn about a mile from an East German guard post just outside Berlin. George told us that he would give us time to reach the city before giving himself up to the East Germans. We drove into Berlin, stayed a couple of days, and then came back. And the interesting thing is that even when we were leaving East Germany the van wasn't searched."

Preparations for my own departure began immediately. I booked a private first-class sleeping compartment on the London-Paris train for New Year's Eve. Then I went to the Air France office in New Bond Street and booked a seat on a Paris-Berlin flight for Sunday. All was now ready. If I could get safely to East Berlin and stay out of Britain for a few months, it would give Michael and Pat plenty of time to cover their tracks.

There was to be one more problem before my departure. During these past weeks I had sent off the rent for Highlever Road regularly each week, explaining in brief notes to the landlady that I was presently involved in a kind of roving commission for a newspaper. The letters, of course, were not posted in Hampstead.

On the Thursday, Pat announced that he intended going back to Highlever Road a few days after my departure to collect the items of property I had left behind. This greatly alarmed me. There was every possibility that the police had stumbled on the Highlever Road flatlet. The fact that no announcement had been made was only to be expected. With the rent being posted off each week the police would naturally just lie in wait for me to return. They would be extremely stupid to do otherwise. I tried for hours to reason with Pat along these lines but it was no use. I couldn't understand why he was so determined to go back there. After all, there was nothing there worth salvaging. A typewriter, a couple of two-way radios that none of us would ever need again, and a few books—nothing worth risking one's liberty for. And it would not end with Pat's arrest. The police would very quickly establish who Pat's friends were, and Michael and Anne would finish up in jail with him. He would be risking at least three people's liberty. But Pat could not be swayed. He had made up his mind.

I remembered that he had once said that he wouldn't mind having the opportunity of standing in the dock at the Old Bailey and telling the authorities exactly what he thought of them for sending a man to jail for forty-two years. It was this apparent indifference of Pat's to arrest and imprisonment that worried me. It was a dangerous flaw in his make-up. If Pat was determined to go back to Highlever Road, I was equally determined that he should not. And I could be every bit as stubborn as Pat.

On Friday morning I put one of my spare passport photographs into an envelope and walked slowly down Hampstead High Street. In Willoughby Road I saw a couple of young boys playing soccer with a large rubber ball. The older of the two was about thirteen. In what I hoped approximated a Central European accent I asked the older boy if he would be kind enough to help a foreigner "who is not knowink vary match about der English." The boy said he would be glad to help. I unscrewed the top of my fountain pen and handed it to him. Then I took the envelope out of my pocket, removed the photograph, and placed it face down on my wallet. I dictated to the boy what I wanted him to write on the back of the photograph. "Bourke. 28 Highlever Road, W.10." I then got him to address the envelope. I thanked the boy, gave him and his companion two shillings each, and walked back to Hampstead High Street. As I made my way up the street I put on my gloves and with the aid of a handkerchief thoroughly wiped both the envelope and the photograph to remove all traces of fingerprints. At the post office I put the photograph back in the envelope, sealed the envelope, stamped it and dropped it in the letterbox.

I went back to the flat and made myself a cup of coffee. The decision was now effectively out of Pat's hands. Whatever doubt there had been about it before, the Special Branch would now certainly be invading Highlever Road within twenty-four hours. There was always the possibility that Pat would not believe this, or would not want to believe it, and the police for their part might keep their discovery a closely guarded secret for as long as possible in the hope that I would return. As time went on and no announcement was made about Highlever Road, Pat might once more start insisting that he should go back there. But I had taken care of that too. Instead of sending the message direct to Scotland Yard I had sent it to a newspaper in Fleet Street. The police would therefore be under constant pressure to allow the story to be printed. Once this happened, Pat would have no more argument. As for Highlever Road itself, it could incriminate only me. All the evidence there pointed to my involvement, and to mine alone. I had insisted that the others all wear gloves when they visited the flatlet. And as a final precaution I had thoroughly wiped the flatlet before leaving.

We had another farewell dinner on Saturday evening, the second one in two weeks, and this time it was for me. Again the wine flowed freely, and we were all in high spirits. The end of the adventure was in sight. Despite our happy mood we found ourselves talking about the consequences of failure. I assured them that if I should be arrested tonight they would have nothing to fear. The police would never get any information out of me. None of them doubted my determination to keep silent, but Michael and Pat expressed the fear that I might have no choice in the matter.

"You will certainly be beaten up," Michael said. "They're very angry over all this. They've been made to look like fools. There are probably people's reputations at stake in this case."

"Not to mention the political pressure," Pat added.

"Well, gentlemen," I said, "whatever happens tonight we will have won. Blake is free, beyond their reach forever. They can't take that away from us."

"Yes," Anne agreed, "they can't take that away from us."

Michael sipped his wine thoughtfully. He looked across at me. "I wonder what's happened to Blake."

"What do you mean?" I asked.

"Well, I wonder what sort of a reception he's had behind the Iron Curtain."

"He might have been liquidated for all we know," Anne said.

There was a brief, awkward silence, then she tried to laugh off her remark. The rest of us laughed nervously with her. She had, in fact, voiced a fear that had been nagging all of us, but none of us was eager to talk about it. The subject was not pursued.

We drove to Victoria Station in the Dormobile that had taken Blake across Europe to East Germany. Michael drove, and Anne and Pat sat with him up front. I sat on the bed in the back of the van.

We arrived at the station at seven-thirty and went straight to the Golden Arrow Bar. The latest time for boarding the train was eighty-thirty, so we had an hour to spare. We got a table to ourselves in a corner, and I ordered three double whiskies and a gin for Anne. By eight o'clock we had had three rounds of drinks, and this, together with all the wine we had consumed at the flat, made us quite drunk.

"You know, Sean," Anne said, "the only trouble with this adventure is that from now on life is going to seem so terribly dull. I mean, how can anything in the future compete with all this?"

"How indeed?" Michael agreed.

We ordered another round of drinks. "You'll be quite drunk going through the barrier," Pat cautioned.

"That's the whole idea," I told him. "If I am to be arrested in half an hour's time I might as well have a good booze-up now. I won't get another chance for a long time."

" 'Tis true for you, faith," Michael agreed, putting on a broad Irish accent. He often did this to remind us that his mother was Irish.

"Well, now, Michael," I said, adopting an equally thick brogue, "I think an occasion like this calls for a song. And what better song to sing in an English bar than the Irish national anthem itself. Do you know it at all, Michael?"

Michael squinted at me over his glass. "Is it codden me you are, Sean? Aren't I after tellen you that me mother is Irish? And sure why should we sing 'The Soldiers' Song' in English at all when we've got the Gaelic?"

"All right so, Michael. One, two, three, four . . ." And so the two of us sang the Irish national anthem in Irish.

"What an extraordinary spectacle!" Anne observed with a smile. "An Irishman and an Englishman singing the Irish national anthem in Irish in a crowded English bar in the heart of London by way of celebrating their rescue of a Communist spy from an English jail and his safe delivery behind the Iron Curtain."

"Nobody would ever believe it," Pat said, laughing.

I thought of the Special Branch men who at this moment were sitting in the dark in my old room at Highlever Road quietly waiting for me to walk in the door, and all the other Special Branch men scattered about the neighbouring streets in Q-cars equipped with high-powered radios. And all on a tip-off given to them by me. They would, of course, assume that this tip-off, like the anonymous telephone call, was an act of spite or revenge by an accomplice in the crime. The young boy's scrawly handwriting would lend weight to this belief. Many adult criminals wrote in a scrawl, as I had discovered during my two years' editorship of the prison magazine. And the police would know that I was not the writer since they would be able to find plenty of specimens of my handwriting at Wormwood Scrubs. The poor bastards might be sitting there for weeks, I mused.

I raised my glass. "Ladies and gentlemen, I give you a toast," I announced. "To Scotland Yard."

"Hear, hear," said Michael.

It was time to go. We made our way towards the platform. The barrier was out of sight in the narrow wooden shed that was built against the railing to house the immigration and customs officials. There was only one entrance to the shed, at the near end. We stopped about twenty yards from this to say good-bye.

"Phone me from Paris tomorrow, Sean," Michael said. "I'll be standing by the phone waiting for your call."

"I'll do that." I shook hands with him. "Good-bye, Michael, and thanks for everything. We'll all have a reunion one of these days."

I shook hands with Pat. "Thank you, Pat, for all those risks you took. Good-bye."

I shook Anne by the hand and then we kissed. "Good-bye, Anne. You were a lovely girl to work with." I looked from Michael, to Anne, to Pat. "If you would like to be sure about my getting through this first obstacle, wait here until the train leaves. If you don't see me being escorted back out of that shed between a couple of plainclothes men, you'll know I've made it."

"We'll wait," Michael said.

I walked across to the shed and went in the door. A few yards along on the left a tall, thin man sat behind a high, narrow desk. I was about to pass him.

"Excuse me, sir. Could I see your passport, please?"

"Oh yes, of course," I mumbled absent-mindedly. I fumbled in my inside pocket, took the false passport out, and handed it to him. He went through it slowly, examining every page. The photograph seemed to interest him least of all.

"Thank you," he said, closing the passport and handing it back to me.

A little farther along was a low counter with three customs men standing behind it. I put my suitcase down.

"Anything to declare, sir?" the first one asked me.

"Nothing at all. A couple of shirts, a pair of socks, and a toothbrush." I started to unzip the case.

"Oh, that's all right, sir," the man said. "How much money are you carrying with you?"

"Just the bare fifty pounds." I reached for my wallet but again he told me not to bother.

"That's all, sir."

I went through the barrier. I felt sure that all customs officers were trained psychologists. Otherwise how could they be so sure of themselves? They were more interested in your face than in your luggage. But that immigration man surprised me. As a matter of routine he would have a photograph of me in his desk. And that was not the only cause for anxiety. During the previous week there had been a story in the papers to the effect that the Special Branch had stepped up their war against the false passport racketeers. Special watch was being kept for the forgeries. I had just beaten them on two counts.

I found my private compartment and lay down on the bed to relax. The steward came in after a few minutes. He told me that he would have to take my passport so that it could be shown to the French immigration officials while I slept. He also gave me a form to fill in—on which, among other things, I had to give a specimen of my signature to be compared with the signature on the passport. I filled in the form and gave it to him with the passport.

"Thank you, sir," he said and left.

I had breakfast on the train at eight o'clock the following morning and at nine I was in Paris. I spent a couple of hours sightseeing and then sought a taxi to Orly Airport. There was a policeman controlling the taxi queue. "Monsieur," he said, and with an elaborate gesture invited me to climb into the vehicle. I found myself wondering how many students' heads this bowing policeman had smashed open with his truncheon in his less polite moments. It gave me a feeling of satisfaction that he was bowing to a fugitive.

At the airport I went up to the exchange counter to convert my francs to German marks. There was a brash American in front of me.

"Here, why didn't that other guy want to change my money?" he asked in a loud voice, nodding at the clerk sitting quietly at the next position.

"Well, I'm afraid he doesn't speak English, sir," the man told him apologetically.

"He doesn't speak English! Why, hell, he *should* speak English, goddammit. This is an international airport, isn't it? I could understand it if it was some hick town."

"Sorry, sir," the man said and changed his money.

I found an empty phone booth and put through a call to Michael. He answered the phone himself. "Well, Michael, so far so good."

"Great, my friend, great!"

"I now have something very important to tell you, so listen carefully."

"Yes, go ahead."

"I have been in contact with my former address. I phoned the landlady. The police are there, awaiting my return. For God's sake, make sure that our friend does not go back there. If he does you will all finish up inside. The responsibility is yours."

"Very well, leave that to me."

"Well, good-bye, Michael. I'll get in touch with you as soon as I possibly can."

"I look forward to hearing from you. Good-bye."

The plane took off at two o'clock, and I was in Berlin shortly after five. There had been a half-hour stop at Frankfurt. Both at Orly and at Frankfurt the passport officials had merely glanced at my passport.

I climbed into a taxi at the Berlin airport and told the driver to take me to the Zoo Hotel on the Kurfürstendamm. The porter at the hotel spoke English, and I started to question him in a very casual way about the procedure for crossing over into the eastern sector. I pretended to be a tourist anxious to see as much as I could while in Germany.

"Oh well, being British, you can cross over whenever you like," he told me. "I, as a West German cannot, but you can." He then gave me directions on how to get to Checkpoint Charlie.

"You call it Checkpoint Charlie too, do you?" I asked, surprised.

"Oh yes," he said with a grin. "It has become part of our language."

I had dinner on the glass-enclosed veranda of the hotel and watched the citizens go by as I went leisurely through a large bottle of red wine. A few tables away from me an American was telling another man that his cousin back home was a "real live cowboy—yeah, the genuine article."

Later I made my way towards Checkpoint Charlie. Berlin was bitterly cold and my mac was proving inadequate. Everybody else seemed to be dressed in a heavy overcoat and fur hat. I stood about fifty yards from the checkpoint and watched. The area was brightly illuminated. Two American soldiers stood on the Western side, well away from the actual dividing line. They had no sentry boxes or huts of any kind. I watched for a quarter of an hour, and during that time one car and two pedestrians crossed over to the East. I was interested to see that the Americans made no attempt to check these people's papers. On the Eastern side, on the other hand, there was a long hut at which everybody had to stop and just before it a sentry box.

This, then, was it. The frontier of the world. The biggest decision of my life was now facing me. The fun and games were over. This was a matter of life and death. What had happened to Blake? Had he been liquidated? If he had, then my death was a foregone conclusion if I crossed that line. Just a few yards' walk. A few yards of concrete, and across it two halves of mankind faced each other in enmity. There was still time to turn back. A prison sentence in England was preferable to death from a KGB bullet. All the rules of logic demanded that I should not take the risk. And yet . . . That frontier held a strange, compelling fascination for me.

I turned away and started to walk slowly back to the hotel. But even as I walked I already knew that I would cross that line tomorrow.

14

Berlin

I booked out of the hotel and walked slowly down the Kurfürstendamm. It was nine o'clock on Monday morning, January 2, 1967. I
had told Blake that I would be crossing at ten. I did some window-
shopping for half an hour and then got into a taxi.

"Checkpoint Charlie," I said.

The driver started up and moved off without a word. Twenty minutes later we were at the checkpoint. The driver took the car right up
to the line, passing the two American sentries on the way. I paid him
off in the car, giving him what amounted to double fare. Money was
now of no value. I got out, and the taxi did a quick u-turn and sped
back into West Berlin.

I threw a quick glance at the two Americans, one on either side of
the road about twenty yards away. They didn't even look in my direction. They seemed more interested in keeping warm in the biting Berlin cold. Even if they had wanted to stop me they couldn't. I was one
step from the Iron Curtain. I looked down at the concrete roadway,
hesitated a moment, and then walked into East Berlin.

A few yards farther on two soldiers with machine guns slung over
their shoulders were sheltering in a sentry box to the right. "Passport,"
they demanded. I handed over my passport and they both scrutinized
it carefully. They apparently spoke no English, for the one who
handed the passport back to me just pointed towards a long, narrow
hut about ten yards farther on and also to the right.

I entered the hut through a door at the near end. This door led into a corridor that extended the full length of the building to an exit door at the far end. Immediately inside the entry door, and facing it, was a glass-fronted office in which stood a Russian Army officer. He went through my passport as carefully as the two sentries had done and then handed me an entry visa on a separate piece of paper.

A few yards farther along there was a low counter behind which stood two East German border guards with revolvers on their hips. They too went through my passport with great care.

Finally, down at the end of the corridor, was another glass-fronted office, where a middle-aged woman was in charge. Here I had to change three West German marks for three East German marks, by way of a sort of entry tax. She too examined my passport, and my entry visa, before changing the money. She smiled as she handed me back the passport, and I felt a little twinge of gratitude, for it was the first smile I had received in East Berlin. The sentries, the Russian officer, and the border guards had seemed determined not to show the slightest pleasure at seeing me. It was as though they resented the British citizen's right to enter East Berlin whenever he liked.

I left the wooden hut and started to walk the remaining fifty yards or so of the restricted checkpoint area towards the nearest street. Halfway along I noticed the three concrete slabs, each about two feet high and half the width of the road. They were arranged in a staggered pattern, two of them on one side of the road and the third on the other side halfway between the first two, so that all vehicles had to weave their way at a crawling pace in and out of these slabs in order to pass. There could be no desperate dash for freedom by any East German in a motorcar.

I had almost reached the street when a voice on my left demanded, "Passport." It was yet another sentry box containing two more soldiers with machine guns. I handed over my passport, and it was again carefully scrutinized, page by page. The passport was handed back without comment, and I walked on.

Five passport checks and three concrete slabs at the frontier of the world. My first contact with communism was not encouraging.

I walked along the street, keeping to the left-hand side. After about twenty yards I passed a large black car parked at the kerb and facing in the same direction as I was headed. I walked on, and after another few yards I heard the engine start up, and then the car cruised slowly past me and stopped again about ten yards farther on. I was just about to pass it for the second time when the rear door opened and a man leaned out. He was wearing a grey overcoat and a matching fur hat. "Mr. Richardson?"

I stopped. "Yes."

"Please get in."

He moved across to the far side and I got in beside him. As I slammed the door after me the car moved off, quickly gathering speed. The man beside me was smiling broadly. "Well, Mr. Bourke, I would have recognized you anywhere. George gave us a very good description of you." His English was grammatically correct but he had a strong accent. He was about forty-five, with greying hair, and looked very Russian.

"How is George?" I asked, trying not to betray my anxiety.

"Oh, he is fine. Yes, fine."

I looked at him, searching his face for some sign, but he just went on smiling.

"By the way," he said, "my name is Vladimir." We shook hands.

The driver sat silently behind the wheel, his large fur hat and heavy overcoat making him look even bigger than he was. His eyes were riveted on the road ahead so that I could not see his face. As we sped through the streets I could not help noticing the startling difference between the two halves of this divided city. In West Berlin the streets were thronged with happy, smiling people and the windows of the modern shops were stocked with a dazzling array of luxury goods. The roads were busy with every make of modern car. Here in East Berlin the windows of the dilapidated shops were empty, and the few people in the streets trudged about hunched and miserable-looking. The lack of cars was almost phenomenal, and those few that did appear seemed all the same model. The whole place was drab and austere, as though the war had ended only yesterday instead of twenty years ago.

In about twenty minutes we arrived at a fenced-off section of the city. This was the Russian compound. Across the entrance was a red and white pole, and standing in front of it was a Russian sentry. Immediately inside this entrance, to the left, was a gateway leading onto a forecourt, and at the opposite edge of the forecourt was a large stone building, the Soviet Command Headquarters. There was yet another sentry standing at this gateway, to the right, and to the left was a guardroom with a window facing onto the road. Inside the guardroom were several more soldiers. I noticed a Russian officer entering the compound ahead of us. Despite the fact that he was in uniform he still had to show a pass to the sentry. As the car stopped in front of the pole, the sentry came across, peered in at us, and seemed to recognize Vladimir. He straightened up, saluted smartly, and raised the pole. We drove in and veered to the right, away from the Command Head-quarters, and as we passed the gate the second sentry saluted us. Two salutes, and Vladimir had not been required to produce a pass. The KGB, I mused, must be a powerful force around here.

We drove slowly along a narrow road. Leading off it on the left were a number of narrow paths lined on either side by comfortable-looking, detached houses. Presently the car stopped at one of these paths and Vladimir got out, beckoning me to follow him. We walked up the path to the end house on the left, and Vladimir opened the two locks on the front door with two different keys.

"Here we are, Mr. Bourke," he announced. "You will be staying here for a few days."

To the right of the hall was a dining-room, and straight ahead a sitting-room. To the left, just inside the door, was a bathroom. Next to the bathroom was a small cloakroom, and next to the cloakroom was the kitchen. We hung up our coats in the cloakroom.

"This way, Mr. Bourke," Vladimir said, and I followed him into the dining-room.

There was a long table in the middle of the floor with a chair at either end. My host pointed to the one farthest away from the door. "Please be seated."

I sat down.

He picked up a briefcase from the sideboard and sat down at the opposite end of the table, facing me. He opened the briefcase and placed it on the floor at his feet. He put his elbows on the table, joined his hands in front of him, and smiled. "Well, Mr. Bourke, you have some documents?"

I pulled out my passport and threw it across the table towards him. He bent down, rummaged for a moment in his briefcase, and came out with a small plastic-framed magnifying glass. With this he went slowly through every page of the passport, paying particular attention to the photograph and the embossed Foreign Office stamp. "Hm . . . very good, Mr. Bourke." He nodded approvingly.

As he placed the passport on the table to his right, I took several more papers out of my pocket. "My train ticket from London to Paris," I said, throwing the ticket towards him. He studied it for a moment. "The carbon copy of my air ticket from Paris to Berlin." I threw it across. "My bill from the Zoo Hotel," and I threw it after the other documents. "And finally," I said, "my entry visa from Checkpoint Charlie." I slid the flimsy piece of paper along the table.

Vladimir looked pleased with my thoroughness but said nothing.

"Oh, by the way," I said as though it were a mere afterthought, "I have something else that might interest you." I reached inside my jacket, took out a postcard-size photograph, and tossed it across the table. "This is a photograph of the window in the cell block through which George made his exit. As you will observe, it could only have been taken from *inside* the prison. Actually, I took it from the window of my room in the Hostel, which, as you will know by now, is inside the wall at Wormwood Scrubs."

As Vladimir studied the photograph his smile broadened a little more. Then he put all the documents into a large envelope and placed the envelope in the briefcase. Once again he put his elbows on the table and joined his hands. He looked at me with a serious expression. "Now, Mr. Bourke, what are your plans?"

I was surprised by the question. I had thought that all the planning would be done by them and that I would have no say in the matter.

"Well," I began uncertainly, "I was hoping that I might be offered hospitality for a few months in order to give my friends in London sufficient time to cover up their tracks thoroughly. George thought that this might be a good idea too."

"Yes, I agree." Vladimir nodded. "The comrades in Moscow think you should go there. You will need a new passport. We shall have to take some more photographs."

"That won't be necessary." I took out my wallet and removed two spare passport photographs. I tossed them across the table. "I brought a couple with me. I thought they might be needed."

Vladimir was impressed and made no attempt to conceal it.

We went next door to the sitting-room. "You will be staying in this house while you are in Berlin," Vladimir announced. "George also stayed here for a week."

"And where is George now?" I asked, searching his face intently for a reaction I hoped would not be there.

Vladimir only smiled. "Oh, he is already in Moscow," he said. "And now I must make a telephone call to Moscow and tell the comrades you have arrived."

He went into the small cloakroom off the hall and I heard him dial a number and say something in Russian. Half a minute later he was talking to Moscow, his voice slightly raised to make himself heard. When he came back into the sitting-room he was looking very pleased. "The comrades in Moscow are delighted that you arrived safely and they asked me to give you their sincere congratulations on the success of your mission."

"Thank you," I said.

"And now," he went on, "I think we must have something to eat. I must apologize for not having a woman here to do the cooking. I shall have to get something from the canteen. But first I must telephone my comrade and ask him to come and relieve me. Excuse me, please." He went back into the cloakroom and made a brief phone call.

Five minutes later the doorbell rang and he went back out into the hall. There was a brief conversation in Russian and then Vladimir came back. "I will go and get some food, Mr. Bourke," he said. "I shall be back in ten minutes." He left, and a moment later I heard the front door slam behind him.

There was the sound of footsteps in the hall and another man came in. I could hardly believe my eyes. He was of medium height and stocky. He wore a brown leather raincoat tightly belted at the waist and a trilby hat pulled well down over his face. His eyes were concealed behind a pair of green-tinted glasses. He looked as if he had stepped straight out of a James Bond novel.

He strode quickly across the room, his hand outstretched.

"Congratulations, Mr. Bourke. It was a magnificent operation."

"Thank you," I said.

"By the way, my name is Edmund."

"My name is Sean."

"Yes, I know," he said. "Welcome to the German Democratic Republic, Sean."

"Thank you."

"Excuse me a moment."

He went to the cloakroom, and when he came back a moment later without his raincoat and hat and took off his glasses, he looked completely different. He was dressed in a crumpled grey suit and green pullover. The sinister aspect was gone, and he might have been a schoolteacher or an office worker.

He seated himself in an armchair opposite me. "Yes, a magnificent operation," he repeated, showing genuine admiration. "This is a bit exciting for all of us here. It isn't every day that something like this happens to us. Indeed, it isn't every year that it happens. I have never known anything like this in all the time I have been posted here." I noticed that his English was much more fluent than Vladimir's. "Even our Chief was quite excited when he heard you had arrived safely. The phone rang in my office, and when I picked it up the Chief said simply, 'Get over here immediately.' I had never heard such urgency in his voice before. I dropped the phone and ran—I actually *ran*—over to his office. When I got there he looked up at me and said, 'He has arrived! Get everything ready!' Yes, your operation has caused a lot of excitement here in Berlin."

"And what was it that you had to get ready?" I asked.

"Well," he said thoughtfully, "there were certain precautions that had to be taken. Here in East Berlin you are a little bit too close to the British and the Americans for comfort. If they found out you were here they might try something. But they have no chance of getting near you now."

"Why's that?" I asked, feeling a little uneasy.

Edmund crossed his legs and leaned back in his chair. "Because this house is now surrounded by six Russian soldiers with machine guns, and they will remain on guard twenty-four hours a day while you are here." He must have noticed the apprehension in my face. "Oh, don't worry," he went on quickly, "the soldiers are not there to prevent you from leaving but to prevent the other side from harming you. They have strict instructions that only two people are allowed to approach this house, Vladimir and myself. Anyone else who tries . . ." He shrugged.

Vladimir returned with some large Thermos flasks containing soup and a meat dish. He also had about half-a-dozen bottles of drink. In the dining-room he filled three glasses with vodka, and we stood up for a toast. "To you, Sean," he said, "and to your successful operation."

"Yes," Edmund added, "to a magnificent operation, and to your future, Comrade Sean."

"Thank you, gentlemen," I said.

During the meal they both listened enthralled as I recounted how the escape had been planned and carried out. From their questions I quickly learned how little they knew about life in England and the liberal conditions that made the escape possible. They were giving me credit on the same basis as if I had carried out the operation under the totalitarian conditions of Eastern Europe.

During the meal we drank plenty of vodka and wine and skipped easily from one subject to another. "By the way," Edmund said presently, "that was a fine job your people did in Dublin a few months ago when they blew up Nelson's Column. We were all delighted here when we heard it on the wireless."

"Yes, very funny," Vladimir agreed, and they both laughed.

"It was long overdue." I smiled. "After all, can you imagine the English tolerating a statue of some German admiral in Piccadilly Circus?"

We started to talk about Berlin, and I hinted at the contrast between the two halves of the city. "Oh, well, the reason for that," Edmund explained, "is that West Berlin has been deliberately set up as a showcase, or a shop window, of the West. The West Germans and their allies pour millions of dollars into West Berlin to keep it going. Oh yes, make no mistake about that."

Next I hinted about the ease with which I was able to leave West Berlin and the restrictions I had met once I crossed the line. Edmund took a swig of vodka. "Don't be fooled by that," he said defensively. "The Americans have got television cameras hidden at Checkpoint Charlie and they photograph everyone going in either direction. Don't underestimate them, Sean. They are very clever people."

"The English are much nicer people to deal with," Vladimir said. "None of the three Western occupying Powers recognizes East Berlin as the capital of the German Democratic Republic, but the English don't try to be too assertive about it."

"No, not like the Americans," Edmund agreed. "Sometimes a party of American military people will drive into East Berlin just to assert their rights under the Potsdam Agreement. They will commit some minor traffic offence, and if an East German policeman stops them they will tell him to mind his own business as they only recognize the authority of the Russians in East Berlin. But the East Germans have an answer for that." Edmund laughed. "They use three police cars to box in the American vehicle and they just keep the Americans trapped for hours until a Russian officer arrives on the scene to rescue them."

Vladimir smiled. "But the English do their best to avoid an incident and accept directions from the East German police for the convenience of it."

We drank three more toasts before the end of the meal: to Ireland, to the German Democratic Republic, and to the Soviet Union.

That afternoon Vladimir went out for an hour, and when he came back he announced that all record of my passage through Checkpoint Charlie had been removed. "Just a precaution," he said, "to be on the safe side."

"And as a further precaution," Edmund added, "Vladimir and I will take it in turns to be with you here in this house at all times. We shall sleep here too."

"Despite all those soldiers?"

"Yes"—Edmund nodded—"despite the soldiers."

I glanced through the sitting-room window at the other houses nearby. "I don't see much sign of the soldiers," I observed.

"Don't worry about that," Edmund said reassuringly. "They are out there all right, well hidden, their gun barrels pointed at all parts of the house."

"A comforting thought," I said quietly.

There were two bedrooms and another bathroom upstairs. One of the bedrooms was assigned to me, and Vladimir and Edmund were to take it in turns to stay the night, sleeping on a couch downstairs in the sitting-room. It was Vladimir's turn the first night. We said good night and I went up to my room.

It was eleven o'clock. I went to the window and looked out. Some of the nearby houses had lights on but there was no sound and no movement. Then I saw a shadow move behind a partly opened upstairs window in the gable end directly opposite me, and a moment later a gun barrel glinted in the pale moonlight. I withdrew from the window to face my first uneasy night's sleep behind the Iron Curtain.

Next day Vladimir announced that he was going out to buy me a complete set of clothing and equipment. "You will need two overcoats," he said, "a heavy one for the winter and a light one for the spring. You will also need some suits, thick ones for the winter and lighter ones for the summer."

"But I have a suit," I pointed out, "and a raincoat."

Vladimir looked at Edmund and they both smiled. "You have never experienced a Russian winter," Edmund said. "If you went to Moscow in your own clothes you would freeze to death, literally."

"You will also need a fur hat," Vladimir went on, "and winter and summer underwear, and fur boots and ordinary shoes, and socks and pyjamas and shirts, and toilet equipment and bath towels and a track suit, and many other things, and a couple of suitcases to carry them all in."

"That's a lot of equipment," I said.

"My Chief has instructed me to spend two thousand marks on you to prepare you for your visit to Moscow," Vladimir informed me. "I shall go to the West to make the purchases. This will be easier."

Remembering the shop windows of East Berlin, I could understand what he meant.

Four hours later Vladimir returned with two large suitcases crammed tight with my new clothes and equipment. I spent another hour trying them on, and, to Vladimir's obvious relief, they fitted reasonably well.

The following day, Wednesday, Vladimir, who I by now realized was the senior of my two hosts, went into the cloakroom and made another phone call to Moscow. He talked for about twenty minutes, and I couldn't help thinking that this direct line stretching across Europe from Berlin to Moscow must follow a very secret route indeed. When he emerged he was smiling broadly. "Well, Sean, the comrades want you in Moscow on Saturday, so you will have three more days in Berlin. George has been informed of your safe arrival and he sends you his congratulations. He also sends a request. He wants me to buy a cardigan for him and bring it with me on Saturday."

That evening when Vladimir came in to relieve Edmund for the night he made another announcement. "Your new name," he told me, "is Robert Garvin. You are from the town of Riga, capital of Latvia. Your patronymic is Adamovich."

"What does that mean?" I asked.

"It means that you are the son of a man called Adam. So your full name is Robert Adamovich Garvin."

The rest of the week was uneventful. Depending on which of them was on "duty," Vladimir or Edmund would go to some distant canteen with the large Thermos flasks to collect lunch or dinner. Breakfast we prepared in our own kitchen. Since no one else was allowed near the house, my hosts had to do the washing-up themselves, a task that I always volunteered to help with.

Vladimir and Edmund were perfect hosts. They would listen attentively to my every utterance and watch my every movement and expression in the hope of being able to anticipate my needs. If I came into the sitting-room and they had the radio tuned to Moscow, they would immediately change over to the BBC for my benefit. (I was to learn later in Moscow that Vladimir was a colonel and Edmund a major. The Chief that they kept referring to was the head of the KGB in East Berlin and had the rank of general. This was an indication of the importance and sensitivity of the Berlin post.)

Vladimir and Edmund were obviously very pleased and felt privileged that Blake and I should pass through their hands. We were very important personages. Only three people in East Berlin knew that I was here, my two hosts and their Chief, the general, and they were determined that I should be well looked after and that Moscow should have no reason to be displeased.

The house was a *safe house*, a place used exclusively for entertaining spies or other important guests of the Secret Service. It was well furnished and decorated, and everything was in the right place, but, as with all *safe houses*, it lacked atmosphere and seemed a little austere. It was a house but not a home.

On Friday afternoon Vladimir announced that I would be leaving for Moscow very early next morning and that he would be coming with me. "You should go to bed early tonight because I must call you at four o'clock."

And so I did all my packing that evening and I was in bed by ten o'clock.

Vladimir roused me from a shallow sleep at exactly four o'clock in the morning. I dressed hurriedly and went downstairs. Vladimir and Edmund were standing in the hallway talking quietly in Russian. Edmund was again in his "uniform" of leather raincoat, trilby hat, and tinted glasses. But this morning there was one subtle change in his appearance. His raincoat bulged slightly under his left arm. I thought of Edmund crossing through Checkpoint Charlie, as he must occasionally do, and I imagined to my secret amusement that every CIA and MI6 agent in West Berlin would be trailing him down the Kurfürstendamm.

Vladimir turned to me, a serious expression on his face. "We are leaving now, Sean. Between here and the car do not speak. No one must hear an English voice."

My God, I thought, they trust no one. We are surrounded by the houses of Russian officers and still no one must hear my voice.

Vladimir picked up my two suitcases and Edmund opened the door. Vladimir went out first, I went after him, and Edmund followed last, shutting the door quietly behind him. The six armed soldiers, invisible all the week, had now put in an appearance. They were standing in the path, their guns at the ready, fingers on the triggers. We moved down the path towards the road, a weird-looking procession, with three of the soldiers in front, three behind, and Vladimir, Edmund, and myself walking in single file between them with me in the middle. The houses on either side of the path were all in darkness, as indeed was the whole Russian compound, and the three soldiers up front were mere silhouettes.

There were three cars drawn up in the road, a driver behind the wheel of each and a second man sitting beside him, six men in all. As we approached, the driver of the centre car got out, took the suitcases from Vladimir, put them in the boot, and then climbed back in behind the wheel without saying a word. Edmund pulled the rear door open and gestured me to get in. At the same time the six soldiers, now standing in an informal group on the path, came to attention at a signal from their NCO and saluted smartly. I nodded my acknowledgement and got into the car. Vladimir exchanged a few brief words with Edmund and then got in beside me. Edmund shut the door after him and then went back and got into the car behind us. The three cars moved off and stopped a minute later at the entrance to the compound. The man sitting beside the driver in the front car showed a document to the sentry, who saluted smartly and promptly raised the barrier.

We left the compound and made our way through the deserted streets of East Berlin, occasionally passing a lone cyclist making his way to or from an irregular shift at his factory or works, his small metal lunchbox strapped to his carrier. As we approached the city boundary a policeman stepped out of a guard post at the side of the road and raised his hand. The car up front stopped, and the man next to the driver again showed his document. The policeman, a German this time, saluted and waved the car on. Our car stopped, and the man sitting next to our driver also showed a document. Again the policeman saluted and waved us on. I turned and looked through the rear window and saw the same thing happening with Edmund's car.

Once clear of the city, we sped in convoy through the East German countryside, my car staying in the middle and Edmund's taking up the rear, its headlights constantly reflected in our rear-view mirror to remind us of Edmund's presence. After about half an hour a cluster of brightly lit buildings loomed up to our right.

"This is the airport," Vladimir told me.

"Oh, we're here already?" I asked.

"No," Vladimir said. "This is the civil airport. We are using a military airfield."

We drove on in silence. After another quarter of an hour we turned right off the main road and found ourselves in wooded country. Twenty minutes later we turned left into a minor road, and after a while the trees began to thin out, and presently we had left them behind us and were in open country.

Way off to the right and well ahead of us the unmistakable white column of smoke from a railway engine was trailing its way slowly across the countryside, clearly visible in the pale moonlight. The smoke was moving towards us, at right angles to our own path, and it seemed we must both converge on some distant level crossing at the same time. Ten minutes later we arrived at the level crossing, and sure enough the barrier was down. The engine chugged its way slowly across our path, dragging one solitary carriage in its wake. The lights of the carriage were on but all the compartments were empty. It looked a little eerie, like some ghost train creeping through the darkness of the night. A shadowy figure in a wooden hut at the side of the road turned a wheel and the barrier was slowly raised to point at the early morning sky like twin anti-aircraft guns. The convoy moved on.

In another fifteen minutes we were at the airfield. There was no wooden pole across the entrance this time. Our path was blocked by a tall iron gate. A soldier emerged from a smaller pedestrian gate to the left and approached the first car. It was a Russian soldier. So this was a Russian airfield, and not a German one. The soldier was shown the document by the man in the front car. He saluted and immediately opened the gate. That document, I concluded, must bear the signature of a general.

Our convoy drove into the airfield and five minutes later came to a halt near a brick building, which was not, I noticed, the control tower. We all got out. Vladimir went into the building and Edmund and I began to walk up and down outside. The other three KGB men stood in a little group apart, and the three drivers formed yet another group. The snow was thick on the ground and it was bitterly cold. Suddenly I felt grateful for my new fur coat and my fur hat.

Edmund looked down at my feet and an expression of dismay came into his face. "Sean!" he exclaimed. "You are not wearing your fur boots!"

"These shoes are quite comfortable," I assured him.

"But you will catch cold," he said, and there was real concern in his voice.

"I don't think so, Edmund."

He shook his head slowly from side to side. "A pity, Sean," he said sadly, "a great pity. I have neglected my duty. I should have been more attentive back in the house and made sure that you wore your fur boots." He looked at me intently for a moment and made a self-conscious effort to force himself to smile, but his eyes remained serious. "Now you will be able to tell the comrades in Moscow how badly we neglected you in Berlin."

His brave attempt at nonchalance was designed to conceal the true earnestness of his remark. It was not a statement but an inquiry, and I knew that a response from me would be welcome. "I can assure you, Edmund," I said, "that my stay in Berlin was most enjoyable and the hospitality I received from you and Vladimir could not have been better. And I shall tell them that in Moscow."

Edmund's face lit up. "Thank you, Sean, thank you very much."

This was my first encounter with that childishly honest seeking-after-approval which I was later to discover was so characteristic of the Russians at all levels. It was an openness and guilelessness that had long since been lost to more sophisticated peoples.

Vladimir came out of the building. "Well, Sean, you will be pleased to hear that your pilot is a general."

"That's very reassuring," I said.

"We take off at seven o'clock," he went on, "and arrive in Moscow three hours later at ten o'clock. But since Moscow time is two hours ahead of Central European time, it will be midday in Moscow when we arrive." He glanced at his watch. "Six-fifteen. We can wait inside for half an hour."

We went into the warm building and Vladimir led us to a large room. It was a classroom with several rows of desks and a lot of diagrams on the walls dealing with navigational subjects. The wall facing the desks was dominated by a blackboard, and hanging directly above it, its lower edge resting on the blackboard's upper edge, was a large framed portrait of Lenin.

Vladimir produced a bottle of vodka and three small enamel mugs. He filled the mugs and handed one each to Edmund and me.

Edmund raised his mug. "To you, Comrade Sean."

"Yes, to you," Vladimir agreed.

The mugs were filled again. This time I proposed a toast. "To the Soviet Union."

"To the Soviet Union," they repeated, and we drank.

I looked up at Lenin's portrait. "That man certainly started something, didn't he?"

"He certainly did," Edmund said earnestly. "A whole new world."

I had learned my second lesson about the Russians in half an hour. In the West nothing was too sacred to be joked about, not even God. But in the Communist world Lenin and laughter could not go together. It was too soon in history.

A young Air Force officer came in and said something to Vladimir. Vladimir made some reply and the officer left. Then Vladimir turned to me. "The general would like a word with me about our flight," he said. To my surprise, he then poured out some more vodka and we continued drinking for another five minutes before he left the room. Even a Soviet Air Force general had to wait while a KGB colonel attended to the more important task of looking after an important visitor like me.

Vladimir returned a few minutes later and said it was time to go. We left the building and got back into our cars, which once more moved off in convoy. We sped along the dark runway to where the aircraft was standing about a mile away. It was a large aircraft with four prop engines, a troop carrier, I thought.

Vladimir took the suitcases out of the boot of our car and climbed up the steps into the aircraft with them. Edmund was chatting to the other three KGB men a few yards away. The three drivers stayed in their cars. Across the pitch-black airfield in the far distance could be seen a small cluster of lights, the control tower and other administrative buildings, I thought. I stood directly under one of the plane's massive wings and looked up. The serial number, in figures three feet high, read: CCCP11123.

Vladimir came down the steps again and went across to where Edmund was talking to the other three KGB men. He shook hands with these three and then he and Edmund came over to me.

"Good-bye, Sean." Edmund smiled as we shook hands. "I hope we meet again. Please give my regards to the comrades in Moscow."

"I will, Edmund," I assured him. "Good-bye."

Vladimir led the way up the steps into the plane and I followed. The body of the plane itself was quite empty and devoid of all fittings. Up front, immediately behind the cockpit, there was a small cabin with a table and two seats on either side of the gangway. Vladimir and I sat at the table on the left. Already seated at the table on the right were three Air Force sergeants with revolvers at their hips. Five minutes later the general and three other crew members came in. The general smiled briefly at Vladimir and led his assistants into the cockpit, the last one through pulling the connecting door shut behind him. The huge plane shuddered as the engines jumped to life, and a moment later we were taxiing to the end of the runway to turn round and face the wind.

Vladimir leaned across the table and at the same time pulled something out of his inside pocket. "Your new passport," he said.

I took it from him. It was an official Soviet passport and much smaller in size, I noticed, than a British one. The only familiar thing about it was the photograph I had supplied. I noted with interest that the official stamp over the photograph was not of the embossed type used by the British but simply a rubber stamp.

Vladimir held his hand out again and I handed back the passport. Of course, it would be too much to expect to be allowed to keep it. It would be needed only in emergencies, such as, for example, if we were forced to land anywhere outside the Soviet Union.

The plane screamed down the runway and was airborne. It quickly gained altitude, banked slightly, and headed east into the sun. Suddenly, because of our height, it was brilliant daylight. I looked out the window, and down below Germany was still cloaked in darkness. An hour later Vladimir glanced through the window and announced that we were over Poland. An hour later still he said we were crossing Byelorussia. I looked down. The whole country lay under a blanket of snow.

At half-past nine we were approaching Moscow. I noticed that the countryside was heavily wooded. The Russian capital had been hacked out of a forest. We were losing altitude, and presently the wheels of our aircraft were pounding on the icy runway.

We were in Russia.

It was Saturday, January 7, 1967. I looked at my watch: exactly ten o'clock. The general had been as good as his word.

"By the way, it is now midday in Moscow," Vladimir reminded me, "so you can put your watch ahead two hours."

There was a car waiting for us actually on the runway. With the driver there was a young man of about thirty. The snow was heavy on the ground and it was bitterly cold. Even my heavy fur coat and fur hat didn't seem adequate. The young man stepped forward, said something briefly to Vladimir, and then we all shook hands. The driver put the suitcases in the boot and we got into the car. We left the airfield by a small back entrance, the young KGB man showing the sentry the necessary authorization.

The airfield was about thirty miles south of Moscow, and our journey to the city was slow and hazardous. The snow ploughs were everywhere, and the snow cleared from the road was piled six feet high on either side. Most of the houses, I noticed, were single-story wooden dwellings. They looked like Christmas cards with their snow-laden roofs and chimneys, the illusion being spoiled only by the ubiquitous television aerials, which sprouted even from the smallest shacks. At regular intervals along the road a little group of people in fur hats would be huddled patiently round a bus stop. Patience, I was to discover, was something that came easily to the Russians.

In an hour we were pulling up outside the Leningrad Hotel. "This is where you will stay for the time being," Vladimir told me, taking my cases out of the boot. He and the young man then took a case each and carried them up to my room on the second floor. It was a small room and the furniture was old-fashioned. There was a green-topped desk with an ornate brass lamp and a white marble blotter. The only concession to the modern age was the telephone.

"And now I must say good-bye." Vladimir smiled. "I hope we meet again, Sean." We shook hands and he left.

"By the way," the young man said then, "my name is Victor." It was the first time he had spoken in English."

"How do you do," I said.

He picked up the phone, dialled a number, and spoke briefly. Then he said in his slow, correct English, "We shall now go and meet George."

That raised my spirits. After a week of this secretive and abnormal life I was longing for some small glimpse of normality again, some contact with the previous order of things. I was also relieved at this indication that Blake was alive, for I knew that my survival was directly connected with his.

Victor led the way downstairs and we waited in the lobby just inside the huge swinging doors. A few minutes later a man came in, caught sight of Victor, and came straight across to us. He was a tall, lean, broad-shouldered man of about forty. "Ah, Mr. Bourke!" He smiled, stretching out a hand towards me. "An excellent operation, Mr. Bourke, an excellent operation. Welcome to Moscow."

"Thank you." I smiled back.

"By the way," he went on, "my name is Stanislav. My friends call me Stan. I hope you will too."

"How do you do, Stan," I said.

He gestured towards the doors. "Well, let us go."

There was a car waiting outside. We drove to the end of the street and turned left. A little later we turned right again and then drew up at the entrance to a lane leading to a block of flats behind the shops that lined the street. We climbed the concrete steps to the third landing.

Stan pressed the doorbell three times, observing a uniform pause between each ring. I noticed that there were two locks on the door.

There was a sound of footsteps inside and then the door was being unlocked. First the two locks were being opened. This, I could hear, was being achieved by a screwing action, the handle of each lock being turned three times. The door opened a few inches, pulling a heavy chain taut, and a middle-aged woman with grey hair peered out at us. She saw Stan and immediately unhooked the chain.

We went in. Stan told the woman in Russian who I was, and all I understood was the name "Robert." Then, turning to me, he said, "This, Robert, is Zinaida Ivanovna. She is George's housekeeper." The woman took our coats and hats.

We were in a spacious rectangular hall off which led five doors. The room to the left, I was to discover, was the housekeeper's. The kitchen was to the right, and next to it the bathroom. The fourth door was shut, Blake's bedroom. The last door, immediately facing us as we came into the flat, was open, revealing a dining-room with a table in the middle set for four. The table was well laden with fruit and wine.

"After you," Stan said, gesturing towards this room.

I went in.

In the far corner to the left was yet another door. I strode across the dining-room and pushed it open. It led to a study. Directly facing me as I looked in was a highly polished mahogany desk, and sitting behind the desk was George Blake. He stood up and came round the desk, his hand outstretched, a broad smile on his face. He was dressed in a new dark suit and looked a lot younger than when I had last seen him in London.

"Well," he said, "I'm very glad to see you."

I smiled and said, "We made it then."

This would normally be the appropriate point at which to bring this interesting adventure to an end. But, also, the story did not end here. In the months that followed, the affair was to degenerate into a sordid tale of treachery, deceit, and betrayal.

15

MOSCOW

The celebration dinner was a good one. There was the traditional Russian soup called borsch made from three different kinds of meat and a lot of cabbage. There were chicken and ham and plenty of wine and vodka and Armenian brandy. Zinaida Ivanovna waited on us. I noticed that when she addressed Stan and Victor she used their Christian names and patronymics: Stanislav Ivanovich and Victor Ivanovich. This, I learned, was the formal mode of address. Blake sat at one end of the table and Victor at the other. Stan and I sat facing each other at the sides.

The first toast was proposed by Blake, and we stood up for it. "To Sean," he announced, "without whose courage and ingenuity we would not be here tonight."

The meal lasted two hours. Stan, I learned, had been the KGB man in the Soviet Embassy in London for a couple of years, hence his excellent command of English. His suit too was English and well cut. His face was lean and muscular and suntanned. His eyes were deep-set and looked straight at you when you spoke and seemed to be trying to penetrate into your very brain and read your innermost thoughts. He carefully weighed everything he said and never seemed to use a superfluous word. This was probably due to the fact that he had qualified as a lawyer at Moscow University before joining the KGB. Victor had also been to Moscow University and taken a degree in history. After that he had been compelled by law to teach for a couple of years and had joined the KGB only recently. Neither Stan nor Victor looked typically Russian and with their clean-cut features could have passed as English or French.

Victor left, and the rest of us adjourned to the study with a bottle of brandy.

"Well, Sean," Stan began, "for the few months that you are in Moscow you will probably want to keep yourself from getting bored. I understand from George that you were editor of the prison magazine at Wormwood Scrubs, and if you like I can get you something in that line while you're here. What do you think?"

"I think that's a very good idea."

"Good. There are a lot of translators employed in our publishing houses whose job it is to translate Russian works into English, but since these people are themselves Russian and learned their English here and have never been to England, they obviously do not have an accurate feeling for the idiom. That is where you come in. Your job would be to read through their translations and correct them."

"Sounds easy enough," I said.

"Would he have to go to an office to do this work?" Blake asked.

"No. I or Victor would collect the manuscripts for him and he could work at home."

An hour later Stan rose to go. "If you like," Blake suggested, "you can go on and I'll walk Sean back to his hotel."

And so it was agreed. Blake and I showed Stan to the door and then returned to the study. Blake went and sat behind his desk again and I sat on the couch to his right.

"Well now," I said, "what happened to you after Michael and Anne dropped you off?"

Blake smiled, moved his chair back from the desk, and crossed his legs. "A very interesting chain of events," he began, "very interesting indeed. I allowed them time to reach the city and then I walked up to the guard post, which was, of course, manned by East Germans. I asked to see a Russian officer. The Germans tried to make me tell them who I was but I refused. I insisted on seeing a Russian officer. Finally they made a call to Berlin, and an hour later a Russian officer arrived. It was now two o'clock in the morning. I told the Russian officer who I was, and he said he would have to go back and report to someone else as he was not in a position to identify me. He instructed the Germans to fix me up with a bed in the guard post and left. At exactly nine o'clock in the morning the door burst open and three Russians came in. The one in the middle was a man that I had been in contact with years before when I was with the Secret Service in Berlin. 'It's him!' he shouted. 'It's him!' And he ran forward and threw his arms around me. Now that man had been asleep in bed in his flat in Moscow six hours before. The KGB had put through an urgent call from Berlin to the KGB Headquarters in Moscow and asked for someone who would be able to identify me. In just six hours they had got this man out of his bed, rushed him to a military airfield near Moscow, flown him in a jet to Berlin, and driven him out to the guard post. Six hours!"

"That's efficiency," I agreed.

"After that," Blake went on, "the procedure was much the same as in your own case. I stayed a week in the safe house with Vladimir and Edmund and was then flown in a special aircraft to a private airfield outside Moscow used by Government Ministers." He pulled open the drawer of the desk and took out a black folder. "Have a look at this," he said, passing the folder across.

It was a dossier on the escape made up of cuttings from British newspapers and teleprinter messages sent out by the major news agencies. I went carefully through it and noticed that every reference to myself was heavily underlined in red ink.

I handed it back. "You know, there cannot be many men in this world who have had the privilege of reading their own dossiers from the files of the KGB. It's a weird feeling, like looking at your own obituary."

Blake walked me back to the hotel. We said good-bye on the steps after exchanging telephone numbers and arranging to meet again next day.

Victor was assigned as our general guide and helper under Stan, and it was he who collected us in a chauffeur-driven car next day, Sunday. We went on a tour of the snowbound city. "You can get a very good view of Moscow from the Lenin Hills," Victor told us. "I think we should go there." He gave some instructions to the driver.

The Lenin Hills are not really hills but some sloping land at the western edge of the city dominated by Moscow University. In front of the university there is a viewing wall about three feet high beyond which the ground falls away steeply to the river. Standing at this wall, one does indeed have an excellent view of the city, and it is a popular spot for foreigners.

Now as we approached, Victor was craning his neck forward and scrutinizing the dozen or so cars parked near the viewing wall. Then he turned abruptly to the driver and said something, and the car accelerated and we sped past the line of people leaning over the wall. "I'm sorry about that," Victor said. "There were a couple of Western diplomatic cars parked there. You must not be seen, of course."

On Tuesday evening Blake phoned me at the hotel. "I say, Sean, would you like to come round to dinner tonight?"

"Yes, I'd love to."

"Good. I've got something interesting to show you. A little surprise."

"I can hardly wait."

Blake laughed. "You still don't know the way to my flat, do you?"

"No, I don't."

"I'll meet you in half an hour outside the Ministry of Transport, that big building at the top of the street where your hotel is."

"Right. I'll be there."

We met outside the Ministry and trudged slowly through the snow to Blake's flat. He opened the door himself, using two keys, turning each through an angle of three hundred and sixty degrees twice.

The dinner table was set for four again. "This time," Blake explained, "I have decided to invite Zinaida Ivanovna and her daughter Sofia to join us. You haven't met Sofia yet. She lives here too, sharing her mother's room. She's twenty-five and works as a translator at the Ministry of Foreign Trade—her English is very good. A bit on the buxom side, I'm afraid. Not my cup of tea at all. Oh yes, the surprise. Come with me."

I followed him to his bedroom, which was next to the dining-room. He turned his back on me and opened the wardrobe. He reached in, took something out, and appeared to be making some adjustment to his suit. Then he turned round to face me. Pinned to his jacket were the insignia of two orders.

"What on earth are they?" I asked.

Blake pointed to the first one. "The Order of Lenin," he announced proudly.

"Good God! That's the highest they can give you, isn't it?"

"Yes, the highest. It's the equivalent of a knighthood. It was presented to me at a special luncheon yesterday by the Minister for State Security on behalf of the Soviet Government."

"They must value your services highly."

Blake shrugged. "They have not been displeased with me."

"And what's the other one?" I asked.

"That is the Order of the Red Banner. It was awarded to me while I was still working in Berlin, but for obvious reasons it could not be presented to me at the time." He laughed.

"No, obviously it couldn't," I said.

Zinaida Ivanovna and Sofia were so thrilled with Blake's medals that they persuaded him to wear them during dinner. And so he sat there at the head of the table, smiling broadly and looking very pleased with himself. There were many toasts and once again Blake proposed, "To Sean, without whom we would not be here tonight."

I had dinner at Blake's flat almost every day after that. At the end of the second week, when Stan was eating with us, Blake suggested that I should move out of the hotel and into his flat. "After all, Stan," he pointed out, "this is quite a large flat and Sean could have the study. The couch in there folds down flat to make a bed, and Zinaida Ivanovna could as easily cook for two of us as for one. And it would also save you all the trouble of having to send Victor to the hotel every day to interpret for him."

Stan thought about it for a moment. "It is not a bad idea," he agreed, "but I would have to get permission from my chiefs."

A week later the permission was given and I moved into Blake's flat. A few days after that, at the end of January, Stan came to see me, looking very concerned. Blake came into the study with him.

"Sean," Stan began, "I'm afraid I have some bad news for you."

"Oh?" was all I could say.

"Yes, the flat in Highlever Road has been discovered by Scotland Yard and you have now for the first time been publicly named as the man wanted for questioning. Your photograph is on all front pages."

"Oh, I see," I said, trying to conceal my relief. "Well, it was bound to happen sooner or later."

"But it is a pity it had to happen at all," Stan said. "This changes your position drastically." He was pacing up and down the full length of the room, his hands behind his back, his eyes on the floor, carefully weighing every word he uttered. Behind those smooth, intelligent features there was, I knew, a very sharp mind.

"I don't see how it does change anything," I argued. "It was inevitable, and my intention has always been to return to Ireland and fight extradition. If I had sprung a member of the IRA from prison I would not be handed over to the British. The answer given by the Irish authorities in such cases is that the matter is *political*. Well, George Blake was as much a political prisoner as any IRA man."

Stan paused at the end of the room and looked at me with those penetrating eyes of his. "But there is a difference here. George Blake is a Communist and Ireland is a Catholic country. Ireland is also economically dependent on Britain. Laws can be given different interpretations to suit the convenience of governments. And there will be a great deal of pressure on the Irish Government."

"That's a chance I'll have to take," I said. "And anyway we've gained something from this development. Now that the police know definitely that I'm the culprit they will be concentrating their efforts on looking for me, their net will be spread much less wide, and my friends will have an even greater chance of escaping detection."

"I agree entirely," Blake put in. "Michael and Pat are not criminals and they are not known to be friends of this man here"—he nodded in my direction—"so, although they had little chance of being caught before, they have even less chance now. The police will now concentrate on checking up on his known friends"—he nodded at me again— "including those he knew in prison, and so Michael and Pat are in the clear. As I see it, this discovery of Highlever Road and his established guilt"—another nod in my direction—"is a blessing. It is the best thing that could have happened from the point of view of our friends in London."

"Yes, you may have a point there," Stan conceded reluctantly.

"When will we see the papers?" I asked.

"I'll get a cable off to London for them tomorrow," Stan said.

The papers arrived in a few days, and sure enough my photograph was on the front pages. MAN WHO HELPED BLAKE STILL IN LONDON was the banner headline in one paper. It was accompanied by a full-length photograph of me, taken during my trial in Sussex in 1961.

"Well," Stan observed, "since they believe you are still in London, let's keep it so that they go on believing that. When you want to write to your family we'll send the letters to London in a diplomatic bag and have them posted there."

Progress Publishers of Moscow gave me a test to establish whether I would be suitable for editing work. It was a rough English translation of an article that had appeared in some Russian magazine. It was about a heroic Russian worker named Ekaterina Borisovna. She was director of a large collective farm and also a local councillor. She led an industrious life, to the glory of the Soviet Union. One passage in the article, describing the collective farm, said: "The many-voiced hubbub of a thousand white hens filled the huge barn, their red cocks swaying in the wind." I made a note at the bottom of the page. "In English, 'cock' is a slang word for the male sexual organ, or penis. Therefore, to talk of the hens with their 'red cocks swaying in the wind' is to suggest that Ekaterina Borisovna kept some strange birds. On the other hand, 'cock' is also an abbreviation for 'cockerel,' the male bird of the species, but it is difficult to imagine why these sturdy creatures should sway in the wind, unless, of course, they were drunk. I think the word you are looking for is probably 'comb.' "

I was accepted for the job, and the first manuscript I was given (and the only one, since after that I did no further work) was a translation of a work entitled *Scientific Communism—A Popular Outline*, written by a Russian professor of political science. This also had one or two amusing ambiguities: "The power of man's muscle, wind, and water was gradually replaced by electricity."

The KGB gave me an allowance of three hundred roubles a month. As there were two and a half roubles to the pound, this meant that I was getting a hundred and twenty pounds a month.

About twice a week Blake and I would have dinner with Stan in a Moscow restaurant. Certain restaurants had to be avoided since they were frequented by Westerners. The phone would ring and Stan would tell us he was on his way. Blake and I would leave the flat and wait in the street near the lane. A few minutes later a black Volga car would sweep up, Stan sitting beside the driver, looking very debonair in a dark English suit. Blake and I would jump in the back and the car would then speed off towards the centre of Moscow. On the way home from these dinners Stan would be dropped off at a different address on each occasion. He was divorced and had a lot of women friends. He was the nearest thing to the James Bond image that I was to encounter in Russia.

Blake spent most of his day writing long memoranda for the KGB, and Stan would call at about six o'clock each evening to collect them. He would bring with him a portable tape recorder, and he and Blake would spend about two hours in Blake's bedroom, conversing in low tones. Blake was giving the KGB every scrap of information he had been unable to pass on before his arrest, as well as details of the methods employed by the British to investigate and interrogate him.

From the moment I moved into Blake's flat I found myself face to face with a complete stranger. Gone was the ever-ready smile, the patient and understanding disposition, the willingness to listen and sympathize. Blake was sullen, intolerant, arrogant, and pompous. The George Blake that we had all known in Wormwood Scrubs had never really existed. It had been a deliberately false image, calculatingly projected for his own long-term benefit. In Moscow, George Blake had suddenly, dramatically, reverted to type.

From the outset he was determined to let me know that the flat was his, that he was the boss, and that I was allowed to live there only because he had bestowed the privilege on me. He refused to call me Sean, insisting on addressing me as Robert. The fact that Stan called me Sean made no difference. For Blake to call me Sean would have been an undue familiarity for a man in his exalted position. Such a familiarity had been all right in Wormwood Scrubs when he needed my help.

He never missed an opportunity to assert his superiority. One morning I was sitting at the desk in the study (now my room) editing the manuscript. I had the radio tuned into the BBC World Service and was listening to some pleasant background music. Blake was next door in the dining-room, writing his notes for the KGB. The connecting door was shut.

Suddenly he stormed into the study, an angry expression on his face. "I say, Robert, would you mind turning that radio down a bit! It's impossible for me to concentrate." He stormed out again.

The radio was already at a low volume but I turned it down anyway. It was now almost inaudible. Five minutes later the door burst open again. Blake's face was flushed with indignation. "Now look here, Robert, I do wish you'd turn that radio off. It is quite impossible for me to write."

I turned the radio off. It was Blake's flat.

His attitude to Zinaida Ivanovna and her daughter was no less superior. One evening, when I was in the kitchen chatting with the two women, Blake strode in. "I wish to make an announcement," he said pompously in English, then switched to Russian. As he spoke, I could see the women's expressions changing from surprise, to bewilderment, to anger. He switched back to English. "Having made my announcement in Russian, I shall now translate it for your benefit. With effect from today, all noise and all movement in this flat is to cease by eleven o'clock at night at the very latest. I do not consider it at all unreasonable that I should demand to be allowed to sleep at eleven o'clock. I cannot do this if people are walking about and making noise. That is all I wish to say. Good night." He turned on his heel and stalked out.

Zinaida Ivanovna mumbled something to her daughter and Sofia interpreted.

"My mother and I are thinking of leaving and going back to our own flat. My mother can come and do the cleaning and cooking each day and go home at night."

But they didn't leave. They were afraid of the KGB and didn't want to do anything to displease them. I knew this was their reason for staying, because every time Stan came to the door the two women would scuttle away to their room and stay there until he left.

Another side of Blake's true character quickly showed itself: his vanity. He turned out to be the vainest man I had ever met in my life. But he was more than vain. He was a narcissist, unashamedly in love with his own image. In his determination to preserve his schoolboy figure he devoted at least one hour a day to physical exercises, which he performed completely stripped in front of a full-length mirror. Several times I found him dancing by himself. When the dance step required him to turn his back on the mirror he would look over his shoulder and admire himself from behind, so reluctant was he to lose sight of his body for a moment. He often said that if he had not been a spy he would have liked to be a priest. "Those beautiful robes that bishops and cardinals wear would really appeal to me," he said, laughing. Once I saw him genuflecting before the mirror, the golden silk bedspread draped over his shoulders like a benediction cape. He caught sight of me in the mirror and wheeled round to give me an elaborate blessing.

He had great illusions of grandeur and loved to strut about the flat in his crimson dressing-gown, a glass of champagne held delicately between his fingers. Sometimes he would stride into my room, brandishing a bottle of champagne in one hand and two elegant-looking glasses in the other, and say in his cultured Foreign Office voice, "I say, Robert, what is your attitude to a glass of champagne?"

His thinning hair caused him some anxiety and he often spoke of getting a wig. Another source of discontent was the irregular pattern of small blue scars on his forehead, acquired when he jumped from the prison wall and smashed his head on the gravelled road. He would carry these scars to the grave with him, and I knew that he would always hold it against me for having caused him to fall awkwardly that night.

Yet another facet of Blake's real character soon became evident, and indeed helped to explain his other strange behaviour. This was his physical and emotional weakness. As a man Blake was quite inadequate. He was terrified of coming face to face with physical violence or bloodshed. Since Moscow is a place of much drinking and many drunkards, sometimes, on the way home late at night, Blake and I would encounter a drunk staggering along the pavement. Blake would promptly leave me, cross to the other side of the street, and rejoin me when I had gone well past the drunk. In the presence of children he became hopelessly soft. He would linger near a playground to watch the children at play, and when walking through the streets his eyes were constantly darting from one young person or group to another. Sometimes he would even stop and look round and keep staring after them until they had disappeared out of sight. On one occasion Victor brought his six-year-old son to the flat, and Blake fussed over him and fondled him with a maternal devotion that was embarrassing to watch.

One Sunday it was arranged that Blake and I should go driving in the country for the day. Victor was due to call for us at ten o'clock in the morning. At nine o'clock I went into the kitchen, where Blake was busily preparing sandwiches to take with us. He looked up as I came in. "This is not easy, you know," he said, frowning. "I have to prepare sandwiches for the three of us, and for the driver too. It's a lot of work."

"I'm sure it is." I smiled.

Blake dropped the knife he was holding and straightened up. "So you think that's funny, do you?" he demanded, his face going red.

"Nobody said anything about it being funny," I replied.

His whole body started to shake. "So you think it's funny, do you?" he repeated. "Well, damn you!" He picked up a plastic container full of eggs and threw it. It crashed into the cabinet about two feet clear of my head and the eggs splashed on the floor. "Damn you! Damn you! Damn you!" he cried, and his voice was almost a sob. He picked up half-a-dozen apples, rushed to the door, and proceeded to throw them one after the other against the wall at the opposite side of the hall. "Damn you! Damn you! Damn you!" he kept screaming, his face contorted in an agony of frustration and fury. Then he ran into his room and slammed the door loudly behind him. His actions were those of a hysterical woman, and the whole incident was acutely embarrassing. But I had not failed to notice that despite his fury Blake had aimed that container well clear of me. He refused to leave his room for the rest of the day, and Victor and I had to go for the drive by ourselves.

One evening, about three months after my arrival in Moscow, Blake had a visit from a KGB man with whom he had had dealings years before in Berlin while working for the British Secret Service. They spent a couple of hours in Blake's room, talking about old times over a bottle of champagne. Blake's door was at right angles to the kitchen door and only a couple of feet from it. Like so many things Russian, doors were often shoddily made and failed to close properly. I was in the kitchen making a cup of tea. The kitchen door was open. The voices of Blake and his friend reached me quite distinctly.

"And how is Robert?" the KGB man asked presently.

"Oh, he's not too bad," Blake replied.

"And what are his plans?"

"Well"—I could just visualize Blake shrugging indulgently—"you see, Robert is just, well, just an Irish peasant. He doesn't know what he wants, that's the trouble. But anyway we're trying to condition him to stay here, to settle down in Russia. We're working on it."

When the KGB man left, Blake came into my room with a bottle of champagne and two glasses. "I say, Robert, what is your attitude to a glass of champagne?"

I allowed a week to elapse so as not to make Blake suspect that I had overheard him and then approached him in his room. "Well," I began, "I have now been in Moscow more than three months and I think it's time I reminded Stan that my stay here is supposed to be temporary. I want to return to Ireland."

"Oh, do you?" Blake tried to sound surprised.

"That has always been the idea, as you know."

"And what about Michael and Pat?"

"What about them?"

"By returning to Ireland you would be putting them in danger," he said resentfully.

I controlled my anger with an effort. "Now look here," I said in a level voice, "it's *my* future we're discussing, not other people's. Michael and Pat are at this moment free men, living and working in their own country among their own friends. They're in no danger from me or from anyone else. I'm the one with a price on his head. I'm the one on the run, living in a strange country among strange people. I'm already accepting all the blame and drawing the police away from the others, and I'm not complaining about it. But I'm not going to spend the rest of my life as a hunted man living in a country that I don't want to live in. I want to go back to Ireland and face extradition and return to a normal way of life. I want to be Sean Bourke, an Irishman, not Robert Garvin, a non-person. My future may not be important to you but it is very important to me."

"Very well," Blake said sullenly, "I'll pass your remarks on to Stan."

But by June nothing more had been said or done about my departure. I did, however, write a couple of letters, but since I could not put an address on them and therefore could not get a reply, it was not a very satisfying exercise. Stan would come into my room with the notepaper and envelope in a plastic folder. He would also have a bottle of Quink ink. Both the stationery and the ink were bought in London. "When you have written the letter, put it in the envelope and put the envelope back in the folder," he would say. "I mustn't touch either the envelope or the notepaper because my fingerprints are probably on record in London." The same procedure applied to Blake. He would be given stationery bought in Cairo. Our letters would then be flown in diplomatic bags to the two capitals, to be posted by the KGB men on the spot. I left my letters unsealed when I handed them to Stan, and to my surprise I noticed that Blake was expected to do the same.

By the summer my relations with Blake were distinctly cool. I knew that he was actively spying on me and making regular reports to the KGB on my moods and attitudes. One day when he was out I went into his room to borrow a book. His latest memorandum, comprising some ten pages, was lying quite openly on the writing table. This was

an unusual act of carelessness for him, since he normally locked everything away in his wardrobe before leaving the flat. I glanced at the top
page. It was about me. It was a review of our life in Wormwood
Scrubs. And there it was again: "But whatever else might be said,
Bourke is first and foremost an Irish peasant."

Blake's mother was due to arrive in Moscow on Friday, July 21, to
spend a month with her son. The KGB decided that she should not
meet me nor find out that I was in Moscow. My presence behind the
Iron Curtain was to be kept a closely guarded secret. "If the British
know definitely that you are here," Stan told me, "they might make a
formal request that you be handed over to them, and that would embarrass our Foreign Minister."

It was arranged that I should go for a holiday on the Black Sea
while Mrs. Blake was in Moscow. And so, almost at the same moment
as Mrs. Blake's plane was coming down at Moscow Airport, mine was
taking off for the Caucasus. The man coming with me was a KGB
officer named Vladislav, Slava for short. He had the same rank as
Stan, but that was where the similarity ended. Slava was conspicu-
ously short, of stout build, and looked very Russian. He had the Slav's
snubbed nose and full mouth and eyes set well apart, and his cheek-
bones were slightly pronounced. All of his clothes were Russian. Like
all the KGB officers I had met so far, he was patently honest and
sincere and went out of his way to be helpful. He also possessed that
charming Russian characteristic of seeking approval which I had first
encountered in Berlin.

It was the first time Slava had met me, and he was determined not
to do anything wrong. He insisted that I wear dark glasses all the time
lest I be recognized by foreign tourists. "We must be careful," he
cautioned. "Your photograph has been in all the newspapers in Europe."

When we arrived at Adler Airport—the nearest piece of flat land to
the seaside resort of Sochi—we were met by a KGB car. "That is the
car over there," Slava announced, after comparing its number with a
small diary in his hand.

The man in the car was the head of the Sochi office of the KGB. He
introduced himself as Vladimir. To my surprise, he drove the car himself, the first time I had been in a KGB car that was not driven by a

chauffeur. We made our way along the winding coast road at the foot of the Caucasus, and in forty minutes we were in Sochi. Vladimir was a skillful driver.

Sochi is a town full of rest homes, where in the summer Soviet citizens from all parts of the country go for their holidays. Each rest home, or sanatorium as it is called, belongs to a particular industry, and only the employees of that industry can stay there. No foreigners are allowed. The KGB arranged an exception in my case. Rooms were waiting for Slava and me in Zapolyaria Sanatorium, which belonged to the workers of the copper mines up in the Arctic.

These sanatoria are peculiar to Russia and could exist only in that society. You would have to be brought up on them to appreciate them. They would never be accepted by a Westerner. The whole attitude is paternalistic, but then so is Soviet society in general. Today's Russians have never known anything else. The sanatorium, then, is a microcosm of Soviet society.

At Zapolyaria a hefty nurse banged on your door at seven in the morning and a minute later the commanding voice of a physical-training instructor boomed out of the loudspeaker in your room. "Good morning, comrades! The time is seven o'clock and it is a beautiful day. Stand in the middle of your room, heels together, arms by your side. Touching your toes, with me . . . begin: One, two, three —up! One, two, three—up! Come on, comrades, get right down there now, come on, right down, the day is only beginning!"

Each sanatorium has its own stretch of beach, fenced off from the sanatorium on either side. That first morning as I lay sunning myself on our crowded piece of beach, the regimentation of sanatorium life was brought home to me with a shocking abruptness. At precisely eleven o'clock half-a-dozen loudspeakers started to blare out the command: "All right, comrades, on your feet!" I raised myself on an elbow and looked around me. A thousand human beings, men, women and children, instantly got to their feet. About thirty yards away a burly P.T. instructor was standing on a raised platform, feet apart, hands on his hips, surveying his obedient flock. Fixed to the rail in front of him was a microphone. "All right, comrades," he commanded, "with me . . . begin!" And he led the vast crowd through a series of exercises. Slava, who had been lying on a large bathtowel a few yards away, was on his feet and following the actions of the instructor with the same enthusiasm as everyone else. I lay back, closed my eyes, and pretended to be asleep. The session went on for a quarter of an hour. Shortly afterwards the voice of another instructor rang out, farther away this time, and when I looked in the direction of the sound I saw that the people of the neighbouring sanatorium were having their lesson.

In the dining-hall eight persons were allocated to each table, but the tables held only four and so the meals had to be served in two shifts. Those on the first shift were expected to be out in half an hour, so Slava arranged for us to be on the second shift. The food was plain and wholesome, with the accent on soup, potatoes, and bread. Breakfast was difficult to distinguish from lunch and would often consist of boiled meat, mashed potatoes, and semolina pudding.

Every sanatorium had a "cultural organizer." His task was to arrange excursions, dances, concerts, and other communal activities. Our cultural organizer would march into the dining-hall every morning at breakfast-time with a long typewritten list clipped to a board. "*Dobrei utra, tovarischi!*" (Good morning, comrades!) he would shout. When complete silence had descended on the hall he would proceed to read out the programme of activities for the day, a task that sometimes took as long as ten minutes. Once a week you had to "stand by your beds" for room inspection. The superintendent and an entourage of half-a-dozen lesser officials, all dressed in long white coats, would then trail from room to room to ensure that everything was in order.

I religiously shunned all organized activities and made a point of trying to break as many rules as possible. You were required to be in by midnight, when the doors of the sanatorium were locked for the night. I usually got back at one or two in the morning and kept banging on the door until one of the night staff came to let me in. The only special facility that I did take advantage of was the water massage. Slava and I had applied for this at the compulsory medical examination on our arrival, and the doctor had entered the necessary authorization in our small blue record books, which we had to take with us everywhere we went. The water massage and other special treatments were carried out in a clinic in the grounds of the sanatorium. In front of the entrance to the clinic there was a small lawn, and in the centre of the lawn, resting on a five-foot-high pillar, was a bust of the Russian psychologist Pavlov, gazing down benignly at the dog and the monkey nestling affectionately against his breast. He looked a little bit like George Bernard Shaw.

I had the water massage twice a week, on Tuesdays and Fridays. There was a large, oblong tank finished in white tile which the nurse would fill with lukewarm water. Dressed in my bathing trunks, I would lower myself into the tank, gripping the hand-rail on either side. Then the nurse, a pretty brunette, would go over every inch of my body with a thin, powerful water jet coming from a rubber hose attached to a pump. She missed nothing.

After only a few days at the sanatorium everyone was wondering what this strange *Anglichanin* (Englishman) was doing in their midst. Everyone was given the same story, even the superintendent. I was an Englishman who had been working for years as a journalist in South Africa. The South African Government didn't like the left-wing views I frequently expressed and had ordered me to leave the country. I was now having a well-earned rest as a guest of the Soviet Union. This made me a great hero in the eyes of the superintendent, and he never lost an opportunity to shake hands with me.

Slava could stay in Sochi only a week and had then to return to Moscow. During that week we made a number of trips by boat to other towns along the coast. Before taking me anywhere Slava would first check with the local KGB office to get a detailed account of the movements of any foreigners who might be in the area. "We cannot have dinner in the Magnolia Hotel tonight," he would say, "because there is a party of English people staying there."

One day we were travelling from Sochi to Sukhumi, capital of the tiny autonomous republic of Abkhasia in Georgia. The hydrofoil, skimming along over the calm surface of the Black Sea, was halfway to its destination when Slava pulled his diary out of his pocket. "By the way, Sean," he said, flicking through the pages, "we shall arrive in Sukhumi at two o'clock and will be leaving again at six. A party of American tourists will arrive at five and will leave at nine. We and they will be in the town together for only one hour, so we are unlikely to meet. However, during that one hour between five and six we shall have to be careful."

Before returning to Moscow, Slava arranged with the KGB in Sochi to look after me for the remainder of my stay. Even they were not told my true identity but were led to believe, like the people in the sanatorium, that I had come from South Africa. A young man of about thirty-two named Valodya was assigned to me. He laid on every facility. If I wanted a car I had only to pick up the telephone, and by the time I reached the front door it was already waiting. And there were plenty of girls. The Sochi office had a huge black car, a Zim, which is normally used by Soviet Ambassadors abroad. In a country where very few people have any sort of car, this easily impressed the girls. The Zim would sweep up to the front door of the sanatorium, Valodya sitting beside the chauffeur and two girls in the back. "Robert, hello!" he would shout. "What are you standing there for? Jump in! Don't keep these lovely girls waiting!" And then the car would speed off down the middle of the drive, people jumping out of its path on both sides and Valodya laughing at the top of his voice all the way. The Sochi KGB were much more relaxed and informal than their comrades in Moscow. It may have been the climate and the seaside way of life.

I met plenty of girls. There was Svetlana, a student doctor from Kiev, blond, beautiful, and twenty-two. And there was her friend Sonya, dark, twenty-four, and a student engineer. Neither of them spoke English, but that was no obstacle. There was Natasha, a brunette of twenty-three who worked in Sochi as an Intourist guide. Her English wasn't bad. Then there were Ekaterina, Nadia, and Golina. Valodya and I would take the girls to a restaurant—the favourite was a Georgian restaurant at the top of a tall peak in the Caucasus called Bolshoi Ahun—and later we would split up. If it was before midnight I might take the girl to the sanatorium—thus breaking another rule— or Valodya would use his power to arrange a room at a hotel in the town.

But for all his humanity and hard living Valodya did not neglect his duty as a KGB officer. "As with most people in a seaside town, our work is pretty seasonal," he explained in his ponderous English. "In the summer a lot of foreign tourists come here, and that keeps us busy. In the winter there are very few tourists, and we can relax. At the moment I am permanently stationed in the Sochi Hotel. I have a lot of Western tourists to keep an eye on."

One day he came to see me unexpectedly at the sanatorium. He pulled a little red notebook out of his pocket and selected a page. "Robert," he said, "what is a filtering plant manager?" I explained as best I could what I thought a filtering plant manager was. "Well," he went on, "we have an Englishman from somewhere near London who describes himself as a filtering plant manager. He is staying at the Magnolia Hotel so we must avoid that restaurant for a couple of days." During my weeks in Sochi, Valodya was to make many references to that little red book.

It was originally planned that I should stay in Sochi for a month and return to Moscow on Saturday, August 19. But the day before my departure Vladimir, the head of the Sochi office, came to see me at the sanatorium and told me that he had just received a message from Moscow saying that I should stay another week. Mrs. Blake, I assumed, had decided to delay her departure for London.

The following Saturday, August 26, Valodya accompanied me to the airport. He came with me right to the plane, and we said our farewells at the bottom of the steps. Halfway up, I glanced back over my shoulder. Valodya had his little red notebook in his hand and was writing down the registration number of the plane.

Victor was waiting for me at Moscow Airport with a car. "How is George?" I asked as we sped towards the city.

"Oh, he is fine," Victor said. "His mother left only yesterday. He is very happy to have seen her again."

Blake was at the flat when I arrived. "Well, well, well," he said, beaming. "I must say, Robert, the Black Sea seems to have done you a great deal of good. I've never seen you looking so well. And what a suntan! You're positively bronze!"

"I don't feel too bad either," I told him. "I had a very nice holiday. Very nice indeed."

"That sounds interesting. What did you do?"

I told him all about Sochi, going into considerable detail about the girls.

"My, my!" he exclaimed. "It sounds like something out of *A Thousand and One Nights*, or out of James Bond for that matter."

"Just a month in the life of Sean Bourke." I laughed. "And how did you get on yourself?"

"We had a wonderful time," Blake said. "My mother and I spent the first three weeks in the Carpathian Mountains. We stayed in a little chalet by a lake and went bathing and boating every day. The weather was marvellous. Then we came back to Moscow. Stan put a car at our disposal and we went into the country almost every day. My mother enjoyed herself tremendously." He filled two glasses with brandy and handed me one. "By the way," he went on, "my mother was able to give me some very interesting information about the activities of the police while we were in hiding in London. The Special Branch were at her house within an hour of the escape. They asked her if she knew anything about it, and she admitted straightaway that you had asked her for seven hundred pounds to finance the operation. A few days later an Inspector flew out to Bangkok to talk to Adele, and she confirmed my mother's story. So, you see, they were on to you from the start." Blake grinned.

"I see."

"The Special Branch were furious with you," he went on. "They did everything they could to discredit you in the hope that if she knew where you were hiding she would give you away. The Special Branch Inspector in charge of the investigation told my mother that you were an evil man and that you were likely to come back and try to blackmail her. That, in fact, was the explanation he gave her for keeping a permanent watch on the house."

"Coming from the police, that doesn't surprise me at all," I said.

Blake sipped his drink. "There is something else that will interest you, Robert. A book has been published about me called *Shadow of a Spy*. The last few chapters deal with the escape, and you are named as the brains behind it. Just before publication it was serialized in the *Sunday Express*. Stan is going to bring the papers and the book on Monday."

"I look forward to reading them," I said.

Blake then told me that he had got tired of Zinaida Ivanovna's cooking and persuaded the KGB to move her and her daughter out of the flat.

I started to unpack my case. At the bottom there were some photographs wrapped in a towel. I had taken them in Moscow during the winter and spring, and a girl named Anna, who had been trying to teach me Russian, had got them developed for me. They were perfectly ordinary photographs of Moscow and the surrounding countryside. Some of them had even been taken by Victor and showed Blake and me posing together. I had forgotten that they were in my case until I arrived in Sochi. I unwrapped the photographs and was just about to put them in the desk drawer when Blake caught sight of them. He dashed across the room and snatched the photographs from my hand. "I haven't seen these, have I?" He frowned. "I better have a look at them." Without another word he took the photographs to his own room. Next day I got them back with the comment that they had not come out too well.

Stan called on Monday and, as usual, went straight to Blake's room. I felt instinctively that the time had come for some decision to be made about me. It was now almost the end of August and I had been in the Soviet Union eight months. If Stan didn't make a move soon I would take the initiative myself. I had known for a long time that I was being spied upon by Blake and that I was the subject of lengthy discussions in his room. I felt that I was going to be discussed tonight and that the discussion would have a direct bearing on my position. I put on a pair of carpet slippers and went quietly to the kitchen. I left the kitchen door ajar. I filled the kettle and put it on the gas stove to boil. Then I walked across to the cabinet where the cups and saucers were and slid back the glass front. The cabinet was near the kitchen door, and from where I stood the voices of the two men reached me quite clearly. They were discussing the book *Shadow of a Spy*. The topic was brought to a close and the conversation turned to me.

"How did Sean enjoy his holiday?" Stan asked.

"Well, he made it sound as though he had a great time," Blake answered. "He talked of wild dinner parties at restaurants and mentioned about six girls that he had been to bed with. But that's probably a lot of lies."

"Oh, I don't think so." Stan sounded surprised at this insinuation. "You see, I told the people in Sochi to lay everything on for him. After all, Sean had been cooped up in this flat for seven months. He needed a break."

There was a short silence. Blake, I imagined, must be very disappointed that his little bit of poison hadn't worked. But he was not going to give up so easily.

"By the way, Stan," Blake said, "there is something you should know about. When he got back on Saturday he was unpacking his case and I was in the room with him. Hidden away at the bottom of the case, wrapped up in a towel, he had a lot of photographs. As he took them out of the case he tried to hide them from me, but I spotted them just in time and took them off him. Now the point is this. I know for a fact that he did not have these photographs before he went on holiday. Do you think he made contact with someone from the West while he was in Sochi, got these photographs developed, and then passed on copies of them to this foreigner?"

Stan thought for a moment. I knew he was turning this question over very carefully in his highly disciplined mind. "Well, I don't really think so," he said slowly.

The kettle started to boil, and I went to the stove and made the tea. Then I went back to the cabinet.

"Yes, I think that's the best idea," Blake was saying. "You'll go out and tell him yourself, will you?"

"Yes, I think I should," Stan answered.

I picked up the teapot and a cup and saucer and went back to the study. I sat behind the desk in the hope that it would give me some slight psychological advantage. A few minutes later Stan knocked on the door. He was very polite and never entered my room without knocking.

"Come in," I called.

He pushed the door open. "Good evening, Sean. How are you?" He took a couple of paces towards me, his hand outstretched.

I stood up, leaned over the desk, and shook hands with him. "Not bad, Stan, and you?"

"All right," he said.

"Please sit down." I nodded towards the couch.

He sat sideways, to face me, his left arm lying along the back of the couch. He had a serious, almost troubled, expression. "Sean, now that you have been in Moscow eight months, and the summer is finished, and you've had your holiday, you must be giving some thought to your future."

"I seldom think of anything else."

He hesitated a moment. "We have been thinking about it too, and our conclusion is that you should stay in the Soviet Union for at least five years."

The words fell on my ears like thunder. I felt numbed. It was exactly the same sensation I had felt as I stood in the dock at Sussex Assizes and the judge pronounced sentence: "Prisoner at the bar, you will go to jail for seven years." I stared at Stan without speaking. My face felt flushed, and I knew I looked angry.

"I'm sorry," he said. "Don't take it too badly."

"How do you expect me to take it?" I asked, unable to control my resentment.

"But what other course is there?" Stan looked as troubled as he sounded.

"What other course is there?" I repeated. "I made it perfectly clear from the beginning, even in Berlin, that I wanted to stay here for only a few months and then return to Ireland. You accepted this when we first spoke about it here in this flat eight months ago."

"Yes, that's very true." Stan's voice was quiet and conciliatory. "But a lot has happened since then. You have become a well-known figure. Your photograph is frequently in the papers and people write about you in books. You would be recognized wherever you went. It would even be difficult for you to get from here to Ireland without running the risk of being arrested. And remember, Sean"—his voice became even more solemn—"you have the safety of other people in your hands. That is a big responsibility."

I looked at him sharply. "Are you suggesting that I would betray my friends to the police if I was arrested?"

Stan sat up straight. "No, of course not," he said quickly.

"I'm relieved to hear that. The police would get no information out of me. I would die first."

Stan leaned back on the couch once more. "I accept without hesitation that you would not give information under physical force. Unfortunately, though, you would not be dealing with ordinary policemen. The people who would be dealing with you would not be interested in beating you up. No, they are much more subtle than that. They can give you a drug that will make you talk without your even knowing it. And to make matters worse, this drug could have a permanent effect on your health."

My scepticism must have shown.

"I can assure you, Sean, I have personal knowledge of this. They got hold of one of our men in London a few years ago and gave him the full treatment. He told them everything they wanted to know. They didn't even bother putting him on trial. When they had finished with him they just put him on a plane for Moscow. The man's nervous system was so badly affected by the drug that he has become a permanent invalid. He now has a pension for life from our Service."

I felt like jumping to my feet and shouting at the top of my voice, "For God's sake, you're not talking to a child!" It wasn't that I thought the British Secret Service incapable of such a thing. There was no reason for believing that MI6 was any different from the KGB or the CIA. All secret services existed to bypass the normal legal procedures. If a London constable took the law into his own hands it was called "un-English," but MI6 were not bound by such nice standards. They existed to do all those *un*-English things that had to be done for the sake of preserving the things that *were* English. No, what annoyed me was Stan's apparent belief that I could be so easily frightened. But I was also a little disappointed. The man sitting before me was a colonel in the KGB, the world's most powerful and most efficient secret service. He was not just a spy, or even a master spy, but a master of master spies. As head of the British section of the KGB, he had the job of controlling and directing the Blakes and the Philbys and the Macleans. The clumsiness with which this clever man now tried to frighten me was unexpected. But at the same time it was reassuring. It showed that he was, after all, human, a man of flesh and blood and emotions, and not just an automaton, not just a machine.

"Don't look so depressed, Sean." The concern in Stan's voice was genuine. It was obvious that he did not enjoy this particular task.

A vague plan was already beginning to form in my mind, and I decided to start playing for time. I would not say anything that would put Stan in a corner and force the hand of the KGB. "Well"—I shrugged—"how would you feel if you had just learned that you had to stay in a particular country for five years whether you liked it or not?"

"But I can assure you that you can have a free choice about where to live. Every town in every one of the fifteen republics of the Soviet Union is open to you. And we will give you every assistance to pursue a worth-while career in publishing."

I shrugged again and said nothing.

Stan stood up to go. "Well, think about it anyway, and I'll see you again in a few days."

I stood up too, and we shook hands and said good night.

A few minutes later I heard the locks of the front door being wound open and the mumble of voices in the hall. "Well, good night, Stan," Blake was saying in his sugary voice. "It was nice seeing you."

The door shut, the locks were wound home again, and then Blake was walking across the dining-room towards my room.

"Well, Robert," he said, smiling, seating himself in a straight-backed chair against the opposite wall, "I understand you've been having an interesting discussion."

I looked at him coldly. "Yes, I've just been sentenced to five years' imprisonment."

Blake's smile vanished. "Well, I would hardly put it like that."

"Wouldn't you? Well, that's how I put it."

"But you've been told that you can go anywhere you like in the Soviet Union. The Soviet Union is a very big place."

I kept my eyes on his. "If I'm told that I must stay in a country against my will, that makes me a prisoner. The size of the prison is not relevant."

Blake looked hurt. "But if you were to return to Ireland you would be handed over to the British and you would finish up in prison anyway."

I leaned forward over the desk. "If I were given a free choice in the matter, I would rather spend the next five years in an English prison on porridge and goulash than here on champagne and caviar."

"Do you really mean that?" he demanded angrily.

"Yes, I do. It's a price I would willingly pay for the privilege of living once more in the Western world among my own people."

"But you've been told that you can go back in five years." Blake was getting angrier and raising his voice.

"For Christ's sake, give me credit for some bit of intelligence," I shouted. "This five years is just a delaying action. If I'm a prisoner today, why should I be any less a prisoner in five years' time? The idea is that I should be kept in this country for the rest of my life—and you know it."

"I don't agree," Blake said indignantly. "You never know what changes might occur in five years."

I picked up a ruler and pointed it at him. "Listen. The only way that it would be possible for me to set foot on British soil without going to prison would be for the British to have a Communist revolution. And I don't want that to happen because then Britain would be as bad as this God-forsaken bloody country and I wouldn't *want* to go back there. There would be no point."

Blake stood up. I could see that he was making an effort to control his temper. "And what exactly don't you like about this country?" he demanded. He was being hypocritical, for I knew that he disliked living in Russia as much as I did.

"Everything," I said.

He hesitated for a moment. "But at least you would be free here."

"Free!" I laughed ironically. "Now you're making a mockery of the word freedom. Nobody is free in this bloody country. The Russians don't know what the word freedom means." I stood up. "There is only one mind and one conscience in the Soviet Union, and that's the Communist Party. The people are treated like children. They are told what to think and what to say and what to feel. They read in their so-called newspapers exactly what the Party wants them to read; they hear on Radio Moscow what the Party wants them to hear; they see on their television screens just what the Party wants them to see. And everybody is afraid to complain. They are frightened and intimidated without even fully realizing it, because they have never been otherwise and don't know any different. To the Russian people Lenin is God. For fifty years, by command of the Communist Party, the Russian people have prostrated themselves before the image of Lenin in every corner of the land with a fervour and devotion that their forefathers would never have displayed before their icons and their crucifixes. And by God, if the Party decreed tomorrow that Lenin was anti-Communist, these same people would tear down his statues and burn his portraits in the streets!"

I was trembling with anger. Blake was visibly shocked, but in view of my mood decided not to pursue the point.

"Well, anyway," he said in a quieter voice, "whatever you might think of this country and its people, you yourself could have a very comfortable life here. You could have a good job, a car, a nice apartment, security for life. Here you would be a privileged and honoured citizen. Back there you would be just an ex-convict."

"I'd rather dig trenches for the rest of my life in Britain or Ireland, than live in luxury here against my will! And I've had experience at digging trenches."

Blake shrugged resignedly. "Well, it's entirely up to you. They can hardly keep you here against your will. It would be more trouble than it's worth. If you don't want to stay here, then obviously you must go."

"It's not as obvious as all that," I said, watching Blake's face very closely. "It is not the only alternative."

Blake looked at me sharply. The thought, obviously, had already been in his mind.

"Oh, well, I shouldn't worry about anything like that," he said reassuringly. "They can't very well do that. After all, I am living here too, and I would know about it." Then his expression abruptly changed and his eyes grew cold. The pretence of concern for my well-being vanished as suddenly as it had been assumed. "I'll tell you one thing," he said coldly. "If this was fifteen years ago, the question of your leaving would not have arisen, I can assure you of that." A faraway look came into his eyes. "No indeed, the question would not have arisen."

Blake, of course, was talking about the reign of terror under Stalin, when the murderous Beria was head of the KGB. Suddenly I realized that Blake himself had begun to work for the KGB while Stalin and Beria were still in power. Blake had worked for Beria! Now I could understand that faraway look in his eyes. He actually longed for those days of intimidation and murder.

"You're quite right, the question would not have arisen—Because I would not have been stupid enough to come to this country while that mass-murderer Stalin and his psychopathic hatchetman Beria were terrorizing the Soviet Union. No, the question would not have arisen." I could see that Blake was making an effort to control himself and I knew that I could say these things with impunity. Stalin had been denounced and Beria had been shot. The new generation of KGB officers, men like Stan and Slava, were embarrassed by the past.

"I think you're being extremely foolish about this whole business," Blake said finally and went back to his own room.

Stan phoned next day and Blake spoke to him for a few minutes. "Oh yes, he's fine, Stan, fine," I heard him say. Then Blake called me. "I say, Robert, Stan would like to talk to you."

I took the phone. "Hello, Sean here."

"Hello, Sean. How are you feeling?"

"Not bad, not bad at all."

"You're not feeling too depressed?"

"No, I'm not."

"Oh, good. I'm very pleased to hear that." Stan spoke with sincerity. His concern was genuine. "I'll call you again later in the week," he said.

"All right, Stan." We said good-bye.

Blake had been hovering in the background. "Well, just imagine that!" he exclaimed. "The KGB ringing up to ask you how you feel. Actually concerned about you. My, my. It wouldn't have happened a few years ago. Things *have* changed." There was a look of real amazement on his face. He found it difficult to understand that there could be men in the KGB with a sense of ordinary human decency, men who were not as ruthless as Blake himself. And that faraway look came into his eyes again.

Blake spent all of that day reading *Shadow of a Spy*, which Stan had brought the night before, and the following morning passed it on to me. The book was written by E. H. Cookridge, himself a former Intelligence officer. It covered all of Blake's life, from his childhood in Holland to his escape from Wormwood Scrubs Prison. The section dealing with his work in Berlin stated that Blake was the one who had betrayed the "Berlin Tunnel" to the KGB. This was a tunnel, dug by the CIA, and MI6, going from West Berlin deep into East Berlin. Its purpose was to enable the British and Americans to tap the underground telephone cables linking East Berlin with Moscow. According to Cookridge, this tunnel had been in use for some time before it was "blown" by Blake; it had been one of the West's greatest triumphs in espionage.

I finished the book that evening and took it back to Blake. "Well," I said, pushing his room door open and going in, "it was certainly interesting. So you were the one who told the KGB about that tunnel?"

Blake pushed his notes aside and leaned back in his chair, smiling broadly. "My friend"—he tilted his head backwards and looked down his nose pompously—"the KGB knew about that tunnel before the first spadeful of earth was dug out of the ground. I saw to that."

"Did you?" I tried to sound impressed. "So all those top-secret messages that the British and Americans listened into that year were all specially laid on for the purpose by the KGB?"

"Naturally." Blake gave a triumphant little grin and turned back to his writing.

Stan called on Friday. My short experience of Secret Service work had taught me at least one lesson: the value of knowing what an enemy or potential enemy was thinking and planning. I put on my slippers and went to the kitchen. I left the door ajar and very quietly put the kettle on the stove. With a cup in my right hand I stood near the door and listened.

Stan and Blake were discussing Mrs. Blake's next visit to Moscow in December. She would travel overland by train from Holland and go right on into East Berlin. There she would be met by Vladimir and flown from East Berlin to Moscow. The discussion went on for almost half an hour.

"Very well," said Blake finally, "that is that problem out of the way."

There was a short silence. Then, lowering his voice, Blake went on, "Now then, about our friend. When you left Monday night I went into his room to talk to him, as I told you I would. We had a long discussion about what you had said to him. He completely accepted your decision, there is no doubt at all about that. He even said that he would now settle down to learning Russian in earnest. I was quite surprised that he accepted the situation so readily. Now, this is the point. On Wednesday I lent him *Shadow of a Spy*, in which he himself, of course, is mentioned. Immediately he had finished reading it his whole attitude changed. He no longer wanted to stay in the Soviet Union. He hated the Soviet Union and wanted to go back to the West. His change of attitude was almost incredible."

Stan listened in silence.

"There is no doubt at all in my mind," Blake went on, "about what his motives are. He doesn't hate the Soviet Union at all. This book has given him ideas. The only reason he wants to go back to the West is so that he can make money out of all this."

Stan still said nothing. He wasn't being very helpful to Blake. I couldn't help drawing a comparison between the two men at that moment: Stan—strong, resolute, exuding self-confidence; Blake—weak, erratic, unsure of himself, playing Iago to Stan's Othello.

Getting no comment from Stan, Blake went on, "Of course, we must remember, Stan, that at the moment the whole world believes that the KGB organized the escape and that our friend was only used. This means great prestige for you people. Now, if he is allowed to go back to the West and tell his story, you people will no longer get the credit."

I could hear Stan getting to his feet. He started to pace up and down. This was a sure sign that he was troubled. Blake's poison was beginning to work. A whole minute elapsed. Then Stan spoke for the first time.

"I don't think that part of it matters so much," he said thoughtfully. "You see, no matter what Sean might write, people will always believe that we had something to do with the escape. No, my only concern is for those other people in London."

Stan continued to pace up and down. Blake knew that he had him on the run. Then he struck.

"As I see it, Stan," he said slowly, his voice as cold as ice, "you are faced with only two alternatives. You can go out there now and tell him that he must stay in this country for at least five years whether he likes it or not—and if you like I will tell him for you. Or you can . . ." The sentence remained unfinished.

Stan stopped dead in his tracks. My whole body went numb. My heart was pounding against my ribs. It was so loud in that awful silence that I thought Stan and Blake must hear it. "Finish the sentence," I whispered, "finish the sentence! For God's sake, finish it! Anything would be better than this terrible silence." But Blake had already said what he wanted to say, and beyond that there was nothing else that could be said.

Hardly aware of what I was doing, I turned off the gas under the kettle and made my way back to my room. I was feeling dazed. I sat behind the desk, staring straight in front of me. My first instinct was to run, to leave the flat and run into the streets and keep running. But where could I run to? I was in a strange city in a strange land, among an alien people. There was nobody out there that I could ask for help. Though I had never harmed or wanted to harm the Soviet Union, I was now their enemy. With a few treacherous words, Blake had made me their enemy.

Why? I asked myself, Why? What had I done to Blake? In what way had I ever tried to harm him? In what way had I tried to harm communism? But, of course, it wasn't that. Blake's action had nothing to do with ideals or noble causes. The only thing at stake for Blake was his personal vanity, his only motive was an insatiable thirst for power. Blake needed the KGB a lot more than the KGB needed him. The KGB was his muscle, his strength, his backbone. Without the KGB he was just a weak, insignificant little man. Blake liked to play God. For years he had used the KGB for his own selfish ends. He had used them to enable him to wield the power of life and death over other men, stronger men than himself. This was the only way he could ever achieve power. This power had not been a means to an end, but an end in itself. Blake needed this power to survive. It was his life's blood. Without it he was nothing.

And now his power was gone. But not quite. I was to be the final sacrifice on the altar of Blake's vanity.

How would they do it? They would hardly shoot me here in the flat. That would mean carrying the body away. No. There would be a drive into the country. That would not rouse my suspicions. We had driven into the country many times during the winter and spring and we had gone for long walks in the forest. "I say, Robert, they have very kindly put a car at our disposal for the afternoon. What about a trip into the country?" They would allow me to walk ahead. There would be a whispered instruction behind me, a rustling of clothing, and then oblivion. Even in Russian prisons capital punishment was carried out in this way. The condemned man thought he was being taken to see the doctor or some other official. He walked down a long corridor. Then the guard dropped behind, and a moment later the sentence of the court had been carried out.

Would Blake come with them? Yes, he would have to, otherwise it would look suspicious. The grave would already be dug and waiting —a dark, damp hole deep in the forest, the freshly dug clay piled up around the edges, and lying crumpled on the bottom a still-warm body dressed in a smart English suit. No coffin. The wet clay would be shovelled in on top of the soft flesh. And the only sign of any disturbance in the calm autumn forest would be a small patch of fresh earth standing out briefly against the backcloth of yellow autumn leaves. Was this how all Blake's victims died? It was unofficially said that there had been forty-two of them, one for each year of his sentence. Blake had always denied this in Wormwood Scoubs, and at that time I had believed him.

I could kill Blake, if I had a gun. If I knew beyond doubt that my death was imminent I could take him with me.

At this moment I needed a distraction, any distraction, to take my mind off Blake's treachery. I had a small record player on the window sill to the left of the desk and beside it a pile of records. I flicked through them. Tchaikovsky's "Piano concerto No. 1." The wrong mood entirely. Beethoven's "Fifth." God, no! Finally I selected the "Appassionata" played by Richter. But it didn't help. The music was like a weak anaesthetic fighting a losing battle with an excruciating pain. Blake's treacherous words kept penetrating my brain.

Blake frightened me. If a man wanted to harm me because he hated me I could understand it and cope with it. Hate was something tangible. I was capable of hatred myself. But I knew that Blake did not hate me. He had no reason to. He could send me to my death with a glass of champagne in his hand and a smile on his face. I had never met anyone like him in my life before.

I heard voices out in the hall.

"Well, good night, Stan. It was nice seeing you. Have a nice week-end."

The door shut, the locks were wound home, and the chain rattled onto its hook. A minute later I heard Blake's quick, effeminate footsteps on the dining-room floor as he crossed to my room. He pushed the door open and came in. He was wearing his red dressing-gown. In one hand he held a bottle of champagne; in the other, two glasses.

"I say, Robert, what is your attitude to a glass of champagne?"

"I wouldn't mind one at all," I said.

"Oh, jolly good." He put the two glasses on the desk in front of me and filled them up. He handed me one, picked up the other, and went to the couch. He sat at the far end, facing me, and leaned back in an elaborate pose of leisurely relaxation, his left arm hanging loosely over the back of the couch. He raised his glass. "To you, Robert."

"Thank you," I said. The bubbling champagne tasted bitter in my mouth.

"Ah!" Blake sighed, looking rapturously at his glass. "Champagne and beautiful music! What more can one ask for?" He looked at me and smiled. The tiny blue scars on his forehead stood out darker than ever, a brutal and mocking reminder of my own folly.

On Sunday, Blake and I went to the Ararat Restaurant, not far from the Bolshoi Theatre, for lunch. It was a habit we had got into during the past few months. Being near Blake now was quite distasteful, but I was determined to make him talk as much as possible in the hope that I might glean some sort of meaning for his actions. I made up my mind to take full advantage of this occasion as I now felt sure that whatever happened it was likely to be the last time we would sit down to a meal together.

We had roast chicken and a bottle of red Georgian wine. I had insisted on paying for the meal so that I could order a second bottle. I steered the conversation round to communism and the Soviet Union. I just *had* to know how Blake's mind worked. I *had* to be sure that I was not making some dreadful mistake. This was my last chance. Halfway through the second bottle of wine I started talking about means and ends.

"If the end is good enough," Blake declared, "*any* means are justified to bring it about."

"And do you think that communism justifies the use of any means to achieve it?" I asked.

"Most certainly."

"Very well," I said, "let's take a hypothetical situation. Supposing that half the population of the world had to be killed before communism could be achieved. Would that be justified?"

Blake poured some wine into his glass and then, noticing that mine was almost empty, filled it up. He put the empty bottle to one side and looked at me. "Yes, my friend. It would be fully justified."

I sipped my wine thoughtfully. I didn't want to sound impatient lest he should become suspicious. "But I thought," I said, "that communism was supposed to be for the benefit of mankind. How do the dead half of the people benefit?"

Blake shrugged. "They don't, of course. That is unfortunate, perhaps. But the surviving half of the population *do* benefit. This makes it worth while to sacrifice the other half."

There was a silence. I had to be careful how I asked my final question. "So I take it then," I said casually, "that you agree with Stalin and Beria?"

Blake looked long and thoughtfully into his glass. "Yes," he said slowly, "I do agree with them. It may be that innocent people died, but it was worth it. If they hadn't died there would have been a lot more bloodshed in the long run." He looked up at me. "The end justifies the means."

I paid the bill and we left the restaurant. Blake rushed on ahead of me. He was a fast walker and never bothered to modify his pace for my convenience. It was up to me to keep up with him if I so chose. Now as he raced ahead of me I found myself looking at him more intently than I had ever done before: narrow shoulders and slim, graceful body; quick, effeminate walk; long, black, greasy hair hanging over the collar of his shirt, a red patch of scalp showing through his thinning crown. I was filled with revulsion. I had to make an effort to stop myself from shouting out my feelings at the top of my voice.

We turned left and headed up Marx Prospect towards Dzerzhinsky Square. At the Metro station Blake stopped and leaned on the rail at the edge of the pavement. The KGB Headquarters dominated the square at the opposite side. It was a seven-story buff-coloured building, forming a whole block unto itself, its ground-floor windows barred and carefully screened to a point well above eye level. Directly in front of it, in the centre of the square, was the statue to the founder of the Russian Secret Service: Felix Edmundovich Dzerzhinsky, 1877–1926. He was a great humanitarian and loved children. At the left-hand side of the square, at right angles to the KGB office, was the huge department store that specialized in children's goods. This shop was called Detsky Mir (Children's World). At the top of this building, near the roof, the name was spelled out in large neon letters.

Blake looked from the KGB office to the department store, and his eyes travelled slowly upwards and came to rest on the neon sign. He forced a smile. "How very appropriate," he said.

"What?" I asked.

"The KGB office being next to the Children's World."

"Oh?"

"Yes, my friend, all this Secret Service work is so utterly childish. One big game. It makes me laugh."

"Except that these children play for real," I observed.

Blake snorted. "In London we used to call our office the Wimbledon Club."

"Why's that?" I asked.

"Because it was all balls and rackets." He turned his back on me and rushed away.

How very transparent this master spy had suddenly become! The reason he now tried to denigrate the work of the Secret Service was because he no longer belonged. At the height of his power and glory he had contrived to work for two Services, so that he might have a double measure of power. He had betrayed the British, and now even the Russians had no further use for him. He had been deprived of his reason for living.

That evening I was in my room, sitting behind the desk, thinking of my position. Whatever was going to be done about me would be done within the next few days, possibly tomorrow. By now I had no further illusions about Blake and I had made up my mind what I must do. And yet, I thought, there must be some small spark of decency in his make-up. Nobody could be as ruthless as that. Perhaps if I were to confront him, face to face, one man to another? That way all possible doubt would be removed. After all, he owed me a favour.

I went and knocked on Blake's door.

"Come in."

I pushed the door open.

Blake, resplendent in his crimson dressing-gown, was standing before his full-length mirror, his back to me. "Yes?" he said without looking round.

"I want to return to Ireland," I said. "I hope I can count on your support."

Blake turned on me abruptly, his face flushed with anger. "My support!" he shouted. "My support! Why should *I* give you *my* support?" He spat the words at me contemptuously. "I don't think you should be allowed to leave the Soviet Union. If you want to leave this country, that's *your* funeral. Don't come asking *me* for help." He tilted his head back and looked down his nose at me, his hands on his hips.

Russia was the only place in the world where Blake could have spoken to me like that. It was the only place where he would have dared to do it.

Without a word I turned and left the room.

16

A Gamble with Death

At three o'clock next day I left the flat, telling Blake that I was going ✿✿
for a walk. It was Monday, September 4, 1967. I walked up Khmel- ✿✿
nitsky Street, crossed the junction with New Square, and entered
Kuibysheva Street. On the left I passed the green-and-white-painted
headquarters of the Communist Party of the Soviet Union, its privacy
protected by white screens on all the windows, and on the right,
GUM, the huge State department store whose dismal interior of long,
narrow corridors and overhead galleries reminded me of Wormwood
Scrubs Prison—except that the shop assistants at GUM smiled a lot
less than the screws at Wormwood Scrubs.

I entered Red Square. At the far side was the front wall of the
Kremlin, with the main entrance to the Kremlin itself and the Kremlin
clock overhead. Halfway along to the right, in front of the Kremlin
wall, stood Lenin's Mausoleum, squat and solid like an air-raid shelter.
Way off to the right, up at the north end of the Square, was the tall
red-brick Historical Museum. Immediately to my left, looking like
something out of a fairy tale with its onionlike domes, was the beautiful St. Basil's Cathedral, built in the 1550s by Ivan the Terrible to
celebrate the seizure of Kazan. It dominated the south end of the
Square. In front of the cathedral and slightly to the left of it was the
round stone platform with eight steps leading up to it, on which the
czars beheaded their enemies. As I looked now there was a small knot
of people standing on the eighth step and gazing in over the low
wrought-iron gate at the small round block in the centre on which the
condemned man laid his head to await the axe.

Hundreds of people, alone and in groups, were strolling about the Square, leisurely treading its smoothly worn cobblestones. The usual knot of sightseers were gathered in front of the Mausoleum just staring at its black marble entrance with the five golden letters overhead that spelled Lenin. The Mausoleum was flanked by two sentries.

The Kremlin clock, Radio Moscow's tinny, pre-puberty version of deep-voiced Big Ben, chimed out the hour of four. Two sentries, accompanied by their escorting NCO, emerged from the main entrance of the Kremlin and goosestepped towards the Mausoleum to relieve the two already there. There was a flurry of interest from the people on the Square, and many of them hurried across to line the path of the strutting, robotlike soldiers and to crowd in front of the Mausoleum to watch the changing of the guard. Here and there a tourist camera was quickly raised to eye level and lowered again.

The Moscow River flows past the south wall of the Kremlin and is separated from it by the Kremlin Embankment. The boundaries of this embankment are formed by two bridges that span the river, one at either end of the Kremlin wall, thus making the embankment the same length as the wall itself. The bridge at the western end leads into Borovitskaya Square, and the one at the eastern end into Red Square. The stretch of the riverbank between these two bridges on the opposite side of the river is called the Maurice Thorez Embankment. Halfway along this embankment, facing the Kremlin across the river, is the British Embassy.

I looked up at the Kremlin clock again: five past four. I turned left and walked past St. Basil's towards the river. I crossed the bridge to the far side and descended the steps to the embankment. I strolled slowly along towards the Embassy, occasionally glancing across the river at the Kremlin, the golden domes of its three cathedrals and the Ivan the Great bell tower gleaming brightly in the mid-afternoon sun.

The British Embassy stands back a little from the street and has a gravelled forecourt, which is separated from the pavement by a wall surmounted by railings. There are two gateways, one used as an entrance by the Embassy cars and the other as an exit. Outside each gateway, and just clear of it, there is a sentry box used by the police guards in bad weather. The top half of the sentry box is glass-panelled to enable the policeman to see in all directions. In fine weather the policemen stroll up and down the pavement.

As I approached the Embassy I could see that the gateway nearest to me was unguarded. The policeman who should have been there was up at the other gateway, talking to the second policeman. With them was the officer in charge. I walked past the unguarded gateway, glancing at the Embassy building without turning my head. I wanted to make sure that the Embassy was open, for once I stepped onto that forecourt I would have defied the KGB. I walked past the second gateway and the three policemen and continued on to the bridge at the other end of the embankment. At the bridge I turned round and started to walk back. My decision was made.

The three policemen were still gathered at the same gateway, talking. I walked past them. At the second gateway I turned abruptly to my right and hurried across the forecourt. Out of the corners of my eyes I could see the three policemen breaking away from each other and staring after me with startled expressions on their faces. I climbed the steps of the Embassy and hurried in the door. On the right, sitting behind a desk, was a middle-aged man in a brown sports coat. I knew he was the receptionist by the cut of his features. Unlike a Russian, the Englishman carried his class clearly stamped on his face.

I put the palms of my hands flat on the desk and looked at him. "Is this the British Embassy?"

"Yes," he answered.

"Good. My name is Sean Bourke. I am wanted by Scotland Yard in connection with the escape of the spy George Blake from Wormwood Scrubs Prison in London. I have come to give myself up."

He looked at me blankly for a moment and then, with typical British unflappability, he said, "Well, would you care to go round next door to the Admin Block?"

I nodded towards the front door. "I think it would be extremely unwise for me to go back out there."

He stood up. "Very well, I'll get someone to come and see you. You can wait in there." He indicated a door opposite the desk.

I went in. It was a waiting-room, furnished like all waiting-rooms with some couches and armchairs and a couple of low tables. There was one window overlooking the forecourt. The view was obscured by a white curtain that extended above eye level. I moved the curtain and looked out. The policemen had resumed their proper positions guarding the gateways; the officer in charge was standing with one of them and staring at the Embassy door.

I sat down with my back to the window. On the table in front of me was a copy of the *Daily Express*. The big black headline on the front page was about a murder.

The door opened and a man came in. He was tall and slim and dressed in a dark suit. I stood up.

"Good afternoon," he said. "Can I help you?"

"I hope so," I told him.

"Please sit down," he invited, seating himself in an armchair opposite me. "In what way can I help?"

"Scotland Yard are looking for a man named Sean Bourke in connection with the escape of George Blake from Wormwood Scrubs," I said.

"Oh, and you know all about it, do you?" he asked.

"I *am* Sean Bourke."

He frowned. "Oh, I see. Hm . . . I think I had better go and talk to someone about this. Will you excuse me a moment, please?"

"Of course."

"Thank you. I'm sorry to leave you alone like this. Won't be long."
He went out.

A few minutes later the door opened again and two other men came in. One was in his late thirties and the other was about twenty-five. They were both dark-haired and dark-suited and, like the first man, looked every inch English. The older man did the talking.

"I'm David," he said, "and this is Paul."

We shook hands.

"Well, what exactly is the problem?" David began.

"My name is Bourke, Sean Bourke. Scotland Yard want to see me about the escape of George Blake from prison in London. I've come here to give myself up."

David smiled, and young Paul, standing a little behind him, smiled too. "And what do you want us to do?" David asked.

This question surprised me. "Well," I said. "I was hoping you might be able to help me get back to Britain."

"Have you got a passport?"

"No."

"How did you get to this country?"

"With a false passport."

"Where is the false passport now?"

"The KGB have it."

"But you're not even British, are you?"

"No, I'm Irish."

David looked at Paul and they both smiled. David shrugged. "How do you expect us to be able to help an Irishman?"

"But it's the British who want me," I protested, "not the Irish."

David shrugged again, and Paul just went on smiling. I looked plaintively from one to the other, and my heart sank at the indifference I saw there.

"Where is Blake now?" David asked.

"He's living here in Moscow and I share his flat."

"What's the address?"

"I'd rather not say. It's a KGB flat, and I'm still in Moscow."

"Hm . . ." David looked at me thoughtfully for a moment. "Will you excuse us?" he said.

"Of course." I stood up as they left.

Five minutes later David was back with another man. This was an older man, about forty-five, with grey hair. He was in his shirt sleeves and looked as though he had hurried from his desk somewhere in the Embassy.

"This is Mr. Harris," David said, introducing him. "He is the Consul and may be able to help you."

"Good afternoon, Mr. Bourke," the Consul said, shaking me by the hand. "Please sit down."

I sat with my back to the window, and David and the Consul sat facing me.

"I understand, Mr. Bourke, that you have no passport," the Consul began. He was much more friendly and down-to-earth than the other three.

"That's right."

"And you came to Moscow with a false passport?"

"Yes."

"You are an Irish citizen, aren't you?"

"I am, yes."

He thought for a moment and then leaned forward and pushed a pad towards me. "If you would care to write down your full name and date and place of birth and your address in Ireland, I'll see if I can get you a passport." I wrote the information he wanted and handed it to him. He studied it for a moment and nodded. "Very well, Mr. Bourke, if you would care to call back in about a week I should have something for you."

I stared at him in open dismay. "Call back in a week! If I leave this Embassy I shall be dead in twenty-four hours!"

"Well, you got yourself into this, didn't you?" David said calmly.

"But what else can we do, Mr. Bourke?" the Consul asked. "I shall have to get in touch with our Foreign Office in London and ask them to approach Dublin, and we shall then have to wait for Dublin to send on a passport."

"But I came here today in defiance of the KGB," I said desperately, "and I rushed into this Embassy while the police had their backs turned. Can't you give me asylum?"

"We can't give you asylum, Mr. Bourke." The Consul's voice was genuinely sympathetic. "You are an Irish citizen, and if we tried to make representations to the Russians on your behalf they would just laugh at us. They would tell us to mind our own business."

"Isn't there any embassy in Moscow that acts for Ireland?" I asked.

The Consul shook his head. "I'm afraid not. Ireland is not represented in any Communist country."

I stared at him in disbelief for a moment and then forced myself to ask the final desperate question. "Isn't there anywhere at all I can hide?"

He looked at me sadly. "No, Mr. Bourke, there's no place you can hide, not in *this* country."

Very slowly I got to my feet. I turned to the window and pulled back the curtain. The two policemen were standing resolutely in the centre of their gateways. The officer was standing next to the one on the right—the gateway through which I had fled. All three had their backs to the street and were glaring grim-faced at the Embassy, their holsters strapped to their hips. I lowered the curtain and turned back to the two diplomats. They too had got to their feet.

"Gentlemen," I began, "you are unlikely ever to see me or hear from me again, and I would like to take this opportunity to say something that I hope will be passed on to the right quarters." I spoke in a calm, resolute voice. "I did, in fact, break George Blake out of prison. I did it entirely on my own. The KGB were in no way involved. The operation cost only a small sum of money, which I was able to borrow from friends, but these friends had no idea what I wanted the money for.

Blake and I left the country immediately, travelling to Berlin on false passports that I had procured earlier. We crossed into East Berlin at the British checkpoint and made contact with the KGB. We stayed a week in East Berlin and were then flown to Moscow in a military aircraft. I have since been sharing a flat here with Blake. It was never my intention to stay in Russia for more than a few months, but now they are reluctant to let me go. It has been said that Blake was responsible for the deaths of forty-two British agents. I, like so many other people, was persuaded by Blake that this was not true. But now I think differently."

I walked to the centre of the room and turned round to face them once more. "One night last week I overheard Blake urging the KGB to murder me."

David stared at me, and the Consul emitted a low, almost silent whistle.

"Blake," I went on, "is an utterly ruthless man. He is completely devoid of any conscience. Not only does he want me dead, but I now know that he would willingly pull the trigger himself." I paused. There seemed nothing else to say. "Well," I concluded, "that's all. I hope my remarks will be passed on." I took a couple of steps towards the door and then noticed the ventilating grill just to the right of the doorjamb. "I suppose this place is bugged?" I asked.

David nodded. "Yes—we assume it is, anyway."

"Just as well," I said. "Perhaps Blake will hear the recording himself. That will be *some* satisfaction."

We stood facing each other in silence for a moment. The two diplomats had the sort of solemn expressions on their faces normally worn by prison governors and chaplains as they watch a condemned man walk to the gallows. David, I thought, was looking solemn because it would have been indecent to do otherwise in the circumstances. But the Consul seemed genuinely upset.

I turned my back on them, pulled the door open, and left the room. In the hall three men were standing in a little group with the receptionist, talking in low voices. They fell silent when I appeared and stood staring at me. I walked quickly to the front door and descended the steps to the forecourt. The policemen were still in position, their backs to the street, and all three were now looking at me. I walked across the forecourt to the gateway on the right, the one where the officer was waiting. He made no move until I stepped onto the pavement, onto Russian soil. Then he blocked my path. I looked at the epaulets on his shoulders. He wore a large star, the insignia of a major.

He said something in Russian, but the only word I could make out was passport. I looked at him blankly for a moment and then said, "*Ni ponimaiu.*" (I do not understand.) He glanced over my shoulder at the Embassy and then beckoned me to move along the pavement with him. We walked about five yards, where we were out of sight of the Embassy windows. He turned to face me again, a very determined look on his face. He said something in Russian.

I shrugged. "*Ni ponimaiu,*" I repeated. "*Ya Anglichanin. Angliskii tourist.*" (I'm an Englishman. An English tourist.)

He held out his hand and uttered one word: "Passport."

"*Nyet,*" I said. I pointed in the general direction of the Leningrad Hotel. "Passport—*Leningradskii Gestinitsa.*" I pulled my diary out of my pocket and pointed at a telephone number. "*Telefon, Leningradskii Gestinitsa.*" In fact, a foreign tourist in Moscow did have to leave his passport at his hotel.

The major looked at me intently, his eyes slightly narrowed. He was trying to make a decision. He wanted to believe me, for his own sake. After all, it was he who had allowed me to get past him into the British Embassy, onto foreign soil. He gave me a doubtful look, then saluted and walked away.

I could hardly believe it. It must have been obvious that I had deliberately evaded them to get into the Embassy. Otherwise why should I have passed the gate where the three of them were standing and walked on to the second, unguarded gate? The major must desperately have wanted to believe me.

I started to walk back along the embankment the way I had come. It was the loneliest walk of my life. I had believed that once I entered the British Embassy I would be safe. That small patch of British soil stood for decency and legality and the English way of life. I had not expected to be turned away, and I could see in the eyes of the men I had spoken to that they believed my death to be imminent.

Within a very short while the KGB would know what I had done. At this very moment the major was probably phoning Dzerzhinsky Square from one of the sentry boxes. Would I make it to the bridge? I felt like running but I dared not. I left the pavement and crossed the road to the river wall. I leaned over the wall and looked down at the fast-flowing river. At this moment the only choice seemed to be what form my death should take. Should I cheat the KGB and rob Blake of some small personal satisfaction? For a full minute I stared, almost unseeing, at the rushing water below. Then I turned my back on the river and walked back to the pavement.

I made my way slowly towards the bridge. Just beyond the bridge, parked outside the Bucharest Hotel, I could see a large touring coach. It had to be foreign because the Russians didn't have such luxury vehicles. Instead of climbing the nearest flight of steps to the street above, I carried on under the bridge and stood about twenty yards from the hotel. Painted on the side of the coach in large gold letters were the words EXCELSIOR TOURS BOURNEMOUTH. The people were getting out of the coach. English people. I wanted to run across to them, to ask them for help. But how could I? I had broken their laws, aided their enemies. They would have no interest in helping me. And anyway my experiences in Sochi had taught me that not far from every party of foreign tourists in the Soviet Union there lurked a KGB man. The last couple got out of the coach and followed the others into the hotel. I kept staring after them until they had disappeared through the door. I took one last long look at those golden English letters and then walked away and slowly climbed the steps to the street above.

I crossed the bridge and walked up behind St. Basil's into Red Square. There was still a little knot of people on the top step of the execution platform. I made my way across to the Mausoleum and moved slowly from one group of sightseers to the next. I was listening for an English voice. I wanted to make one last contact with the Western world so that I would at least have the satisfaction of knowing that the truth about Blake would reach Britain and in particular Michael and Pat and the others who had helped us. But the only foreign tongues I could distinguish were French and German. I reflected on the irony of the situation. For almost a year, on the instructions of the KGB, I had scrupulously avoided all contact with British and American citizens. Now when I searched for them they were not there.

The Kremlin clock struck six. It was an hour since I had left the Embassy, and if the KGB already knew about it, one of the first places they would come looking for me would be Red Square. The sentries came goosestepping out of the Kremlin, and I turned my back on the Mausoleum and made my way towards the north end of the Square. I crossed Marx Prospect to the Bolshoi Theatre and headed up Pushkin Street towards the boulevard. In the boulevard I turned left, crossed Pushkin Square, and carried straight on. Somewhere along the boulevard, I remembered, was the Soviet Journalists' Club. Perhaps some of them occasionally invited a British or American colleague along for a drink. A quarter of an hour later I was there.

The Journalists' Club, like the British Embassy, was set back a little from the street and had a forecourt, but unlike the Embassy it was not detached. It looked like it might at one time have been flush with the buildings on either side and then suddenly been pushed back by some giant hand. I stood on the pavement near the entrance to the forecourt and waited. Every five minutes or so a group of men would enter or leave, and I listened carefully to their voices. Nobody spoke English. I looked at the cars parked at the kerb. They were all Russian Volgas.

Finally, in desperation, I walked across the forecourt and entered the club. Just inside the door on the right, a stout, middle-aged woman sat on a chair. She, I knew, was there to examine all passes. In the Soviet Union you needed a pass, complete with photograph, for every-thing—to enter a library, or an office block, or a hospital, or a club. The woman looked up at me questioningly and said something I did not understand. In very halting Russian I told her that I was looking for an English journalist, "*Angliskii zhyrnaleest*," but she just looked at me uncomprehendingly.

In a room to the right about twenty or thirty reporters were being briefed by an Army colonel. The door was open, but none of them paid any attention to me. Two men came in, showed their red-covered passes to the woman, and started to walk on across the hall. The woman called after them, and I made out the words "This comrade." The men turned and looked at me. I smiled briefly, waved my hand in a gesture of dismissal, and left the building.

I walked on up the boulevard to Arbat Square. I looked at my watch: seven-thirty, two and a half hours since I had left the Embassy. The KBG *must* know by now.

Outside Arbat Metro station there was a phone box. I went in, inserted a two-kopeck piece, lifted the handset off the hook, and dialled the number of the flat.

"Hello." It was Blake's voice.

"Hello. This is Sean here."

"Oh, hello." His voice was questioning.

"Now listen carefully," I said. "I have something very important to tell you. I have just been to the British Embassy and asked them to help me get back to Ireland."

There was a short pause at the other end of the line, then Blake's voice exploded into the phone. "You have done what!" he shouted.

"I have been to the British Embassy," I repeated.

"You have been to the British Embassy!"

"Yes."

Blake seemed to be choked with dismay and anger. "You fool! You complete and utter fool! What did you do that for?"

The anger welled up inside me. "Because I'm sick and tired of you and the KGB and this cloak-and-dagger life!" I shouted. "I'm sick and tired of being a pawn in your little game of revenge against the British Secret Service! I'm sick of the whole bloody thing! I want to return to a normal life. I want to go back to Ireland on an Irish passport made out in my own name, and I want to be myself again."

"And how do you think you're going to achieve that?" His voice was heavy with sarcasm.

"The British have asked me to call back in a week to collect an Irish passport. "I shall then go to the Soviet Foreign Ministry and apply for an exit visa. From now on it's going to be all aboveboard. I'm having nothing more to do with you or the KGB."

"And do you think you're going to get away with that?" Blake demanded incredulously.

"I'm going to try," I said. Of course he was right. Every Western Embassy in Moscow would now be closely guarded by the KGB, as would the Foreign Ministry. I would not get near the British Embassy.

I could hear Blake inhaling angrily through his teeth. "You are even more stupid than I thought you were!" He spat the words at me contemptuously. "And that's really saying something."

"You may think so," I said, "but I don't agree."

"You never told *me* you were going to do this, did you?" he demanded.

This question was not as stupid as it sounded. It was an exercise in self-preservation. It was taken for granted that the telephone in every safe house was tapped, and Blake wanted the KGB to hear me exonerate him.

"Why should I tell you? Why should I tell you anything?"

"You *are* stupid!" Blake shouted. "You really are stupid! You are a stupid fool!"

I could feel my face flushing with anger. My grip tightened on the handset. "You know, I can't understand you," I said. "I can't understand you at all—*comrade!* Any other man in your position would be standing up and waving flags for me. Any other man in your position would be shouting at the top of his voice, 'Let him go, let him go! If the man wants to go home, for God's sake, let him go! He has done me a great favour and he is at least entitled to that much!' But not you, oh no, not you. I just *can't* understand you."

There was a moment's silence as these words sank in. Then Blake, almost overcome with fury, started to stammer and stutter. "How . . . d-d-*dare* you t-t-talk to me like that!" His voice was almost a scream. "How d-d-*dare* you! How d-d-*dare* you! What gives you the right to say things like that to me! What gives you the right! Do you think I have no one else to consider but you! How d-d-*dare* you! How d-d-*dare* you!"

At that moment I realized that Blake was mentally unbalanced. Only a madman could betray you and then ask you how dare you object. I said nothing.

After what seemed a long pause Blake spoke again, this time in a calmer voice. "And what are you going to do now?"

"I'm just going to wander through the streets for the next week and then go back to the British Embassy for my passport."

"But you can't do that. You can't just wander through the streets. The police will pick you up." Now he was just stalling me to give the KGB time to trace the call.

"I'll get by," I said.

"But why not come back to the flat and wait here, and you can still go to the Embassy in a week's time?"

God, I thought, he really must think I'm stupid! Or else he's frightened and trying to reassure the people listening in that he's on their side.

"I'd rather not," I said. "I want to be alone with my thoughts."

"I see. And where are you calling from?" He was getting desperate now.

"A phone box somewhere in Moscow." I hung the handset back on the hook, watched it swing to and fro a couple of times, and then left the box.

I went into the Metro station and caught a train going west. I had no clear idea what I was going to do or where I was going to go, but I wanted to get as far away as possible from the centre of the city. The train was fairly crowded at Arbat station. At Smolenskaya a lot more got in. At Kievskaya the same thing happened. And again at Studencheskaya and Kutuzovskaya. At Fili more got out than in, and at Bagrationovskaya the train was noticeably less full. From there on the train became emptier and emptier. We went through Fili Park, Pionerskaya, Kuntsevskaya, and finally reached Molodyozhnaya, the end of the line. I followed the few remaining passengers up the escalator to the street.

I was in a residential suburb at the western edge of the city. Blake had been right when he said I couldn't just wander through the streets for a week. Nobody could do that in Moscow. A policeman could demand to see your papers at any time, and I had no papers. You couldn't stay in a hotel without a passport even if you were a Russian, and Russians were forbidden by law to check into a hotel in their own town. I looked at my watch: eight o'clock. I had to get out of sight before midnight, before the streets became empty and I became conspicuous in my solitude. I remembered the forest on the edge of Moscow. I used to go for strolls there in the spring and early summer. There was a park over at the eastern edge of the city called Izmailovo Recreation Park. It was really a fenced-off section of the forest with lots of paths and other facilities added. Beyond the fence was the open forest. There was a Metro station at Izmailovo Park, but I would not go by Metro as this would involve travelling across the centre of Moscow, through the busiest stations.

There was a taxi rank just along the street from the Metro station. I went up to the first taxi and got in beside the driver. You were expected to do this. To sit in the back seat would be to put the driver in a different class from yourself, and the driver, after all, was your comrade. Even Army generals and heads of Ministries felt they had to be seen sitting next to their chauffeurs.

"*Metro stantsia Izmailovskii Park, pozhalista,*" I said.

Without a word the driver started the car and we moved off.

In half an hour, we were at the park. The fare was two roubles seventy kopecks, and I gave the driver four roubles. That left me with five roubles in my wallet, the equivalent of two pounds, but money meant the same to me now as it had at Checkpoint Charlie. It made no difference whether I had five roubles, five thousand roubles, or even five million roubles. Money could not buy what I wanted.

I strolled on past the Metro station, past the park, and then left the pavement and walked into the forest. I was plunged into sudden darkness. I raised my left hand and kept the forearm about six inches in front of my face as I staggered and stumbled onwards, deeper and deeper into the forest. Gradually my eyes became accustomed to the darkness, and the trees nearest to me as I walked were no longer mere shadows but were distinguishable for what they were, tall straight birches, their pale bark standing out in the faint light from the stars overhead.

I kept on walking for an hour, the sound of the city's traffic growing fainter as I went. I came to a clearing, edged by undergrowth and some low bushes. I plucked at the undergrowth and broke some of the thinnest and leafiest branches off the bushes and spread them on the ground under a birch. I stood perfectly still for a moment, listening. The silence of the forest was complete. Then I lay down on my bed of leaves. I was wearing only a thin summer suit and an open-necked shirt. It had been a fine sunny afternoon when I left the flat, so I had taken no raincoat with me. But now the chill of early September hung in the air and I felt cold.

What I was doing had no logical basis. It could only prolong my life by a day or two at the most. There was no place I could go, no place I could seek refuge. Every room in every house in every city, town, village, and hamlet throughout the Soviet Union was allocated and controlled by the State. And at this moment every citizen, every man, woman, and child, in his relationship with me, was an agent of the KGB. The man at the British Embassy had been right. There was no hiding place, not in *this* country.

I found myself thinking about home—about my childhood in Limerick and the Christian Brothers' School and the boys I had played truant with and the school policeman from Cork who used to chase us. And I thought about my very first crime: a pot of strawberry jam out of a railway wagon at the age of twelve; two years' probation at the Limerick Juvenile Court, and in my stupidity and bravado an insolent look for the ancient Court Clerk as I signed the forms. "You'll be back," he had said in a quiet, confident voice. And, of course, I was. Daingean Reformatory and then Borstal. And this was how my life was to end—in a cold Russian forest on a bed of leaves. My mother's parting words came back to haunt me and mock me. "Don't ever do anything against John Bull. That's your mother's advice to you now, and you have only one mother." I had often wondered what a condemned man thought about during his last hours.

I made no attempt to sleep, for I dreaded the agony of waking from temporary oblivion to face the stark reality of my fate all over again. Better to stay awake. At the moment my senses were dulled by the sheer hopelessness of my plight, and this dullness served to lessen my mental anguish in some small measure. The night grew colder, and the heat of the day's excitement gradually ebbed out of my body. I found myself curled up in the foetal position, the last resort of the lonely. The forest was my womb, but a cold inhospitable womb that would soon deliver me up to a hostile world.

Every half an hour throughout the night I got up and did five minutes' exercise to keep myself warm. As the dawn filtered through the trees to light the forest I stood up for the last time. I walked for an hour and then discovered that I was not alone. A number of men and women from suburban Moscow were out picking mushrooms, their bodies well wrapped against the early morning chill, baskets in hand and eyes firmly on the ground. When I met these early morning visitors to the forest I pretended that I too was searching for mushrooms.

I wandered through the forest for three hours and then started to feel the first pangs of hunger. I found a rough track and followed it until I reached the main road. I was in a quiet suburb. I went into one of those all-purpose shops that the Russians call a *gastronom*, which sell everything from chocolate to salted herring, from milk to vodka. I bought a kilogram of salami and a bottle of milk. In a kiosk I bought a copy of *Pravda*. As usual, the front page carried a large photograph of some heroic Soviet worker (*rabochi*) standing grinning next to his machine. That was the Russian idea of a pin-up. But I only wanted the paper to sit on in the damp forest.

All round me people were rushing to work and children were going to school. There were long queues at the bus stops and the tram stops as office workers waited patiently to be taken to the centre of the city. I went back into the forest, sat on my copy of *Pravda*, and ate my breakfast. The salami would last me all day and even extend to breakfast next day. A kilogram, I had learned, was approximately two pounds. After breakfast I carefully wrapped the remaining salami in its greaseproof paper and put it in my jacket pocket. I had finished the milk and thrown the bottle away.

I continued wandering through the forest for the rest of the morning. There was nothing else to do.

In the afternoon I decided to phone the flat again. There was nothing to be gained by this, but it would at least relieve the boredom and at the same time Blake might quite unintentionally give me some clue as to what the KGB were doing. At any rate there was nothing to be lost.

I left the forest and boarded a tram going south, a route that was still well away from the city centre. After about half an hour I got off. The call, of course, would be traced, and I was now sufficiently far away from the suburb where I intended sleeping again that night. I went into a phone box and dialled the flat.

Blake answered. "Hello."

"Hello. Sean here."

"Oh, hello, Sean. How are you?" That was the first time he had called me Sean since I moved into his flat. His voice was very friendly.

"I'm fine," I told him, "fine."

"But how are you keeping, Sean? Where are you sleeping?"

"I'm sleeping on a park bench," I lied.

"But that must be extremely uncomfortable. You haven't even got a coat. You must be cold."

"I've done it before."

"But what are you doing for food? You know, Sean, I'm really worried about you."

It was a good attempt at sounding concerned, but I knew that Blake's only purpose in asking these questions was to give the KGB time to reach me before I hung up. But I was a long way from Dzerzhinsky Square.

"There's no need to be worried," I told him. "I can look after myself."

"But you can't go on sleeping out like this. There's no point. I mean, it's quite silly when you come to think of it. Why don't you come back here?"

"I'd rather not."

"But why? This must be preferable to sleeping on a bench."

"I explained my reasons why last night."

"I do wish you'd reconsider, Sean."

"No, I won't do that."

"And what are you going to do now?"

"Carry on sleeping on a park bench."

"I do wish you'd come back here, Sean. I really do."

Of that I had no doubt at all. I looked at my watch. I had been in the box five minutes.

"Now, look," I said, "neither of us is a fool. We are both intelligent men, and I know as well as you do that your phone is tapped and that at this moment a car is on its way here. So I'll say good-bye."

There was a short silence at the other end as the realization dawned on Blake that I had seen through his performance.

"Well, will you call again, Sean?"

"Yes, I'll call tomorrow." I hung up.

I jumped on the first tram that came along and headed back towards Izmailovo Park. All I had learned from that conversation was that Blake had been instructed to keep me talking as long as possible. His friendly tone meant nothing more than that he was anxious to carry out that task to the best of his ability. And anyway it wasn't difficult for him to sound pleased—he now had every reason to be pleased. My action in going to the British Embassy had worked in Blake's favour and had guaranteed that the death sentence he demanded would now come easier to the KGB. I didn't blame Stan. I thought he was genuinely concerned for my well-being. But I knew that hidden away in the dark corridors of every spy headquarters there was a faceless little man who wielded the power of life and death over other men. He might be a nice respectable family man living quietly in suburbia, and he might never have met the man who was to die, but it was his job to sign the execution order. He might not even particularly like doing it.

I got out of the tram and went to the newspaper kiosk. I bought several copies of *Pravda* and *Izvestia* and half a dozen of those magazines called after the different republics of the Soviet Union. These would be my mattress and my blankets for tonight. I went back into the forest.

I spent another sleepless night, and it was colder than the night before. Again I got to my feet every half hour and did exercises to keep warm. The newspapers and magazines helped a little, but not much. The magazines I spread on the ground to keep the damp at bay, and the newspapers I used to cover myself. I wondered how long I could survive.

Next morning at six o'clock I was again pretending to be looking for mushrooms with my unwelcome neighbours. At eight o'clock I sat under a tree and took a few more bites out of the thick salami sausage. Then I went walking again. On and on I walked wearily, round and round in ever-diminishing circles. I could hardly think any more. I stumbled through the forest like an unseeing automaton.

At two o'clock I went back to the shops. I had to get some more milk. I couldn't face the soggy, tasteless salami without it. I bought the bottle of milk. Fifteen kopecks for the milk and fifteen kopecks as a deposit on the bottle. Everything was very dear in the Soviet Union. A pair of shoes cost a full week's wages, and a roughly made suit cost a month's wages. But then missiles and anti-missiles and anti-anti-missiles and spaceships and all the other paraphernalia of East-West competition cost a lot of money too. The shoes and the suits and the cars could wait.

I stuffed the bottle of milk into my jacket pocket. I now had the milk protruding out of one pocket and the salami out of the other. My suit was crumpled and creased, and I had a two-day growth of beard, and my hair was matted and my shoes were caked in mud. People were beginning to notice me, to give me a look that lingered just a fraction of a second too long. I went to the kiosk to buy a fresh supply of *Pravda*s and *Izvestia*s and magazines for tonight's bed. *Pravda* had another picture of a heroic worker on the front page.

A police jeep approached but I made no attempt to conceal myself, and I was surprised, almost pleasantly surprised, at how little I cared whether I was picked up or not. But the jeep passed me by and its occupants gave me no more than a casual glance.

I went back into the forest and found a smooth-backed tree to lean my back against. I put a *Pravda* on the ground and sat on the heroic Soviet worker. I unwrapped the salami and took a reluctant bite, leaving a clear trail of parallel teeth marks on the soggy grey-brown meat. I washed it down with milk. How long could this last? How long before I died of exposure or hunger or both? I had one rouble left in my pocket, enough for tomorrow's food. Again the realization came to me that the choice now lay only between the different forms of death. After I had spent my last rouble tomorrow I would go deeper and deeper into the forest and would not come out again. How long would it take? Three days? Four? The nights were getting colder—it shouldn't take *too* long. And the alternative? A bullet. That would be quicker, much less painful. Why cling stubbornly to life when the only thing to be gained was a more painful death? I looked at the salami and the teeth marks, hesitated a moment, then threw the meat violently into the undergrowth. I stood up and walked out of the forest.

I got on a train at Izmailovo Park station and got out four stops later at Kursk station, the nearest station to the flat. I walked to our street and went into a phone box about ten yards from the lane leading to the block of flats. I dialled the number.

"Hello." It was Blake.

"Hello. Sean here."

"Hello, Sean. How are you?"

"Fine."

"Sean, I'm worried about you. You're getting nothing to eat, are you?"

"I'm not doing too badly."

"But the nights are getting so cold. You can't go on like this."

"Why can't I?"

"Well, you'll catch a cold, you'll get ill."

"I've got great stamina."

"That may be so, but no one can survive those conditions for very long. It really is very foolish."

Blake was good at his job. He gave nothing away. We were both playing a game and each knew that the other was aware of it. We were each searching for a chink in the armour of the other. At that moment I could not help reflecting on how things had changed since that first night that I had spoken to Blake by two-way radio at Wormwood Scrubs.

"I'll manage," I said.

There was a short pause, then he said, "Look, Sean, why don't you come back here? You can't go on running forever. Why not come back now?"

"I think I might as well."

"You will? You're coming in?"

"Yes."

"Oh, good. Good boy. That's very sensible." The relief in Blake's voice was genuine.

"I'll be there in half an hour," I told him. I hung up.

In fact it would take me only three minutes to reach the door of the flat, but I had a reason for lying. I walked up the lane, went through the front door of the block, and very quietly climbed the stairs. I paused on the landing outside the flat and put my ear to the door. The telephone was in the hall, and Blake was now dialling a number.

"Hello. Stan? He's coming in. Yes, he's on his way now. He should be here in about twenty minutes or so. Yes . . . yes. Well, I suggest that you send someone along to watch him arrive and make sure he isn't being followed. You will? Good. Very well, I'll call you when he arrives. Good-bye."

I allowed five minutes to elapse and then rang the bell.

Blake opened the door. "Well, well," he said, grinning. "You're back. You got here early."

"I caught a bus."

"Come in, come in. My, you look a bit rough. You'd better have a bath while I get you something to eat."

The dining-room door opened, and Victor came into the hall. "Hello, Sean."

"Hello, Victor."

"Victor has been sleeping here for the past couple of nights," Blake explained. "We weren't sure what had happened to you, or whose hands you had fallen into, so they sent Victor along shortly after you phoned."

Victor was wearing a dark suit instead of his usual sports jacket, and I could see the bulge under his left arm.

"Well," I said, "I could do with that bath, so if you'll excuse me."

"Of course, of course." Blake smiled.

While I was in the bath I could hear the crackling of bacon being fried in the kitchen next door and the mumble of voices as Blake and Victor talked.

The meal was a good one—four rashers of bacon, two eggs, fried tomatoes, a pot of tea, and bread and butter. Blake was waiting on me.

He looked very pleased with himself, as indeed he had reason to be. This was his moment of triumph. He was plying me with questions in a good-humoured fashion. Whom did I meet at the Embassy? Didn't they try to persuade me to stay? Where had I been sleeping? I told him as much about the Embassy as I wanted to and the whole truth about my stay in the forest. Victor stood silently in the background.

When I had finished eating Blake suggested that I should try and get some sleep. "Get your head down for a few hours. You look like you need it."

I went into the study and made up my bed on the couch. I pulled open the desk drawer. As I had expected, all my personal effects were missing. All the photographs taken in Moscow and several rolls of negatives, as well as the first part of the escape story I had already started writing. This part dealt only with life in Wormwood Scrubs.

I heard Blake moving about in the hall and then he was talking on the phone. I pulled the study door open and listened.

"Hello. Stan? He's here. Yes, he arrived about three quarters of an hour ago. He's gone to bed now. No, I don't think so, Stan. I think it's the wrong psychological moment. Later on in the evening perhaps. All right, Stan. I'll see you then. Good-bye."

For a spy, Blake had an extraordinarily loud voice that carried very clearly.

I went to bed but only pretended to sleep. Stan arrived about two hours later. I heard Blake receive him and usher him into his own room. A few minutes later Blake came to the study, pushed the door quietly open, and looked in. He stood there for about half a minute, listening to my breathing, then left.

I got up and went to the door. "He's sound asleep," I heard him say. Then all three of them started to discuss me, but at this distance I could only make out Blake's words. Stan and Victor spoke much more quietly. Blake was telling them that he had read what I had written about Wormwood Scrubs Prison and that none of it appeared to be damaging to anyone. "But this passage which I've marked here is significant, I think," he went on. "Listen: 'I pulled the cell door to but didn't lock it. It was not that I wanted to leave again, but there is a vast psychological difference between being confined to a room whose door is locked and one whose door is not locked. There may be no desire to push the door open, but the knowledge that it *can* be opened makes the room seem infinitely less intimidating.' I think that tells us something about his thinking."

I went back to bed. I lay there for another two hours, listening to the murmur of voices from Blake's room. Then I got up and dressed. I put the bedding away in the cupboard and folded the couch back into its normal position, making as much noise as possible in the process. I wanted them to be aware that I was up and about. Five minutes later I heard footsteps in the dining-room, and all three came in.

"Hello, Sean," Stan said, and to my surprise he held his hand out.

"Hello," I said as we shook hands.

"I must be going now, Sean," Victor said. "Good-bye."

"Good-bye, Victor."

Blake went to let Victor out and then came back.

I looked at Stan. "Well," I said, "when does the inquest begin?"

"Oh, there's no question of an inquest, Sean. I'd just like to have a chat with you, if you don't mind." He didn't smile, but his tone was pleasant and even conciliatory.

I shrugged. "Very well."

We all sat down. I didn't sit behind the desk this time. There seemed no point, no advantage to be gained. The play-acting was over so far as I was concerned.

Stan sat in the middle of the couch, and I sat on a straight-backed chair facing him. Blake sat in another straight-backed chair to my right, facing in towards Stan and me.

"Well," I said, "where do I begin?"

Stan frowned briefly. "Don't make it sound so formal, Sean. You're not talking to a policeman. I hope we can talk frankly to each other, like friends."

"Well," I began, "as you know by now, I dodged past the policemen on Monday to get into the British Embassy. I asked them to get me an Irish passport from Dublin in my own name so that I can go home to Ireland in a perfectly legal manner and return to a normal way of life. That's all I want. They took my particulars and said that they would do what I asked and that I should call back in a week."

"But there was really no need for you to do that," Stan said quietly.

"I think there was. It's *my* future life and happiness that's at stake, and no one else's. And it's up to me to act in my own interests as I see fit. When I came to Moscow in January you agreed that I should stay here for only a few months. That was clearly understood. And then last Friday you told me that I would have to stay here for at least five years."

Stan had a hurt expression on his face. "But, Sean, I only meant you to *consider* the proposal. I asked you to think it over. I'm very disappointed that you didn't ask *me* to help you instead of going to the Embassy like that. If you were in such a hurry to go home you should have told me, and I would have arranged it for you."

I was looking intently at Stan as he spoke, searching for a sign, some small hint of what he was really thinking. Did he know more about my visit to the Embassy than I had chosen to tell him? Had the waiting-room been bugged? Indeed, did it need to be bugged? Did the KGB have their own man in the British Embassy? After all, they had had Kim Philby and he had been Deputy Head of MI6. Were there other Philbys still in London? Even if there wasn't a KGB man in the Embassy itself, had some double agent at MI6 Headquarters in London already passed on the details of my denunciation of Blake to his KGB contact at the Soviet Embassy for transmission to Moscow? All these thoughts raced through my mind as I searched Stan's face for a sign. But all I saw there was the honesty and sincerity that had always been there.

"Stan, I considered, and still consider, that in the long run this is the best way out for everyone. I am relieving everyone of a great deal of trouble and inconvenience. Now you don't have to go to the trouble of issuing me false travel documents and all the rest of it. This is much simpler. I do everything the legal way. Everything aboveboard. I go back to Ireland and fight extradition."

Stan shrugged. "Very well, Sean, if that's how you want it. The decision is yours." He paused for a moment, then went on, "By the way, would you mind having a look at some photographs and see if you can recognize the diplomats who spoke to you? It's entirely up to you. You needn't do it if you don't like."

"I have no objections at all," I told him.

Stan pulled a long envelope out of his pocket and handed it to me. It contained about a dozen postcard-size photographs. They were formally posed and looked as if they might have been copied from passports. Superimposed at the bottom of each was the person's name spelled phonetically in the Russian alphabet. Without hesitation I picked out the four diplomats I had spoken to, and also the receptionist.

Stan studied them. "Hm . . . do you think any of them were MI6?"

"I wouldn't be at all surprised. I'd say David was almost certainly MI6, and probably Paul too."

Stan showed the two photographs to Blake. "You wouldn't know them, I suppose?"

Blake glanced at them briefly and shook his head. "No, I was before their time. And certainly this fellow Paul is much too young to have been around in my day."

"How did they treat you at the Embassy, Sean?" Stan asked next. "I mean, what was their general attitude to you?"

"With the exception of the Consul," I told him, "they were a load of snotty-nosed bastards. They seemed to be rather pleased that I was in trouble."

"I see." Stan put the photographs back in his pocket. "And did they try to find out your address?"

"Yes, David wanted to know it, but all I told him was that I was sharing a flat with George Blake somewhere in Moscow."

Stan nodded. "Well, I'm glad you didn't give them the address anyway." He lit a cigarette, took a deep pull, and then slowly exhaled. "And what are your plans now, Sean?"

"Well," I said hesitantly, "I want to go back to Ireland."

"Very well, I'll make the necessary arrangements. I don't think it would be a good idea for you to get your passport through the British. This would enable them to know too much about your plans, and they might try to intercept you on your way to Ireland. I think we should try and get you a passport through some other channel. Will you leave it in my hands?"

I could hardly believe Stan's tone. "Yes, of course," I said, "whatever you say."

"Thank you, Sean."

I glanced at Blake. He looked bewildered and angry but remained resolutely silent.

"And are you in a desperate hurry to leave," Stan went on, "or can you wait a few more months?"

"Well, now that I know definitely that I'm leaving and that you're going to make the arrangements, I suppose another few months won't make any difference."

Stan looked relieved. "I'm glad you see it that way. You've been in the papers a lot lately, and I think it would be in your own interests to let things cool off a little before making the move." He paused to light another cigarette. He was a chain smoker. He leaned back in the couch and blew the smoke thoughtfully at the ceiling. "Well now, gentlemen, the position seems to be this. Up until Monday the British did not know that you two were here. Your letters from Cairo and London had them confused. But now that they do know, they are going to be looking for you. There is a real danger that MI6 and even the CIA will try to get you. I suggest, therefore, that you should leave Moscow for a while. I shall arrange a tour of the Soviet Union for you. You'll enjoy the tour anyway, so it will be mixing business with pleasure. You can stay away at least a month."

"That sounds very interesting," Blake said, forcing himself to smile.

"Very interesting indeed," I agreed.

"Yes, it should be." Stan nodded. "You can start with the Baltic states and work your way right across to the far east, as far as Tashkent. I think you'll enjoy it."

"I'm sure we will," I said. "When do we start?"

"Perhaps in a week. I'll have to make a lot of preparations." Stan looked thoughtfully from me to Blake and back to me again. "In the meantime," he went on, "we shall have to give you a bodyguard." He saw me frown. "Oh, don't worry, Sean, this is not surveillance but protection. In the interests of your own safety you should have a bodyguard while you're waiting for your tour to begin. We can't take any chances with the other side." He stood up to go. "The bodyguard will begin first thing in the morning." He paused a moment and looked at me. "Oh, and by the way, Sean, please don't go to the British Embassy again, for *my* sake. If you do you will be causing a great deal of trouble for me personally."

"Very well, Stan, I promise you I won't."

We shook hands and said good night. I remained in the study and let Blake show Stan to the door. I thought they might have a few things to say in private.

I still could hardly believe the turn events had taken. I had feared, even up to the moment Stan said good night, that the whole discussion was merely a prelude to my arrest. And instead of being arrested I was now being offered a tour of the Soviet Union. Still, perhaps it was too soon to jump to conclusions. I was still in the Soviet Union. There was plenty of time. And there was always the possibility that the British, believing me dead, might make public my denunciation of Blake. My position was still precarious.

There was no doubt at all in my mind that Blake was just as surprised at Stan's attitude as I was myself. His friendly, almost fawning, treatment of me when I came back from the forest had had a note of rejoicing in it. Was he rejoicing in anticipation of a final triumph?

From the moment Stan left the flat Blake reverted to his sullen, resentful self. And a few days later I knew I had been right. We were discussing the forthcoming tour and my return to Ireland.

"You know, Robert, you're a very lucky man," he said, a look of anger and frustration on his face.

"Oh, why's that?"

"You took a great risk going to the British Embassy. You're lucky you weren't shot."

"Oh, am I? Well, I'm not going to thank the KGB or anybody else for not murdering me in cold blood."

"You're still a lucky man. They could have just taken you out and bumped you off. Nobody would be any the wiser. You would have just disappeared, that's all. No questions asked. You're lucky. You gambled with your life and you won. The KGB think you are a very brave man. They told me so."

"Brave—bollocks! For me the choice was very simple. I would rather be dead than spend the rest of my life in the Soviet Union against my will. It had nothing to do with bravery."

So the question of being shot *had* been openly discussed. No wonder Blake had been so jubilant when I returned from the forest.

Our bodyguard consisted of four men and two girls. They installed themselves in a house overlooking the front door of our block of flats. As soon as Blake or I set foot in the street they were behind us, keeping at a discreet distance. They worked in two shifts, two men and a girl to a shift. They followed us everywhere—into shops and restaurants and cinemas, onto buses, trams, Metro trains, and even riverboats. The girl's function seemed to be to pose as the girl-friend of one of the men while the other man kept in the background. I had wondered at first how they would cope if Blake and I jumped on a bus without warning, but this proved to be no problem at all. If our bodyguards were not close enough to get on the same bus they would just stop on the pavement and within half a minute they would be close behind us again, in a KGB car. Blake and I debated how they were able to do this and concluded that the large black handbag that the girl always carried must have contained a small two-way radio. Their purpose really was to guard us and not just to keep an eye on us. They made no attempt to conceal themselves from us, and after a while we decided to make their job easier by telling them in advance exactly where we were going and what our route would be.

A week went by but there was no sign of the tour beginning. Stan seemed to be in no hurry to arrange it. Then something happened in London that was to force the KGB's hand. On Saturday, September 16, Vladimir Kachenko, a young Russian scientist studying at Cambridge, was being escorted aboard a Moscow-bound plane at London Airport by the KGB men attached to the Soviet Embassy. The police intervened and took Kachenko off the plane. A diplomatic incident had begun. I first heard the news on the BBC World Service and told Blake about it.

There followed loud protests from the Soviet Embassy, to which the police replied that it had appeared to them that Dr. Kachenko was being taken aboard the plane against his will and that he also appeared to be drugged. Furthermore, several people had seen him being bundled into a car on a London street. He was now, they said, in hospital receiving treatment.

On Monday, September 18, Kachenko went voluntarily to the Soviet Embassy to join his wife there. Mrs. Kachenko called a press conference at the Embassy at which she vigorously denounced the conduct of the British police. She said she had written to the Prime Minister about it.

The following morning, Tuesday, September 19, she received a reply from Mr. Wilson in which the Prime Minister rejected the allegation that the police had behaved improperly. "It appeared to the police," he wrote, "that your husband was being put aboard the plane against his will. If, as you say, this was a mistaken impression resulting from the fact that your husband was ill, then the proper course would have been for the authorities at the Soviet Embassy to ask for our help with the problem."

That afternoon, Vladimir Kachenko and his wife boarded another plane at London Airport and flew back to Moscow.

While all this diplomatic manoeuvring was going on in London, it was having repercussions in our flat in Moscow. On the Monday, while Kachenko was still in the Soviet Embassy in London, our phone rang and Blake answered it. Stan was calling from Dzerzhinsky Square, and he and Blake talked for a whole hour. Their conversation related to Kachenko. Blake would repeat some English name questioningly and then tell Stan whether the name was familiar to him. He identified three members of the staff at Cambridge as being MI6 agents. "Oh yes," he would say, "I know him. Dr. —— is a Cambridge don. His task is to try and recruit students from Communist countries to work as agents for MI6 when they return home. Yes, I met him when I was studying Russian at Cambridge."

The list of names supplied by Kachenko to the KGB at the London Embassy, and immediately radioed to Moscow, was a lengthy one. I counted at least ten. There were two hyphenated names, and I was surprised to hear Blake at one stage say, "Yes, I believe she was a WRAC officer." The door of my room and the dining-room door were wide open, and I could hear everything that was said.

Finally Blake put the phone down and came straight to the study. "Well," he said, grinning, "I suppose you heard all that."

"I could hardly help it," I said.

"It's this poor fellow Kachenko."

"What's the story behind it then?"

Blake grinned again. "Well, it seems that MI6 were trying to recruit him. They thought that they had won him over, but the KGB were in on it too, and they also were trying to use Kachenko. In the end Kachenko was heading for a nervous breakdown so the KGB decided to get him back to Moscow. MI6, who, of course, had been trailing Kachenko, saw the KGB picking him up, and the police were instructed to go to his rescue at London Airport."

"So that's what the police meant when they said that several people had seen Kachenko being bundled into a car?"

"Exactly. The several people were MI6 officers. They thought Kachenko was being taken to Moscow against his will so they decided to have him taken off the plane by the police and give him an opportunity to ask for asylum. But they miscalculated. Kachenko wanted to go back to Moscow. In fact he's flying back tomorrow."

"So there are some red faces in MI6 today?"

"Yes, quite a few, I'd say." Blake laughed. "You see, this is a game that both sides are playing all the time, but the important thing is not to cause a public incident, because once that happens the Foreign Secretary becomes involved. He's the one who has to answer the Protest Note. The Russians are pretending to be furious but secretly they're delighted to see the British embarrassed."

It is an established practice in international relations that when one side suffers a loss of face at the hands of the other, a determined effort is made to redress the balance. This is usually done by creating a counter-incident. The British had made an embarrassing mistake and the whole world knew it. It was important for them that attention be drawn away from this mistake as speedily as possible.

And so, on Wednesday, September 20, the day after Kachenko flew back to Moscow, the British Foreign Office released the story of my visit to the British Embassy in Moscow. I first heard the news on the BBC World Service. I listened nervously as the announcer read the Foreign Office statement, but to my great relief no mention was made of my denunciation of Blake. It was stated simply that I had gone to the Embassy to ask for help in getting home and had been told to call back in a few days but had failed to do so.

Stan called that night and confirmed that the Foreign Office statement had been released for the sole purpose of drawing attention away from the Kachenko incident. "We also believe," he said, "that if Kachenko had agreed to stay in Britain, the British Secret Service would have quietly offered to hand him back to us in return for you, Sean." Stan started to pace up and down the room. "This is all very embarrassing. Ten foreign correspondents called at the British Embassy today and their stories will be in all the newspapers in Western Europe tomorrow." He pulled a bundle of papers out of his pocket and glanced at them one after the other. "Some of the things they say are not very flattering. There are suggestions that you are in some sort of trouble." The papers he held in his hand were copies of all the stories filed by the correspondents that afternoon. "Anyway," he concluded, "this now means that you must definitely leave Moscow within a couple of days.

You now have the newspapers as well as the other people looking for you."

That Saturday night, September 23, Blake and I caught the overnight train from Moscow to Leningrad, the first leg of our tour. We were accompanied by Slava. Almost at the same moment that we were boarding the train in Moscow, I was "seen" at Orly Airport in Paris and an urgent signal was flashed to Scotland Yard. The British and Irish Special Branches were immediately alerted to watch all points of entry into both countries. And as they watched, Blake and I and Colonel Vladislav Komarov slept peacefully in our bunks in our private compartment on the Moscow-Leningrad express.

We arrived in Leningrad at nine o'clock in the morning and were met by a KGB officer with a car. Our rooms were already reserved for us in the October Hotel. We stayed in Leningrad a week and were provided with two Intourist guides who spoke English. The reason for the two guides was that Blake's tastes and mine differed so greatly. His idea of having an enjoyable time was to spend hours and even days touring the art galleries. I preferred to visit breweries and champagne plants. However, I did go with Blake and Slava to the ballet. During that week we saw two, *Swan Lake* and *Spartacus*, and the opera *The Bronze Horse*. Each time we sat alone in the imperial box, which had been reserved for us by the local office of the KGB.

My guide's name was Valentine, a twenty-five-year-old brunette. One day when we were driving back from the coast, where we had spent half an hour gazing out over the Gulf of Finland, she suggested that I might care to see her flat. I said yes, and she told the driver where to go. I stayed the night. I phoned Slava at the hotel to tell him I would not be back, otherwise I imagined there would have been a manhunt. Next day Blake was a little envious of my adventure. "Well," he said, adopting that strained smile that was now so familiar, "that puts you one up on me, Robert."

Our stay in Leningrad was to be the pattern for the whole tour. At every airport or railway station we were met by a KGB car and taken to our reserved rooms at the town's best hotel. We would then spend a few days touring the town and surrounding district as VIPs. When we visited a factory or other plant we were met at the gate by the director and shown round by him personally, after which we would adjourn to his office for drinks. Our hosts were always told that Blake and I were "important officials from England visiting the Soviet Union as guests of the Soviet Government." And the more success I had with the In-tourist guides, the more envious Blake became of the "Irish peasant," and the more difficult he found it to conceal his envy. "Ah well, it's the luck of the Irish," he would say and quicky change the subject.

We travelled by train from Leningrad to Vilnius, capital of Lithua-nia. We arrived at three in the morning and were met by a pleasant young Lithuanian named Paul. We spent four days in Lithuania. Our guide in Vilnius was a local teacher of English who was a devout Communist and very proud of his country's economic achievements under communism. But Vilnius itself was a tumbledown old town of narrow streets and dilapidated houses and unmade roads. I was inter-ested to learn that the local power station, like the power stations in Ireland, burned turf.

On our second day we drove into the country to visit a health resort in the forest. It was a long journey, and we would have to spend the night at the resort and return to Vilnius next day. On the way we stopped at Kaunus, former capital of Lithuania, for lunch. We also drank a certain amount of brandy. Later we stopped again at a café and drank more brandy. We now had only an hour to go before we reached the resort. Paul was sitting in front next to the driver, and Blake, Slava, and I were in the back, with Blake in the middle. Up to this point nobody had mentioned my visit to the British Embassy, but now that our tongues were loosened with drink it was almost inevi-table that the matter would come up. It started quietly with a discus-sion of the British Foreign Office move in releasing the story of my visit to the Embassy. Then Slava said, "I must say, Sean, I was very disappointed, your doing a thing like that. Very disappointed indeed."

"Naturally you're disappointed," I said. "But as I saw it, I was act-ing in my own interests. I was supposed to be staying here for only a few months and then suddenly I was told that I must stay for at least five years. I think that gave me the right to normalize my position. If there had been an Irish Embassy in Moscow I would have gone there, but there wasn't, so the logical choice was the British Embassy. I don't see any reason to apologize for what I did. I'm an Irish citizen who wants to go back to Ireland."

"That is all right," Slava conceded. "Of course you are an Irish citi-zen who wants to go back to Ireland, but the way you went about it is very unprofessional—very unprofessional indeed. You could never be one of us, you could never be one of our organization. Never."

I made an elaborate sign of the cross. "Thanks be to God for that. You have just paid me a great compliment."

"The trouble with you," Blake said angrily, "is that you're so selfish. You're thinking only of yourself. Those other people in London will be in danger if you go back to Ireland, but that doesn't seem to worry you."

"If anybody around here is selfish," I retorted, "it's you. You are no more concerned about those people in London than you are about me, except in the respect that you wouldn't want them to be arrested so that you could have the last laugh on the British. That's why you don't want me to leave Russia—because if I were extradited from Ireland the British Secret Service would be one up on you. So don't try and kid me. Give me credit for some bit of intelligence."

"And do you *want* to give the British the last laugh?" he demanded. "Do you *want* to help those people?"

"What do you mean, *those people*. You make it sound as though I shouldn't like them or something."

"And do you? Do you like them? Look at the trick they played on me—forty-two years!"

I threw Blake a sidelong glance. "Yes, it was a long sentence all right, but you weren't exactly nicked for shoplifting."

"And you like them for that, do you?" Blake persisted.

I turned in the seat to face him. "I think it's the highest possible compliment to the freedom-loving English people and to the English way of life that the conditions existed in that country whereby it was possible for us to do what we did. There is hardly another country in the world where we could have done it—and you bloody well know it."

Blake knew I was right, but he would never admit it. "Freedom-loving English people!" he sneered. "What utter nonsense!"

"You can mock at English freedom if you like, but without it you wouldn't be a free man today."

"Rubbish! I'm free today not because of the English way of life, but because of your bravery and the bravery of the other people who helped us." Blake was being insincere, partly because he could never acknowledge that he had betrayed a decent way of life, and partly to impress and reassure the two KGB officers in the car.

"Bravery—bollocks!" I said contemptuously. "Bravery, like everything else, is relative. It does not require much bravery to defy the authorities in England, because you know that you're not going to be dragged out of your bed in the middle of the night and shot. There was no bravery needed to throw a rope ladder over an unguarded prison wall in London. You're lucky the situation wasn't reversed and you weren't doing your sentence in a Russian prison, because then you would never have escaped. And you would have been wasting your time asking anyone to spring you. That would *really* require courage."

"Nonsense!" Blake lied. "Of course you could escape from a Russian prison, and of course you could find people like yourself and Michael and Pat who would be prepared to help."

"I'll believe that when I see Russian students parading in Red Square in protest against writers being sent to Siberia."

"You know, for someone who's had all the help you've had in this country," Blake said angrily, "you're not very grateful. You're here in this country and enjoying this country's hospitality on *my* say-so, do you realize that?" He started to jab his thumb against his chest. "On my say-so! On my say-so!"

I felt no anger at Blake's words. Since I had discovered his treachery I had felt at a distinct advantage in my dealings with him, and now I was going to use that advantage for the first time. Blake's phony performance had gone far enough. I allowed about ten seconds to go by. There was complete silence in the car, and the only sound to be heard was the wind whistling against the windscreen and the closed windows as we sped through the forest. Darkness had descended, and the car's powerful headlights lit up the trees, which came right up to the edge of the road on either side. Looking straight in front of me, my eyes on the back of the driver's head, I spoke in a quiet, almost reflective voice.

"Before you go any further, Mr. Blake, I think you should know one or two things that I know and in this way you might be saved a great deal of embarrassment. It's no use pretending to be concerned about me or pretending to admire my bravery, because I happen to know that you have nothing but the utmost contempt for me. I once heard you say to a KGB officer that I was just an Irish peasant who didn't know what he wanted."

I glanced at Blake. There was a look of confusion and embarrassment on his face. I knew what he was thinking. If I had overheard that remark, what else had I overheard?

"W-w-well," he began uncertainly, "when I used the word peasant I was naturally referring to your love of your own country, your attachment to that land. That's all I meant." The anger and indignation had gone out of his voice. Now, for the very first time since I arrived in Moscow, Blake was on the defensive.

"Don't go on insulting my intelligence, please." I spoke quietly, without any note of triumph in my voice. If there was to be any triumph over Blake it would have to wait until I reached the safety of the West—if I ever did reach it.

Slava leaned forward in the seat and looked past Blake at me. "What's wrong with being a peasant?" he demanded. He was not nearly as angry as he made himself sound, but he felt he had to come to Blake's aid.

"I didn't say there was anything wrong with being a peasant. I'm only saying that this man called me a peasant and I am not a peasant, that's all. And he called me a peasant to show his contempt for me. His words were, and I quote, 'Well, you see, he is *just* an Irish peasant and he doesn't know what he wants.' So you see, if anyone is making a comment on the status of a peasant, it is Mr. Blake here."

"There is nothing wrong with being a peasant," Slava said emphatically. He pointed at Paul. "This man is a peasant. His parents still live as peasants on a collective farm."

Paul turned round in his seat, a questioning look on his face. Slava translated for him, and Paul nodded. "*Da, pravda konyeshna.*" (Yes, that's true, certainly.)

"There you are," Slava went on. "He is a peasant and he is proud of it."

"Good luck to him," I said, "but I don't see anything to be proud of. There is no credit due to a man for being a peasant. A man cannot help being born a peasant any more than he can help being born anything else. None of us can choose the bed we're born in. I certainly wouldn't feel particularly proud to be living in a wooden shack with no lavatory and no running water and doing backbreaking work in the fields all day for a pittance. It's when the man rises above that and, through his own intelligence and determination, achieves a better life for himself that he can *then* feel proud."

Slava sat back to think about this.

"I still think you have a strange way of showing your gratitude," Blake said sharply.

I turned to face him. "Gratitude? Do *you* know what it means?"

"What do you mean by that remark?"

"This," I said, "brings me to the second thing I want you to know. One night I was making a cup of tea in the kitchen and I quite accidentally overheard you and Stan talking. You were discussing me and my desire to return to Ireland, and I heard you say that in your opinion Stan was faced with only two alternatives. I can tell you your precise words. You said, 'You can go out there now and tell him that he has got to stay in this country for at least five years whether he likes it or not—and if you like I will tell him for you.' Yes, you actually offered to give me the order on Stan's behalf."

Blake's face went a deep red, and as I kept looking at him his eyes were slowly lowered until he was looking at the floor. "And did you hear the second alternative?" he asked quietly.

"No," I lied. "The kettle boiled just then and so I made the tea and went back to my own room."

"I see."

"I think you're an extremely ruthless man," I said slowly.

"Do you?" Blake was now almost whispering, his eyes still on the floor, his arrogant superiority gone. His face was filled with the shame he felt at being exposed before Slava as a man who would betray someone who helped him. Even the KGB, after my flight to the British Embassy, were not prepared to stoop to harming me.

There was a moment's silence, and then Slava leaned forward in the seat again and looked across at me. "I still think, Sean, you should not have gone to the British Embassy. I shall never forgive you for that. Never!" With deliberate abruptness he turned his head away and stared straight in front of him at the back of Paul's head, his lower lip protruding in an expression of childish petulance.

Slava did not resent me any more than I resented him, and in a way I admired his dogged determination to be loyal to Blake at all costs. I had learned that if you did the Russians a good turn they never forgot it. Slava's simulated anger towards me was designed purely as a consolation for Blake.

No one spoke during the remainder of our journey through the forest. Blake kept his eyes on the floor, his shoulders hunched forward, his hands in his lap and that pitiable expression on his face. I felt almost sorry for him.

We spent the night at the health resort and returned to Vilnius next day, where we spent one more night. Early the next morning we caught a plane for Odessa.

On our first day there we toured the local champagne plant. Afterwards the director took us to his private room to sample the product. There were seven of us in the party—the director and his deputy, Blake and I, Slava and the local KGB man, and the local Intourist girl-guide. The table was piled high with grapes, apples, and pears. One after the other, the director took eight bottles of champagne out of a refrigerator and invited us to sample them. Each bottle was quickly emptied. We began with dry and went through half-dry, half-sweet, and sweet, and these were followed by four other special types of champagne produced at the plant. The director, a large, stout, jovial man, told us that he had in his lifetime drunk enough champagne to fill the whole room. Looking at his stomach, one could believe it.

We drove back to our hotel, collected our keys at the desk, and went up to the first floor, where our rooms were situated. Slava's room was at one end of the corridor, and Blake's and mine were next door to each other at the opposite end. I was feeling quite merry after the champagne party and was carrying a bottle under my arm that the director had given me as a present. "I'll see you later," I said, going into a toilet near the head of the stairs. Blake and Slava went off towards their rooms.

I emerged from the toilet about a minute later and made my way towards my room. I inserted the key in the lock and tried to open the door but couldn't. I put the bottle of champagne on the floor and tried again. The lock wouldn't turn. "What's the matter with this bloody lock!" I exclaimed, rattling the door handle.

Four young Indians, smartly dressed and well groomed, approached along the corridor and started to let themselves into the two rooms opposite mine and Blake's.

"Why doesn't this bloody door open?" I complained.

"Excuse me, you speak English?" one of the Indians asked.

"Yes, I do. I speak English for the same reason you gentlemen do. It is a legacy of English occupation and the British Empire. Your country and mine, gentlemen, have got one thing in common—we both kicked out the English."

"Oh, where are you from then?" asked one of the others.

"I'm an Irishman," I said, "and I come from the city of Limerick, and my street is called after one of your provinces—Bengal Terrace."

All four smiled warmly. They introduced themselves, and we shook hands.

"And what are you gentlemen doing in Odessa on the Black Sea?" I asked.

"We're in the Indian Merchant Navy," the first one explained. "We are trainee officers. Our ship is being fumigated in the harbour at the moment, and that's why we have to stay in a hotel. And you?"

"Oh, well, I'm—let's say, a tourist."

We went on chatting for a few minutes about life in Britain, where the four young officers had been several times, and then started to talk about Russia. It was almost inevitable that we would get round to discussing the question of hotel rooms in Russia being bugged.

"They're all supposed to be bugged, aren't they?" one of the Indians suggested.

"From what I read in the papers it would appear that at least some of them are." I laughed. "I remember reading some time ago about an English M.P. that the Russians didn't like and so they planted a bird on him in his Moscow hotel and photographed them in bed together. The M.P. lost his wife and his parliamentary seat."

Slava emerged from his room at the far end of the corridor and started to walk towards us.

"I suggest we go back to talking about India," I said quietly. "And don't look over your shoulders."

"Why?" asked one of the Indians.

"Because the man approaching us is a policeman."

"Hello, Robert," Slava greeted me. He was frowning and obviously displeased with me.

"Hello, Slava. These gentlemen are trainee officers in the Indian Merchant Navy."

Slava nodded at the four of them in turn but still didn't smile.

"So your ship is being fumigated?" I said, addressing no one in particular.

"Yes," said the first Indian.

"And you can't stay on it while that's being done?"

"No, I'm afraid not."

We started to talk about India and its economic problems and Slava joined in. It was clear that he was determined not to leave me alone with my new acquaintances, so I picked up my bottle of champagne. "Well, gentlemen, I'm off."

"Perhaps we'll see you later?" one of them suggested. "Our room is just opposite yours if you'd care to join us for a drink."

"Thanks," I said.

I gave the key a couple more violent turns and this time the lock opened. At the same moment Blake's door opened and he came out into the corridor. I went into my room. Slava and Blake followed me in. I sat down on the bed and they sat down in two chairs facing me. This time there was no gentle leading up to the subject, no polite preliminaries.

Slava looked angry. "Sean, I thought we agreed before this tour started that we would avoid contact with foreigners."

"We did. But those men spoke to me first. What do you expect me to do—ignore them?"

"You needn't ignore them, but at the same time you don't have to spend a quarter of an hour talking to them. You could be polite to them and then let them go on their way. They might have recognized you."

"I doubt it," I said casually.

Slava narrowed his eyes slightly. "What were you talking about before I came along?"

"India."

"Well, they all went very quiet when I appeared. Did you tell them who I was?"

"No, I didn't." I pointedly kept my answers short and factual as a form of protest against this interrogation.

Blake leaned forward in his chair. "What did you tell them about an English M.P. in a Moscow hotel?" he demanded with a sidelong glance at Slava.

I looked at him coldly. "I don't know what you're talking about." I deliberately used the words and the tone of voice normally used by a criminal when being questioned by a policeman. Blake was taken aback by this, but he got my point and did not pursue the matter.

"Well, I wish you would consider *our* difficulties," Slava went on, raising his voice a little. "We are trying to keep you away from foreigners so that you will not be recognized and so that our Foreign

Minister will not be embarrassed any more. That is the whole point of this tour."

"Your problems!" I retorted. "Your problems! That's all you bloody people care about. If you had stuck to our bargain in the first place and arranged for me to leave this country after a few months, there wouldn't *be* any problems. But no, we had to get involved in the cloak-and-dagger routine. You had to have your little victory over the other side, so I was kept here—with a certain amount of encouragement from Mr. Blake here. I'm just a pawn to you bloody people—a pawn in your little game." I snapped my fingers. "I don't mean that much to the Soviet Foreign Office or to the KGB. Nothing would be more convenient for you people than that I should drop dead at this moment. It would be just another untidy loose end out of the way."

Blake's face flushed. "If you think that's their attitude to you," he shouted, "why haven't they just destroyed you?"

I had expected this response, since I had long ago noticed that whenever I made the slightest criticism of the Soviet Union or the KGB, Blake immediately jumped in to reassure them that he did not share my view. He was, I knew, acutely aware of the insecurity of his own position.

"And am I supposed to feel grateful for not being shot?" I demanded.

"What is all this about being shot?" Slava sounded shocked.

"Don't ask me," I said angrily, "ask him. He's the one who brought the subject up. When he says *destroy* he means plain *murder*, but he's just too timorous to use the right word. And I'm not going to thank any bastard for not murdering me."

"What is this?" Slava protested. "What is all this nonsense about shooting and murder? Do you think we do things like that?"

"Oh, for Christ's sake, Slava, don't take me for a bloody fool!"

"What do you mean?"

"What do I mean? Haven't you ever heard of Beria?"

Slava stared at me but said nothing. He looked shocked and embarrassed.

"Yes," I went on, "Beria, the mass murderer. I'm sure you've heard of him. Some of your braver modern poets have certainly heard of him. He's the psychopathic killer who shot all those innocent men on Stalin's orders. So don't look so shocked and incredulous."

For the first time ever I saw Slava's face go red. "Stalin was a great war leader," he blurted out.

"Stalin was a cold-blooded murderer!" I shouted. In my anger I had completely lost control of what I was saying and almost immediately I felt sorry for the embarrassment I had caused this good-natured man sitting opposite me.

"If you think we're so wicked, why haven't *you* been harmed?" he asked in a more subdued voice.

I looked him straight in the face. My anger had gone too. "Because, Slava," I said slowly, "I believe that you and Stan and many of your other comrades in Dzerzhinsky Square are decent, honourable men sincerely searching for an amicable solution to this problem. That is what I believe."

Slava leaned back in his chair, a look of genuine relief on his face. Characteristically Russian, he was pleased and flattered to be assured of approval. "Thank you, Sean," he said.

"I notice you didn't include me in that," Blake said quietly.

I gave him a brief contemptuous look and turned my attention back to Slava.

"Well, anyway," Slava said, getting to his feet, "I would ask you, Sean, to try and keep away from foreigners for the remainder of the tour—as a favour to me."

I stood up. "All right, Slava, I'll do that."

"Thank you, Sean. Good night."

"Good night."

Slava left, and Blake followed him without a word.

Next day we went to visit a fishing village about twenty miles along the coast from Odessa. We were entertained in a fisherman's hut, given an enormous lunch comprising several different types of fish, killed just before going into the pot, and washed down with brandy. That evening, back in Odessa, our local KGB man took us to the circus, where he had already reserved a private box. Afterwards we drove back to our hotel—but it was a different hotel. We had been moved during the day to the airport hotel, where we would spend our last night in Odessa. Slava obviously didn't want me to see those Indians again.

We flew from Odessa to Sochi, the resort where I'd spent my summer holiday. Though we were now well into October the weather was still so warm that we decided to stay a week.

At the airport we were met by my old friend Valodya. He had now been told who I really was and of my part in Blake's escape. There was a new sparkle, a new admiration, in his eyes as we shook hands. "Robert," he said, gripping my hand firmly in both of his, "Robert, I am very glad to see you." He took us to our reserved rooms at the Sochi Hotel.

After a week of October sunbathing on the beaches of Sochi we flew over the Caucasus to Yerevan, capital of Armenia. Yerevan was an unlovely valley town built of local pink stone and surrounded by tall, barren mountains dominated by Mount Ararat, on which Noah's Ark came to rest at the end of the Flood. Yerevan itself was oppressive, and when I looked around at the mist-shrouded hills I felt claustrophobic. Many of the people seemed to be as unlovely as their capital. The women were mostly squat and short-legged and large-nosed. Our Intourist guide, a girl of about twenty-five, had a moustache and a beard and very hairy legs. When she was showing us around I contrived always to be trailing well behind the rest of the party and pretended not to be with them.

Armenian Radio is a national joke throughout the Soviet Union, from the Baltic coast to the Chinese border. The basis of the joke is that you are supposed to tell someone about a mythical question sent in to Armenian Radio and follow this up with an outrageously funny answer supposed to have been given by the radio station. When I remarked to Slava how unfavourably the Armenian girls I had seen compared with the Russian girls, he told me one of these jokes. Someone from Moscow, he said, wrote to Armenian Radio and asked how many trains and buses would be needed to move all the beautiful girls from Armenia to Moscow. The radio station replied that they would have to make a count and this would take some time. A month later the person wrote again and was told that they were still counting. Six more months went by, and Armenian Radio said they still hadn't finished counting. Finally, at the end of a year, the listener wrote again. "Please tell me how many trains and buses it would take to move all the beautiful girls from Armenia to Moscow." Armenian Radio answered, "One bicycle."

We were to spend a total of twelve days in Armenia. The first two days we looked round Yerevan itself. Then we spent three days driving through the mountains, accompanied by an Armenian KGB officer. The scenery was at times magnificent. Our first stop was at Lake Sevan, a huge basin of sparkling blue water hemmed in and contained on all sides by bare, barren mountains of sheer rock. We stayed the night at a hotel overlooking the lake, and next morning continued our journey. We visited the towns of Dilijan, Lermontov, and Kirovakan. In Kirovakan our guide was the Soviet equivalent of a mayor. He arranged the best rooms in the best hotel and then took us to visit the local textile factory. We were shown round by the director, who presented Blake and me with three shirts each, straight off the production line.

Next day we drove back to Yerevan. Instead of going straight to our hotel we went first to the KGB office, a surprisingly large place for such a remote area as Armenia. Blake was expecting letters from his family, and Stan had agreed to forward them to the various towns on our route.

Blake and I stayed in the car. Slava and the Armenian got out. "I'll be back in a moment," Slava said. "I must phone Moscow and let them know how we are, and I shall also see if there are any letters."

Slava was back in a couple of minutes. He handed Blake two letters and then dashed back into the building.

Blake was very pleased with his mail. "Ah, one from my sister and the other from my mother." He looked up at me in the front seat. "Do you mind if I read them now, Robert?"

"Not at all. Carry on."

He ripped open one of the envelopes and read the letter. "Well, that's all right," he said, smiling. "My sister is in good spirits." He opened the other envelope. As his eyes moved down the page the smile slowly vanished from his face. He became flushed and angry-looking. He read the letter twice, put it back in the envelope, and kept staring at the envelope for a full minute. Then slowly, thoughtfully, he put both envelopes in his inside pocket. He spoke not another word to me. There was twenty minutes of total silence as we waited for Slava.

I knew instinctively what Blake had read in his mother's letter. I was walking a tightrope and, like all tightrope walkers, I had developed the super-sensitivity essential to survival.

Finally Slava came out of the KGB office and got in beside Blake in the back seat. "Well, comrades," he announced cheerfully, "we have been invited to take the director's box at the concert hall tonight. Does that meet with your approval?"

"Sounds grand," I said.

"Thank you, Slava."

Without looking round, I knew from Blake's voice that he was not smiling.

At the concert hall we were introduced to the director, who showed us to his private box. I sat in the middle with Slava on my left and Blake on my right. The Armenian KGB officer and a colleague sat behind us. Blake kept his eyes glued to the stage throughout and clapped only half-heartedly. There was champagne in the director's office after the show and then we drove back to our hotel.

Because of some conference that was being held in Yerevan there was a demand for hotel accommodation, and as a result Slava and I had to share a room. Blake had a room to himself, and it had never occurred to any of us that it could be otherwise. It was understood, without having to be discussed, that Blake had a greater desire for personal comfort than either Slava or me.

After we had been in our room about ten minutes Slava asked me to excuse him and went out. I allowed a minute to elapse and went out after him. I made my way noiselessly along the carpeted corridor to Blake's room and stood at his door, my hand closed and raised as though I had knocked and was about to knock again. But there was nobody else in the corridor. I stood perfectly still and listened.

Blake was talking in an agitated voice. "But that's exactly what it says, Slava, I've just told you."

"You are sure there cannot be a misunderstanding?"

"Of course I'm sure. It's perfectly plain language. It says exactly what I have just told you."

"And it is in Dutch?"

"Yes. My mother and I always write to each other in Dutch. Look, Slava, Stan must know about this immediately. I'll translate it tonight and give it to you first thing in the morning, and you can phone it to Moscow."

"Very well, George. You haven't mentioned this to Sean, have you?"

"No, of course not. He mustn't be told about it."

Somebody came out of a room about twenty yards away, and I immediately went back to my own room. Slava came in a few minutes later, a thoughtful expression on his face. He spoke very little, and half an hour later he closed the book he was reading, switched off his bedside lamp, and turned to face the wall. I looked across the room at the back of his head protruding from the blankets and wondered what he was thinking. Then I turned off my own light and settled down to sleep.

Early next morning there was a knock on the door. Slava jumped out of bed and pulled on his trousers. I pretended to be still asleep.

I heard Blake's voice in the corridor. "This is the translation for you, Slava."

"Thank you, George. I'll get it off immediately after breakfast."

"Can you spare a few minutes before we go to breakfast?" Blake asked. "I'd like to have a word with you in private."

"Yes, of course," Slava answered. "I'll be along in a minute."

I continued to pretend that I was asleep but did not overdo it by snoring or breathing too heavily. Slava had a quick wash in the bathroom, finished dressing, and went out, closing the door quietly behind him. I jumped out of bed and hastily dressed, without even stopping to wash. Again I went along to Blake's room and stood at the door.

Blake sounded much more agitated than he had the night before. He was making an urgent plea to Slava. "But I *want* to return to Moscow, I *must* return, and right away. I must make contact with my mother and reassure her."

"But you can do that from here. You can write or even send a telegram."

"No, I want to go back to Moscow. I don't want to continue on this tour with him after that."

"But, George, please, I beg you on behalf of the office, don't go. Stay on the tour. If you go back now it might make matters worse, and, of course, Sean will suspect."

"But you'll be with him, Slava. You two can finish the tour together and you can keep an eye on him. I don't want to stay on this tour after this."

"George, please, as a favour to the office and as a personal favour to me . . ."

I heard footsteps on the stairs and moved away just as a chambermaid appeared on the landing.

Blake stayed in his room, and Slava and I sat down to breakfast together. He rushed through the meal, jumped to his feet, and asked to be excused. "I must go to the office, Sean. I shall be back in about an hour."

Through the window I could see that a KGB car was already waiting for him at the front door. He got in beside the driver, and the car sped away towards the centre of Yerevan. I went back up to my room and lay on my bed.

Slava in fact was gone about three hours, and I began to worry about the instructions that he and the local KGB might be receiving from Moscow. That Slava had been told by Stan to await instructions from a higher level there could be no doubt. That would account for the delay. Would I ever see Moscow again? I felt sure that this was now in the balance.

It was clever of the British—very clever. MI6 had told Mrs. Blake in detail how I had denounced her son in the British Embassy and that I had accused him of trying to have me shot. And they knew that Mrs. Blake, in her anger and shame, would immediately communicate this to her son. But why? I kept asking myself over and over again. Why? There seemed to me only two possible answers. Either they wanted the KGB to murder me, or they believed I was already dead and wanted to avenge themselves on Blake through his mother. I realized that even if I survived, this was a question to which I would never know the answer.

Slava came back just after midday. "Sean, we have an interesting programme for the rest of the day. This afternoon we visit the Palace of the Patriarch of the Armenian Orthodox Church, which is a few miles from Yerevan, and this evening we are invited to the ballet."

We did, in fact, go to the Patriarch's Palace, and that evening sat in the director's box at the ballet. The ballet was a local creation, and afterwards we had drinks with the composer in the director's office. But before going to the ballet we visited the main post office, where Blake, with the help of the local KGB man, sent off a telegram to his mother.

Next morning we moved out of the hotel and were installed in a luxurious villa on a hill overlooking the city. It was a single-story building with six rooms, all leading onto a balcony poised over a swimming pool. Majestic, snow-capped Mount Ararat and its little sister were on our left, hiding us from Turkey, another range of mountains to our right, and below us, in the valley, Yerevan. We had a resident housekeeper to take care of our needs. She was a much-travelled, cultured woman of about fifty and spoke four languages—Russian, French, English, and her native Armenian. We were to spend six days in this villa.

We moved in on a Saturday, and next day, Sunday, October 22, 1967, was the first anniversary of Blake's escape. We had a celebration dinner in a restaurant in the city, and all of us, including Slava and the local KGB officer, drank a great deal of wine, vodka, and brandy.

Blake was keeping his feelings about his mother's letter very much to himself. He was determined that I should not get the slightest hint of what had happened; and, as a man of much experience in double-dealing, he was giving a good performance. He even forced himself to propose a toast "to Robert." "Sean" would really have been too much.

The following day we all had slight hangovers and stayed in bed late. We had a very light lunch on the balcony, and in the evening we were at the opera house, again in the comfort and privacy of the director's box. On Wednesday we visited the cognac plant and were shown barrels of brandy that had been lying in the cellars since 1909.

"Just imagine that!" Blake exclaimed. "They have survived the Russian Revolution and two world wars!"

And they smelled like it too. The air was so heavy with the fumes of the ancient spirit that after a few minutes in the cellars we were all feeling a little drunk.

On Thursday evening we left Yerevan, flew over the Caspian Sea, stopped for an hour at Ashkhabad Airport, and then flew on to Tashkent, capital of Uzbekistan, arriving at one o'clock in the morning, local time. "Adjust your watches, gentlemen," Slava told us. "It is one A.M. in Tashkent, ten P.M. in Moscow, and eight P.M. in London."

We were met by a KGB car and immediately driven to a large private guest-house in the suburbs. This guest-house belonged to the Uzbeki Government and was used solely for entertaining important visitors from other Soviet republics and foreign countries. It was set in spacious grounds and surrounded by a wall. The local KGB man who accompanied us had to show a special document to the gatekeeper before the big green gates were opened to us. The grounds, I discovered, were patrolled twenty-four hours a day by armed policemen with dogs. They even had their own small substation inside the walls. I had discovered, as our tour progressed, that the farther we travelled from Moscow the more determined our hosts were to look after us and create a good impression. In the guest-house the three of us had a small private dining-room all to ourselves.

Next day as I strolled through the grounds and passed the patrolling policemen I couldn't help reflecting on the last time I had walked inside guarded walls and how dramatically my situation had changed since then. At Wormwood Scrubs I was guarded to ensure that I did my punishment as a criminal. Here in Asia a year later I was being protected as an important guest of the State.

The first evening we went to the Tashkent Opera House to see the opera *The Mermaid*, and the following day we did the inevitable guided tour of the city. The contrast between the old mud huts cracked by numerous earthquakes and the tall blocks of new flats springing up all over this ancient city was quite startling.

In the evening we had dinner at the house of a Uzbeki KGB officer and were plied with the Uzbeki national dish pilaf, a mixture of rice and mutton. It is a traditional game for the host to squeeze a lump of rice between his fingers and throw it at his guest, who must catch it in his mouth and then immediately say his name, which, of course, comes out rather garbled. I could see that Blake was not at all keen on this game but he put on a brave face and pretended to be amused. Indeed, I found myself hoping that our host had washed his hands thoroughly before the commencement of the meal.

We visited two other Uzbeki towns, Samarkand and Bukhara. In Samarkand we were given the best suites in the hotel, and when we went on a picnic into the mountains the hotel chef was sent with us to cook our *shashlik*, small pieces of mutton threaded onto metal rods and cooked slowly over a charcoal fire. The hotel manager also gave us several bottles of good wine from his own private cellar.

Bukhara was only an hour's flight from Samarkand. We went there early in the morning and were met by the "mayor," who took us to a large cotton collective for breakfast. The director of the collective received us warmly. He was a big Uzbeki with a wooden leg, a veteran of the Second World War. He still wore an old army tunic and cap. We stayed for lunch too, and the "mayor" made a speech about the economic achievements of their republic.

"Uzbekistan," he declared, "is the main source of the Soviet Union's cotton exports. We are proud of our cotton, our 'white gold,' and it has been good to us. We have fine schools and a fine university. We still have a lot of small houses made from mud, but these mud huts have all got piped gas." He raised his glass of vodka. "Comrades, to peace."

We drank the toast, and then the "mayor" picked up a couple of pomegranates. He threw one each to Blake and me. "And let us hope, comrades," he said, smiling, "that these are the only sort of grenades that any of us will ever have to throw."

That evening we flew direct from Bukhara to Tashkent and went back to the Government guest-house. We decided that we would have a couple of days free from engagements and limited our activities to strolling through the grounds and playing billiards in the games room. That first evening Slava and I found ourselves competing with a couple of High Court judges from Moscow.

We spent a total of nine days in Uzbekistan, and after some discussion decided we would conclude our tour with a couple of weeks' relaxation at the Russian health resort of Kislovodsk.

We left Tashkent at eight in the morning, and four hours later we were in Kislovodsk. "By the way, gentlemen," Slava said as the plane touched down, "you can put your watches back three hours again. It is not midday but only nine o'clock here in Russia."

Slava wanted us to stay at a sanatorium but Blake vehemently refused. I had told him about sanatorium life in Sochi. "No, Slava," he said angrily, "I will *not* stay at a sanatorium. I am going to stay at a hotel even if I have to pay for it out of my own salary. Otherwise I shall just catch the train back to Moscow tomorrow morning."

Slava gave in, and we went to a hotel.

From the meteorological point of view Kislovodsk is something of a phenomenon. The heat from the surrounding mountains keeps the sky perfectly clear for about nine months of the year. It is as though God had drawn a circle in the sky over Kislovodsk and forbidden the clouds to enter. A sort of Sodom and Gomorrah in reverse. It used to be a favourite resort of the aristocracy in the old days and figured prominently in Lermontov's *A Hero of Our Time*. It was November 4 when we arrived, and it was like summer. We spent our days strolling about in shirt sleeves or basking in the sun on the nearby hills.

The town was covered with flags and bunting, and loudspeakers in the streets were blaring out a continuous flow of martial music. This was all in preparation for the fiftieth anniversary of the Revolution. On the big day, November 7, we watched the Red Square parade on television at the hotel.

On Tuesday, November 14, we boarded the Moscow-bound train in Kislovodsk, and thirty hours later, at nine in the evening, on Wednesday, November 15, we arrived back in Moscow. Stan was waiting for us at the station with a car. Slava caught a taxi home, and Blake and I drove to the flat with Stan.

Stan was his usual courteous self and had even taken the trouble to buy some food for us. I went to the kitchen to prepare a light meal, and Stan and Blake remained in the dining-room. I could hear them talking in low voices but could not make out the words. There was hardly any need. The tone, quiet and urgent, was enough to convince me that they were discussing the letter from Blake's mother.

Stan joined us in the meal and was anxious to know all about the tour. Blake and I gave him all the details, and while we spoke I again found myself searching Stan's face for a sign. But he just smiled and appeared to be interested in nothing but our travels. His only reference to the affair was to tell me that while we were on tour my brother Kevin had phoned the British Embassy in Moscow to inquire about me. "And while he was talking, Sean," Stan told me, "there was a woman's voice in the background."

"Probably his wife," I said. To have asked him how he knew so much about the call would have been superfluous.

Stan called again the following Monday and brought with him the English newspapers dealing with my visit to the British Embassy. The story was given great prominence, and there were many photographs of Blake and me. There was also a hint here and there that I might have got into trouble with my Russian hosts for going to the Embassy in the first place. One of the Embassy staff had seen me being stopped by the policeman as I left.

"I'm afraid, Sean," Stan said, handing me the papers, "that I have some bad news for you." I looked at him sharply. "Your mother is dead," he said. "She died in March, but we only discovered it ourselves by reading these papers. I'm very sorry, Sean."

"That's all right, Stan. She was seventy-two and had a peaceful, healthy life."

17

Back to Ireland?

Blake's mother was due to visit him again just before Christmas, and the KGB again decided that I should not meet her. She would be staying with Blake on a permanent basis and so I would be given a flat of my own. While the flat was being prepared I would stay a few weeks in the Warsaw Hotel. The KGB had by now become very sensitive to my reactions and, fearing that I might misinterpret their motives, went to great pains to communicate the decision to me as gently as possible. Slava phoned and asked me if I would care to come with him to the circus, and I said I would. Throughout the evening I could see that he was trying to summon up the courage to tell me something. Then on the way home he put it to me with elaborate nonchalance that it might be a good idea if I did not meet Mrs. Blake.

"She is an old woman, you see, and it might upset her. And if she goes back to the West before you go yourself she would probably talk about how she had met you here. And it might be a good idea to let them think in Britain that you have left the Soviet Union and gone somewhere else. I think this would make it easier for you eventually to return to Ireland."

A few days later Stan asked me if I would care to have dinner with him at the Metropole Hotel. I accepted the invitation, and an hour later he drove up in a KGB car and we went to dinner. It was a big dinner, lasting about three hours, and it wasn't until near the end that he broached the delicate subject.

"As Slava mentioned to you, Sean, it might be a good idea if you did not meet Mrs. Blake. We're trying to get the British to think that you have left this country and gone somewhere else. We mustn't provoke the British by flaunting you in front of people because then they might be tempted to make a formal application to our Foreign Ministry to have you handed over. I have checked on this and have been assured that you will not be handed over in any circumstances, but still we mustn't be provocative."

"That sounds reasonable enough. But how are they going to be convinced that I have left the Soviet Union?"

Stan shrugged. "We have dropped little hints here and there. And also, I think it would be a good idea if you were to write another letter, and we will have it posted somewhere else, in Austria perhaps."

I wrote the letter to my brother Kevin in Scotland. I also wrote another letter addressed to the Minister for State Security, Dzerzhinsky Square, Moscow. I thanked the Minister for the excellent hospitality I had received in the Soviet Union but pointed out that my stay had only been intended to be a short one and that I would never be content until I set foot once again on Irish soil. I told the Minister that I wanted to be in Ireland by the following July at the latest.

Stan was surprised at this second letter but agreed to pass it on. There was no doubt in my mind that it *would* be passed on, and I wanted the Minister to know exactly what my attitude was. I also knew that the Minister, Andropov, was fluent in English.

At the end of the first week in December, Slava came in a car to take me and my luggage to the Warsaw Hotel. I said good-bye to Blake in the hall of the flat. The handshake was cold, and I didn't even try to affect a smile. I was glad to be going.

"Good-bye then."

"Good-bye, Robert. I'll come and see you at the hotel sometime."

In the car Slava told me that there were some repairs being carried out at the flat and that it would be at least two weeks before I could move in. "It might be a good idea," he said, turning to me in the seat as we ploughed through the snow on the Ring Road, "If you were to have someone to act as a sort of guide while you are staying at the hotel. A friend of mine who is a lecturer at Moscow University has promised to help me in this. He knows a young girl student who is studying languages and who is fluent in English, and this girl would welcome the opportunity of meeting someone from Britain so that she can have practice."

"That sounds like a good idea."

"Very well. I am meeting this girl tomorrow and I'll bring her along to see you. Oh, and by the way, I am from Intourist."

"I understand."

"One final point, Sean," Slava said, lowering his voice. "Be sure to avoid restaurants like the National and the other places we have told you about, especially when you are with George. We know for a fact that the Americans at one time planned to shoot Donald Maclean in a Moscow restaurant. Don't tell George this, it might upset him."

"As you say, Slava."

I was installed in Room 207 at the Warsaw Hotel in the name of Komarov. The following afternoon at three o'clock there was a knock on my door. "Come in," I shouted.

Slava entered with a girl. "This is Larisa," he announced. "And this, Larisa, is Robert Garvin."

We shook hands.

"I have explained to Larisa, Robert, that you are a journalist from Britain who has come here to learn Russian."

Larisa was about twenty or twenty-one and had an oval face with large blue eyes set well apart, perfectly shaped lips, and long auburn hair that hung over her shoulders and down her back. She was obviously fashion-conscious and wore a dark green skirt that was as short as was acceptable in Moscow. Round her waist she wore a chain of round chrome links, the last half-dozen links hanging down by her side from the clasp at her hip.

We chatted for about ten minutes and then Slava said he had to go. After I saw him to the door I said to Larisa, "Well, it's extremely kind of you to agree to help me in this way. Getting things like theatre tickets is difficult when you don't speak the language."

She smiled. "Yes, I can imagine. I shall certainly help you with things like that, and of course I am glad to have the opportunity to practice my English."

Her English, in fact, was almost perfect, and her accent was scarcely noticeable. We talked for a couple of hours, and I learned that she was in the philological faculty at Moscow University. Her languages were English, French, German, and, surprisingly, Norwegian. Her home was in a town in the Urals, where her mother was a doctor. Her father, whom her mother had divorced, was a lecturer in history.

We had dinner together in the hotel restaurant that evening and then we went back to my room, where we continued talking for several more hours. It was midnight when I took her back to the university hostel in a taxi.

We met again the next day, and the day after that she phoned to say she was on her way to the hotel with a little present for me. The present was a small green toy dog that barked when you pressed its stomach.

What started as a more or less formal KGB introduction very quickly developed into a deeply personal relationship. I felt I had to be honest with Larisa, and within a few days I had told her the truth about myself. I told her that Blake was now living in Moscow and that Slava and Stan were KGB officers. For a while the pretence was kept up, but gradually it became clear to the others that I had told Larisa the truth and so the pose was dropped. Stan and Slava didn't seem to mind particularly and just asked Larisa not to discuss me with her fellow students.

Stan phoned me at the hotel on Christmas Eve. "Sean, when is this Christmas Day of yours—is it today?"

I was quite taken aback by the question. It seemed incredible that anyone could not know that much about Western customs.

"No," I said after a moment. "Christmas Day is the twenty-fifth, that's tomorrow."

"Oh, I see. Well, I just called to wish you a happy Christmas."

"Thank you, Stan."

"Perhaps you would care to have lunch with me tomorrow to celebrate?"

"I would like to, thank you."

"Very well. I'll be at the hotel at about one o'clock."

The lunch was a good one but bore no relationship to a Christmas dinner. Christmas Day was a normal working day in the Soviet Union, and the restaurant was packed with office workers eating their set one-rouble lunches for which a ticket was bought at the door and surrendered to the waitress. Actually, Russian Christmas had always been celebrated at a later date than the Western Christmas. The restaurant did, in fact, have a tall tree in the middle of the floor and paper chains and several drawings of the traditional Father Christmas. But the tree was called a New Year tree and Father Christmas was called Father 1968. After the Revolution, all the trappings of Christmas had been completely and successfully transferred to New Year's Day.

Throughout the meal Stan seemed quite subdued, and afterwards, when having a drink in my room, he was still quiet and thoughtful. I got the distinct impression that his visit had a dual purpose, that he had something to discuss with me and was finding it difficult to begin. And I felt sure I knew what was on his mind. Only a few days before, the Soviet Government had officially acknowledged to the world that Kim Philby was in Moscow. His story was given a whole page in *Izvestia*, complete with photograph. It had been arranged to coincide with the fiftieth anniversary of the foundation of the Soviet Secret Service. It was a great piece of propaganda, and the KGB and the Government were at the moment basking in the glory of it.

I decided to give Stan a little help. "Stan, you seem very quiet. You're like a man with something on his mind."

"Oh no, I have nothing on my mind."

"I thought you might be worried that I might do something that could detract from the glory of this Philby business."

Stan's face lit up. "Well, now that you come to mention it, I would appreciate it if you would make a special effort to avoid causing us any embarrassment in the next few weeks. It would be a pity if the other side was given an opportunity to use you at the moment."

I smiled. "Don't worry. I shall be very careful. I don't begrudge you your little victory."

"Thank you. Thank you very much."

That evening I took Larisa to the Stanislavsky Theatre to see *Swan Lake*. The dancing was excellent.

By the middle of January 1968 I still had not moved into my new flat, and Larisa suggested that it would relieve the boredom of living in a hotel if I were to go skiing with her for a couple of weeks.

"My dear Larisa," I said, "that is a great bloody idea."

"I'm glad you think so, Sean." She smiled. "There is a sort of guest-house about fifty miles from Moscow that belongs to our university. I can make arrangements for us to stay there, and we can go skiing every day."

"But I have no skis. Shall I buy some?"

"No, that won't be necessary. I'll borrow a pair for you from the university gym."

"Thank you. I shall, of course, have to clear it with Stan."

Stan agreed, and Larisa and I caught a train to the town of Mayazaisk, where a small bus belonging to Moscow University was waiting to take us to the guest-house a few miles away in the tiny village of Krasnovidova. The guest-house was already full with staff and students from the university, but two rooms had been reserved for Larisa and me, next door to each other. My presence as a foreigner caused a bit of a stir, and Larisa was constantly explaining that I was an English journalist who was studying Russian. Larisa herself, I quickly realized, was the most attractive girl in the place, and this made me feel very proud, while making some of the other men envious. We had a table to ourselves in the dining-room, and when Larisa would stroll in front of me dressed in a tight-fitting red blouse and jeans, her lovely hair hanging down her back, all eyes would turn in our direction and there would be whispers of *krasivaya devushka* (beautiful girl).

Larisa was an accomplished pianist and had a good voice. Once or twice during our stay we went to the recreation room, where she would sit down at the piano and play and sing. A crowd would quickly gather round, mostly young men, and at the end of the performance they would be vying with each other for her attention.

Larisa would talk to them politely for a few minutes and then walk across to me and put her arm through mine by way of emphasizing that she belonged to me. She made me feel good.

On the third morning of our stay we went skiing in the forest. The Russian countryside, and in particular the forest, is like a work of art in wintertime, and Larisa, being a very sensitive and artistic person, became almost intoxicated by the beauty of it all. We had been in the forest about an hour, I following the ski tracks made by Larisa in the virgin snow, when she stopped suddenly in front of me.

"Sean," she exclaimed, "look at that tree! Isn't it beautiful!"

The tree in question was a fir, tall and straight and strong. For about the first ten feet of its height it was devoid of branches, save for a short projection lower down, a tiny limb arrested in its growth. The snow-laden branches above, tapering uniformly upwards to the crown, presented an image of conical perfection.

"You're beautiful!" Larisa cried. "Beautiful! I want to touch you." Thrusting her sticks into the snow, she glided forward on her skis and threw her arms round the tree. "You're beautiful," she kept repeating, "beautiful." Then her eyes fell on that short slim branch below and her face lit up. "My darling, let me kiss your beautiful bough." She lowered her face and kissed it, and the thin layer of crisp white snow that covered the limb melted away under the pressure of her warm lips. She straightened up and threw her arms round the tree once more. Then she stood still, her hands slowly caressing the smooth trunk, her cheek pressed against it, her face upturned and her eyes closed. "Oh my God," she breathed, "I'll die! I'll just die!" And her voice trembled with real emotion.

As I stood there awkwardly on my skis, gazing in wonder at this rather moving spectacle, I knew that Larisa in her youthful innocence was blissfully unaware of the symbolism of her own actions in this spontaneous little drama in the snow-covered Russian forest.

She broke away from the tree and glided back towards me to retrieve her sticks. She took off her fur hat to do something to her hair, and at the same moment another party of skiers came rushing by.

"Good God," exclaimed the woman in the lead, "that girl is beautiful! She looks like the Mona Lisa." The others slowed down to gaze briefly at the object of such an extraordinary compliment and some of them mumbled their agreement.

I turned to Larisa. "Did you hear what she said?"

Larisa laughed. "Yes, but she doesn't know much about art, does she?"

I looked at her again in the light of this new observation from a passing stranger. That oval face, those eyes, that hint of a smile, and that long auburn hair unruffled in the calm, windless forest.

"I think she knows a lot about art," I said.

That afternoon we went skiing on the frozen, snow-covered lake nearby. The last of the day-trip fishermen, wrapped in their several coats, had abandoned their tiny holes in the ice and clambered back into their hired bus to be taken back to the town. From the loudspeaker in the village the music of Beethoven drifted across the lake to us. The music stopped, there was a short silence, and then another piece of music began. After the first three bars Larisa stopped abruptly in her tracks and turned to look at me, her face aglow. "Sean," she exclaimed excitedly, "Glinka's 'Hesitation'!" Then she started to sing to the music, and her beautiful young voice, clear as a bell, seemed to fill the countryside.

The setting sun, red and unblurred in a cold, cloudless sky, was just about to dip out of sight behind the silhouetted treetops in the distance as we stood there facing each other in the middle of this frozen, deserted lake, our skis crossed in the snow so that we could be closer together, and there was not a sound or a movement anywhere to detract from the pleasure of Larisa's singing. It all seemed a little unreal, and I felt briefly sad at the thought of one day losing this girl.

On the last night of our stay we went for a long walk along a winding country road. After about half an hour we had lost sight and sound of all signs of human habitation. The sky was perfectly clear, and the stars seemed bigger and more numerous than they had ever been before. (Who ever looks at the stars in a big city?) It was difficult to decide whether the snow-covered countryside, in its night-time pallor, was beautiful or sinister. Neither of us had spoken for about ten minutes, and the only sound to disturb the silence of the night was the crunching of the snow under our feet as we walked.

Suddenly I turned to Larisa and grasped her by the shoulders. "Larisa, I've been in many places and done many things but I've never in my life danced with a beautiful young girl on a deserted country road in Russia in a temperature of thirty degrees below zero on a starlit night. So, my dear Larisa, let us dance."

Larisa got over her surprise and put her arms round me and we danced. I provided the music by singing gently into her ear a song called "Love Me Tender."

"You know, Sean," she said after a while, "if anyone saw us now they would think we were mad."

"And perhaps they wouldn't be far wrong. But what a nice kind of madness."

Next morning we caught the train back to Moscow. Larisa flew to the Urals to spend two weeks with her mother, and I went back to the Warsaw Hotel.

I had now been seven weeks in the hotel, and without Larisa it was more boring than ever. I spent most of my time in the restaurant, eating and drinking. Four days after my return from Krasnovidova I went to the restaurant for lunch at one o'clock and stayed all day. I drank a bottle of brandy and three bottles of wine and made my way unsteadily back to my room at ten o'clock that night. I decided to try and get in touch with my brother in Scotland. I picked up the telephone.

"Da?"

"Anglichanin. Angliski."

"Oh, you are English?"

"Yes, I am. I would like to make a call to Britain, a town in Scotland called Ayr. The number is Ayr 65410."

"It will take about an hour. Good-bye."

I didn't expect to get away with it. I thought that within half an hour there would be a knock on the door and someone from the KGB would ask me what I thought I was doing. But the brandy and the wine had put me in a state of mind where I was past caring. The phone rang again at about eleven o'clock.

"You're through to Ayr. Go ahead," said the voice of an English operator.

"Hello. Is that Ayr 65410?"

"Yes."

"Is that you, Kevin?"

"Yes, it is."

"This is Sean here, calling from Moscow. How are you, for God's sake?"

"I'm fine. My God, am I glad to hear from you!"

"Me too."

"How are you keeping?"

"I'm great, just great."

"Listen, Sean, it's a great relief to hear your voice. We thought we'd never hear from you again. In fact, we thought you had been eliminated."

"Why's that?"

"Well, those reports in the papers about you going to the British Embassy. The rumour here was that you had definitely been shot for doing that. And also I've had the Special Branch along to see me several times. An Inspector told me that they knew definitely that you had been locked up in the Lubyanka prison after your visit to the Embassy."

"None of that's true, Kevin. On the contrary, I was sent on a tour of the Soviet Union. Actually, from the material point of view I am very well off here. I do no work and I get thirty pounds a week."

"And you still want to come back here?"

"Yes, I do. I've made up my mind about that."

"But listen, Sean, you know what's facing you, don't you? The Special Branch have told me that you will get at least fifteen years. The authorities here are very angry."

"I shall return to Ireland and fight extradition on the grounds that Blake was a political prisoner."

"You can forget about that. The Special Branch have told me that your extradition from Ireland is a foregone conclusion. They say it's already been tied up with the Irish authorities."

"That's an insult to the Irish judiciary. Extradition is a matter for judges, not policemen. Can you imagine an Irish judge being a tool of Scotland Yard?"

"I'm just telling you what they told me."

"Anyway, I shall be in Ireland this summer."

"But supposing you *are* extradited under normal Irish law?"

"That's a chance I'm quite prepared to take. I would rather do my sentence and get it over with than spend the rest of my life here. And by the way, the maximum sentence for helping a prisoner escape is five years."

"But when you help a spy escape you can be charged under the Official Secrets Act."

"I'll still take my chances."

"Okay, Sean, that's up to you. I just thought I should warn you, that's all."

"Thanks. Listen, there are a few things I would like to clear up back home *before* I return—just in case I don't get the chance when I get there. I would like your help here, I would like to have a long talk with you in private. Do you think you could come and visit me here in Moscow this summer?"

"I'd like to. In fact, I was going to suggest it."

"Good. We'll discuss the dates and routes and so on by letter. You can write to me here at the Warsaw Hotel. I shall soon be moving to a new flat but the letters will be collected for me."

"All right. I look forward to hearing from you."

"I'll write within a week. Oh, by the way, I don't have to tell you that this phone is tapped, both here and in London."

"You're quite right. You don't have to tell me."

"Good-bye then, Kevin."

"Good-bye, Sean."

I put my feet up on the desk, balanced the chair on its rear legs, and waited for the knock on the door. The reason it had not come earlier, I thought, was because of a slip-up on the part of the hotel's switchboard operator. But now that the call had gone through and been monitored elsewhere in Moscow, I should not have long to wait for the results. And I was completely indifferent—so much so that as I waited I sang "Galway Bay" at the top of my voice. But the knock did not come. I concluded that the tape recordings made by the monitoring service took a little time to reach the right quarters. Also, today was Saturday, so perhaps I would hear nothing before Monday.

But by Monday night there was still no word from Stan or Slava. On Tuesday, Slava came to lunch at the hotel and we spent an hour together in the restaurant and another hour in my room. My call to Scotland was not mentioned. I was puzzled. Did they know or didn't they? If they did, why didn't they say something? Were they waiting to see if I would mention it first? Perhaps they didn't know. Perhaps these tapped conversations took a week or more to find their way to the appropriate official's desk. Whatever the cause of the delay, I decided it would be a wise move to get in touch with Dzerzhinsky Square. I had delayed long enough.

I dialled Stan's office direct. "Hello, Stan."

"Hello, Sean, how are you?"

"Fine, Stan, fine. Listen, I have a bit of news for you. Would you be surprised to hear that on Saturday night I spoke to my brother Kevin in Scotland?"

There was a brief silence.

"Yes, Sean, I *would* be surprised. And disappointed."

"I see. Well, I've written out a full transcript of our conversation for you."

"I'll be at the hotel in an hour."

Stan arrived in half an hour. There were no preliminaries. He looked flushed as he came in the door. "Well, another mess!"

"Why's that, Stan?"

"We have been trying for months to convince the British that you have left the Soviet Union. Your letter from Vienna was part of the process. Now they know again that you are here. They will probably apply for you to be handed over, and this will embarrass our Foreign Minister." He sat down.

"I'm sorry about that, but I've got problems of my own. I've had no contact with my family for more than a year and they didn't know what had happened to me. I have a duty to them too, you know."

"Yes, I know, but if you had discussed it with me I could have helped you. We could have made some arrangement. This way you are causing everyone a lot of embarrassment, including me."

Stan looked genuinely concerned and I felt real sympathy for him. He was, I knew, personally responsible for my actions.

I handed him the transcript. "There really isn't much to worry about," I said. "What transpired between Kevin and myself can't embarrass anyone except the British. As you will see, I reassured him that I was being treated with great courtesy and consideration in this country."

Stan looked up at me wearily. "Sean, I wish when you have a problem like this that you would discuss it with your friends—with Slava or me or George."

"Blake!" I exclaimed. "Discuss it with Blake? Blake's no friend of mine. I respect you and I respect Slava, but I have no respect at all for Blake, so let's not discuss him."

Stan shook his head sadly. "Yes, I had heard that relations between you and George had deteriorated. That is a pity." He stood up to go. "Well, I sincerely hope, Sean, that you regard *me* as a friend."

"I certainly do, Stan."

"Oh, by the way, the newspaper correspondents will know where you are now and they'll be trying to contact you, so we'll have to move you to your flat within a couple of days. In the meantime I'll put a man on duty in the lobby to make sure you are not disturbed."

Though I felt sorry for causing Stan personal embarrassment in the eyes of his superiors, I felt relief at having accomplished what I had. I *wanted* the world to know that I was in the Soviet Union, for therein lay my greatest hope of returning to the West.

A KGB guard was put in the hotel lobby to make sure that I was not disturbed, and three days later Slava came in a car and took me and my luggage to my new flat.

By now it had become clear that the KGB's intentions towards me were honourable and that they were not going to allow themselves to be persuaded by Blake. The painful truth had also dawned on Blake himself, and his attitude towards me once more underwent a dramatic change. So far he had treated me with the utmost contempt and had made no attempt to conceal his feelings, for he had believed that I would never live to tell the tale. But now that the KGB had rejected his advice and I was due to return to Ireland within months, his desperate efforts to back-pedal were almost pitiable to watch. The arrogance and pomposity were gone; he became meek and humble and fawning.

He started to visit me at my flat about twice a week and to bring me little presents. He brought me champagne and wine. He brought me delicacies like apple pies specially cooked for me by his mother. And he brought me bottles of Scotch, which I knew could only be bought in Moscow with foreign currency. He was constantly ringing me up to ask me how I was or to invite me to dinner at a restaurant. And he started to call me Sean again.

All the while he was trying to assess my attitude to him. He would listen to my every word, my every inflection of voice; he would watch my every expression, my every gesture. He was desperately seeking approval, and I could see that it was causing him great pain and embarrassment. He even went to the length of pretending to be critical of certain aspects of Soviet society, condemning the careerists and speaking in derogatory terms about those who would seek to perpetuate the power and privilege of the Party. "Look at these generals riding around in their chauffeur-driven cars. Look at these Ministers with their flats in Moscow and their *dachas* in the country. What has all this got to do with communism?" I found myself in the strange position of disagreeing with Blake on some of these occasions, arguing that material incentives and rewards were necessary to progress.

I wasn't very helpful to Blake and made no attempt to give him the reassurance he wanted—that I would say nice things about him when I returned to the West. In the end, in desperation, he came into the open. We were having dinner in the Metropole, and after the first bottle of wine he started his abject plea.

"I'm afraid, Sean," he said, shaking his head sadly, "that you have not got a very high opinion of me." He stared silently down at the table and waited for my reply.

"Why do you say that?"

He shrugged but still didn't look at me. "Oh, I just get that impression."

"Well, to be honest with you," I told him, "I think you're the sort of person who would find it easy to wield the iron fist. I get the impression that you think we should all be grateful in the Soviet Union for being allowed to *live*—and that includes you and me. Well, I can assure you I feel no gratitude to the Party or to the Government or to the KGB for not beating me, or torturing me, or throwing me into prison, or shooting me. I'm not going to thank any bastard for not doing to me something he has no right to do in the first place."

I could see that my words distressed Blake. His months of trying to ingratiate himself with me appeared to have come to naught. He fingered his wine glass nervously. "Well, I'm afraid, Sean," he said quietly, "that you've got me wrong there. Oh yes, I'm afraid so. My views are entirely the same as yours in these matters, and if you think otherwise then all your—er—past assessments of me will have to be revised too." His voice was almost a whine, and his words were not an argument but a supplication.

After that his efforts at a reconciliation became more and more pitiable. Sometimes he would even try to use Larisa to make me commit myself to a policy of magnanimity towards him. The three of us would be having drinks in my flat and Blake would very carefully steer the conversation round to me and my various attitudes. Then he would turn to Larisa and say something like, "I'm afraid, Larisa, that Sean doesn't think much of me." He would then look self-consciously into his glass and wait for some crumb of comfort to fall from my lips. I usually said something noncommittal like, "Larisa, will you listen to him! He is the great George Blake, the famous secret agent. Why should he care what anybody thinks of him?" Blake would then turn these words carefully over in his mind, desperately searching them for a meagre ray of hope.

I felt no sympathy for him. Blake had urged the KGB to murder me, and they, being more decent than he, had refused his request. He had gambled with my life and lost. And now he was trying to undo the damage, but it was too late. If he were consistent, even in his hostility, I might have some small measure of respect for him. But instead he was humbling himself before me, and the more he humbled himself the greater grew my contempt for him.

My new flat was spacious and comfortable. It had three rooms and a kitchen and bathroom. This was a great privilege, for such a flat could normally be occupied only by a family of six. A family of four would be allocated no more than two rooms. Stan himself, as a single man, was restricted to one room in a shared flat.

I spent my days writing this book, and most evenings and weekends I was with Larisa. I did not tell the KGB what I was doing, and whenever Stan or Slava was due to call I would hide my notebooks in a suitcase. I had written about Blake's attitude in Moscow and about the conversations I had overheard, and I knew that this would not meet with approval. It was my intention to try and smuggle the manuscript to the West.

I was now writing to my brother Kevin regularly, using the Warsaw Hotel as an accommodation address. Slava posted my letters for me. I did not bother to seal them—this would only have caused delay while they were being steamed open in Dzerzhinsky Square. By May, Kevin had made definite arrangements to visit me in Moscow. He would be coming sometime in August. The KGB sent instructions to the London Embassy that he was to be issued with a visa without question.

Larisa was not keen on restaurants, and when we went out it was usually to a cinema or theatre or just for a walk in the park. But we spent most of our time together in the flat. We had many heated arguments about the respective merits and demerits of communism and capitalism. Larisa was as deeply devoted to her system as I was opposed to it. Once when I was particularly vitriolic in my criticisms Larisa's eyes filled with tears. "My God, Sean," she said, "if you knew anything at all about our history you wouldn't say terrible things like that. If you had any idea of the suffering and misery and degradation that our people had to endure before the Revolution you wouldn't be so ready to condemn us. Today in this country we enjoy a freedom and dignity that our parents and grandparents never dreamed of. I am proud of my country and I am prepared to die for it if necessary!"

Larisa and I decided to spend our summer holiday together. She would be free from the university for two months and so we would spend the first month together and the remainder of her holiday she would spend in the Urals.

"One thing I will not have, Larisa," I told her. "I will *not* stay in a hotel and I will *not* stay in a sanatorium."

She looked relieved. "I am glad to hear you say that." She smiled. "I personally would love to stay in a tiny cottage somewhere remote where we can go swimming and walking and fishing and I can do the cooking."

With Slava's help, this is what was arranged. We spent five glorious weeks together in a log cabin by a lake in Byelorussia, not far from the borders of Lithuania. We flew from Moscow to Minsk by Ilyushin jet. At Minsk we were met by a Byelorussian KGB officer named Alexander. He took us in a small biplane from Minsk to a tiny little town called Braslav. Actually, we landed in a field a couple of miles from the town. The field was the airport, and air-traffic control was a caravan in the corner of the field.

"Our roads in Byelorussia are not too good," Alexander explained. "All our towns, big and small, are connected by these biplanes. They are our buses."

At the airport we were met by Valentin, the KGB man from Braslav. He drove us in a jeep, first over a very rough country road and then along a mud track, to our secluded log cabin by the lake. Alexander saw us settled in and then caught the next plane back to Minsk. Valentin, a gangling young man in his early thirties, arranged with the local collective farm to supply us with fresh food daily, and thereafter he called to see us about once a week. I was surprised to learn that a tiny agricultural town like Braslav, a town that was little bigger than a village, with wooden houses and unpaved roads, had two fulltime KGB officers. The tentacles of Dzerzhinsky Square spread far.

The garden of our log cabin stretched down to the lake, and a freshwater stream flowed past our door. The scenery was beautiful, and at sunset the lake became a gold-tinted mirror. Larisa and I would sit on the veranda, sipping champagne, and watch the sun go down, and she would sing Russian songs.

One day I caught a slight cold and Larisa insisted that I go to bed. Then she went to the farm and brought back a jar of fresh honey and a jug of milk still warm from the cow. She put some of the honey in a glass, added some milk, and stirred them together until they were blended. Then she sat on the edge of the bed and spoon-fed me with the delicious mixture, adding more and more honey as she did so.

One day towards the end of our stay Larisa started talking about my return to Ireland. We had, of course, talked about it many times before, and she knew my views. We were sunbathing side by side on the edge of the lake. Her eyes were closed, and her long silken hair was spread out on the grass around her head.

"But they'll put you in prison and they might even beat you! Oh, I can't bear to think of it. I can't!"

"I've told you before, I think I have a good chance of winning in Ireland. And as for being beaten, well, even if I get sent back to Britain I don't think that will happen. Britain is not a police state."

She opened her eyes and turned towards me, leaning on one elbow. "Why can't you stay, Sean? Why? We could be so happy together. This is a big country, a beautiful country. We could go anywhere, live anywhere, do anything. Why do you have to leave?"

"Because I have to be sure of something."

"Sure of what?"

"Sure that I am free."

"But you are free, Sean, you *are*. You are not being kept here against your will."

"I must be sure of that, Larisa, for my own peace of mind. And the only way I can be sure is by putting it to the test. I will never know whether I am free to leave this country unless I actually leave. That's the *only* way I will know."

"But you've got everything here."

"I know that, but no matter how well off I might be here, no matter what comforts are lavished on me, there would always be that doubt, that uncertainty. Can't you see that? I would be in a limbo, like Blake and Philby and Maclean. They're not happy in their enforced exile, and they actually fought for this cause. I have to return to normality, even at the cost of going to prison."

Larisa looked at me through eyes that were already beginning to mist. I took her head in my hands and drew her towards me. Then I lay back, and she rested her head on my chest and very slowly I stroked her hair.

"Perhaps we'll meet again, Larisa, when this is all over."

"I— I—"

I felt a tear fall on my chest and slowly trickle over my ribs onto the grass.

It was the last day in July when Valentin called for us in his jeep and took us back along the mud track to the field where the biplane was waiting to take us to Minsk. Alexander met us at Minsk Airport, and we shared a bottle of champagne with him while waiting to board our jet for Moscow. Stan was waiting for us at Moscow and drove us back to the flat. The following evening I took Larisa to Kazan Railway Station and saw her off on the Urals Express. It would take her forty-eight hours to get home. Russia was indeed a big country.

Kevin was due to arrive in Moscow on Monday, August 12. On the Friday, Blake phoned and invited me to join him for a drink. We met at the Moscow Hotel and spent a couple of hours talking over champagne cocktails. Then he asked me back to his flat for supper. His mother had gone to Holland for a month. He was being extremely attentive to me, and I knew this was an indication of how worried he was about my brother's visit. He realized that once Kevin arrived nothing further could be done to prevent the truth about himself reaching the West, irrespective of what happened to me. Kevin could not be harmed or restrained in any way. His visit to Moscow and the purpose of the visit would be widely known to his friends and to the press before he boarded the plane at London Airport. Indeed, his trip was being financed by the newspaper *News of the World*.

"Well, I hope that you and Kevin have a very nice time," Blake said, showing me to the door. He smiled with his mouth, but his eyes reflected his deep anxiety, and I knew that he bitterly resented the KGB for allowing this to happen to him.

"I'm sure we will," I told him.

As I made my way down the first flight of stairs I heard the sound of the two locks being wound home and then the rattling of the chain onto its hook. Blake was once more alone in his little island of doubt and fear.

It was the last time I ever saw him.

Kevin arrived on Monday, and Stan and I drove out to the airport to meet him. Stan was afraid there might be Western correspondents at the airport acting on a tip-off, and so I wore dark glasses and waited near the entrance to the terminal building while Stan went into the arrival lounge to meet Kevin. But there were no correspondents and everything went without a hitch. We drove back to the flat.

Stan, after having only one drink, rose to go. "Well, Kevin," he said, "I hope you enjoy your stay in Moscow. And, Sean, I shall put a car at your disposal every day while Kevin is here."

"Thank you, Stan."

Kevin and I spent a couple of hours talking about the escape and generally filling in the gaps in each other's knowledge. Then I went to the bedroom and came back with the manuscript of this book, nine thick notebooks containing 200,000 handwritten words.

"Kevin," I began, "the main purpose of your visit is to take this story back to Britain with you. Although your presence here in Moscow will also increase my chances of getting out of here, I at least want to have the consolation of knowing that the truth will reach the outside world."

"Oh? The truth about what?"

"The truth about George Blake."

"That sounds interesting."

"It *is* interesting. Let me tell you about it." For the next hour I gave him a detailed account of Blake's treachery.

"So you see," I concluded, "Blake repaid me by trying to have me murdered."

Kevin looked incredulous. "But why, for God's sake? Why should he want to do that?"

"Because, Kevin, he's a born traitor. Blake does not betray for ideals; he betrays because he *needs* to betray. If Blake had been born a Russian he would have betrayed the KGB to the British. That's how he's made."

Kevin whistled. "Well, that figures."

"How's that?"

"The Special Branch told me that he was no good. I thought maybe it was just propaganda."

"It's no propaganda, believe me."

Kevin picked up the first notebook and flicked through the pages. "But how will I get it out of Russia?"

"With the help of the KGB." I told him. "You are not an ordinary tourist, you are a privileged visitor. Stan will make arrangements for the formalities at the airport to be waived. Just put the notebooks at the bottom of your suitcase and there will be no trouble."

"Right. I'll do that. By the way, where's Blake now?"

"Up to three days ago he was in the flat that I shared with him when I first came to Moscow, but by now he will have moved. I doubt if I will hear from him again."

"Why's that?"

"Secret Service policy—in *every* country. It is assumed that once an individual comes under the control of the other side, every secret he possesses will be divulged, whether voluntarily or otherwise. I have contacted you and you are going back to Britain, and therefore it is assumed that Blake's address will become known to the British. So Blake has to move. It's automatic."

"God, who'd want to be a defector?"

"Who indeed."

Kevin stayed in Moscow a week, living in my flat. He spent part of his day sightseeing and the remainder reading the manuscript.

On the Tuesday, Stan took us to lunch at the River Port Restaurant. It was a lavish lunch with caviar and smoked salmon and chicken, brandy, vodka, and champagne. We discussed the various routes I could take to reach Ireland without touching Britain and the role Kevin could play.

"In fact, Kevin," I said, "all you have to do is apply to the Irish Embassy in London for a passport or travel document on my behalf and then send it on to me. They can't refuse because I'm an Irish citizen."

"With food and drink like this," Kevin said, smiling, "I'm surprised you want to leave at all."

"I'm surprised too," Stan said, "but not because of the food and drink. I'm surprised that Sean wants to take this terrible risk. I honestly believe there is a good chance he will be handed over to the British, and I also believe they will charge him under the Official Secrets Act and give him fifteen or twenty years. Believe me, Kevin, I am only concerned with Sean's welfare. We have nothing to lose by all this, but he has."

"And would he still be welcome to stay here now?" Kevin asked.

"More than welcome," Stan assured him. "I know that Sean is not a Communist, I know that he even dislikes our system, but nobody here minds about that. We've never made any attempt to convert him and we never will. He is welcome to stay here, and he can have his free flat and his thirty pounds a week for the rest of his life. And he doesn't even have to work. He is better off than I am. I can assure you that if I stopped working tomorrow nobody would pay me a penny. But anyway, the decision is entirely Sean's. If he wants to return to Ireland we will give him every assistance."

The day of Kevin's departure arrived. It had been agreed that Stan and I would see him off and that Stan would speed him through the formalities at the airport without a customs check.

Stan called at the flat in plenty of time. "Well, boys, all ready to go?"

We went down in the lift together. I carried Kevin's suitcase. The car was waiting outside the front door, and the driver had the bonnet up and was leaning in over the engine. He straightened up as we approached, slammed the bonnet down, and wiped his hands on an old rag. He took Kevin's case from me and put it in the boot.

Kevin and I sat in the back seat and Stan sat next to the driver.

We left my street, turned onto the Ring Road, and headed out of the city towards the airport. There were one or two minor roads to be negotiated before we reached the main highway. On one of these roads a level-crossing barrier was down and remained down for half an hour. The queue of traffic in both directions got longer and longer, stretching for about half a mile. When the cause of the delay finally appeared it turned out to be a single engine that took three seconds to cross the road.

"A little matter of mixed priorities there, Stan," I said. "Why couldn't the barrier stay up until that bloody old engine was about one minute from the road?"

Stan shrugged his shoulders.

Kevin looked at his watch. "My plane takes off at six and I've got to check in by five. It's now half-past four."

Stan turned round in his seat. "Oh, don't worry, Kevin, you'll make it. We'll take a short-cut." He turned to the driver and said something rapidly in Russian. The driver nodded.

Ten minutes later we left the minor road and turned onto a dual highway. There wasn't much traffic, and for twenty minutes we were doing about seventy miles an hour. Then the engine started to sputter. Stan looked questioningly at the driver. The driver vigorously pressed the starter but the engine would not respond. Finally, when we had slowed down to about thirty miles an hour, he pulled to the side of the road. The driver lifted the bonnet and inspected the engine. He said something to Stan, and Stan translated. "I'm afraid, boys, we have a little trouble with the distributor. It shouldn't take long."

We all climbed out of the car.

Kevin looked at his watch. "It's five o'clock," he said anxiously. "I'm supposed to be checking in now. My wife will be worried if I'm not back in London tonight."

"Don't worry, Kevin," I said. "Five o'clock is the earliest time for you to check in. I'm sure they'll let you check in up to half-past five at least."

"I hope you're right."

"Oh yes, that's quite true," Stan assured him.

The driver had taken the cap off the distributor and was inspecting the leads. By ten past five he still had not repaired the damage. Kevin was becoming quite agitated and kept looking at his watch.

"How far are we from the airport, Stan?' I asked.

"About twenty minutes' drive."

"Can't you use the car radio to call your men at the airport and ask them for help?"

"I am afraid not. Unfortunately this particular car doesn't have a radio."

"In that case we'd better stop a taxi," Kevin said.

"Unfortunately we have taken a short-cut. This is not the main road to the airport and we are unlikely to see a taxi."

Kevin was exasperated. "I've got to be back in London tonight!"

"I'm sorry, but it can't be helped." Stan sounded genuinely sympathetic.

At twenty minutes past five the driver was still under the bonnet working on his distributor. Stan looked impatiently at his watch and went across to talk to him. He appeared to be telling him off for his incompetence, but the driver remained bent over his engine and said nothing.

Kevin looked at his watch. "Twenty-five past five," he said impatiently. "Even if the car starts now I won't be there until quarter to six."

"Let's hope he gets it fixed within five minutes," I said, "then you'll still have a chance. Stan will see to it that you get on the plane all right."

Kevin jerked his head towards the car where Stan was standing over the sweating driver. "I think this is all a fix," he said in a low voice.

I looked at him. "Oh now, Kevin, for heaven's sake, don't start letting your imagination run away with you!"

"Hey, boys!" Stan shouted.

We looked round.

He was pointing along the highway in the direction we had come. "A taxi!"

Sure enough, a taxi was speeding towards us, the first one we had seen on this stretch of road. Stan walked a little way along the road to meet it and raised his hand. The taxi stopped.

"That's a bit of luck," I said to Kevin.

Stan talked to the driver for about a minute and then signalled Kevin and me to come and join them. "I'm afraid, boys, that he only has room for one, so it looks like Kevin will have to go on to the airport alone."

Kevin looked relieved. "Well, that's better than nothing."

I looked into the taxi. Stan was right—there was room for only one more. There were three passengers already in the car, one sitting next to the driver and two in the back seat. They were all men. The driver put Kevin's suitcase in the boot, and then Kevin shook hands with Stan and me and climbed in beside the other men in the back. Stan gave the driver some roubles.

"Cheerio, Kevin," he said. "I hope you catch your plane all right."

"So do I," Kevin answered.

"All the best, Kevin," I said. "See you in Ireland one of these days."

The taxi started up and sped towards the airport.

I looked at my watch. "Half-past five. Do you think he'll make it, Stan?"

"I think so. He should be there at ten to six. I think they'll let him through." He looked over his shoulder at the KGB car and shook his head. "What a pity! I would like to have been at the airport to usher Kevin through without the formalities."

He walked over to the driver, who was still leaning in under the bonnet, and started to upbraid him again. Then he strolled back to where I was standing, an angry expression on his face. "It's not good enough, Sean. As you know, drivers in this country are also mechanics and are responsible for the maintenance of their cars. He should have checked the engine thoroughly before we left Moscow."

Finally the driver got in behind the wheel, pressed the starter, and the engine jumped to life. I looked at my watch. It was exactly six o'clock.

"No point in going to the airport now," Stan said. "I think we should go back to town and I'll go to the office and phone the airport from there. I'll drop you off at your flat first and give you a ring later when I've found out what's happened."

We went back to town.

At seven-thirty the phone rang in my flat. It was Stan. "Well, Sean, I phoned the airport and Kevin caught his flight all right."

"That's a relief. No snags?"

"No, everything is all right. He's on his way to London."

"Good. Thanks." I put the phone down. "Thank God for that," I said aloud. The manuscript, then, had got through. I felt like a new man.

Larisa returned to Moscow a week later and brought me several jars of honey and mushrooms from the Ural Mountains. We had a quiet reunion celebration in my flat with champagne and caviar, and she cooked me a special Urals dish called *pelmeny*.

Stan phoned several times during the next week, and Slava called at the flat to give me copies of *The Times* and to discuss my return to Ireland. I rang Blake's flat about six times but, as I had expected, there was no reply. He had already moved. Everything seemed to be going according to plan.

Then on Tuesday, September 3, fifteen days after Kevin's departure, Stan phoned.

"Hello, Stan."

"Hello, Sean." A pause. "Well, it appears that your manuscript was taken from Kevin at the airport. It is a great pity that you did not ask *us* to arrange for it to be sent to Britain. We could have helped you in this matter." He spoke in a quiet, conversational voice, without any hint of resentment.

"I see."

"It is also a pity you hold these views, but as I told my colleagues there is no point in trying to deprive you of the manuscript because you can simply rewrite the whole thing when you get back to Ireland." Stan sighed. "You know, Sean, you are completely wrong about George. Still, if that's your view you are, of course, entitled to your opinion."

"I see."

"Anyway, Sean, Slava will call along to see you tonight to talk about it."

"Thank you, Stan."

I put the handset back in its cradle and stared at it for a moment. So the car breakdown *had* been a fix. *Unfortunately* this particular car did not have a radio to summon help. *Unfortunately* we broke down while taking a short-cut and could not get help from the dozens of taxis that journeyed to and from the airport every hour of the day along the normal route. *Unfortunately* the one taxi that did come along already had three passengers in it—all men. *Unfortunately* the KGB car was not repaired until six o'clock. It was all very elaborate, but then it would have to be. It was designed to save face. The manuscript could hardly be taken from Kevin with Stan seeing him through the formalities at the airport and me standing in the background. Stan could not be subjected to that embarrassment. Yes, it had been a clever operation. And for the past two weeks the manuscript had been read in Dzerzhinsky Square.

How did they know that Kevin had the manuscript? There was only one answer. My flat was bugged. Every word that Kevin and I had said to each other had been recorded. How would this affect my position, my chances of getting back to Ireland? Stan and Slava had known for some time that I disliked Blake, but they were not sure that I would voice my feelings when I reached the West. Now they had my innermost thoughts about Blake before them in black and white, irrefutable evidence of my intentions.

This was the third time I had upset the KGB: first, my visit to the British Embassy; then my phone call to Kevin; and now this. Could my luck hold out?

Slava called at six o'clock and brought a letter from Kevin. It had been posted the day after his return to London. It should have taken ten days to reach me but had taken fourteen. I concluded that the KGB had wanted to finish reading the manuscript before giving me the letter, as the letter must inevitably refer to what had happened at the airport. The letter was brief and, not surprisingly, showed Kevin's concern for my safety. He explained how the manuscript had been taken from him at the customs and then came a passage that was obviously meant for the eyes of the KGB. "I have of course read the manuscript word for word and know all the things you said about Blake.

My advice to you is to come back to Ireland and not bother to write anything. Forget all about Blake and I will do the same."

I passed the letter to Slava, and he read it. "Huh. I hope he gives us credit for being able to read between the lines."

"I'm sure he does. It's pretty transparent, isn't it? He's obviously worried about me. Perhaps I should get in touch with him straightaway and reassure him."

"Why not phone him?" Slava suggested. "Tomorrow I shall find out the code number that you have to dial from a flat to get through to the foreign exchange, and you can call him tomorrow night."

"Thank you, Slava."

Slava was obviously upset about the manuscript but, like Stan, showed no anger or resentment. "It is a pity you have this opinion of our country," he said, shaking his head. "And it is a pity you write these terrible things about Blake." So he had read it too.

When I asked him where the manuscript was now and when I was likely to get it back he told me that the customs had passed it on to the Press Committee for their consideration. "That is the law of our country," he explained. "The Press Committee have to examine all written material leaving the Soviet Union. It has nothing to do with the KGB. When the Press Committee are finished with your manuscript you will get it back."

This was another exercise in saving face. I knew the manuscript was in Dzerzhinsky Square—otherwise how could he and Stan have read it?

I phoned Kevin the next night.

"My God, am I relieved to hear your voice!" he said. "I thought you were in trouble."

"Well, as you can see, I'm not."

"You know about the manuscript?"

"Yes, Stan told me yesterday. And thanks for your letter."

"I thought you'd be in serious trouble with the KGB. We were all very worried here."

"I don't think there's anything to worry about."

"Now listen, Sean. That business on the way to the airport was all fixed, make no mistake about that. The breakdown was phony and the taxi was phony. And what's more your flat is bugged. It was all a fix."

"Why do you say that?"

"Well, it's bloody obvious."

"But the customs *have* to take manuscripts and pass them on to the Press Committee. That's the law of the land."

"Customs? What do you mean, customs? The KGB were waiting for me at the airport. The moment I put my case on the customs counter a young man in civvies who was standing behind the customs officer said, 'Oh, we have a special room for you. Follow me.' He took me to a room at the back of the customs department and tore my luggage apart. And then he searched *me*—every pocket, even my wallet. He took your manuscript and my own notebook and went into another room. Five minutes later he returned and gave me back my notebook. 'This is your own,' he said, 'you can have this. The remainder we must keep.' Now look, Sean, it's bloody obvious that he knew exactly what he was looking for. My opinion is that when he went into the second room he showed all the stuff to someone who was able to tell him exactly what to give back to me and what to keep. The man in the other room must have been someone who is known to you, someone who even knows your handwriting. Perhaps it was Slava or Victor, or even Blake himself?"

"I see. Well, I shall pass your remarks on to Stan and see what he says."

"Yes, do that. And are they still going to send you back to Ireland?"

"Of course. Why shouldn't they?"

"I hope you're right. If their intentions towards you are so honourable, why do they play tricks like this?"

"You still can't be sure that it *was* a trick."

"Oh, for heaven's sake, I'm not a fool. The whole thing was childishly clumsy. Now listen carefully. I've made a decision. If you are not back in Ireland by the end of November at the latest, the KGB and the Soviet Foreign Ministry are going to be caused a hell of a lot of embarrassment. I've got a plan all worked out in detail. There will be thousands of leaflets printed, and there will be continuous picketing outside the Soviet Embassy in London, and if necessary the windows of the Ambassador's car will be smashed while the Ambassador is in it. I'm deadly serious about this. They can have it the hard way if they like—and you can tell Stan what I've said."

Kevin knew as well as I did that our conversation was being monitored, and he was speaking for the benefit of the KGB.

"Oh, I don't think all that will be necessary," I said, also speaking for their benefit. "I consider Stan and Slava friends, and there's no doubt in my mind that they'll arrange my return to Ireland."

"I just hope you're right, that's all. I've been in touch with the Irish Embassy in London and you will have a travel document in a couple of weeks."

"All right, Kevin."

"Thanks very much for calling."

"That's okay."

"Let me know when your travel document arrives. And don't forget to tell Stan what I said."

"I'll do that."

I wrote a transcript of the conversation and gave it to Slava. He and Stan were incredulous at the suggestion that there was anything phony about the journey to the airport. And they thought Kevin's plan of campaign was childish and unnecessary. They could hardly have reacted otherwise.

A month went by and there was still no sign that my manuscript would be returned to me. I was not particularly concerned. All I wanted to do was get back to Ireland. The book could always be re-written.

Stan and Slava became more attentive than they had ever been before. They were constantly ringing me up to ask me how I was and to inquire if I needed anything. They also took me to dinner regularly, reserving a private dining-room at the Metropole or the Praga. On these occasions the manuscript would be discussed, and Stan and Slava would very gently suggest that I had perhaps misunderstood Blake's words and intentions. They were concerned solely about my attitude to Blake. My criticisms of Soviet society didn't seem to bother them. But then why should they care? Half the world already criticized their country anyway. I found myself admiring these two men for their unswerving loyalty to Blake and for their tenacious efforts to defend him, and I also found myself contrasting them as men with the traitor whom they were compelled by duty to support.

The travel document arrived on October 10. It was issued by the Irish Embassy in London and valid for one month and one journey, from Moscow to Ireland "by the most direct route." It was agreed that

I should leave Moscow on Monday, October 21, and travel to Dublin via Amsterdam.

On Thursday, October 17, Stan took me to lunch at the Arbat Restaurant. We began eating and drinking at two o'clock and went on until ten. By now I had become accustomed to the KGB habit of elaborately paving the way for an announcement that might cause unhappiness. I was wondering what announcement Stan was going to make, and then at nine o'clock he made it.

"I think, Sean, it would be a good idea if you left your manuscript behind you. When you have arrived safely in Ireland we will send it on to you. If you take it yourself you might be arrested when you arrive in Dublin and the manuscript confiscated."

"That makes sense," I agreed.

We had a farewell dinner at my flat on Sunday, October 20. Larisa and I acted as hosts to Stan and Slava.

Slava brought my air ticket and exit visa and forty American dollars. "You fly from here to Amsterdam," he explained. "You have a two-hour wait there at the airport and then catch your connecting flight direct to Dublin. You don't have to go through immigration at Amsterdam so there should be no difficulty. I think forty dollars should be enough for the journey, don't you?"

"More than enough, Slava. Thanks."

The phone rang and I went to answer it. It was Kevin.

"Well, Sean, are you still coming home tomorrow?"

"Yes, everything is arranged. I'll be in Amsterdam about midday, as I've told you."

"Good. I'll be waiting for you in Dublin. I've taken the precaution of telling the press that you're coming. I think the more people who know about it the more likely you are to arrive."

"A very wise move. Thank you."

"I've arranged for a television team to meet you at Amsterdam. They're from Granada Television in England. The man who will approach you is a reporter with a programme called 'World in Action.' I told him that you'd be carrying a copy of *Pravda*."

"Okay, I'll remember that."

"See you in Dublin."

"Yes indeed."

Stan said that he would call to collect Larisa and me in the morning and take us to the airport. I would not be seeing Slava again, so we said good-bye as he and Stan left.

"Good-bye, Sean," he said, shaking me warmly by the hand. "I wish you every success and I hope we meet again."

"I hope so, Slava. Good-bye and thank you."

Next morning Larisa was waiting with me in the flat. Stan was due in about ten minutes. She opened her handbag and took out a plain gold ring. "Until we meet again, Sean." She slipped the ring on the third finger of my right hand.

I gazed down at it. Knowing the hazards of shopping in Moscow, I realized that Larisa must have queued for hours to get it.

Stan arrived and we went down in the lift to the street. My luggage consisted of a briefcase containing a spare shirt, a set of underwear, a pair of socks, and the green dog Larisa had given me at the Warsaw Hotel. All my other belongings I left behind in the flat.

As the airport came into sight Stan said something to the driver and the car slowed down. Then he turned round in his seat to look at Larisa and me. "I think we should say good-bye some little distance from the entrance. There might be correspondents there, and Larisa and I should not be photographed. Oh, and by the way, Sean, if you see me in the departure lounge afterwards, pretend you don't know me."

The car stopped about a hundred yards from the entrance to the terminal building and we all got out.

I shook hands with Stan. "Good-bye, Stan."

"Good-bye, Sean. And remember, you are free to turn back right up to the moment the plane takes off."

"Thank you."

I looked at Larisa.

"I'll be up on the balcony to watch you take off," she said.

We kissed, and I hurried away towards the terminal building.

I filled in the customs form, saying I had nothing to declare, and handed it to the woman customs officer together with my travel document and exit visa.

"Have you any currency?" she asked.

"Yes, forty dollars."

"Well then, why didn't you declare it?" she demanded aggressively.

"Well, I—"

A man who was standing next to her glanced down at my exit visa and then whispered something in her ear. Without another word she handed me back my papers.

I climbed the stairs to the departure lounge. I had about half an hour to kill before my flight was called so I went along to the bar for a drink. Five minutes later Stan appeared. He had a drink a few tables away from me, then went into the lavatory, and after that moved non-chalantly about the departure lounge. I pretended to ignore him but I could see that he was studying all the other passengers.

My flight was called, and I started to walk down towards the gate. Stan was walking towards me, and as we passed each other he said in a half whisper, without turning his head, "Good-bye, Sean. Good luck."

"Good-bye, Stan, and thanks."

At passport control a young frontier guard was quite openly photo-graphing everyone on my flight. This was not normal routine, and I again found myself admiring the KGB for their thoroughness. The frontier guard in the cubicle carefully scrutinized my papers. He handed me back my travel document, kept the exit visa, and pulled back the little metal barrier to let me pass. I had to wait with the other passengers at the other side of the barrier until everyone was present and correct, and then a frontier guard escorted us all together across the thirty yards of tarmac that separated us from our plane. A frontier guard officer was waiting at the bottom of the steps.

I looked across at the terminal building. Larisa was standing alone on the balcony, her auburn hair blowing in the cool autumn breeze. She waved her hand and I waved back. I allowed the other passengers to go aboard first and kept looking at Larisa. Then I climbed the steps, paused a moment on the top one, gave one last wave, and entered the plane.

Most of the other passengers were American tourists, loudly discussing their adventures in the Soviet Union. We fastened our safety belts. The jet screamed down the runway, lifted itself off Russian soil, and headed west.

At Amsterdam, as I entered the arrival lounge, a tall, fair-haired young man walked up to me.

"Excuse me, are you Mr. Bourke?"

"I am."

"Oh good. I'm from Granada Television. Your brother told me that you would be expecting me."

"That's right."

"Well, we'd like to do an interview. Would you care to come along to our hotel?"

"I'd love to."

At passport control the immigration officer glanced briefly at my emergency travel document and allowed me to enter Holland. No visas, no questions. I was back in the West.

At the hotel I was introduced to the other members of the television team. The cameras were set up and we did the interview.

Then the phone rang. It was Kevin, to tell me that there was fog at Dublin Airport and planes were being diverted to London or Belfast.

I cancelled my flight and spent the night in Amsterdam.

Next morning I flew with the television team to Düsseldorf. We spent two hours there and then boarded a Pan American airliner for Ireland.

Four hours later we were approaching Shannon Airport. I looked out of the window. Below me I could see the Clare Hills. That was where I used to hide from the police and sleep in haybarns years ago when I played truant from school.

The plane came in low over the muddy estuary of the Shannon, and a minute later its wheels were pounding on the runway. It taxied up close to the terminal building and came to a halt. The television crew went out first to record my arrival. Then I stepped out onto the platform.

A large crowd of newsmen up on the balcony were shouting and waving and pointing cameras at me. I walked down the steps onto Irish soil. The date was October 22, 1968: the second anniversary of George Blake's escape.